Enhancing the Well-being of Children and Families through Effective Interventions

of related interest

The Developing World of the Child
Edited by Jane Aldgate, David Jones, Wendy Rose and Carole Jeffery
Foreword by Maria Eagle MP
ISBN 1 84310 244 7

Approaches to Needs Assessment in Children's Services
Edited by Harriet Ward and Wendy Rose
Foreword by Professor Al Aynsley Green
ISBN 1 85302 780 4

Safeguarding and Promoting the Well-being of Children, Families and Communities
Edited by Jane Scott and Harriet Ward
Foreword by Maria Eagle MP
ISBN 1 84310 141 6

Family Support as Reflective Practice
Edited by Pat Dolan, John Canavan and John Pinkerton
ISBN 1 84310 320 6

Child Welfare Services
Development in Law, Policy, Practice and Research
Edited by Malcolm Hill and Jane Aldgate
ISBN 1 85302 316 7

Culture and Child Protection: Reflexive Responses
Marie Connolly, Yvonne Crichton-Hill and Tony Ward
ISBN 1 84310 270 6

The Child's World
Assessing Children in Need
Edited by Jan Horwath
ISBN 1 85302 957 2

Child Neglect
Practice Issues for Health and Social Care
Edited by Julie Taylor and Brigid Daniel
Foreword by Olive Stevenson
ISBN 1 84310 160 2

Developing Good Practice in Children's Services
Edited by Vicky White and John Harris
ISBN 1 84310 150 5

Supporting Parents
Messages from Research
David Quinton
Foreword by Right Honourable Margaret Hodge
ISBN 1 84310 210 2

Child Development for Child Care and Protection Workers
Brigid Daniel, Sally Wassell and Robbie Gilligan
Foreword by Jim Ennis
ISBN 1 85302 633 6

Fostering Now
Messages from Research
Ian Sinclair
Foreword by Tom Jeffreys
ISBN 1 84310 362 1

Enhancing the Well-being of Children and Families through Effective Interventions

International Evidence for Practice

Edited by Colette McAuley,
Peter J. Pecora and Wendy Rose

Foreword by Maria Eagle MP

Jessica Kingsley Publishers
London and Philadelphia

First published in 2006
by Jessica Kingsley Publishers
116 Pentonville Road
London N1 9JB, UK
and
400 Market Street, Suite 400
Philadelphia, PA 19106, USA

www.jkp.com

Library of Congress Cataloging in Publication Data
Enhancing the well-being of children and families through effective interventions : international evidence for practice / edited by Colette McAuley, Peter Pecora and Wendy Rose ; foreword by Maria Eagle.-- 1st American pbk. ed.
p. cm.
Includes bibliographical references and index.
ISBN-13: 978-1-84310-116-1 (pbk. : alk. paper)
ISBN-10: 1-84310-116-5 (pbk. : alk. paper) 1. Child welfare--United States. 2. Child welfare--Great Britain. 3. Crisis intervention (Mental health services)--United States. 4. Crisis intervention (Mental health services)--Great Britain. 5. Family policy--United States. 6. Family policy--Great Britain. I. McAuley, Colette. II. Pecora, Peter J., 1954- III. Rose, Wendy, 1944-
HV741.E54 2006
362.76'81--dc22

2005031665

British Library Cataloguing in Publication Data
A CIP catalogue record for this book is available from the British Library
ISBN-13: 978 1 84310 116 1
ISBN-10: 1 84310 116 5

Printed and bound in Great Britain by
Athenaeum Press, Gateshead, Tyne and Wear

Contents

List of Figures

List of Tables

Foreword

In the United Kingdom, current government policy is explicitly aimed at increasing opportunities for all children and improving the outcomes for our most vulnerable children. There is an ambitious programme of change underway that focuses on building services around the needs of children and young people and transforming the delivery of those services. This involves not just children themselves but also their families and the local communities where they live, and requires the development of strong partnerships locally and across government. In this sense, the well-being of children is everyone's business.

To bring about the improvement we all desire in the lives of vulnerable children, a fundamental question asked by politicians, policy makers and professionals alike is what do we know about what makes a difference? Which services help and in what circumstances? At which populations should services be directed – at the individual child, their families or the community as a whole? Which services have been proven to bring about signs of significant improvement? Which are valued by families? Are there some that make little or no difference or indeed do more harm than good ? Are services effective for all children and families? Are they sensitive to those children with additional needs because of disability or ethnicity or other factors in their lives? Answers to these questions are critically important so that we can be confident about where and when to direct our resources and so that we can see tangible improvements in children's outcomes.

I therefore welcome the increasing attention being given to reviewing the effectiveness of work with children and families. The development of this volume was initially inspired by an international seminar on intervention, sponsored by the Government and held at Cumberland Lodge, Windsor, in 2001, that led to the international collaboration between UK and US researchers. This is the first time that such a comprehensive review of the contemporary evidence about service effectiveness has been undertaken, drawing on research from both sides of the Atlantic so that we can begin to learn from each other's experience. All of the contributors are internationally recognised experts in the field of child welfare. Undoubtedly, this book will play an important part in helping to build our knowledge, both in the UK and the US. The conclusions drawn suggest we are only just embarking on a lengthy but crucial journey to gather the evidence base we need to help national and local partnerships in making critical decisions about the way we plan, resource and deliver services to improve children's lives.

Maria Eagle MP, Parliamentary Under Secretary
of State for Children, Young People and Families, UK

Preface

The original impetus for this book was a meeting of international child welfare research experts in Windsor in 2001, which was organised by the Department of Health and chaired by Wendy Rose. There was a clear consensus that we needed to further develop our thinking about interventions to be offered to children and families and what we know about their likely benefits. Immediately after attending that meeting, Colette McAuley spent a sabbatical at the School of Social Work, University of Washington and the Casey Family Programs Research Unit, Seattle. There she began discussions with Peter Pecora about the development of an international collection of evidence on the effectiveness of some of the principal child welfare interventions of particular interest to policymakers, managers and practitioners. There clearly was a serious preoccupation with developing evidence-based practice on both sides of the Atlantic and it was hoped that the presentation of evidence from both countries would stimulate further international comparison and learning. And so the idea for this book was born.

The editorial team brought together expertise and interest in the area of researching outcomes in child welfare in their respective countries as well as concern about the need to use research to inform policy and practice developments. All three of us are founding members of the International Association for Outcome-Based Evaluation and Research on Family and Children's Services, and have been inspired by the work of this international fellowship of researchers. Not only have fellow members supported and encouraged us but some have contributed to the book as authors.

One of our first challenges was to agree the selected areas to focus upon, given the breadth of child welfare. We were extremely aware of many other areas that we would have wanted to include if issues of length, time and manageability had not prevailed. In selecting the contributors from our respective countries, we invited internationally recognised writers in their fields of expertise. This was important as we were asking them not only to summarise the available evidence succinctly, but also to comment upon the nature of the evidence available and provide critical judgement as to what messages could be taken from that body of evidence. Our idea met with considerable enthusiasm largely due to its perceived timeliness. We were incredibly fortunate to attract internationally recognised experts to contribute and it has been a pleasure to work with them over the past couple of years to bring this volume to completion. Our hope is that this book will provide useful and easily accessible evidence along with the opportunity to compare findings across countries and thus contribute to advancing our knowledge in this complex field.

Colette McAuley, Peter J. Pecora and Wendy Rose

Experience of Child
Welfare Interventions

PART ONE

Child Welfare
in the UK and US

CHAPTER 1

Effectiveness of Child Welfare Interventions

Issues and Challenges

Peter J. Pecora, Colette McAuley and Wendy Rose

Introduction

Child and family services in the United Kingdom, Europe, the United States and many other countries are at an important nexus of development. A foundation of qualitative and quantitative research studies is gradually being established which has produced documentation that certain intervention approaches are supported by research – this is a key part of what is necessary to implement *evidence-based practice*. In the US, while the emphasis on using evidence-based practice models is originating more with state and county agencies, the US federal government requirement that each state's services be measured using a common set of performance standards and its modest support for child welfare research are contributing to this shift. The ability of some child welfare interventions to be manualized and formatted for larger-scale replications is resulting in cautious optimism that evidence-based practice approaches may indeed be possible in some areas. (See, for example, the Blue Skies Project at www.aecf.org; Chamberlain 2003; Cohen, Mannarino and Zhitova 2003; Henggeler *et al.* 1998; Jensen *et al.* 2005).

In the UK since the 1980s there has been considerable interest in exploring the effectiveness of specialist services for children in need and their families and the impact that processes of service intervention may have on their lives; examples of such services are child protection, residential and foster care, and leaving care.

However, UK government policy since 1997 has been increasingly directed at improving the outcomes for all children and minimizing the risk to children of loss of opportunity. This has given added impetus to the interest in effectiveness of interventions. It has broadened the focus from the provision of specialist services for children in need to strengthening the universally provided services of health and education, and targeting those children and families in the population who may be at risk of exclusion, disadvantage and other difficulties. It has been expressed as a strategy to shift the focus 'from dealing with the consequences of difficulties in children's lives to preventing things from going wrong in the first place' (HM Government 2004b, p.2). Knowing what works has acquired more importance as major national programmes are established, because of the implications both for government resource allocation decisions and for the government's record of policy achievement.

Evidence of Effectiveness of Interventions

A number of relevant reviews of research about children in need and their families already exist – although they are not strictly reviews of programme effectiveness. For example, the UK government has produced reviews of research on child protection (Department of Health 1995a), residential care (Department of Health 1998b), the Children Act 1989 implementation (Department of Health 2001d) and supporting parents (Quinton 2004) among others. There have also been some reviews that have focused on the effectiveness of child welfare interventions. The Barnardo's What Works series (e.g. Alderson *et al.* 1996) has been followed by reviews of the effectiveness of family support (Statham 2000) and child protection services (Macdonald 2001). *Children and Society* has also devoted a special edition to evaluating the effectiveness of community-based initiatives (Lewis and Utting 2001, p.1).

Alongside this, the UK government and research foundations have recently initiated a series of major research studies on outcomes and costs of child welfare interventions. Evidence on the effectiveness of child welfare interventions is accumulating also in North America. Reviews of the evidence on early childhood interventions (Gomby *et al.* 1995; Guralnick 1997, 1998; Karoly *et al.* 1998; Reynolds 2004), home-visiting services (Gomby *et al.* 1999; Olds *et al.* 2000), family support (Comer and Frazer 1998), child maltreatment (Chaffin and Friedrich 2004; Corcoran 2000), multisystemic family therapy (Littell 2005; Littell, Forsythe and Popa 2004), family foster care (Geen 2004; Pecora and Maluccio 2000), and residential care (Whittaker 2000) among others have recently become available. But many gaps exist and there are many unanswered questions about the dynamics of parent, child and family behaviours and how best to address those that may be harmful.

Challenges in Measuring Effectiveness in the Social Welfare Field of Child and Family Services

While an exhaustive discussion of methodological and other challenges to measuring effectiveness in these programme areas is beyond the scope of this chapter, some of the major challenges are described below, drawing from the research experience of the editors, from issues presented in the chapters and from other sources:

1. Theoretical frameworks that can guide research or the interpretation of the data are sometimes not available. One of the clearest examples of this is how the family-based services field has struggled to articulate a specific logic model of therapeutic change and to make sense of conflicting research findings (e.g., Pecora *et al.* 1995; Walton, Sandau-Beckler and Mannes 2001).

2. Interventions are developed and show positive results in sheltered environments but then are not ready to be rigorously tested in community settings with a wide range of complexities or barriers. In contrast, a number of projects involving Family Group Conferencing (see www.americanhumane.org), Functional Family Therapy (see www.strengtheningfamilies.org/html/programs_1999/01_FFT.html), Treatment Foster Care (Chamberlain 2003) and Multisystemic Therapy (Henggeler *et al.* 1998) are attempting to carefully implement large-scale replication projects in a variety of communities.

3. Lowering the costs of evaluation studies by using agency administrative data has been hampered by the limited inclusion of outcome indicators in those information systems and/or modest rates of completion by workers. The data lack reliability if there has been insufficient training to ensure common understanding or validity if too few workers have completed a particular data element.

4. Infrequent use of related agency administrative databases hamper the ability to measure key programme outcomes. For example, in foster care, the employment of young adults who have recently left care is a crucial outcome to track (Goerge *et al.* 2002); educational achievement is often a key indicator of adult success; and former service recipients who are involved in juvenile justice or receiving public assistance are judged as being less successful.

5. Over reliance on cross-section ('snapshot') or exit data instead of longitudinal cohort data. A growing number of authors have provided compelling arguments concerning the dangers of over-relying on cross-sectional or exit data (Courtney, Terao and Bost 2004).

6. Too few studies have been able to collect detailed service usage and programme fidelity data. Consequently, programme fidelity (adherence by staff to the treatment model) is infrequently measured and we are therefore unable to determine if the intervention was actually implemented according to a certain set of standards for type, dosage and quality (e.g., Kirk, Reed-Ashcraft and Pecora 2003).

7. Small sample sizes hamper or prevent the use of multivariate approaches and analyses of key subgroups (ethnicity, level of problem severity, service dosage). For an example of how the use of multivariate approaches was successfully attempted, see Ryan and Schuerman (2004).

8. More meaningful child well-being indicators are missing from some research studies. Instead status measures, such as number of children reunified or time elapsed between termination of parental rights and adoption, are used.

9. Relatively few follow-up studies have been completed that enable measurement of intermediate and more distal programme outcomes. This is beginning to change in early childhood interventions (e.g., Reynolds 2004) and family foster care (e.g., Courtney and Dworskey 2005; Pecora *et al.* 2005).

10. When follow-up studies have been completed, some of the positive short-term programme results are shown to fade over time (Smith, this volume).

11. A common set of standardized diagnostic measures that assess behaviour, educational functioning, satisfaction, self-esteem, and other central dependent variables have been used infrequently. (See, for example, Mason *et al.* 2003.)

12. Youths in care, caregivers, alumni and front-line staff are often not involved in study design and data interpretation to help ensure that researchers gather meaningful information in respectful ways. (See Sinclair 1998, or the Better Together curriculum for youth and parent involvement at www.casey.org.)

13. For new or underexplored problem areas, few qualitative studies have been completed that would help the field understand better the programme model, the dynamics of treatment, consumer perceptions of service and what is working and why. The National Service Framework in the UK (Department of Health and Department for Education and Skills 2004) will incorporate the views of children and their families as

well as studies of process into their evidence base for the development of effective services (see Sloper and Statham 2004).

14. Few experimental or quasi-experimental programme studies have been completed to evaluate more definitively different practice models or specific interventions. The need for substantial investment in research on effectiveness in the UK is more fully discussed in Chapter 26.

15. Control group contamination through contact with experimental group families or through shared social network members may be undermining group comparisons. Programmes employing experimental designs typically recruit participants from specific sites and randomly assign participants within sites. The reason for this approach is legitimate, to maximize between group comparability at baseline. However, the likelihood is fairly high that demographically comparable subjects, sharing a common life circumstance (pregnant or parenting young children) and living in the same neighbourhood, will have overlapping social networks. Within these networks, informal patterns of sharing resources and information may actually play a more important role than formal services, a fact established at least for African-American women (Neighbors and Jackson 1984, as cited in Chapter 7).

16. Are we learning from failed experiments? There are very few replication studies being conducted that would help the field deepen our knowledge and determine if an intervention can be implemented with different populations or the same populations but in different kinds of communities. Just because an intervention fails in one community or for one type of client does not mean that it will be ineffective in another setting or client group.

17. Comparison groups are not always utilized. For example, the researchers may not be able to compare their sample (if appropriate) with the general population of youths of similar age, gender or ethnicity, nor may they be able to use other benchmarking data from similar programmes and more similar populations of youth or caregivers.

18. Current statistical approaches could be bolstered with more advanced statistical methods that would help address better some certain research questions – such as for whom is this intervention the most effective? What aspects of a programme are most linked with improved outcomes? What are the effect sizes that would better gauge the relative power of the intervention? For example, in the case of home visiting, the programme's positive benefits measured in the form of 'effect sizes' are modest (see Chapter 7).

19.   Single interventions may not be sufficiently powerful by themselves. For example, several authors have argued that home visiting alone is insufficient to meet the needs of vulnerable families; thus programme impact is compromised when quality community services are not available or accessible (Ramey and Ramey 1993; Weiss 1993, as cited in Chapter 7).

20.   Some interventions may not be acceptable to families, may stigmatize users or are not seen as helpful. Consequently, these interventions do not effectively engage parents in interventions and have high drop-out rates. Unfortunately, this appears to hold true for some of the most disadvantaged families (Smith in this volume).

21.   Some interventions are comprehensive but also individually tailored, leading to variation within the treatment group on specific intervention components received. This makes it more difficult to tease apart specific and overall effects of early interventions (see Hanson, Morrow and Bandstra in this volume; Kirk *et al.* 2003).

Why it is Important to Gather Evidence from both the UK and the US

Countries differ in their culture, history, values, intervention approaches, policies, and programme structures. Those differences can be crucial in determining whether evidence from one country is applicable to another. The broader field of child and family services, however, may advance more quickly if a careful consideration of evidence and ideas from more than one country is considered.

While a review of research from countries other than the UK and US was not possible due to the limitations of this book's size, research in Canada, Ireland and elsewhere is cited in many chapters and it would be very useful to review this in more depth to understand the full extent of international resources in these areas. Having a broad understanding is important for future service delivery and research commissioning because it helps policymakers, programme designers and evaluators be aware of mistakes made by other countries and, perhaps most importantly, how a successful programme is designed and implemented.

How this Book is Structured

The next two chapters provide a policy and programme context for child and family services in the UK and the US. Chapter 2 focuses specifically on the legislative, policy and practice context in the UK, particularly since the introduction of the Children Act 1989. Chapter 3 is devoted to the legislative, policy and practice context of child welfare research in the US. These three chapters comprise an overview – Part One of the book.

Part Two ('Evidence on Interventions with Vulnerable Children, Young People and Families'), Part Three ('Evidence on Therapeutic Interventions with Children who have Experienced Abuse/Neglect'), Part Four ('Evidence on Foster Care, Adoption and Transitions for Children and Young People'), and Part Five ('Innovative Approaches in Schools and Community Programmes') contain the evidence on effectiveness of the selected interventions. We lead with a slightly larger 'foundation' chapter in each topic area that is written by one or more UK contributors, and then one or more US contributors summarizes the research evidence from that country. Each of the chapters addresses:

- the intervention
- the evidence available on its effectiveness
- the limitations of that evidence
- implications for policy, practice and research.

In Part Six the editors provide an overview of the state of evidence of effectiveness of child welfare interventions and relate this directly to the UK Assessment and Intervention Frameworks (Department of Health, Department for Education and Skills and Home Office 2000b; Department of Health 2002f). The broader implications for service planning, policy and practice will be considered. Recommendations as to future evidence needs to inform practitioners are also addressed.

This book covers a wide range of the most common areas of intervention offered to children and their families. It provides an overview of existing international research evidence on the effectiveness of such interventions in an easily accessible volume. We hope that the summaries provided will also stimulate further specialist reading. Obviously, similar evidence needs to be gathered regarding other approaches to intervention as we continue to build our knowledge base about what makes a difference to the lives of children and families. Nonetheless, we are confident that readers will learn much about the state of the art with respect to each of the selected areas and be more aware of some of the key cross-cutting research, policy and practice challenges.

CHAPTER 2

Child Welfare in the UK

Legislation, Policy and Practice

Wendy Rose, Jenny Gray and Colette McAuley

Introduction

In this chapter we present a broad perspective on child welfare in the United Kingdom to provide a context for the evidence chapters that follow. We begin by offering selected demographic characteristics of children before moving on to consider in more detail the characteristics of vulnerable children who, with their families, are likely to be users of child welfare services. The legislative and policy context is then addressed with policy relating to assessment and effective interventions being discussed in greater depth. The importance government places on evidence-based services is explored.

Vulnerable Children in the UK

Children account for a quarter of the total population in England. In 2003, there were 11 million children under 18 years. Around 3.66 million of these children were estimated to be vulnerable. This figure represents a decrease from four million since 1997. 'Vulnerable children' are defined as those who would benefit from extra help from public agencies in order to achieve the best life chances. Vulnerable children are usually living in poverty, defined as households with less than half the average household income (see Table 2.1).

Under section 17 of the Children Act 1989 (England and Wales), children whose development is impaired or likely to be impaired or who are disabled and in need of services are defined as children in need. There are estimated to be 376,000

Table 2.1: Children in the UK: selected facts and figures
National child demographics[a]

Population on the UK by respective countries in 2001	49.2 million England; 2.9 million Wales; 5.1 million Scotland; 1.7 million Northen Ireland
Child population in UK under age 16 in 2001	11.9 milliion (20% population)
Stepfamilies with dependent children in Great Britain 2000/2001	8% of families with dependent children
Dependent children in Great Britain living in lone parent families in 2002	20% of all dependent children

Vulnerable children in England [b]

Children who would benefit from extra help from public agencies, usually living in households with less than half the average household income in 2003	3.66 million
Children in need in 2003	376,000
Children on child protection registers in 2003	26,600
Children looked after at 31 March 2003	61,000
Children in foster care at 31 March 2003	41,100
Children in residential care (including secure units) at 31 March 2003	5900
Children in care placed for adoption at 31 March 2003	3400

a   Source: National Statistics (2003)
b   Source: Department for Education and Skills (2004a)

children in need known to children's social services in England at any one time. Children's services are provided through local government units (150 in England). They are responsible for ascertaining if children are indeed children in need, ensuring services are provided and supplying central government with information about children in need in their area.

Children on Child Protection Registers

At 31 March 2003, there were 26,600 children and young people whose names were on child protection registers in England. This represented a rate of 24 children per 10,000 in the population aged under 18. Over the past decade there has been a significant decline in the registration rate which has been attributed in part to the impact of the Children Act 1989 and in part to the introduction of new statistical returns following government guidance on safeguarding children (Department of Health, Home Office and Department for Education and Employment 1999). Since 1999, children have been registered where they have been deemed to be at continuing risk of harm and require a child protection plan. This change was introduced in a context of providing services at an earlier point to children in need, which is discussed later in this chapter.

There was a spread across the age ranges with a similar proportion (29%) of children on the register being in the 1–4 years, 5–9 years and 10–15 years categories. A further 11 per cent were aged under one year while only 2 per cent were aged 16 years or older. Although more boys than girls were on the register at 31 March 2003, the rates of registration are very similar for both sexes (24 per 10,000 for boys and 23 per 10,000 for girls).

Neglect is the most frequently used category, accounting for 39 per cent of children registered during 2002–03 (see Table 2.2). Physical abuse accounted for 19 per cent of registrations followed by emotional abuse (18%) and sexual abuse (10%). Between 1999 and 2001, the percentages in the category of neglect had steadily increased. The number of cases categorized as emotional abuse has been fairly stable. In contrast the use of the categories of physical abuse and sexual abuse have generally fallen.

Table 2.2: Children on the child protection registers in England at 31 March 2003 – reasons for registration

Predominant reasons for reasons for registration	Percentage of children registered
Neglect	39
Physical abuse	19
Emotional abuse	18
Sexual abuse	10
Mixed categories	15

Source: Department for Education and Skills (2004b)

During the year 2002–03, there were more girls than boys on the child protection register in connection with sexual abuse. Sexual abuse accounted for 12 per cent of girls on the register at 31 March 2003 and 8 per cent of boys. The rate was 3 per 10,000 girls and 2 per 10,000 boys in the population. In contrast there were more boys than girls on the register in connection with physical abuse. Seventeen per cent of boys on the register at 31 March 2003 were registered in connection with physical abuse compared with 15 per cent of girls. The rate was 10 per 10,000 boys and 9 per 10,000 girls in the population.

Of the 26,600 children on child protection registers on 31 March 2003, 83 per cent were of a white background, 6 per cent of a mixed heritage background, 5 per cent black or black British, and 3 per cent Asian or Asian British. The remainder were of other ethnic origins. One per cent were registered before birth.

Looked After Children

The Children Act 1989 defines the basis on which the state provides out-of-home care for children in need. This may either be on a voluntary basis as a service to assist parents or as the result of a court order. Both groups of children are known as 'looked after children'. They may be placed in a range of different placements including foster care or a residential setting. The responsibility of parents for their children does not cease when they become looked after. During the period the child is looked after by a local authority, parental responsibility is shared with that authority.

Almost 61,000 children were looked after in England at 31 March 2003, representing 55 per 10,000 children aged under 18 years. Over 65 per cent were the subject of a compulsory care order. Sixty-five per cent were in the 5–15 age range. Fifty-five per cent were boys. The majority (81%) of children were white, while 8 per cent were of mixed heritage, 7 per cent were black and the remaining 2 per cent were Asian.

Foster family placements were the most frequent substitute care option for children in England, a pattern reflected throughout the UK. Around 68 per cent of all looked after children in England were placed in foster families. Almost 10 per cent were looked after in children's homes (including secure units). This represents an increase in usage of foster care and a decrease in the use of residential provision since 1999. The greatest percentage increase of children in foster care is to be found in those living in kinship care arrangements. Finally, 3400 looked after children were placed for adoption in the year ending 31 March 2003, representing a 5 per cent decrease from the previous year. This departs from the upward trend in adoptions evident in the previous three-year period.

Outcomes for Looked After Children

Over several decades there have been continuing concerns about children growing up in out-of-home care (for example, Kahan 1994; Parker *et al.* 1991; Sinclair and Gibbs 1998). The reasons for their being unable to remain at home often relate to causes such as abuse or neglect, associated with parental problems of substance misuse, mental ill health and domestic violence (Cleaver *et al.* 1999), but these early adverse experiences may have been compounded by inadequacies of the care system such as inappropriate placements, frequent moves, patchy educational provision or dislocation from family and friends. Since 1997, government policy has been specifically aimed at improving outcomes for these vulnerable children through initiatives and programmes such as Quality Protects, Choice Protects and Every Child Matters.

The government's statistical collections have been designed to assist in the collection of information about outcomes for children looked after. Two particular areas of concern have been educational achievement and difficulties with offending behaviour.

It is estimated that 27 per cent (9200) of looked after children of school age during 2001–02 held statements of special educational needs (SENs). (In England children are deemed to have special educational needs if they have a learning difficulty which calls for special educational provision to be made for them.) Compared with national figures for all children in England, looked after children are almost nine times more likely to have a statement.

Looked after children of the age of criminal responsibility are three times more likely to be cautioned or convicted of an offence than others. Almost 10 per cent of children looked after for a year or more who were aged ten or over had been convicted or subject to a final warning or reprimand during the year. This compares with a figure of 3.6 per cent for all children.

Child Welfare Legislative and Policy Context

The Children Act 1989 provides the overarching legal framework for work with children in need and their families. This was a major piece of reforming legislation, consolidating and modernizing numerous previous child welfare statutes. The 1989 Act lays out the duties and responsibilities for local authorities and the courts to safeguard and promote the welfare of children in need. The Children Act 1989 was the first piece of legislation to take a developmental approach to children in that the duties were framed in relation to impairment of and significant harm to children's development. It was also a child-centred piece of legislation in that, for the first time, children's views had to be taken into account when decisions were being made about their lives. The Act recognized that children are best brought up with their families, but that from time to time some parents would need help through the provision of services. It also recognized that some children are not able to live with their families. The Act emphasizes the importance, in these circumstances, of working with children and families towards reunification and, where necessary, if children cannot return home to their birth families, of making decisions about an alternative permanent placement. This emphasis has been strengthened and modernized in subsequent legislation: the Children (Leaving Care) Act 2000 and the Adoption and Children Act 2002. The Children Act 2004 has broadened responsibilities towards children, both nationally and at a local level, with a view to improving the outcomes for all children, not just those with identified additional needs. The 2004 Act established the office of Children's Commissioner in England, thus completing the quartet of Children's Commissioners, one in each nation in the United Kingdom. At the same time, it places a duty on each children's services authority in England to make arrangements to promote cooperation with relevant agencies to improve the well-being of all children in the authority's area, having due regard to the importance of parents and others caring for them.

Government Policy About Assessing Children's Needs

In April 2000 three major government departments in England – the Department of Health, the Department for Education and Employment and the Home Office – took the unusual step of jointly issuing national guidance on assessing children in need and their families (Department of Health, Department for Education and Employment and Home Office 2000). The purpose was, in part, to assist local authority social services, working in collaboration with health, education and other community agencies, to meet one of the government's national objectives for children's social services (Department of Health *et al.* 1999) under the Quality Protects programme: 'To ensure that referral and assessment processes discriminate effectively between different types and levels of need and produce a timely service response' (p.20).

The guidance was issued to address increasing government concerns about poor assessment practice in children's social care, evidenced in a number of research studies (such as Department of Health 1995a) and government inspection reports (such as Social Services Inspectorate 1998 and 1999), as well as to promote a more broadly based approach to the assessment of need and provision of services to vulnerable children.

It was emphasized that assessment was not an end in itself but the beginning of a process leading to an improvement in the welfare or outcomes for a child or young person who was defined as 'in need' under the Children Act 1989. Following initial gathering and sifting of information about a child and his or her family, the process would involve careful analysis, decision making and planning, intervention and review. Fundamental was the acknowledgement of the significant relationship between assessment and effective intervention, as the words of the Department of Health headline read 'Better Assessment Leading to Better Services' (Department of Health *et al.* 1999).

English social services departments and partner agencies were required to implement the new framework for assessing children in need and their families, by incorporating it into their local policies and operational practice from April 2001. In

Wales it was implemented from 2002 and in Scotland a national approach to the introduction of an Integrated Assessment Framework was under development in 2005. At the same time, a common assessment framework was being developed in England and Wales for use across all agencies working with children to identify children's additional needs to ensure that they receive services at an earlier stage (Department for Education and Skills 2005c). The common assessment framework has been piloted in England with the intention of national implementation by 2008.

Findings from the major research study undertaken by Cleaver and colleagues in England and Wales confirmed reports from a number of sources, including national dissemination and training events, about the early experience of implementing the Assessment Framework (Cleaver and Walker with Meadows 2004). Staff working with children in need and their families were generally very positive about the framework. Information in children's social services was being gathered well according to the dimensions of the framework. However, difficulties were being encountered by practitioners when it came to analysis, judgement and decision making about when and how to intervene. Practitioners (and their managers) were displaying a lack of confidence and some uncertainty about what services might make a difference and about which services to use in which circumstances. Such feedback has strengthened the commitment of policy makers, working with practitioners and researchers, to address issues of intervention and to explore how to assist practitioners in their day-to-day decision making. This has been given added impetus through a range of government initiatives, such as the Change for Children programme, aimed at improving the evidence base of service provision; another primary example is the National Service Framework for Children, Young People and Maternity Services, a fuller discussion of which can be found in Chapter 26.

Assessment as the Route to Effective Intervention

The Assessment Framework has been developed to take account of the complex inter-relationship of factors in the inner and outer world of the child and family which can have an impact on a child and to provide a conceptual map for practitioners to use in the process of gathering and analysing information about what is happening (Rose 2001). The framework is, therefore, a way of understanding a child within the context of the family and the wider community in which he or she is living. It consists of three systems or domains (see Figure 2.1):

- the child's developmental needs
- the parents' or caregivers' capacities to respond appropriately to those needs
- family history, wider family and environmental factors.

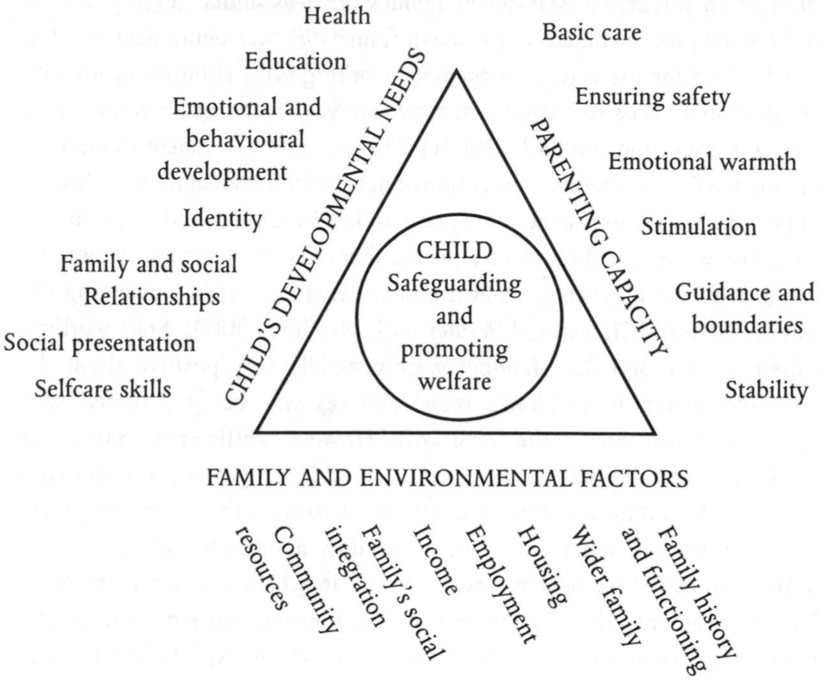

Health

Education

Basic care

Emotional and
behavioural
development

Ensuring safety

Emotional warmth

Identity

Stimulation

Family and social
Relationships

CHILD
Safeguarding
and
promoting
welfare

Guidance and
boundaries

Social presentation

Selfcare skills

Stability

CHILD'S DEVELOPMENTAL NEEDS

PARENTING CAPACITY

FAMILY AND ENVIRONMENTAL FACTORS

Community resources · Family's social integration · Income · Employment · Housing · Wider family · Family history and functioning

Figure 2.1: Assessment Framework

Reproduced from Department of Health *et al.* 2000, p.17

The framework is underpinned by a developmental approach to children's needs. Practitioners are expected to distinguish a child's needs according to the age and stage of development a child has reached and the range of factors and experiences which may have influenced that particular child's developmental progress. The guidance expects that: 'Plans and interventions should be based on a clear assessment of the developmental progress and difficulties a child may be experiencing and ensure that planned action is timely and appropriate in terms of a child's developmental needs' (Deaprtment of Health 2000b, p.11).

It was recognized that the effectiveness with which a child's needs are assessed will be key to the effectiveness of subsequent actions and services and, ultimately, to the outcomes for the child. As Jones (1997, p.521) succinctly describes this relationship: 'Treatment is intimately bound up with assessment, relying on it as a house relies on its foundation.' Saunders, Berliner and Hanson's guidelines on treatment for

American practitioners working with child abuse problems (2001, updated 2003) reflect on the relationship between assessment, intervention and outcomes:

> A basic principle of all clinical practice is that assessment should precede the initiation of interventions. Based upon the results of the assessment, a treatment plan should be developed that is tailored to the problems and needs of individual family members as a whole. The likelihood of a successful outcome is enhanced substantially when effective interventions are matched correctly to specific problems discerned through appropriate assessment. (p.14)

Furthermore, as Jones argues (Jones 1998), 'There is good reason to suggest that the quality of the work in the investigation phase sets the tone for subsequent intervention' (p.111).

Following appropriate assessment, the critical issue for practitioners is the decision about when to act and which services or interventions are likely to be most effective for a particular child and his or her family in order to achieve the best possible outcomes in the circumstances.

An Intervention Framework for Vulnerable Children and their Families

The guidance on assessment (Department of Health *et al.* 2000) leaves the practitioner at the point of making decisions about a plan of intervention. In developing a more integrated and coherent approach to practice with children and families, policymakers and researchers addressed some of the issues involved in ensuring an effective service response. Their considerations focused on whether they could develop a framework for intervention which would help to inform and guide the practitioner in making those critical decisions, and which would build on the developmental/ecological perspective of the Assessment Framework. Evidence gathered over many years suggested that the involvement of the child's family as an active participant was crucial to the success of any intervention programme (Bronfenbrenner 1976, and others). Involving parents as partners could reinforce the positive effects of child-directed services and help to sustain the effects over time. However, research evidence also strongly indicated that 'for children from the most deprived groups no strategy of intervention is likely to be effective that focuses attention solely on the child or on the parent–child relationship' (Bronfenbrenner 1976, p.250). Bronfenbrenner argues that this calls for 'measures that will effect radical changes in the immediate environment of the family and child' (1976, p.250). This argument, reinforced by many other research studies since the late 1970s, has now been enshrined in government programmes addressing child poverty and exclusion, such as Sure Start (Tunstill *et al.* 2005). The concern with improving children's outcomes initially took a long-term perspective, interested in the impact on children's development over time and into adulthood, ensuring that children grew up to fulfil their potential as citizens. However, that narrower perspective has now been broadened to encompass the concept of children's well-being, as important as their well-becoming, reinforced by the children's rights perspective and by valuing childhood as an experience in itself (Ben-Arieh 2002, and others). It is reflected in the government's commitment to improving the lives of children, young people and their families (HM Government 2004b). This broader approach has suggested not only a reframing of the objectives and ambitions for children in policy terms, but also has required consideration of the development of new measures or indicators in evaluations of the effectiveness of interventions and their impact on children.

Policymakers, concerned with improving practitioners' interventions in children's lives, were interested in the developing work of Prilleltensky and Nelson and their colleagues in Canada (Prilleltensky and Nelson 2000; Prilleltensky, Nelson and Peirson 2001), which focused on the interrelationship between child, family and community wellness. They drew on their work to construct a framework for conceptualising intervention to assist practitioners in their decision making and planning (see Table 2.3). This was incorporated into the new approach to assessment, planning, intervention and reviewing called the Integrated Children's System, which is being rolled out for national implementation by 2006 (Department of Health 2002f).

Summary: An Evidence-based Approach to Intervention

The development work on the Integrated Children's System came at a time when increasing emphasis was being placed on the importance of an evidence-based approach in public policy which, in social care, was seen as playing a crucial part in driving up standards and improving the protection afforded to some of the most vulnerable children and adults in society (Department of Health 2000b). while there was government concern to ensure that the provision of social services was no longer a 'postcode' lottery, other interests also prevailed, such as achieving best value from resources under pressure and ensuring effective delivery. This resulted in the increasing use of government-determined measures of social services performance, primarily as a tool for controlling and managing resources. In the 1990s these measures focused more on inputs and outputs than on outcomes of child welfare services (discussed by Tilbury 2004). However, the government commitment to ending child poverty, tackling social exclusion and promoting the welfare of all children 'so that they can thrive and have the opportunity to fulfil their potential as citizens throughout their lives' (Department of Health et al. 2000, p.x) has reinforced the policy interest in outcomes and the search for evidence of what can make a positive difference to the lives of vulnerable children.

Table 2.3: Framework for effective intervention

	Child	Parents/carers	Family	Community	Society
Universal	Immunization programme	Antenatal classes	Maternity and paternity leave	Children's Participation Programme	Accessible child care
	Junior citizenship programme	Guidance on helping children learn to read		Community Safety Strategy	Child tax credit
	Connexions support				
	Health and education				
	Leisure facilites				
Targeted	School action for children with special educational needs	Home-visiting programmes	Drop-in centres	Sure Start	Child support for divorced and separated parents
	Children's Fund	Parental education classes	Family centres	Credit unions	
		Marital counselling		Community development projects	Parental leave arrangements
		Parenting Plus			
Specialist	Schools' pastoral support programme	Cognitive behavioural therapy	Functional and structured family therapy	Neighbourhood renewal	Child welfare legislation e.g. Children (Leaving Care) Act 2000
	Play therapy	Child behaviour management			
	Multisystemic approaches	Foster carers' training			
	Group work for sexually abused children				

Reproduced from Department of Health 2002f, p.26

Contemporary children's policy in the UK is being driven by an ambitious government change programme in children's services, requiring local implementation within a national framework, which aims to improve the outcomes for all children and narrow the gap between those who do well and those who do not (HM Government 2004b). In England and Wales, the five outcomes which are considered key to securing well-being in childhood and later life are:

- being healthy
- staying safe
- enjoying and achieving
- making a positive contribution
- achieving economic well-being.

In Scotland, interestingly, they are expressed slightly differently as being:

- safe
- nurtured
- healthy
- achieving
- active
- respected and responsible
- included.

The achievement of improved child outcomes requires local change programmes which focus on improvement and integration of universal services, early intervention targeted to promote opportunity and to prevent problems arising, and specialist, high quality help to be available where problems have arisen. For policymakers, managers and practitioners, therefore, the imperative becomes even greater to work with researchers to build knowledge about the service interventions that are most effective in enhancing the well-being of children, young people and their families, and the communities in which they live.

CHAPTER 3

Child Welfare in the US

Legislation, Policy and Practice

Peter J. Pecora, James K. Whittaker and
Anthony N. Maluccio

Introduction

This chapter provides a broad perspective on child welfare in the United States to place in context the detailed and specific evidence chapters which follow. Selected demographic characteristics of children are provided, along with the key mission and objectives of child welfare services. Major national legislation related to child and family issues is summarized, and the extent to which policy and practice are guided by research is discussed. Drawing from innovative projects and programs across the country, we conclude with a discussion of current policy issues in child welfare services.

Vulnerable Children in the US

Child Maltreatment

Children make up a crucial but slowly decreasing proportion of the US population. A total of 72,894,483 children under the age of 18 were living in the US in 2002. Almost one in four (23.4%) were children of color under 18 in 2002 (see Table 3.1).

Table 3.1 Children in the US: selected facts and figures

National child demographics

Child population under age 18 in 2002[a]	72,894,483
White children under 18 in 2002[a]	76.6%
Non-white children under 18 in 2002[a]	23.4%
Children and youth under 12 in 2000[b]	66.4%
Children and youth age 12 and older in 2000[b]	33.6%

Who cared for America's children in 2002?

Both parents[c]	68.7%
Mother[c]	22.8%
Father[c]	4.6%
Grandparent[c]	1.8%
Other relative[c]	1.1%
Foster parent[c]	0.3%
Non-relative[c]	0.8%
Number of women with no husband present who were raising their own children under 18 years[d]	8,145,233

Our most vulnerable children

Children living in families with incomes below the poverty line in 2002[e]	12 million
Children living in extreme poverty in 2002[e]	5 million
Referrals for possible child abuse or neglect in 2002[f]	1.8 million
Children substantiated or indicated as abused or neglected in 2002[f]	896,000 victims
Children who died as a result of abuse or neglect in 2002[f]	1400 (1.98 deaths per thousand)
Children in foster care on September 30, 2003 (family and non-family settings)[g]	523,000
Children in family foster care as of September 30, 2002 (78.2% of all children in care)[h]	416,024
Children in non-family foster care as of September 30, 2002 (21.8% of all children in care)[h]	115,976
Children adopted from the public foster care system during the fiscal year ending September 30, 2001[i]	46,668
Children waiting to be adopted from the public foster care system as of September 30, 2001[i]	126,000

a   Source: US Census Bureau, Population Division (2003).
b   Source: US Census Bureau (2000).
c   Source: US Census Bureau (2003a).
d   Source: Estimate from US Census Bureau, American Community Profile (2003).
e   Source: National Center for Children in Poverty (NCCP), Columbia University (2003) US Census Bureau (2003)[1]
f   Source: US Department of Health and Human Services (US DHHS), Children's Bureau, Administration on Children, Youth and Families, National Clearinghouse on Child Abuse and Neglect Information (2003b), p.xiii.
g   Source: US DHHS, Administration for Children and Families, Administration on Children, Youth and Families, Children's Bureau (2005a).
h   Source: www.acf.hhs.gov/programs/cb/dis/afcars/publications/afcars.htm.[2]
i   US DHHS, Administration on Children, Youth and Families, Children's Bureau, Adoption and Foster Care Analysis and Reporting System (AFCARS) (2003), p.4. See www.acf.dhhs.gov/programs/cb/publications/afcars/ Adapted from Child Welfare League of America (2004a), p.1

In 2002 nearly two million US children were reported as abused and neglected. Compared to 1990 reports, this represents an increase of some 46 percent in officially reported victims.[3] The major types of child maltreatment and the percentage of substantiated reports are included in Table 3.2.

Table 3.2 : Percentage of children with different types of substantiated child maltreatment in the US in 2002

Percentage of children experiencing a type of maltreatment	*Percentage of child victims*[a]
Neglect (including medical neglect)	60.2
Physical abuse	18.6
Sexual abuse	9.9
Emotional or psychological maltreatment	6.5
Other type of maltreatment (e.g., abandonment, threats of harm to the child, congenital drug addiction)	18.9

a   The maltreatment type percentages will total more than 100 percent because many children were victims of more than one type of maltreatment and were coded multiple times.

Reproduced from US DHHS, Children's Bureau, Administration on Children, Youth and Families, National Clearinghouse on Child Abuse and Neglect Information (2003), p.22

Child Placement Rates and Dynamics

The US federal government (US DHHS) estimated that in 2002 532,000 children were placed in foster care in family and non-family settings, and 813,000 children were served throughout that fiscal year (US Department of Health and Human Services, 2004a).[2] A sizable number of youth enter adulthood by emancipating from out of home care; 19,008 youth exited foster care during fiscal year 2001 in that manner. As shown in Table 3.1, the numbers of children in placement have risen substantially since 1980, but they have shown a slow and steady decrease since 2000, with the decrease in out-of-home care population numbers attenuated by lower reunification rates. A disproportionate number of children of color are placed in foster care, especially African Americans, Native Americans, and Hispanics (Chibnall *et al.* 2003; Hill 2001; Hines *et al.* 2004). People of color are underrepresented among child welfare staff (see www.cwla. org), and there are insufficient services to ensure that children achieve permanency by returning home or being placed with guardianship or adoptive families.

Child Welfare – Legislative and Policy Context

Mission of Child Welfare Services

Historically, the mission of child welfare has been to respond to the needs of children reported to public child protection agencies as abused, neglected, or at risk for child maltreatment. Recently, there has been more emphasis on looking beyond public and private child welfare agencies to involve communities as a whole in the protection and nurturing of children. In addition, there has been an increasing effort to formulate collaborative community strategies aimed at preventing and responding to child abuse and neglect. Our knowledge of the risk/protective factor interplay at the child, parent, family, neighborhood, and community levels has grown to include the need to look beyond the typical parent–child dyad (Child Welfare League of America 2003).

Goals of Child Welfare Services

The field of child welfare services is gaining more clarity and consensus about its mission. There are a primary goal and two secondary goals for child welfare services. First and foremost, the primary goal is to protect children from harm. The secondary goals are to preserve existing family units, which include birth family and relative families, and to promote children's development into adults who can live independently and contribute to their community – a goal which may require a variety of permanency planning alternatives such as family reunification, placement with relatives, different forms of guardianship, adoption, and *planned* long-term foster care or kinship care with legal safeguards such as guardianship (Pecora *et al.* 2000; US DHHS, Administration on Children, Youth and Families, Children's Bureau 2003a).

There is some debate in the field about placing child safety as a goal superior to family support. Indeed, many family advocates and some researchers argue that without a simultaneous emphasis on child safety and family support, neither will happen in an equitable manner. Since 1998 reports have been submitted to Congress which document state performance (McDonald, Salyers and Shaver 2004; US DHHS 2003, 2004b; US Government Accounting Office 2004).

Advances in Child Welfare Policy

Child welfare policy is slowly but steadily being shaped by advances in a variety of areas, including research and practice in risk, resilience, and protective factors. For example, landmark books like *Neurons to Neighborhoods* reinforce infant and young child stimulation principles outlined by earlier pioneers and made them accessible to a broader audience (Shonkoff and Phillips 2000). Berrick *et al.* (1998) emphasize the importance of paying attention to child development fundamentals like attachment theory and social learning in designing child welfare policy and programs. Advances in the treatment of child abuse and neglect have emphasized how children with varied psychological make-up and differing amounts of social supports respond differently to various healing approaches (Briere 1992). Additionally, ecological and diversity perspectives underscore the vital roles that broader community networks and environments play in services and healing.

Over the past five decades major research studies (e.g., Fanshel and Shinn 1978), "program scandals" (Wooden 1976), class action lawsuits, and effective advocacy by adoptive parents precipitated a wide range of policy reforms. These include:

- strategically focused family-centered services to strengthen parenting

- child-centered early intervention and remedial services based on increased understanding of early brain development

- attempts to embed substance abuse treatment services within child welfare, or at least to strengthen linkages across service delivery systems such as mental health, education, and juvenile justice

- use of least restrictive placement environments that facilitated the closure of hundreds of residential institutions, and

- permanency planning for children to secure a stable family if their birth parents are unable to care for them within a reasonable period of time (e.g., Casey Family Programs 2003a; Maluccio, Fein and Olmstead 1986).

Two other significant transformations bear mentioning. First, service system leaders in child protective services, family support, and foster care have identified community collaborations as essential for effective services (Larner, Stevenson and Behrman 1998; Morgan, Spears and Kaplan 2003). Second, the field has recognized the need to move children of all races and ages to a more permanent family situation, while also being cognizant of the need to nurture child development if children remained involved in the child welfare service system.

Key Child Welfare Policy and Legislation

A number of public policies influence program provisions and impact the families served by child welfare services. These are listed in Table 3.3.

Current Policy Challenges

There are a number of policy challenges facing child welfare services, some of which are underscored by the mixed success the US is having in meeting the basic needs of children, ensuring their safety, health, relationships and opportunities, while supporting families as the foundation for positive child development.[4]

Early Intervention Services are Underfunded and Lack Federal Leadership

The critical importance of early intervention services has long been recognized in helping families avoid involvement with the child welfare system or placement of their children. Best practices for early intervention programs involve a range of family-centered services focusing on meeting the needs of the child within the context of his or her family and larger environment.

Clearly, with better prevention strategies in place, we could help families avoid their children entering the child welfare system.[5] However, in order to implement these strategies, a more unified leadership with a cohesive plan for family support is needed at the federal and state levels. We must also raise the public profile of the importance of affordable child care and increase awareness among policymakers about the importance of *family economic security* in preventing children from entering the child welfare system.

Family Support Services are not Backed by Coherent Funding Strategies

The goals of family support services include enabling families to raise their child at home by reducing stress, and through strengthening and enhancing care giving capacities (Walton, Sandau-Beckler and Mannes 2001). Utilization of formal support services by family caregivers plays a significant role in reducing the burdens and stress associated with caring for a child and in helping families obtain services for unmet needs. Such services usually are jointly financed by the federal and state

Table 3.3: A select list of child welfare-related federal legislation[a]

Policy legislation	References
Supplemental Social Insurance (SSI)	Social Security Administration (2000)
Child Abuse Prevention and Treatment Act of 1974 (P.L. 93-247)	Light (1973), Stein (1984)
Juvenile Justice and Delinquency Prevention Act of 1974 (P.L. 93-415)	Costin, Bell and Downs (1991, pp.71–2)
Title XIX of the Social Security Act	
The Education of All Handicapped Children Act of 1975 (P.L. 94-142)	Costin, Bell and Downs (1991, pp.300–303), Singer and Butler (1987)
The Individuals with Disabilities Education Act (IDEA) (began as the Education for All Handicapped Children Act of 1975—PL 94-142)	Parish and Whisnant (2005), Kirk, Gallagher and Anastasiow (1993, pp.51–2), Ramey and Ramey (1998)
P.L. 101-476 (Act modifying services for special education students)	
Title XX of the Social Security Act (as amended by the Omnibus Reconciliation Act of 1981)	Mott (1976)
The Indian Child Welfare Act of 1978 (P.L. 95-608)	Plantz *et al.* (1989)
The Adoption Assistance and Child Welfare Act of 1980 (P.L. 96-272)	Pine (1986)
Independent Living Initiative (P.L. 99-272)	Mech (1988)
P.L. 99-457 (mandates health, rehabilitation, education, and social services to children who have special needs from birth)	
Family Support Act of 1990	
1990 Farm Bill (P.L. 101-624)	www.thomas.loc.gov; www.connectforkids.org
Personal Responsibility and Work Opportunity Reconciliation Act (PRWORA). This funds the Temporary Assistance to Needy Families (TANF)	
Adoption and Safe Families Act of 1997	
More recent child welfare legislation	
Foster Care Independence Act of 1999 (P.L. 106-169) and the Educational Training Voucher Provisions	Child Welfare League of America (2004b)
Keeping Children and Families Safe Act	
The Adoption Incentive Program (P.L. 108-145)	Child Welfare League of America (2004b)[b]

Continued on next page

Table 3.3 cont.

Policy legislation	References
Adoption Opportunities Program (Title II of the Child Abuse Prevention and Treatment Act, P.L. 108-36)	
Runaway, Homeless, and Missing Children Protection Act	
Legacy Provisions in the American Dream Downpayment Act	
Extending food stamps to eligible immigrant children	
Protect Act (Amber Alert System)	
The Howard M. Metzenbaum Multi-Ethnic Placement Act (MEPA) of 1994 (P.L. 108–382) Interethnic Adoption Provisions (IEPA) of 1996 (Section 1808 of the Small Business Job Protection Act of 1996 mended the Multi-Ethnic Placement Act of 1994)	See US DHHS[c]

a A number of other pieces of legislation are important to child welfare services but are not summarized in this figure; these include the Social Security Act of 1935, amendments to the Act passed in 1939, 1950, 1962, 1965, 1967, 1974, 1983, some of which are also known as the title amendments of Title IV-A, IV-B, IV-E, IV-F, and V. These title amendments established, terminated, or altered a wide range of income assistance, medical, social service, and other programs. For more information, see Costin *et al.* (1991), DiNitto and Dye (1989), Stein (1991).

b Child Welfare League of America (2004b).

Sources: Compiled from Pecora, Whittaker, Maluccio and Barth (2000), and summaries prepared by the Public Policy Team of Casey Family Programs with the consultation of Children's Defense Fund, Child Welfare League of America, American Public Human Services Association, and the Alliance for Children.

governments, often with Medicaid resources, and typically administered by state or county governments. Not surprisingly, there is tremendous variability in the level of funding allocated for family support, and in the types of available services (Parish, Pomeranz and Braddock 2003).

Block-granting of Key Child Welfare Funding Mechanisms Requires Additional Discussion

A number of federal leaders have submitted proposals to Congress under which states would be allowed to use federal foster care funds, not only to support children in out-of-home care, but also to support child abuse prevention and post-adoption services. These and other proposals can be seen as efforts to address the family support issue raised above. But the downside to these proposals is that the overall budget support for children's services would decrease if all of them were to be enacted. Based upon what occurs with block-granting of Medicaid and food stamps, families would no longer have an entitlement.

Policy and Funding to Treat Mental Health and Substance Abuse Problems Must be Redesigned

Fragmented funding streams and policies fail to encourage effective treatment of comorbid conditions that are much more common in the United States than previously thought (Kessler and Magee 1993). For example, substance abuse problems are present in a significant percentage of the families where children are placed in out-of-home care (Besharov 1994). Many agency administrators are diverted from other activities in order to "braid" or cobble together multiple sources of funding to cover the costs of programs; their efforts highlight the critical need for more coordination at the federal and state levels to maximize the effectiveness of existing resources (Johnson, Knitzer and Kaufmann 2003).

Differential Response Approaches to Child Protective Services Intake Need Additional Testing.

New intake approaches are attempting to divert low-risk families to supportive programs other than Child Protective Services. These approaches need further testing and evaluation in order to inform policymakers' decisions concerning the roles of law enforcement, medical, legal, and social services personnel, as well as the role of voluntary agencies.

Kinship Care Funding, Licensing and Practice Policies Need to be Aligned

More than six million children live in households headed by grandparents or other relatives. US Census data tell us that 2.4 million grandparents are taking on primary responsibility for the basic needs of their grandchildren (US Census Bureau 2005). Kinship caregivers often lack the information and range of supports required to fulfill their parenting role (Children's Defense Fund 2004). Twofold legislation was recently introduced by Senator Hillary Clinton to provide special tax breaks for these once-again parents and, perhaps more importantly, to establish "kinship navigators" to advise these parents.

Increase Tribal Access to Federal Child Welfare Services Funding and Improve Existing Infrastructure

Consistent with their cultures, Native American tribes have exercised jurisdiction over their children, but they have seriously underdeveloped services. Tribal entities need to build a variety of services infrastructures such as management information systems and quality improvement programs. However, Native American tribes are not allowed to access Federal Title IV-E funds directly; this diminishes the effectiveness of tribal foster care programs.

Agency Policies Should Promote Better Assessment and Support of Gay, Lesbian, Bisexual, and Transgendered Youth in Out-of-home Care

Mallon (1999) and others have described how child welfare service delivery systems have not encouraged staff members and foster parents to protect and nurture gay, lesbian, bisexual, and transgendered youths. Such youths are vulnerable to victimization, depression, suicide, and placement disruption because of their sexual orientation. Special efforts are needed both to assess the needs of these youths and to devise supportive services for them.

Cross-systems Collaboration Needs Strengthening

When the risk factors and other root causes of a parent's need for child welfare services are identified, a more integrated approach to family support and children's services is essential. Economic supports, education, mental health, domestic violence, law enforcement, juvenile justice, and child welfare services all need to work more toward a common purpose. For example, morbid conditions such as depression and drug abuse require interdisciplinary approaches.

Transition Policies and Support for Emancipating Youth Must be Overhauled

Too many graduates of the foster care system are under-trained and underemployed. Many of these people are part of a large group of "marginalized youth." Alumni of foster care vary widely in their level of preparation for emancipation from foster care in terms of education and income.

Independent living preparation must be redesigned to start at age ten, not at the current age of 17. A comprehensive transition plan should be developed for every child. It should include planning for supportive relationships, community connections, education, life skills assessment and development, as well as planning for identity formation, housing, employment, physical health, and mental health (Massinga and Pecora, 2003).

Permanency Planning Needs Strengthening

Child welfare policy needs to be refined in ways that increase the likelihood that more youths will achieve and maintain permanence in a reasonable time period through foster care, reunification, relative placement, guardianship, or adoption. This includes crafting policies to ensure that kinship care families have access to resources needed to raise healthy children in stable home environments. Adoption policy must address more thoroughly how to better respond to the legal concerns expressed through the MEPA and IEPA legislation discussed in Table 3.3.

Policymakers Need to Recognize Racial and Ethnic Disproportionality in Outcomes

Disproportionality and the disparities in outcomes for children of color in the child welfare system are slowly being recognized as major ethical, policy, and program issues. Because major forms of racial disproportionality exist in provision of services and achievement of permanency outcomes, our goal should be to remove race and ethnicity as a predictor of outcome in child welfare services (Hill 2001).

Performance-based Contracting has not been Fully Implemented

State and county policies to promote evidence-based practice models and performance-based contracting have been hampered by a lack of knowledge of baseline conditions, sound target goals, and infrastructure funding gaps, as well as a lack of information about what practice models are currently evidence-based. Quality improvement systems must be in place to enable agencies to steadily improve (Mordock 2002; Pecora *et al.* 1996).

Child Welfare Policy, Practice and Research Evidence

The relationship between current research evidence and developments in policy and practice is not as strong as it needs to be, despite new successes in formulating evidence-based polices and program models. The Cochran and Campbell Collaboratives are systematically reviewing the evidence base for various program areas, and have done tremendous work in moving the field forward. For example, promising practice "registries" compare and report various program models to showcase those that have the strongest evidence base. Unfortunately, there is still a shortage of funding for evidence-based policies and programs, but it is slightly improving as some state agencies implement performance-based contracting and consider evidence-based program models (which remain too rare in the field). More research funding must be targeted to answer policy and fiscal concerns about outcomes and program effectiveness.

Conclusion

We have reviewed historical and current policies and legislation in American child welfare in the US. A number of critical issues requiring reform have been discussed. The utility of a risk and resilience model for policy reform has been explored. Models that consider the developmental processes of children and families may be useful in future child welfare reform initiatives. Policy experts would be wise to consider this framework as debate about ways to reform child welfare services continues.

Acknowledgements

This chapter draws on material in the third edition of *The Child Welfare Challenge*. We appreciate the advice from that textbook's other co-authors Richard Barth and Robert Plotnick. Special thanks to Fran Gutterman, Adrienne Hahn, Martha Jenkins and Betsey Rosenbaum of Casey Family Programs, and the legislative advocacy staff of the Child Welfare League of America for the policy briefs and position statements that informed the legislative policy section. Finally, foster care alumni, practitioners, and foster parents have taught us much about the real impacts of policy. We appreciate the time they have devoted to improving the child welfare system.

Notes

1. In 2001, 16.3 percent of children under age 18 lived in poverty — more than any other age group in America.

2. These data are from the federal Adoption and Foster Care Analysis and Reporting System (AFCARS), which used data from 45 state and other jurisdictions, including Washington, DC and Puerto Rico, to derive these estimates. US DHHS, Administration for Children and Families, Children's Bureau (2004,p.1). See www.acf.hhs.gov/programs/cb/dis/tables/entryexit2002.htm; for total children served in 2002, see www.acf.hhs.gov/programs/cb/dis/afcars/publications/afcars.htm. Note that AFCARS data are periodically updated, therefore, the data cited may not match the data on the current website.

3. There were three million reports involving the welfare of approximately five million children in 2001 and 1.8 million in 2002. For federal child maltreatment statistics, see US DHHS, Administration for Children and Families, Children's Bureau (2004). In 2003, nearly three million US children were reported as abused and neglected, with 906,000 confirmed victims (US Department of Health and Human Services, Administration for Children and Families, Children's Bureau, National Clearinghouse on Child Abuse and Neglect Information 200JC, pp.5, 21)

4. This section draws from policy briefs and position statements prepared by Casey Family Programs (2004) and Child Welfare League of America (2004b).

5. See Chapters 5, 7, 9, 23 and 25.

PART TWO

PART TWO

Evidence on Interventions with Vulnerable Children, Young People and Families

CHAPTER 4

Early Interventions with Young Children and their Parents in the UK

Marjorie Smith

Introduction

This chapter is being written at a time when there is, in the UK at least, a huge proliferation of interventions designed for young children or their parents. This largely
reflects the increasing political interest in parenting and interventions to lift children
out of poverty and poor childrearing environments, as well as to improve their health,
well-being and future prospects.

It is now accepted that experiences during the early years are of crucial
importance in determining later outcomes for children. In the first three years of a
child's life brain development is at its most rapid, and there is evidence that
appropriate stimulation and experiences are formative in neurological development
and the child's later ability to learn. Equally, there is evidence of the lasting negative
impact of poor environments, or environments lacking in stimulation, on children's
later development. There is some evidence that the first three years of life are
important not only in relation to intellectual development but also to later mental
health and well-being. It is known that there is considerable continuity between early
behaviour problems and later behaviour problems (Moffit et al. 1996). In particular,
conduct disorder in young children predicts later antisocial behaviour, and this is
associated with poor outcomes in a number of other areas (Maughan and Rutter
2001; Scott 1998). Emotionally stressful environments are also known to be
associated with a risk of poor outcomes such as behaviour problems and low
self-esteem for young children (Eisenberg 1998). For example, it has been suggested

that if young children are exposed to high levels of stress, such as might result from domestic violence or abusive situations, the effects of consistently high levels of stress hormones can be damaging (Gunnar 1998).

The aim of interventions with young children or their parents has been to target known risk factors, to try to prevent or ameliorate negative outcomes for the child or family. Most interventions have been targeted at particular groups of children or their parents – usually only mothers – and not at all children or all families. These groups 'in need' are normally identified by known risk factors, including material factors such as poverty or poor neighbourhoods; family factors such as poor parenting, family violence or poor maternal mental health; or child factors such as developmental delays or behaviour problems.

There are two varieties of interventions for young children and their parents in the UK. The first are 'home grown' interventions, and these are usually developed and used locally, and of relatively small scale. Many of these have originated in the voluntary sector, and have the advantage of being designed to meet local needs. At the same time, these projects operate on low budgets and only a small minority have been evaluated, so much of the current activity is of unknown effectiveness. The second type of interventions is 'imported' intervention programmes, usually developed in the US although there are recent examples from Canada and Australia (such as Triple P: the Positive Parenting Programme). In some cases these have had quite widespread application within the UK, and a few have been systematically evaluated on UK populations, but the majority have not.

Although interventions in the early years are usually aimed at improving the life chances of children in some way, it is not always children who are the direct focus of the intervention. Interventions may directly involve the child, the parents (nearly always the mothers), or both. Some interventions may aim to improve the children's life chances by intervening to improve maternal health or well-being in pregnancy, before the child is born. The majority of parenting programmes do not involve children directly at all, but some will be designed to improve child behaviour through changing the mother's behaviour and response to child behaviour, and will take a skills approach. Others will aim to do the same thing, through a parent education approach, while some programmes use a combination of parenting skills and education. Another set of interventions, also with the same aim of improving young children's life chances by improving the quality of their parenting, will aim to do this less directly, through improvements in maternal mental health or self-esteem, and there will be little, if any, direct focus on the child.

Other interventions to improve children's life chances may aim to do so even less directly, through changes in the local environment. For example, new community facilities or local services may be created or more family friendly employment opportunities developed. At the broadest level, interventions for young children and their parents can be effected on a national level, through the tax and benefits system, or through government funding for services which support families with young children. Sure Start, which will be discussed later in this chapter, is a good example of a government-initiated intervention at a national level, albeit one that aims to be effective through changes at the local level.

The Nature of the Evidence

Most reviews of interventions in the early years (for example, Guralnick 1997; Meisels and Shonkoff 1990; or, in the UK, Macdonald and Roberts 1995; Pugh, De'Ath and Smith 1994) come to the same conclusion: that few interventions have been systematically evaluated in any way, and even fewer evaluated in a scientifically rigorous way, such as by a randomized control trial (RCT) (Oakley 1996). In the few instances in the UK where interventions have been rigorously evaluated, this has usually been in relation to short-term or immediate outcomes. 'Effectiveness' has been normally assessed by comparing standardized measures made before the intervention, with the results on same measures repeated close in time to the end of the intervention. The expectation is that short-term or intermediate improvements will indicate or predict better long-term outcomes, although there are many examples of short-term gains that have 'washed-out' over time. No rigorous and longitudinal evaluations of early years' interventions in the UK have been identified.

Where evaluations have been carried out in the UK, they are commonly based on parents' perceptions of whether they or their child have benefited from the intervention, and there is no objective or standardized assessment of whether there have been changes in line with the aims of the intervention. As Oliver and Smith pointed out (2000), the concept of 'effectiveness' is open to different interpretations. Parents may feel or believe that they or their children have been 'helped' in some way, and may perceive and rate their children's behaviour as improved. This may well be a valid outcome of an intervention if mothers feel more confident, competent and relaxed in their role, but changes in perception are unlikely to be the sole aim of an intervention, and most interventions have some other aims. The stated goal of most interventions for young children or their parents is to produce change in child behaviour, child outcomes, adult behaviour, or combinations of these.

The recent government policy emphasis on parenting (Henricson 2003) and the subsequent proliferation of parenting programmes have identified a significant group of parents who actively seek to attend parenting programmes to help them in the task of bringing up their children (Barlow and Stewart-Brown 2001) but, as described earlier, most interventions have been designed for, and targeted at, specific groups of young children or their parents identified as 'in need', usually on the basis of some known risk factor. These are not generally parents who 'volunteer' for parenting programmes. This may go some way to explaining why many parenting programmes tend to report relatively low participation rates and high drop-out rates. Spencer (2003) points out that only 10 per cent of a group of parents invited to attend a parenting group expressed a definite interest in doing so, and in another study involving parents who had already identified their children as having behaviour problems, only 30 per cent agreed to participate in a randomized control trial. Drop-out rates from parenting programmes such as the Webster-Stratton tend to be of the order of 50 per cent or higher and, where such information is available, it is clear that there is social patterning in drop-out, with more disadvantaged parents less likely to complete the course (Spencer 2003).

There is scant systematic information on whether drop-out rates for parents from ethnic minority groups are higher, but as minority ethnic groups tend to be over-represented among the disadvantaged population, this would follow the known pattern of characteristics of those who do not participate or drop out. The fact that most parenting programmes have a white middle-class origin may result in a lack of sensitivity or 'fit' of the programme to those parents from other social or cultural groups, with the result that parents may feel the programme is not relevant to them, or that their way of parenting is being disapproved of.

There is very little information on the effectiveness of any UK interventions designed specifically for young children or their parents in minority ethnic groups, and indeed relatively few interventions in the UK that would come into this category. A recent review of 'what works' in parenting programmes for or including minority ethnic parents did not include a single UK-based study (Barlow, Shaw and Stewart-Brown 2004).

One further caveat should be added in relation to the nature of the evidence, and this relates to evidence of effectiveness from studies in the US being applied to the UK. It has sometimes been assumed that where particular interventions have been shown in the US to be effective, that this will also be the case in the UK. This is despite differences in culture (including parenting behaviour), the main minority ethnic groups, education and the infrastructure of health delivery. It is also probable that in 'translating' a programme to make it suitable for use in the UK, other subtle changes of unknown significance are also introduced.

We do have some evidence of interventions delivered and evaluated in both countries. For example, evaluations of the effects of the Webster-Stratton parenting programme delivered in the UK (Scott *et al.* 2001) have produced similar results (including take-up and drop-out rates) to those conducted in the US (Webster-Stratton, Hollinsworth and Kolpacoff 1989). A less consistent picture emerges in relation to findings on the effectiveness of out-of-home day care for disadvantaged families. The conclusions from a review of eight US studies of the health and welfare effects of day care were broadly positive, identifying beneficial effects on children's

IQ, behaviour and school achievement, as well as positive effects on maternal education, maternal employment, and the interaction of mothers with their children. Most of the interventions reviewed included parent training/education (Zoritch, Roberts and Oakley 2002). In contrast, results from a well-conducted RCT on the effects of day care provision in the UK (reviewed in more detail later in this chapter), did not identify any such positive effects, at least in the short term (Toroyan et al. 2003). It should be noted, however, that the UK study did not include any parent education or training component.

Evidence of Programme Effectiveness

The evidence included here is not comprehensive, but rather focuses on independently evaluated 'home grown' interventions in the early years and UK applications of interventions originating elsewhere and whose effectiveness on UK populations has been systematically assessed. Interventions are grouped according to their main focus and those included under each subheading are generally large scale, well known and available at a range of sites. This has excluded some small-scale interventions such as Bookstart and the Family Literacy Programme, aiming to increase early literacy skills and school readiness in young children, and so prevent early school failure. Where these have been evaluated, most appear to have been effective, perhaps as a result of their very specific and focused aims. Also excluded are some relatively well-known parenting education programmes, such as PIPPIN (Parents in Partnership – Parent Information Network) and Parenting Positively, which report generally positive effects in terms of parental self-report but which have not been independently evaluated.

Maternal Health and Social Support

The large majority of interventions for expectant mothers, very young children or their parents that might come under the heading of maternal health and social support are home based, and will be discussed in Chapter 6. One exception is the New Parent Information Network (NEWPIN), which is partly home based and partly centre based.

NEWPIN was designed to provide social support for vulnerable women under stress where there is a danger of family breakdown. NEWPIN place a particular emphasis on alleviating depression in mothers with young children. Mothers are usually referred to the scheme by health visitors, GPs or social workers, although a few are self-referred or referred by those already in the programme. The scheme is unusual in that it now runs groups for fathers as well. The programme is largely centre based, and there are now 19 NEWPIN family centres in the UK, but it also includes an initial home visit. Following this, the mother is matched with a volunteer 'befriender'. The intervention is a mixture of social involvement in therapeutic support groups, therapy (which includes one-to-one counselling for those who want it) and training in the form of a personal development programme. NEWPIN family centres can be used as drop-in centres, and have crèche and playroom facilities for children. Two independent evaluations of NEWPIN have been conducted (Cox *et al.* 1991; Oakley *et al.* 1995) and both came to broadly the same conclusions, although neither was particularly rigorous. It was noted that participation rates were generally low: in one of the evaluations less than half of those referred had made any use of NEWPIN, and most users had been fewer than five times. The greatest gains, in terms of self-reported well-being, were made by those who had the greatest involvement with the centres (Cox *et al.* 1991), although about half of those who had used the service at all felt that NEWPIN had helped them. Mothers who were referred but never used the service reported that it did not meet their needs or address their problems.

Parenting Skills

This category covers a large group of interventions or programmes for parents and, especially, mothers. These range from those designed for parents who have been identified as having severe difficulties in parenting their children (for example, Mellow Parenting), to those who self-identify as having difficulties with parenting or, more usually, who identify their children's behaviour as problematical (for example, the Webster-Stratton Programme; Parenting Positively); to those who lack confidence in their parenting skills, or are simply interested in being better parents (PAFT – Parents as First Teachers; Parenting Matters). Some programmes, such as the Webster-Stratton programme, have been used in both clinical settings for parents whose children have identified behaviour problems, and for self-referred parents in community settings.

MELLOW PARENTING

Mellow Parenting is a programme developed in the UK by a group with expertise in child psychiatry, psychology and social work (Puckering *et al.* 1994). Its application is increasing, particularly within specialist clinical environments, and training in the programme is now coordinated through a professional association.

The Mellow Parenting programme is designed for families with children aged under five, who are experiencing stress and relationship problems with their children. The 13-week centre-based parenting support groups are focused on the development of parenting skills, using a mixture of group work, video feedback sessions and workshops. The aim is to empower parents who may have experienced poor parenting themselves to find better ways of relating to their own children.

In a relatively small-scale evaluation involving parents with multiple problems and often with a history of abuse or emotional deprivation, Mellow Parenting was shown to be associated with improvements for both participating mothers and their children. These were in mother–child interaction, maternal well-being, mothers' perceptions of their effectiveness and confidence in parenting and child behaviour, language and intellectual abilities. It was also noted that attendance was high in these multi-problem families. The changes achieved were still evident at an 18-month follow-up (Mills and Puckering 2001).

INCREDIBLE YEARS PARENTING PROGRAMME

This video-based social learning parenting programme, which originated in the US and is probably better known in the UK as the Webster-Stratton programme, has been used in a number of settings in the UK (Webster-Stratton and Hancock 1998). The programme has been used as part of a randomized evaluation of the effectiveness of community- versus hospital-based support for children with behavioural problems (Harrington *et al.* 2000), and it has also been systematically evaluated when delivered in the context of a normal service setting (Scott *et al.* 2001). In the latter evaluation, the programme was used with groups of parents of children aged three to eight years of age who were referred to child and adolescent mental health services because of their child's antisocial behaviour.

Parents were allocated either to a parenting group, or to a waiting list control group. Before entry to the study, and again between five and seven months later, parents were interviewed and completed questionnaires about their children's antisocial behaviour, and a direct (videotaped) observation was made of parent–child interaction during a structured play task. Before the start of the intervention, children's mean scores (in both groups) were above the 97th percentile for conduct disorders, compared with population norms.

After the intervention period, parents who had been part of the parenting groups rated their children as showing much less antisocial behaviour than before the groups, while there was no change in the ratings of those who were part of the control group. At the same time, independent ratings of parents' behaviour showed that those who had participated in the parenting groups were more likely to praise their children and less likely to give ineffective commands than those in the control group. It should be noted, however, that not all parents wanted to be considered for the study – nearly a fifth did not want to take part, and, of those who did and were allocated to the parenting groups, a further 18 per cent attended four or fewer sessions, and were considered to have dropped out.

PARENTING MATTERS (FORMERLY PARENT LINK)

These parenting courses, run by Parentline Plus, are open to parents of children of all ages, rather than just the parents of young children. Parents are told about the course and whether there is one available in their locality when they call the Parentline Plus telephone helpline. Alternatively, parents may be told about the courses by their GP, health visitor or social worker. The course comprises 12 weekly sessions of two and a half hours each, and is experience-based, encouraging parents to share their experiences and ideas in relation to specific topics. A small 'independent' evaluation, but not independently peer reviewed or published, suggested that in addition to improvements in children's behaviour (as rated by the parents themselves), parents benefited from the intervention in terms of improvements in their self-esteem, stress reduction and improvements in family relationships (Davis and Hester 1996).

Pre-school

While it could be said that pre-school is not an intervention, pre-school educational programmes focused directly on children have been used with the aim of enhancing child development or intellectual outcomes, or 'readiness to learn' in children from disadvantaged environments. A number of rather small studies have suggested that good quality pre-school programmes can have a positive influence on both educational and social outcomes, at least in the short term. The evaluations included here are those either conducted in the UK or that apply to programmes or interventions that are available on a national basis in the UK.

HIGH/SCOPE INSTITUTE UK

Much attention has been given to the results of this relatively small-scale intervention (Perry Preschool Project/High/Scope Education), which took place in Ypsilanti, Michigan US, on four cohorts of children recruited between 1962 and 1965. The children involved were African-American pre-schoolers aged between three and four years, from low-income families, identified as at risk of school failure. The original programme was a two-year programme of two and a half hours, five days a week, of intensive academic stimulation, in small groups with a high staff ratio. The programme content was organized on Piagetian principles of child-initiated learning, with children selecting their own activities. Children were encouraged to 'plan-do-think' for each activity. Parents were also involved, through both home visits by teachers and monthly small group meetings.

The reason that this small intervention has received so much attention is that it was a RCT (although the rigour of this has been questioned by Farran 1990), it was rigorously and longitudinally evaluated and it has been shown to be effective in the long term, even though there were no cognitive differences between intervention and control children in the middle-school period (Berrueta-Clement *et al.* 1984; Schweinhart, Barnes and Weikart 1993; Schweinhart and Weikart 1980; Schweinhart, Weikart and Larner 1986).

High/Scope is an example of a US-designed intervention that is now in use in the UK. High/Scope Institute UK aims to improve the quality of young children's lives by training adults to work with children in the early years. Courses comprise seven teaching blocks of a week's duration, carried out over an eight-month period. The approach that is taught is very similar to that of the original intervention programme. It is now estimated that a quarter of a million children in the UK attend settings where the High/Scope approach has been used. Despite this number, there do not appear to be any UK-based evaluations of effectiveness.

THE EFFECTIVE PROVISION OF PRE-SCHOOL EDUCATION (EPPE)

There is one substantial study of the effects of pre-schooling in the UK (Sylva *et al.* 2004). Sylva and colleagues conducted a five-year longitudinal multilevel project involving over 3000 children who were recruited when they were aged three years and followed until they were aged seven. The study was conducted in 141 different settings (nursery schools and classes, integrated centres, local authority day nurseries, private day nurseries and playgroups) and included a group of 'home' children who did not attend any pre-school. Assessments of children's cognitive development were made using standardized psychometric tests, and socio-emotional adjustment was assessed by means of standardised ratings made by pre-school staff. Assessments continued until the end of the first stage of primary education (Key Stage 1). The design of the study enabled conclusions to be drawn about the benefits of pre-schooling at the institutional level (do some types of pre-school provision produce better results than others?); the centre level (do some individual centres produce better or worse results than others?); and at the level of the individual child (what are the characteristics of individual children or their backgrounds that influence the outcomes, or that interact with the type or quality of provision?).

Results from the pre-school period indicated that overall children who attended pre-school did better in both cognitive development and aspects of social behaviour than those who did not. Starting younger was related to better outcomes for children than those who started when they were older, but there was no difference associated with whether children attended full-time or part-time. Pre-school was also found to be effective in reducing the educational risks for socially disadvantaged children, and the most significant gains were made by children in the most disadvantaged groups. This applied to the risks of developing learning difficulties or social behavioural problems at primary school, as both were significantly reduced.

Analyses of the pre-school data also indicated that both the type and quality of pre-school were important factors in children's developmental progress. Integrated centres (where education and care are combined) tended to produce better cognitive outcomes for children, while integrated centres and nursery classes promoted better social outcomes for children. For disadvantaged children, environments where there was a mix of children from different social backgrounds promoted better outcomes than did settings where most of the children were disadvantaged.

There were differences between individual settings in their 'effectiveness' in promoting child outcomes, and these were related to assessments of the quality of the setting made using standardized rating scales. In general, settings that were effective in promoting cognitive development in children were also effective in promoting social behavioural development. Case studies of a small number of 'effective' settings identified five aspects of practice that appeared to be particularly important. These were the quality of the adult–child verbal interactions; staff knowledge and under-standing of the curriculum; knowledge of how young children learn; adults' skill in supporting children in resolving conflicts; and helping parents to support children's learning in the home.

The positive effects of pre-schooling remained evident at the end of Key Stage 1, although some of the benefits had diminished in strength over the two years that children had been at school. When the children reached the age of seven, the effect of the duration of pre-school attendance was still evident, although more so in academic skills than in social or behavioural outcomes.

Out-of-home Day Care

Out-of-home day care has been used as an intervention in cases of poor environments or problems at home, such as maternal depression, with the aim of improving the health and welfare of both children and their mothers. It is notable that in a UK review of interventions involving random or quasi-random allocation of participants, on the effects of out-of-home day care on children, the eight included studies were all from the US (Zoritch *et al.* 2002).

Since then, however, one study evaluating the effectiveness of providing day care for young children has been published in the UK (Toroyan *et al.* 2003). The aims of the study were to improve the health and welfare of disadvantaged families, but a primary outcome was to move families out of poverty by increasing maternal employment. The study, which had a RCT design, was conducted at one 'model' early years day care centre (designated by the government as an 'early excellence centre') situated in a deprived area of London. The 120 families with 143 children who had applied for places were randomly allocated to either a centre place or whatever other child care they could find for themselves. The centre provided highly flexible quality day care, integrating education with care and offering extended hours.

Eighteen months after the start of the trial, although the intervention group mothers were somewhat more likely to be in employment (67% were, as opposed to 60% of the control group mothers) and worked more hours per week, they were less likely to have a weekly income of more than £200. Children in the intervention group did have slightly higher mental development scores (but not statistically significantly so). At the same time, they had experienced more ear infections and were more likely to have visited a doctor or nurse in the previous month.

The authors identify a lack of statistical power, as a result of smaller sample numbers than expected, as one of the weaknesses of the study (Toroyan *et al.* 2003). They conclude by questioning the assumption that paid employment provides an immediate route out of poverty and recommending that, in addition to the provision of day care, policies to reduce family poverty must tackle low pay and the benefit structure.

Sure Start

The major UK government initiative Sure Start, launched in 1999, while not an intervention as such, must also surely be mentioned. Sure Start is not a single intervention, but a programme comprising (among other things) a large number of different interventions, located in different disadvantaged areas. The central aim of Sure Start is 'to improve the health and well-being of families and children, before and from birth, so children are ready to flourish when they go to school' (Glass 2001, p.14). This will be achieved by helping the development and coordination of services in disadvantaged areas, so that they are available for all families with young children in the area, community driven and professionally coordinated and flexible at the point of delivery. By March 2004 it was anticipated that 400,000 children in the UK had access to 524 Sure Start local programmes.

There is a comprehensive programme of assessment and evaluation being conducted alongside the development of this initiative, to assess how effective Sure Start is in meeting certain key targets. The evaluation is taking place on a national basis across all schemes, but in addition each individual scheme is required to carry out their own local evaluation. As Glass (2001, p.18) says, 'the evaluation will be concerned with whether a multi-agency, community based programme of early intervention makes a difference to school performance – rather than the detailed contribution of each element of the programmes'.

The first outputs from the National Evaluation of Sure Start (NESS) have appeared, and these relate to the experience of setting up the schemes and their implementation, as well as the first results relating to effects at the community, family or child level (NESS 2004). The evaluation team caution that, 'with such ambitious goals, it is clear that the ultimate efficacy of [Sure Start] cannot be determined for quite some time' (NESS 2004, p.4), but rather disappointingly are only able to report one significant finding in the impact study, based on the comparison of more than 8000 families from 75 Sure Start areas with 3000 families in 50 comparison areas. This was that in Sure Start areas mothers were observed to treat the child in a warmer and more accepting manner than in comparison areas.

Conclusion

Although there are now a considerable number and type of different interventions for children in the early years and their parents, this is a relatively recent development, and it remains the case that the UK has lagged behind the US in the development and evaluation of interventions. It has been concluded that interventions in the early years can improve outcomes for children and their parents in a number of ways, but most reviews are of interventions developed for US populations and rely on studies carried out there. Since there are significant differences between the two cultures in a number of important areas, such as child care and health care, as well as economic and demographic differences, it is questionable how applicable any conclusions drawn from these reviews are in a UK context. As a result, within the UK, there is little 'hard' evidence of the effectiveness of such interventions.

In most of the areas where evaluations have been systematically and independently conducted, the results look promising (rather than conclusive) and suggest that specific interventions can be used as a means of achieving positive outcomes for children and their families – the possible exception relates to the provision of day care as a means of improving the financial circumstances of families. Given the multiplicity and complexity of other factors that impinge on and influence child development, it should be seen as encouraging that it appears that specific interventions can also have a positive impact.

Despite this generalization, there is a lot that is not yet known about effective interventions in the early years. We still have a lot to learn about how to design interventions or programmes that are acceptable to families, do not stigmatize and are seen as helpful, in order to engage parents effectively in interventions and maintain participation to avoid high drop-out rates. This often applies particularly to the hard-to-reach parents who are deemed to 'need' help or support with parenting. We also have much to learn about how interventions work, in terms of 'active ingredients' or the mechanisms that achieve change. Given the substantial increase in the number and type of interventions now available in the UK, and the goodwill and positive energy in those who promote them, it seems timely for some more energy to be expended in finding out systematically which of these interventions are most effective (including cost-effectiveness) in achieving a particular aim, for which groups (and how to expand this to other groups) and how the intervention works.

CHAPTER 5

Early Interventions with Young Children and their Parents in the US

K. Lori Hanson, Connie E. Morrow and Emmalee S. Bandstra

Introduction

From a public policy perspective, there is a strong consensus among parents, advocacy groups, professionals, and policy makers that early intervention makes a difference (Gomby *et al.* 1995; Guralnick 1997; Knitzer 2001; US Public Health Service 2000). The nearly 50-year history of early childhood intervention has been closely intertwined with public policy, federally funded programs, and legislative mandates (see Meisels and Shonkoff 2000; Shonkoff, Lippitt and Cavanaugh 2000). Although credited with creating and supporting many early interventions currently available in the United States, public legislation has evolved in a piecemeal manner, resulting in policies and programs that are fragmented and uncoordinated. Several initiatives have developed to prevent young children from living in poverty, as well as to address social, economic, and racial disparities in the areas of education and health (e.g., Head Start, Early Head Start, State Children's Health Insurance Program). Others focus on ensuring children's safety (e.g., Child Protective Services) and meeting the special needs of children with disabilities (e.g., Individuals with Disabilities Education Act).

Creating a cohesive, integrated system of service delivery is essential, as reflected in the US Surgeon General's report that "children and families are suffering because of missed opportunities for prevention and early identification, fragmented services, and low priorities for resources" (US Public Health Service 2000, p.6). The combination of reduced funding for early interventions at the federal level and increased local awareness of the critical importance of the early years has led to increasing state and local investments. As differing service systems evolve from one locality to another, issues of fragmentation are further exacerbated and make it nearly impossible to estimate how many infants and young children are receiving various early intervention services. There has been a proliferation of coalitions, commissions, and oversight groups focused on early childhood interventions and issues, such as school-readiness, infant mental health, early child care quality and availability, universal pre-kindergarten, and maternal–child health. These groups assert the importance of the early years in shaping children's later health and educational success, and advocate for funding of related service programs.

Developments from within professional fields related to early intervention have informed advocacy efforts and inspired policy changes and increased resources and supports. For example, in 1994, the National Center for Infants, Toddlers and Families at Zero To Three published the Diagnostic Classification of Mental Health and Developmental Disorders of Infancy and Early Childhood (DC:0-3; Zero to Three National Center 1994), the first systematic, developmentally based diagnostic framework. Providing a uniform language for evaluating and labeling difficulties experienced in early childhood has enhanced scientific dialog and resulted in improved financial coverage of early mental health assessment and intervention services through Medicaid and other payment systems.

Early childhood intervention has been broadly defined as:

> multidisciplinary services provided to children from birth to 5 years of age to promote child health and well-being, enhance emerging competencies, minimize developmental delays, remediate existing or emerging disabilities, prevent functional deterioration, and promote adaptive parenting and overall family functioning. (Shonkoff and Meisels 2000, p.xvii)

Common interventions in early childhood include both focused and comprehensive approaches, such as developmental assessment and intervention, early childhood education, maternal–child health services, home-visiting programs, and parenting education. The scope of interventions ranges from preventive approaches aimed at the general population to techniques focused on identified problems and families in crisis. Given this broad scope of prevention and early intervention, as well as the number and variety of risk factors impacting young children in society today, it is likely that some aspects of early intervention are applicable to all of the more than 20 million children under the age of five currently living in the US (US Census Bureau, Population Division 2005).

Prevention is focused on enhancing protective factors and resilience and reversing or reducing known risk factors. Approaches to preventive intervention are categorized into "universal," "selected," or "indicated" (Institute of Medicine 1994). The *universal* approach aims to serve all young children to ensure optimal development. Examples include developmental monitoring in the pediatric care setting, infant care classes within hospitals and birthing facilities, and media campaigns emphasizing the importance of talking to infants. The *selected* approach is focused on early intervention with young children considered at risk due to various family or environmental stressors, such as children with depressed or substance-abusing parents and families living in poverty. Examples of selected interventions include low-birthweight infant developmental follow-up clinics and home-visiting programs for infants of teen parents. Finally, the *indicated* approach is designed to address the needs of children or families experiencing identifiable behavioral health problems, such as attachment disorders or other severe emotional problems. Examples include dyadic psychotherapy and live or video interactive guidance.

The basic premise underlying early intervention is that preventing or minimizing difficulties early is not only attainable, but preferable to treating problems arising later. Another important contextual assumption is that intervening with infants and young children necessarily involves intervention with parents. Ecological theories of development emphasize the interactional nature of influences of the child, family, and broader social environment (Bronfenbrenner 1989; Sameroff and Fiese 2000). This systems theory tends to be less linear and less focused on blaming the parenting or family environment than more traditional cause-and-effect developmental theories (Halpern 2000), thereby offering more points of entry for intervention. The implication for intervention is that one must not only approach the child in the context of the family, but also the family in the context of the broader community and environment.

The Nature of the Evidence

The relatively robust support from general developmental research for the influence of caregiver relationship qualities and behaviors upon child health and developmental outcomes has positively contributed to advocacy for more widely available early intervention programs to enhance such factors. Despite strong support from parents, professionals, and policymakers for early intervention, scientific research conclusions are somewhat less robust (Guralnick 1997). Unmistakably, several exemplary intervention studies have demonstrated strong scientific evidence for both short- and long-term effectiveness (e.g., Infant Health and Development Program, High/Scope Project, Nurse Home Visitation Program, Abecedarian Program). However, many methodological challenges must be overcome in conducting early intervention research. As community-based early intervention services have become more widespread, and some even mandated, it has become increasingly difficult to identify appropriate comparison or control groups. Comparisons must be made between specific interventions and the current standard of care available within the particular community studied, rather than between treatment and no treatment groups. Additionally, because early interventions tend to be comprehensive but also individually tailored, there may be variation within the treatment group with regard to the specific intervention components received. This makes it more difficult to tease apart specific and overall effects of early interventions.

Evidence of Program Effectiveness

Lessons From General Developmental Research

General developmental research implicating specific protective and risk factors has informed the content and design of early interventions to increase resilience (Werner 2000) and decrease risk. The most influential protective factors related to interventions in infancy and early childhood involve the parent–child relationship and other parenting characteristics.

Since infants and young children are especially dependent on the world around them to meet their physical and emotional needs, interventions commonly aim to promote nurturing relationships. Decades of early childhood research support the critical importance of providing social and emotional support and stimulation, thereby promoting early brain development (Schore 1996). Aside from the impact on present quality of life, research findings have indicated the importance of the quality of early attachments to later child social behavior and school achievement (Barnard 1997; Erickson and Kurz-Riemer 1999). Caregiver sensitivity to infant cues is a key factor related to forming secure attachment relationships (DeWolff and van Ijzendoorn 1997). Parental sensitivity and responsiveness together result in the capacity for reciprocity: the ability to interpret infant cues accurately and respond appropriately to the child's emotional needs.

Other parental behaviors important to child outcomes include social and cognitive growth-fostering techniques, such as talking, singing and reading to babies; facilitating exploration; and creating opportunities for mastery (Erickson and Kurz-Riemer 1999; Hart and Risley 1995). In the toddler years, parents must balance their responses to the child's conflicting needs for exploration/autonomy and closeness/attachment (Lieberman 1993). Specific knowledge of newborn capacities, developmental sequences, and age-appropriate expectations enhances successful parenting skills. Parental well-being and family social supports also act as important protective factors contributing to positive parenting and child outcomes (Osofsky and Thompson 2000).

Lessons from Early Intervention Research

Because of the wide variety of interventions implemented and evaluated, early intervention research has generally led to broad conclusions, rather than specific guidance for intervention content. Multiple resources are available to locate specific prevention and early intervention programs, many with objective evaluative ratings. Although a review of specific programs is beyond the scope of this overview, Tables 5.1 and 5.2 contain a list of such resources and a selection of frequently cited programs. The remainder of this chapter will highlight findings regarding overall effectiveness, as well as some guiding principles for best practice.

Early childhood intervention studies have consistently resulted in modest but positive outcomes, emphasizing the overall value of such programs, especially with the addition of cost-benefit methods that document long-term savings (e.g., Karoly *et al.* 1998). Several reviews have found interventions to account for about 10 percent of variance in outcomes (Erickson and Kurz-Riemer 1999) and average effect sizes of one-half to three-quarters of a standard deviation (Guralnick 1997). Methodological difficulties, such as inadequate outcome measures, limited funds to evaluate and sustain longitudinal studies, perceived ethical barriers to designing well-controlled studies, low sample sizes, attrition, substandard or inconsistent service delivery, insufficient staff training, and staff turnover, have contributed to the modest scientific findings in many studies (e.g., National Research Council and Institute of Medicine (NRCIM) 2000; Shonkoff and Meisels 2000).

Outcomes positively impacted by early intervention include child development domains of cognitive functioning/IQ and achievement, social-emotional competence, health, behavior, and peer interactions (Barnett 1995). Parental outcomes have also been favorably affected, indicating improved parent–child relationships and attachment; parenting skills, knowledge, and behavior; and individual parent capacities, such as literacy and employment (Brooks-Gunn, Berlin and Fuligni 2000). The wider environment is impacted by improved child, parent and family functioning, as indicated by long-term results of reduced child maltreatment, delinquency, and violence, as well as economic savings for the community (Karoly *et al.* 1998; Yoshikawa 1995). The field has recently entered its "second generation" of research, with a movement to assess differential effectiveness (i.e., which children benefit most from what interventions and how). It is also increasingly recognized that the limits of traditional quantitative analyses can be effectively balanced with qualitative parent, child, and staff perspectives when evaluating interventions. While conclusive results are not yet available, some common characteristics of effective early intervention have emerged.

Early interventions with children at risk may offer the greatest impact and long-term cost savings, suggesting the selected approach to early intervention may be preferable to universal. Many intervention programs have been designed for particular at-risk groups (e.g. children living in poverty, children with disabilities, children of substance-abusing or depressed parents, children exposed to violence, and children of teen parents; see examples in Shonkoff and Meisels 2000; Zeanah

Table 5.1: Selected resources for locating effective early intervention programs

Resource	Description	Website
Center for the Study and Prevention of Violence	Blueprints for model programs	www.colorado.edu/cspv
Comparison Matrix of Science-Based Prevention Programs: A Consumer's Guide for Prevention Professionals (US Department of Health and Human Services)	Description of various rating systems and matrix of programs	Visit "Publications" link at www.model programs.samhsa.gov
Development Services Group	Office of Juvenile Justice and Delinquency Prevention's model programs guide and database	www.dsgonline.com
Emerging Practices in the Prevention of Child Abuse and Neglect (Administration for Children and Families)	Program reviews and rankings	Can be accessed at National Clearinghouse on Child Abuse and Neglect Information nccanch.acf.hhs.gov
Model Programs (Substance Abuse and Mental Health Services Administration)	National Registry of Effective Programs	www.modelprograms. samhsa.gov
Prevention Decision Support System (Center for Substance Abuse Prevention)	Community-based logic model planning tool	www.preventiondss.org
Prevention Pathways (Center for Substance Abuse Prevention)	Model programs and programs for specific populations	www.preventionpath ways.samhsa.gov
Promising Practices Network on Children, Families, and Communities	Proven and promising programs, searchable by program benchmark/outcome	www.promising practices.net
Strengthening America's Families (Office of Juvenile Justice and Delinquency Prevention	Effective family programs for prevention of delinquency	www.strengthening families.org
Western Center for the Application of Prevention Technologies (Center for Substance Abuse Prevention)	Planning and best practices (Step 6)	www.casat.unr.edu/ westcapt
Zero To Three Programs and Services (for Professionals)	Professional education, program consultation, and parenting education resources	www.zerotothree.org

Table 5.2: Selected early intervention programs for infants/young children and their parents

Program	Program type	Prevention approach
Carolina Abecedarian Project	Comprehensive	Selected
CEDEN Family Resource Center/Healthy and Fair Start	Home visitation	Indicated
Chicago Child-Parent Centers (Reynolds)	Comprehensive	Selected
Child and Family Resource Programs (previously Syracuse Family Demonstration Project)	Comprehensive	Selected
Clinical Infant Programs (Fraiberg, Leiberman)	Comprehensive	Indicated
Comprehensive Child Development Program	Home visitation	Selected
DARE To Be You	Comprehensive	Selected
Early Head Start Program	Educational	Selected
Families and Schools Together	Comprehensive	Selected
Focus on Families	Parent training	Indicated
Head Start Program	Educational	Selected
Healthy Families America (developed out of Hawaii Healthy Start)	Home visitation	Selected
Healthy Start (to reduce infant mortality)	Home visitation	Selected
Helping the Noncompliant Child	Parent training	Indicated
High/Scope Perry Preschool Project	Educational	Selected
Home Instruction for Parents of Preschool Youngsters (HIPPY) www.hippyusa.org	Home visitation	Universal
HOMEBUILDERS	Comprehensive	Indicated
Infant Health and Development Program	Comprehensive	Selected
Making Parenting a Pleasure	Parent training	Universal
MELD	Parent training	Universal
NICASA Parent Project	Parent training	Universal
Nurse Family Partnership (previously Prenatal and Early Childhood Nurse Home Visitation)	Home visitation	Selected
Nurturing Parenting Program	Family skills training	Selected
Parent-Child Development Centers	Comprehensive	Selected

Program	Program type	Prevention approach
Parents Anonymous	Comprehensive	Universal
Parents as Teachers	Parent training	Universal
Raising a Thinking Child: I Can Problem Solve	Parent training	Universal
Starting Early Starting Smart www.health.org/promos/sess	Comprehensive	Selected
Strengthening Multi-Ethnic Families and Communities	Parent training	Indicated
The Incredible Years Parents and Children Training Series	Comprehensive	Selected
Yale Child Welfare Research Program	Comprehensive	Selected

2000). Within at-risk groups, the highest functioning children tend to make the most progress through participation in early intervention (Guralnick 1997). In addition, children with environmental risk factors appear to fare better than those with biological risk factors (Erickson and Kurz-Riemer 1999).

Interventions that benefit vulnerable families most are comprehensive, including a range of service components within the context of family-friendly service settings and focused on the multiple needs of young families throughout early childhood (i.e., prenatally to school entry) (Halpern 2000). Programs combining parenting support with child-focused educational activities seem to demonstrate the best outcomes with regard to child development and academic achievement (Gomby *et al.* 1995; NRCIM 2000; Shonkoff and Meisels 2000). Furthermore, "two-generation" programs, focused specifically on adult outcomes for parents (e.g., literacy, employment), as well as child and parenting outcomes, tend to demonstrate the best long-term benefits for families.

Meeting the individual needs of parents and other significant family members enables families to provide a more supportive caregiving environment for young children (Osofsky and Thompson 2000). For example, providing an integrated service program within the pediatric health-care setting has been found to increase caregiver access and utilization of needed mental health and substance-related treatment, with long-term implications for optimizing family and child well-being (Hanson *et al.* 2003; Vogel *et al.* 2003). Discrete or narrow interventions alone are too limited to make a notable impact, but when delivered in the context of a continuum of family support services, more pathways for change are created, leading to a stronger combined effect.

Service integration requires a sophisticated, carefully designed approach to meeting the needs of individuals, families, and communities (see Hanson *et al.* 2001 for a resource guide regarding how to build an integrated service program). Service components most relevant to families of young children include health, education and development, parenting support, substance-abuse and mental health services for caregivers, and connection with community resources and social services. Typically, agencies directly provide the services most closely related to their own mission and expertise, and link families to other services through a case management model and cooperative agreements or subcontracts with other providers. Ongoing assessment and reduction of barriers to service utilization are critical to ensuring access to needed services. Evaluating the effectiveness of comprehensive, service integration programs is challenging because it is not feasible to determine which of the multiple intervention components engender change. Perhaps the synergy of well-integrated interventions is the key to making enduring progress in child development within at-risk families and environments.

Early childhood intervention is most effective when it begins earlier (ideally at birth, but at least by the age of two), provides adequate intensity, and continues for an appropriate duration (Gomby *et al.*1995; Halpern 2000). Intensity takes precedence over duration, as programs with infrequent contacts have generally not been shown to be effective. Erickson and Kurz-Riemer (1999) suggest that early intervention must involve a minimum of 11 contacts over three months. After an initial period of intensity, it may be appropriate for contacts to be scaled back to meet the individual needs of the family. Cost-benefit considerations must be taken into account regarding intensity and duration, as most services cannot be made available on an indefinite basis (NRCIM 2000).

In the context of comprehensive, integrated services, it is necessary to offer individualized service delivery, based on the child's developmental level and the family's needs and goals. A tailored treatment or service plan can be developed collaboratively with parents, selecting desired components from a "menu" of services, as suggested by Hanson and colleagues (2001). This partnership approach allows for family choice and empowers parents to make changes for their infants and young children. Early intervention is more effective when family needs and resources are matched to well-defined goals for the child and family, rather than simply providing generic "family support" without clear objectives (NRCIM 2000). In addition, offering an array of interventions in a flexible manner helps overcome many barriers to service access. This may involve offering services at non-traditional times (i.e., evenings, weekends), or across multiple settings. For example, home visiting often increases participation, as well as offering services in other convenient, non-stigmatizing settings (e.g., pediatric health clinics, child-care settings).

Given theoretical and developmental research findings regarding the importance of early caregiving relationships, it is not surprising that effective interventions also tend to be relationship focused. It takes time to develop trusting relationships with parents, and the quality and continuity of these therapeutic relationships are critical to success. Interventionists must model the warmth, responsivity, and consistency they hope to facilitate within the parent–child relationship (Hanson *et al.* 2001). Family-centered services place an emphasis on engaging families when and where they are most ready and available, starting with services families prioritize for themselves (Osofsky and Thompson 2000). For example, being active and reliable in meeting immediate concrete needs is important in itself, but also affects how parents experience relationships with early intervention programs (Halpern 2000). Additionally, given the growing racial, ethnic, and cultural diversity in the US, it is critical for programs to ensure services are culturally appropriate, utilize a strength-based orientation, and communicate respect for each family's values and beliefs (US Department of Health and Human Services (US DHHS) 2000).

Provider knowledge and skills are essential to the effectiveness of early intervention programs (NRCIM 2000). An interdisciplinary team approach ensures the availability of a wide range of health, mental health, developmental, educational, and social services to meet diverse needs of young children. The higher the risk of the families served, the more sophisticated staff members must be to create an impact. Some contend that professional staff are superior to paraprofessionals in achieving intervention goals (Halpern 2000), while others claim paraprofessionals can be as effective when well trained and supported by professional supervision (Musick and Stott 2000). However, no one would debate that all early intervention staff require specialized training and limited caseload assignments.

Model early intervention programs are generally theoretically grounded, with clearly defined goals and objectives for families (NRCIM 2000). A sound theoretical framework provides guidance in determining children's needs, factors important to parenting, and avenues for facilitating desired family outcomes. In addition, given the modest strength of overall early intervention findings, it is important to define reasonable expectations for program outcomes, recognizing there are no instant solutions to many complex social problems (Meisels and Shonkoff 2000). Emde and Robinson (2000) discuss the importance of designing intermediate goals and intervention activities by envisioning and working backward from the desired long-term developmental outcomes.

Well-defined program outcomes and evaluation are critical, and must be closely tied to the theoretical program design. Whether implementing a well-established intervention or a new approach with a family or working on a larger programmatic scale, practitioners must continually assess progress and effectiveness of the overall program and its components. To be effective, quality of program implementation must be high, and outcomes should be closely related to intervention activities (NRCIM 2000). Quality controls are important not only to heighten effectiveness, but also to avoid potentially negative effects. With frequent assessment of program fidelity and effectiveness, interventions can be modified for improvement when indicated.

Conclusion

Significant developments in early childhood research have led to increased knowledge of the critical, formative nature of the early years in relation to biological mechanisms, brain development, and social-emotional functioning in young children. Despite a burgeoning knowledge base, the implementation of this knowledge into policy and community practice has not kept pace with the needs of children growing up in today's society. The canvas of the family system in the US has changed dramatically in the past few decades, with both parents working and having less time to spend at home in many families, often with the added burden of economic hardship and poverty, increased cultural diversity and ethnic disparities in developmental outcomes, and concerning levels of family and parent dysfunction (NRCIM 2000). The field of early intervention is broad in scope, and scientific refinement is critical to the process of defining the most efficacious intervention modalities for specific early development concerns. Why does early intervention matter? Because "Early pathways, though far from indelible, establish either a sturdy or fragile stage on which subsequent development is constructed" (NRCIM 2000, p.384). Accordingly, early intervention with young children, particularly those at risk or showing signs of impaired developmental progress in any domain, is the most viable mechanism for improving a child's lifelong potential.

Research to date has begun to lay the groundwork for establishing guidelines for effective interventions, although much work remains. Early intervention programs have consistently demonstrated modest but positive outcomes, especially with regard to the long-term cost savings of preventive intervention programs for at-risk children. Intervention is most successful when identification and services are initiated as early as possible, are intensive in duration, are individually tailored, and are integrated with other identified behavioral health service needs.

Concepts of early intervention and "best practices" to date often focus on specific, single modality interventions. There is great need in this field to establish more fluid and integrated systems of care for families with young children, especially for families with multiple needs. This includes providing preventive intervention and mental health services to families and children in more accessible and widely utilized settings, such as pediatric health clinics or early childhood education centers. In the US, a number of promising federal, state, and private early childhood initiatives have been explored, but the availability of integrated systems of care varies dramatically among communities, and funding for comprehensive service delivery remains poorly coordinated. Interventions, few and fragmented, often overlap, compete, and leave important needs unaddressed, clearly indicating a need for systematic change (Carnegie Corporation 1996; Gomby *et al.* 1995; Halpern 2000).

Given the overall positive findings regarding the general effectiveness of early intervention, future research must move beyond the simple question of "does early intervention work?" To advance the field, results must be relevant to guiding both programmatic and policy decisions (Guralnick 1997). We need to know what interventions work best, for which children and families, based on what outcome measures, and at what cost. However, in the real world, neither the early interventions delivered nor the children and families served are homogeneous in nature, posing challenges for researchers to overcome through creative methods and design. Ideally, the strength of scientific findings is bolstered most by the application of prospective, longitudinal designs that use randomized controlled trials. Currently, in the US, where public laws dictate some services for children with disabilities, so-called "no treatment" control conditions are rarely if ever found, and the ethical implications of randomizing treatment can often be overcome only when offering two different but potentially beneficial interventions. Frequently, studies compare a particular intervention to the "standard of care" in a particular community, but this standard likely varies across communities and over time. Quasi-experimental design and analyses of specific intervention components and participant characteristics will likely be what informs the field as we move forward.

Informed by child development theory, promising practices, and increasingly more sophisticated quantitative and qualitative research, early intervention professionals, advocacy groups, and policymakers should continue to strive for successful interdisciplinary service delivery partnerships and systems of care to address the diverse needs of early childhood. This will require quality implementation of comprehensive service programs, with resources for ongoing evaluation of effectiveness and quality improvement.

Acknowledgements

This report would not have been possible without the support of the US Department of Health and Human Services Substance Abuse and Mental Health Services Administration (SAMHSA), Casey Family Programs, the Healthy Start Coalition of Miami–Dade, and the Health Foundation of South Florida. The content of this publication does not necessarily reflect the views or policies of these organizations. Responsibility for the content of this report rests solely with the named authors.

CHAPTER 6

Home Visiting for Parents of Pre-school Children in the UK

Jane Barlow

Introduction

UK government policy has over the past decade increased its focus on support for families, and parenting in particular. The government Green Paper 'Supporting Families' (Home Office 1998) points to the need to ensure that all families have access to the advice and support they need, and to tackle the more serious problems of family life. The Children Act 1989 points to the need to protect children from abuse within the family, while avoiding unnecessary weakening of family ties. It emphasizes the importance of family support and partnership with parents, and requires local authorities to give family support a high priority in terms of resource allocation. Since then *Every Child Matters* (HM Treasury 2003) has set out the government's proposals for protecting children and maximizing their potential, and the government initiative Sure Start (Department for Education and Employment 1997) is intended to provide a number of services, some of which include the use of home visiting, as part of a range of local area-based services to improve support for families and parents.

Home visiting has a long history in the UK, extending back to the development of universal health visiting. The use of home visiting to deliver an intensive and structured programme of care to families with young children, however, has a more limited history in the UK, beginning in the 1970s with the Child Development Programme (Percy and Barker 1986) and Home Start (van der Eyken 1990). Since then, home visiting has proliferated in the UK with the development of a range of professional and non-professional (volunteer) programmes. While the number of families that currently benefit from such home-visiting programmes in the UK is not known, a recent survey of parenting programmes more generally showed that there was considerable variability in their availability across the country (Henricson *et al.* 2001).

UK-based home-visiting programmes have many features in common perhaps most importantly being the aim to improve outcomes for parents and children by providing families with social support, practical assistance, and education about parenting and/or child development (Gomby, Culross and Behrman 1999). These programmes differ, however, with regard to their focus, the level of services offered (i.e. onset, intensity and duration), who the service is provided by (i.e. professionals or non-professionals), the populations that they serve, and the model underpinning the programme.

This chapter provides an overview of the evidence concerning the effectiveness of currently available home-visiting programmes for parents of pre-school children in the UK.

The Nature of the Evidence

There is now a plethora of research on home-visiting programmes, but much of the available evidence has been conducted outside the UK, predominantly in North America (Bull *et al.* 2004). While there is evidence of the effectiveness of home-visiting programmes in the UK, there is considerable diversity as regards the type of evaluations that have been undertaken, and indeed their rigour. While some programmes have been evaluated using rigorous study designs (e.g. randomised controlled trials or RCTs), many have involved the use of observational or less scientific study designs (e.g. qualitative and process evaluations). Much of this evidence does not permit us to be conclusive as regards the effectiveness of home-visiting programmes in the UK. However, in conjunction with the work being undertaken internationally, it is becoming increasingly possible to identify the features associated with more effective home-visiting programmes (e.g. MacLeod and Nelson 2000).

Evidence of Programme Effectiveness

Introduction

The following section will review evidence concerning the effectiveness of UK-based home-visiting programmes for parents of young children. The programmes reviewed have been selected because they provide exemplary models of a number of different types of home-visiting programme. The choice of programmes was also influenced by the fact that there only are a limited number of evaluations available of the effectiveness of UK-based home-visiting programmes. The Community Mothers Programme, which was established and evaluated in Ireland, was included because it represents an extension of the UK-based First Parent Visitor Programme (see below).

The Child Development Programme

The Child Development Programme (CDP) (Percy and Barker 1986) began in 1979. By 1993 the programme had been adopted by 18 NHS provider units across the UK (Emond *et al.* 2002). The CDP is delivered by specially trained health visitors, and the fundamental premise of the programme is that of 'empowerment' in which the parent is recognized as an equal in the partnership with the home visitor and an expert on his or her own child.

The approach of the programme is behavioural as opposed to cognitive or psychodynamic, and visits are semi-structured, the content of each visit being left to the discretion of the parent and home visitor. Visits are made every four or five weeks and are of 40–60 minutes' duration. The programme focuses on six areas – health, language, cognition, socialization, nutrition and early education, and the home visitor aims to encourage behavioural change in one or more of these areas by supporting and reinforcing the strategies decided upon by the parent. A Child Progress Form is completed jointly each month prior to decisions being made about what the mother would like to do during the coming month to help her child's progress.

During the following visit, the home visitor and parents discuss the progress that has been made in meeting these goals. The programme has a strong nutritional focus, and time is spent during each session discussing in a non-judgemental way what the child has eaten and drunk in the past 24 hours. Parents are also asked about their view of the child's health during the past month. Humorous illustrated materials are used covering the six areas mentioned above in order to present sensitive parenting issues in an informal way, and to illustrate different methods of handling problems and promoting development (Percy and Barker 1986).

One of the only rigorous evaluations of this programme showed higher immunization rates, and less time spent in hospital in the intervention children. In addition, intervention children showed greater concentration, better social behaviour, and better language development and communication skills than comparable control children. The effects of the programme on the mother were not assessed using standardized outcome instruments, but evidence from interviews suggest that the programme was also beneficial for parents (Percy and Barker 1986).

'First Parent' Home Visitor Scheme

While the CDP showed some positive outcomes, the health visitors delivering the intervention experienced considerable difficulty in integrating the more intensive visiting with their existing caseload. It was therefore agreed that in the second phase of the programme one health visitor would visit all the primiparous families from four or five health visitors in the same or adjoining clinics (Percy and Barker 1986). This First Parent Visitor Programme (FPVP), as it became known, comprised a programme of regular home visits by a specially trained health visitor to first-time parents from deprived areas. The FPVP is based on the CDP (Percy and Barker 1986), and aims to support and advise the mother, who is visited at home antenatally (during the third trimester), at the statutory primary birth visit, three weeks postnatally, and then every five weeks up until the eighth postnatal month. Approximately 20 per cent of families experiencing ongoing difficulties continue to receive the service until the child is two years of age. As with the CDP, the emphasis of the FPVP is on empowerment, and the programme is delivered using written materials including cartoons (Percy and Barker 1986).

An evaluation of the effectiveness of this programme was undertaken using both prospective and retrospective data, in which four comparison areas were matched on social, economic and demographic profiles with three areas receiving the FPVP (Emond *et al.* 2002). Retrospective data were collected from a total of 2113 families, and prospective data from a total of 459 families. Overall, the evaluation did not show any clear advantage for the FPVP over conventional health visiting.

As regards child health there were no differences in developmental outcomes using the Bayley Scales when the child was aged one and two years, and both height and weight Z scores were lower in the FPVP children at two years of age than in comparison children. There were no differences in immunization rates, uptake of child health surveillance or use of hospital services, and a higher proportion of families who received the FPVP were registered on the local child protection register than comparison families. There were, however, lower accident rates in the FPVP group in the second year of life and an increased use of electric socket covers. As regards maternal outcomes, women who received the FPVP were more likely to have changed partners, but also had a wider support network than comparison women. The FPVP group also consulted with their GPs less often, and was more likely to have breast-fed their infant, and to have given their infant fruit-juice drinks. There were, however, no differences between the groups as regards self-esteem, locus of control or rates of depression (Emond *et al.* 2002).

Community Mothers Programme

While the FPVP was evolving and being implemented in health authorities in England and Wales, resource limitations in Ireland meant that the programme could not continue. A decision was therefore made to implement the programme using non-professional experienced mothers, and the Community Mothers Programme was launched in Dublin in 1983 (Johnson, Howell and Molloy 1993). The programme is based on the CDP and the aim is for experienced mothers in disadvantaged areas to give support and encouragement to first-time parents. Local public health nurses identify potential community mothers. Suitable individuals undergo four weeks of training, focusing on the concepts underpinning the programme, and the training provides the volunteers with an opportunity to meet with other community mothers and to discuss methods of delivering the programme. Following training, each community mother works under the guidance of a family development nurse, and provides support to approximately five to 15 first-time parents (Johnson *et al.* 1993).

An RCT was undertaken to assess whether non-professionals could deliver the programme effectively. A total of 262 first-time mothers living in a deprived area of Dublin were randomly allocated to receive either standard support from the public health nurse or standard support plus a monthly visit from a community mother on a monthly basis up until the infant's first birthday. The intervention was delivered by 30 community mothers living in the same community as the study participants. The results showed a range of benefits in terms of child outcomes. The intervention children were more likely to have received their primary immunizations, be read to on a daily basis, be exposed to nursery rhymes, and have cognitive games played with them (e.g. hide and seek, singing and number games). They were less likely to begin cows' milk before 26 weeks or to receive inappropriate energy intakes or inappropriate amounts of animal protein, non-animal protein, wholefoods, vegetables, fruit, and milk.

There was, however, no significant difference between the groups as regards number of days spent in hospital and, among those admitted to hospital, intervention children had a longer mean stay. There was also a range of improvements as regards maternal health. Mothers in the intervention group had a better diet than controls and were less likely to feel tired, miserable or to want to stay indoors. They were also less likely to have negative feelings about the previous year in which their child was born and more likely to have positive feelings.

The results of a seven-year follow-up showed that the beneficial effects were sustained, and that some of the benefits had extended to subsequent children (Johnson *et al.* 2000). Thus, children in the intervention group were less likely to have had an accident requiring a hospital visit, but more likely to have been admitted to hospital because of illness. They were more likely to visit the library weekly and to have their homework checked by their mother. Subsequent children were more likely to have received influenza and polio vaccination. Mothers in the intervention group were more likely to disagree with statements such as 'Children should be smacked for persistently bad behaviour' and 'I do not have much to be proud of', and to make positive statements about motherhood, compared with the control group. It should be noted, however, that there was significant attrition at the seven-year follow-up (only 33% of the original sample were interviewed), and that these results may not therefore be generalizable.

Home Start

In addition to the Community Mothers Programme, there have been a number of other home-visiting programmes delivered by volunteer non-professionals. Home Start was one of the first volunteer home-visiting programmes in the UK. It was started in 1973 in Leicester by an experienced volunteer and voluntary work organizer who had been influenced by early intervention programmes in the US, in particular Head Start (Gibbons and Thorpe 1989).

Home Start is a voluntary organization that aims to provide support, friendship and practical assistance to families with children under five years of age who are experiencing problems. Families are visited at home by a volunteer and the emphasis of the programme is on encouraging parents' strengths, reassuring them about their capabilities, and encouraging them to widen their network of relationships and to use existing community services (Gibbons and Thorpe 1989). There is also a range of group activities available in addition to individual home visiting. In June 2003 there were over 300 Home Start schemes in the UK, and over 100 internationally.

There have been numerous surveys and qualitative evaluations of Home Start since its inception, showing positive results. Surveys show that Home Start offers support to families with a range of presenting problems including maternal isolation in addition to more complex problems such as maternal depression, and that a significant minority of referrals to Home Start comprise vulnerable families facing severe difficulties (Gibbons and Thorpe 1989). A further survey showed that approximately 22 per cent of parents receiving the Home Start service were 'high risk' in the sense that children had been on the child protection register, or under a Supervision Order, or on the verge of being taken into residential care. While qualitative evaluation of the Home Start programme to date suggests that it has made a positive difference to parents in terms of meeting the physical, emotional, social, and educational needs of children, and in encouraging confidence in and respite from parenting (van der Eyken 1982), more recent research has pointed to the need for more objective evaluation (Oakley, Rajan and Turner 1998).

Following this, a study was conducted in collaboration with Home Start to establish appropriate outcomes measures (McAuley 1999). More recently an evaluation of its effectiveness and cost effectiveness using quantifiable outcome measures alongside in-depth interviews was carried out to assess whether the input from volunteers resulted in objectively measurable changes in outcome (McAuley *et al.* 2004, in press). This quasi-experimental study comprised 80 mothers under stress who were receiving Home Start and 82 mothers in similar circumstances from England and Northern Ireland. The mothers' parenting stress, mental health, self-esteem and social support, and their children's emotional and social development, were assessed as well as the mothers' use of services at baseline and 11 months later. At follow-up, the majority of the mothers were experiencing less parenting stress, exhibiting fewer depressive symptoms and showing higher self-esteem, and there was evidence of improvement in their children's development. More social support was available to them. However, the mothers in both groups showed similar levels of improvement. Interviews with the mothers suggested that, although they valued the service, the intensity and type of support may have contributed to this outcome. The evidence did not suggest a cost-effective advantage for Home Start either.

The Family Partnership Programme

The Family Partnership Programme (originally called the Parent Advisor Programme) was established in 1985 for children with disabilities. The programme has now developed and is provided as a routine service funded by the local health authority to children of a variety of ages and problems (Davis and Rushton 1991). It is provided by a range of professionals (e.g. health visitors, nursery nurses and school nurses) who have received approximately eight days of formal training in the skills of relating to parents and enabling the helping process of parenting issues and of child behavioural management.

One of the central aims of the Family Partnership Programme is to establish a trusting relationship with parents based on a partnership. This involves the sharing of power and pooling of expertise and is predicated on the helper adopting a number of attitudes, including respect, genuineness, empathy and humility. The aim of this process of empowerment is the building of parental expertise and self-efficacy, and it involves active listening, empathic responding and a variety of challenging techniques intended to help parents recognize and change some of their ways of understanding the world, and to manage identified problems. Programme providers receive regular supervision on both an individual and group basis.

Referrals to the service are received directly from parents in addition to a range of professionals in health, social, voluntary and education services (Davis et al., 1997). The service is provided to parents of pre-school children with multiple psychosocial problems who are living in socio-economically deprived areas. The visits are conducted on a weekly basis, for one hour, for as long as is necessary to meet the parents' needs. The intervention depends upon the development of a trusting and respectful relationship with the parents, and the programme aims to promote and support the parents' own exploration of identified problems and to help them establish aims and effective problem management strategies.

An RCT of the programme showed increased parental self-esteem, decreased levels of parental stress and emotional difficulties, more positive parental constructions of children, improvements in the home environment and decreased child behavioural problems (Davis and Rushton 1991). Further evaluation is currently being undertaken of the clinical effectiveness of the Family Partnership Programme in providing early intervention for families of children with emotional/behavioural problems, and of its long-term effectiveness as part of the European Early Promotion Project (see below). This is a mental health promotion intervention that comprises a universal and an indicated component both of which consist of home visits. The universal component consists of trained primary health-care workers conducting 'promotional' interviews immediately before and after all new births. The aim of the promotional interview is to promote positive interaction between parent and child as a key element of healthy psychosocial development during infancy and childhood, and to facilitate the transition to parenthood of first-time parents. For example, the health visitor might ask, as part of a promotional interview, how the mother felt when she learned that she was pregnant. Positive feelings would then be endorsed and negative feelings explored further and talked about (Puura *et al.* 2002).

Screening is also carried out to identify families whose children are at risk of developing mental health problems. The targeted component of the European Early Promotion Project consists of the health visitor working intensively using the Parent Partnership Model with families who have been identified using the screening as being at increased risk of mental health problems.

The European Early Promotion Project

The European Early Promotion Project (see above) has been evaluated as part of a large multicentre trial in Europe and the UK. Early findings have shown that the training improved the capacity of the primary health-care worker to identify families in need and to make accurate judgements about need. The results also indicate that in the UK, trained health visitors were seen by parents as being significantly more helpful and there were benefits in some countries for families at two years in terms of mother–child interaction, the home environment, and the functioning of the parents and children. (European Early Promotion Project 2005; Puura *et al.* 2002).

Postnatal Support Workers

The majority of home-visiting programmes in the UK are provided on a targeted basis. A recent study, however, evaluated the effectiveness of a brief (ten three-hour sessions) home-visiting support programme for *all* postnatal women (Morrel *et al.*

2000). The support workers aimed to provide effective practical and emotional support including helping the mother gain confidence in caring for her baby and reinforcing midwifery advice on infant feeding. The support workers had all achieved their national vocational qualification postnatal care award and completed training in domiciliary care and care of young children.

This study showed that there were no significant improvements in health status among the women in the intervention group and poorer self-perceived health as regards physical and social functioning and physical role limitation. The intervention group were also significantly more depressed. There were no significant differences between the intervention and control group as regards social support or rates of breast-feeding. There was also little difference between groups in the use of NHS services and costs, but there was an additional cost for the support-worker service (Morrel et al. 2000).

Home Visiting Delivered by Health Visitors

Two recent studies have been undertaken to evaluate the effectiveness of home-visiting programmes delivered by specially trained health visitors. The first involved five health visitors trained in the use of the listening model visiting disadvantaged mothers in the home, beginning when the baby was approximately ten weeks old. The focus was on the woman and her needs, with practical support and information available on request. On average, women received ten hours of support during seven home visits plus additional telephone contacts. This intervention was evaluated as part of an RCT that compared the Support Health Visitor (SHV) intervention with Community Group Support or standard services. The results show that that this intervention had little impact on any of the major outcomes measured, including childhood injury, maternal smoking or maternal depression. However, SHV women had different patterns of health service use (e.g. less use of GPs) and fewer anxious experiences of motherhood than control women (Wiggins et al. 2004).

The second study is an evaluation of a home-visiting service that has been established in GP practices across two counties. Forty health visitors were trained to deliver an intensive home-visiting programme to pregnant women who were experiencing significant environmental and psychological difficulties, with a view to improving maternal and infant mental health and reducing the risk of poor parenting. The home visitors were trained in the Parent Partnership model (see above), in addition to a number of methods of improving parent–infant interaction including infant massage (Onzawa et al. 2001), dialogical baby dance (Maattanen 2001), a modified version of the Brazelton Neonatal Assessment Scale (PIPPIN 2000), and the use of songs and music (PEEP 2000).

All the home visitors received twice-monthly, group-based supervision that aimed to help them to think about what was happening in the families with whom they were working and to contain the anxiety that such intensive work with complex families might engender. The aim of the supervision sessions was to reinforce and support the home visitors in the use of their skills to engage families, understand them, and enable the helping process. The sessions were also intended to help them reflect on any difficulties, using principles from a range of psychotherapeutic approaches.

This home-visiting programme is currently being evaluated as part of an RCT in which consenting women have been randomly allocated to the intensive home-visiting service or the standard treatment control group. Women allocated to receive the new service were visited weekly by a home visitor beginning during the second trimester and ending one year postnatally. The process data from this evaluation showed that home visitors perceived the intervention to have made significant difference in terms of important aspects of maternal and child functioning, including maternal mental health, domestic violence and interactions with children. In-depth interviews with women who had received the service showed a high level of satisfaction across the board, and provided moving testimony concerning the impact of this intervention on the lives of vulnerable women and children. However, the quantitative results showed no differences in the babies at 1 year on any parent-report measure, but differences favouring the group that received home visits were observed on an objective assessment of maternal sensitivity ($p<0.04$) and infant cooperative-ness ($p<0.02$). The authors recommend, however, that this result is treated with caution due to the large number of outcomes measured. There was a non-significant increase in the likelihood of intervention group infants being the subject of child protection proceedings, or being removed from the home (6% in the intervention arm compared with none in the control group). The authors treat this finding as a positive outcome given the evidence showing that abused children adopted in infancy fare much better than children adopted after 4 years of age (Kaniuk, Steele and Hodges 2004).

Evidence of Effectiveness

A recent review of home-visiting programmes concluded that there is 'enormous variability in outcome for many home-visitation programmes' and that the variation occurs 'across programme goals, programme models, programme sites, and across families within the same site' (Gomby 2000, p.1431). This is also true of UK-based home-visiting programmes. There are, however, a number of themes emerging from the evidence concerning the children and young people for whom these programmes are most effective.

Perhaps most importantly, the UK evidence supports the findings more generally that home-visiting interventions appear to have greater impact for children of women at higher risk (e.g. unmarried women, women on low incomes, teenage mothers). Home-visiting programmes that are offered to women who are already coping, or to women who are not experiencing adversity, may not only fail to produce positive outcomes but may also lead to regression (Gough 1993; Morrell *et al.* 2000). This may be due in part to the failure to mobilize 'normal' support and coping mechanisms as a result of the intervention (Morrell *et al.* 2000). These programmes also appear to be effective for children with emotional and behavioural problems (Davis and Rushton 1991). There is, however, currently insufficient evidence concerning their effectiveness with children from ethnic minority families.

While the effectiveness of these programmes may not necessarily depend on who delivers the programme (i.e. professional as opposed to non-professional), there is increasing evidence to suggest that outcomes are determined by the emphasis that is placed on the establishment of an honest and trusting relationship. For example, many of the most successful of the included home-visiting programmes (e.g. Family Partnership Programme, First Parent Visitor Programme and the Community Mothers Programme) all emphasize the importance of the home visitor/client relationship.

A recent review of reviews of ante- and postnatal home-visiting programmes concluded that those programmes that are restricted to a narrow range of outcomes are less effective than those with a more comprehensive approach in which the multiple needs of families are addressed. It also pointed to the greater effectiveness of more intensive programmes that are delivered over longer periods of time (Bull *et al.* 2004).

Conclusion

Research on home visiting is important because:

> a significant proportion of some of the most difficult and costly problems faced by young children and parents today, are a direct consequence of adverse maternal health related behaviours during pregnancy, dysfunctional infant care-giving, and stressful environmental conditions that interfere with parental and family functioning. (Olds and Kitzman 1993, p.53)

There is also increasing recognition of the need for a shift of focus from child protection to family support and improved parenting (Department of Health 1996b), and for interventions to reduce the harmful effects of the social and physical environment on the health and development of mother and child (Report to the NHS Central Research and Development Committee 1995).

Research on the effectiveness of home-visiting programmes in the UK in particular is still limited and, as with the US, findings have been mixed. The evidence to date suggests that some UK-based home-visiting programmes can be effective in improving a range of outcomes for both children and parents and are a potentially effective means of working with 'hard to reach' families.

While the evidence from the UK alone is limited, the broader evidence base (e.g. Bull *et al.* 2004) supports the use of such programmes as part of children's services policy. For example, home-visiting programmes of the nature examined in this chapter may have a significant role to play as part of the new government initiative 'Sure Start', which provides a range of locally based services to improve support for families and parents of pre-school children living in areas of deprivation (Department of Health 2001). Home visiting is one of the most potentially effective means of working with 'hard to reach' families, and it seems likely that these programmes will be an important means of meeting the needs of some of the most difficult and deprived families in the UK. They may also have a role to play during the antenatal and immediate postnatal period in the primary prevention of problems which have their roots in parenting and children's early experiences, including emotional and behavioural problems, and as part of mental and physical health promotion programmes.

There is evidence that home-visiting programmes have limitations, and also of ineffectiveness (e.g. Morrell *et al.* 2000). The reasons for this are only just beginning to emerge, and future evaluations of home-visiting programmes in the UK should include the collection of descriptive and process data, in order to enable further assessment of the factors that contribute to their success or failure.

CHAPTER 7

Home Visiting for Parents of Pre-school Children in the US

Maureen Marcenko and Fredi Staerkel

Introduction

Home visiting as an intervention strategy for vulnerable families in the United States is rooted in early 19th century "friendly visitor" programs that sought to improve the health and welfare of poor urban families (Arnold *et al.* 1989). Not until the late 1970s, when David Olds conducted the now landmark Elmira nurse home visitation study (Olds *et al.* 1986), did the effectiveness evidence through rigorously conducted research begin to emerge. The next two decades would witness a burgeoning of home-visitation programs, utilizing a variety of models, with accompanying effectiveness studies. When *The Future of Children* published its winter 1993 issue examining model home visitation programs with research evidence, they estimated that 200,000 children and families were enrolled in the programs whose primary goals were preventive. Six years later, in the spring/summer 1999 issue, *The Future of Children* reported that over a half million children were enrolled in the six program models reviewed. It is impossible to estimate how many families are being reached today by home-visitation programs in the US. A visit to the National Center for Children and Families and Communities website (www.nccfc.org), which is Olds's nurse home visitor program, identifies one or more of their model programs in every American state. Clearly, home-visitation services are ubiquitous in the US.

Yet there is considerable diversity in home-visitation models. Reporting on a survey of almost 2000 agencies providing home-visiting services in the US, Powell (1993) concludes that there are significant variations within and across programs. Although most programs see their goal as improving child and parent outcomes, they differ in assumptions about the root causes of poor outcomes; strategies for change;

content of the visits; and the host, intensity, and staffing of the program. This degree of program variance has led to the observation that home visiting is a service delivery strategy rather than a particular service (Powers and Fenichel 1999).

The theory base underlying home-visiting programs also is varied but, at the highest level of abstraction, most can be conceptually located within an ecological framework that takes into account interactions between child, family, and community factors. Theories of child development, attachment, and social learning figure prominently among programs, as a pathway to both child and family well-being. Furthermore, home-visitation programs can be linked to the public health tradition of primary and secondary prevention.

The Nature of the Evidence

After nearly two decades of rigorous research on home-visiting programs in the US, the jury is in: "When program benefits were demonstrated, they usually accrued to only a subset of families originally enrolled in the programs, they rarely occurred for all of a program's goals, and the benefits were often quite modest in magnitude" (Gomby *et al.* 1999, p.6). Gomby and her colleagues call their analysis of home-visiting program results "sobering" and recommend that program expansion be reassessed in light of the most recent findings regarding efficacy. Despite a lack of compelling evidence supporting the benefit of home visiting for young children and their parents, there is a widely held consensus in the early childhood field that home visiting should be retained, albeit with more modest expectations (Gomby *et al.* 1999; Shonkoff and Philips 2000).

In a special issue of *The Future of Children* in 1999, the outcomes of six well-studied home-visiting programs were published. All six models had at least one randomized trial, across a number of program sites, and at least two or more years of follow-up data. The results of these model programs provide the basis for our analysis in this chapter. After a brief discussion about the parameters of home-visiting programs, potential explanatory factors will be explored by whether they are policy- and community level variables or conceptual and programmatic issues. Based on our analysis, in the final section of the chapter we offer suggestions regarding the future of home visiting in the US.

The six home-visiting programs reported on in the 1999 (Volume 9) issue of *The Future of Children* lend credence to the aforementioned observation. The programs are briefly described below.

1. *The Nurse Home Visitation Program.* The NHVP serves women less than 29 weeks pregnant, who are pregnant for the first time and have at least two of the following risk factors: unmarried, less than 12 years of education, unemployed. Women are followed through pregnancy and during the

two years post partum. Program components includes a standardized protocol delivered by public health nurses and aimed at health-related behaviors, care of children and life-course development (Olds *et al.* 1999).

2. *Hawaii's Healthy Start Program.* Begun in 1975, this program uses paraprofessional home visitors to help parents employ non-abusive parenting strategies, enhance parent–child interactions, promote healthy child development and ensure that the family has a regular primary medical provider. Families are screened and assessed at the time of delivery and those identified as high risk are offered home-visiting services (Duggan *et al.* 1999).

3. *Parents as Teachers.* PAT began in 1981 with five primary goals:

   (a) increase parental knowledge of child development

   (b) ensure children are ready for school

   (c) prevent child maltreatment

   (d) increase parenting confidence and competence

   (e) foster a home-school-community partnership.

   Parent educator home visitors offer regular (monthly, biweekly, or weekly, depending on needs) home visits, monitor children's development, link families to community resources, and encourage families to participate in group meetings (Wagner and Clayton 1999).

4. *The Home Instruction Program for Preschool Youngsters.* HIPPY is a two-year program for families with pre-schoolers and parents with limited education. Developed in Israel and brought to the US in 1984, the goal of this program is to prepare children for school by enhancing the home literacy environment, parent–child verbal interactions, and encouraging parents to help their children learn. Home visitors are paraprofessional and usually live in the same neighborhood as the families served (Baker, Piotrkowski and Jeanne 1999).

5. *The Comprehensive Child Development Program.* The CCDP was developed in 1989 for low-income families with newborns and was designed to enhance the infants' physical, social, emotional, and intellectual development. It required families to remain involved for five years. Paraprofessional home visitors meet with families twice per month, and provide case management and child development services including health/dental care services, developmental screening and diagnosis, child

development activities, parenting education, mental health and substance abuse treatment, and vocational/employment services (St. Pierre and Layzer 1999).

6.   *Health Families America.* The HFA, launched in 1992, is a national initiative to prevent child maltreatment. Services are offered to all families with newborns to reduce the stigma of targeted services and the frequency of visits depends on family needs. The goal is to reduce child maltreatment, encourage healthy cognitive and emotional child development, and assist parents with life-course issues. Home visitors are professionals who receive periodic standardized training (Daro and Harding 1999).

The authors of each chapter in this book have been charged with providing the evidence on effectiveness on a particular intervention; in our case, this is home visiting in the US. Since the data from several rigorously studied programs have been competently analyzed by Gomby and colleagues (1999), we would like to use this space to interrogate the possible reasons home-visiting programs have not consistently delivered on their promise to reduce child abuse, improve parenting, and increase child well-being. Such an analysis can potentially contribute to the discourse on early intervention services for vulnerable families.

Evidence of Program Effectiveness

Policy and Community Factors

Several authors have argued that home visiting alone is insufficient to meet the needs of vulnerable families, thus program impact is compromised when quality community services are not available or accessible (Ramey and Ramey 1993; Weiss 1993). The premise of this line of reasoning is that home visiting represents but one component of a system of care required to produce positive outcomes for families at risk of unhealthy development and, when other needs such as housing or health care are not met, the effectiveness of home visiting is not fairly tested.

The role of available, accessible, and quality community services as a necessary condition for home-visiting success is a testable hypothesis, but to our knowledge, no researchers have measured this construct in their evaluations. A proxy measure might be the rate at which program participants with an identified need for a particular service receive that service. Clearly, this meets the available and accessible criteria, if not the quality criterion. Some programs report service receipt but not whether there was an identified need; this makes it difficult to assess the extent to which program participants overall were able to access *needed* community services (Goodson *et al.* 2000).

One of the most striking findings regarding service use was reported by the evaluators of the Comprehensive Child Development Program (CCDP) (Goodson *et al.* 2000). Even though case management was a core element of the CCDP intervention, and the dose met the planned level, program participants were no more likely to receive community services than control group families. This is an interesting finding because it suggests that if a service is available in a community, the added value of case management is negligible. In other words, "if you build it" and people value it, they will access it. Maybe our efforts should be focused on building and disseminating a network of quality services that meet expressed community needs, while flexibly providing case management to families requiring additional assistance accessing services.

An alternative hypothesis for the low level of home-visiting efficacy that has not received attention in the literature is the possibility of control group contamination through contact with experimental group families or through shared social network members. Programs employing experimental designs typically recruit participants from specific sites and randomly assign within sites. The reason for this approach is legitimate: to maximize between group comparability at baseline. However, the likelihood is fairly high that demographically comparable subjects, sharing a common life circumstance (pregnant or parenting young children), and living in the same neighborhood, will have overlapping social networks. Within these networks, informal patterns of sharing resources and information may actually play a more important role than formal services, a fact established at least for African-American women (Neighbors and Jackson 1984). Wagner and Clayton (1999) identified a similar phenomenon among the largely Latina sample they studied in their evaluation of the Parents as Teachers home-visiting program. Add to the mix that home-visiting programs have been operating in some of these communities for a decade or more, the conditions for a true experiment are critically compromised.

Another community-level explanation for the disappointing showing of home visiting is that it cannot overcome the pervasive negative effects of poverty (Weiss 1993). Basic needs such as housing and food must be met before mothers can either attend to or incorporate new parenting knowledge and strategies. Along these lines, Chaffin, Bonner and Hill (2001) conducted a very instructive analysis of statewide family preservation and support programs to assess their effectiveness at preventing child maltreatment. A particular strength of this work was the authors' attention to level of client risk, program characteristics, and control for surveillance bias. The results showed these programs were not effective at preventing child maltreatment, and, furthermore, center-based services were associated with fewer cases of substantiated maltreatment than home-based services (Chaffin *et al.* 2001). In addition, among the client group at highest risk for maltreatment, programs focusing on basic needs and mentoring were more effective than programs designed around child development, parent education, or case management strategies (Chaffin *et al.* 2001).

These findings buttress the argument that poverty and its attendant problem of meeting basic needs must be addressed in order prevent child maltreatment. In fact, if we did nothing else, insuring that all families have their essential needs for food, clothing and shelter met might be the most effective means of preventing child maltreatment.

A guaranteed income program in the US is unrealistic; it simply is contrary to our historical conception of poverty as a personal problem, best solved through structured incentives. Recent changes in welfare policy provide a contemporary case in point in that the benefits are time limited and linked to employment activities (Administration 1996). The history of home-visiting programs is consistent with this perspective. As Halpern (1993) notes "the most important formative influence on early intervention services in the US has been the tendency to view poverty as an individual and local problem" (p. 160). Rather than addressing the underlying causes of poverty, inadequate income, and economic opportunity, the preferred approach has been the provision of services to remediate individual deficiencies and health-compromising behaviors (Halpern 1993). In the case of home visiting, targeted services are expected to produce change in mothers' behaviors, leading to greater self-sufficiency, and improved child health and developmental outcomes (Olds *et al.* 1997).

Conceptual and Programmatic Issues

If home-visiting programs are built on the assumptive foundation that children experience poor outcomes because their mothers lack knowledge and resources (Hebbeler and Gerlach-Downie 2002), then the role of the home visitor is to teach and facilitate access to community services. Indeed, the core elements of most programs have been curricula on child development, teaching and modeling parenting skills, and case management. Prima facie, the logic of the model seems unassailable. However, there has been some interesting qualitative work examining the content of home visits, providing important insights concerning the emphasis of the intervention in practice and the corresponding assumptions regarding change.

Based on multifaceted longitudinal data from parents and home visitors, as well as videotapes of home visits, Hebbeler and Gerlach-Downie (2002) concluded the program under examination was operating from a flawed theory of change. Home visitors, working from the assumption that all parents desire to be good parents, saw the goal of the intervention as helping parents feel good about themselves as people and as parents. Little attention was given to parent–child interaction, which could have been a behavioral indicator of parenting expertise and a point of intervention (Hebbeler and Gerlach-Downie 2002).

Drawing on the burgeoning work in infant mental health, Halpern (1993) also sees the therapeutic opportunities inherent in parent–child interaction, particularly for women who have experienced adversity. Based on a psychodynamic framework and deeply rooted in attachment theory, this approach uses the parent–child relationship as the backdrop against which the parent's own past trauma can be examined, understood, and resolved. Thus, the parent becomes psychologically healthier, and this leads to improvements in the parent's relationship with the child (Cohen *et al.* 1999).

Taken together, the findings regarding the content of home visits, and the potential negative impacts of past trauma on current parenting, suggest that greater attention to parent–child interaction may be a productive focus of home visits for some families. Supportive interventions with the intent of making women feel good about themselves may be inadequate to overcome the painful effects of early trauma awakened in the context of the present parenting relationship. Careful assessment and skilled practitioners are a critical adjunct to this work, but colleagues in the infant mental health field have produced the intervention technology from which to borrow (Cohen *et al.* 1999; Kelly and Barnard 1999).

Any analysis of the limitations of home visiting must address program attrition. Hovering around 50 percent for most programs, this level of drop-out, coupled with the fact that among those who remain most do not receive the intended program dose, signals a problem with the priority or value participants assign to the program. Attrition is a multifaceted issue, difficult to tease apart with the available data. We have chosen to examine the content of home visiting as one potential factor in attrition.

Putting aside the obvious legitimate reasons for attrition, such as moving or work and school conflicts, which Duggan *et al.* (1999) found accounts for about 14 percent of drop-out, it seems reasonable that in order to continue services participants must get something they value from the visits which they cannot get elsewhere more easily. In most program models the parent–home-visitor relationship is the foundation upon which the intervention is built. In fact, interventions generally are assumed to occur within the context of this relationship. However, if the underlying assumption is that mothers targeted for home-visiting services lack supportive networks of family and friends and the home visitor fills that void, then this assumption warrants testing. Few studies have examined the dynamics of this relationship. One study found it nearly impossible to evaluate the impact of the home visitor–parent relationship due to the high turnover among home visitors (Rector-Staerkel 2002).

As noted previously, home-visiting programs are very diverse on a number of levels, including program content, but most provide case management and parenting or child development knowledge. Earlier in the chapter we discussed the negligible effect of case management. Consequently, if this is the focus of the visit, it is not difficult to understand why participants discontinue service.

The majority of programs employ standardized curricula to deliver child development information or parenting skills (Gomby *et al.* 1999). Several programs have noted a tension that occurs in the home visit when families are dealing with a crisis they find most pressing but the home visitor has to cover prescribed content. This also poses significant problems from a methodological perspective, when the hypothesized pathway to specific outcomes is the acquisition of knowledge and skills contained in the curriculum. Furthermore, generalizability of research findings demands program standardization.

From a practice perspective, however, this could be viewed as an opportunity. By making the dilemma transparent, clients and home visitors can engage in modifying the intervention to meet the needs of the client population better. Again, the experiences of program families can be used propitiously to create new intervention strategies. The challenge for researchers then becomes measuring the impact of this flexible program model.

Conclusion

We want to preface this section of the chapter by saying that we do not know what home visiting should look like in the future in the US. The answer to that question lies in communities and neighborhoods across the US. We intend to argue, as others have (Minow 1994; Weiss 1993), that home visiting should be part of a comprehensive and coordinated set of supports and services based on the unique culture, strengths, needs, and challenges of each community.

The evidence on home visiting suggests it is time to move away from testing stand-alone programs to investigating the efficacy of an integrated network of community-based services. Even if it were desirable to study home visiting, it is no longer feasible to isolate the effects of a single program. Home visiting has become ubiquitous in some communities, with multiple agencies offering their own form of the service. This point was clearly illustrated in the evaluation of Hawaii's Healthy Start Program (Duggan *et al.* 1999) where 28 percent of the control group families had received some home-visiting services after the first year of the study.

We would like to suggest, however, a set of guidelines that can shape the process by which community-based services are designed and delivered. First and foremost is the need for authentic community input and control. Interventions that address felt community needs, using culturally congruent approaches, and building on community assets, have the potential of maximizing impact. For instance, earlier in this chapter we discussed the role of family and friends in some communities as primary sources of parenting advice and information. Might it be possible to capitalize on this dynamic by employing strategies to increase grandparents' current knowledge of parenting? Intervention viewed from this perspective recognizes the uniqueness of each community and opens up new opportunities to develop innovative approaches.

Second, current epidemiological data regarding the social, emotional, and physical health risks of a community are essential for planning efficacious early intervention services. Program focus and content informed by reliable community level data are likely to have the greatest impact. Olds's intervention in upstate New York was so successful in part because the intervention was able to reduce cigarette smoking, which was particularly high (55%) in the target population (Olds *et al.* 1986a). The same intervention was less effective in Memphis where only 9 percent of the sample smoked (Olds *et al.* 1999). Reasons for the differential impact are more complex than the prevalence of cigarette smoking alone, but it demonstrates the diversity of risk among communities and thus the need for locally relevant data and approaches.

Third, it seems consumer choice and input ought to play a larger role in the design and delivery of early intervention services than is typical of home-visiting programs. Just as there are differences among communities, there is variety in the preferences and needs within communities. The importance of choice and program flexibility is most apparent in the high level of attrition in the majority of programs. Collaborative relationships between clients and home visitors help focus and prioritize the intervention and reduce the dissonance of competing agendas.

The goal of this chapter was to interrogate some of the reasons home visiting has not delivered on its promise. We recognize that the factors contributing to home-visiting outcomes are complex and may vary by program and by community. While our purpose has been critical in nature, it is not meant to dismiss home visiting as an approach to early intervention. We believe there is a role for home visiting within a robust system of community-based services.

CHAPTER 8

Support for Young People and their Families in the Community in the UK

Nina Biehal

Introduction

Since the 1980s, studies in both the UK and the US have consistently pointed to high rates of admission to care for older children and teenagers (Packman and Hall 1998; Pecora, Fraser and Haapala 1991; Triseliotis *et al.* 1995b; Wells and Biegel 1991). In England, for example, 42 percent of new admissions are aged 10–15 years (Department of Health 2002d). Despite these high rates of entry, teenagers often receive little social work attention prior to admission so that many admissions are emergency placements which occur once families have reached crisis point (Fisher, Marsh and Phillips 1986; Packman and Hall 1998; Sinclair, Garnett and Berridge 1995; Triseliotis *et al.* 1995b).

The Children Act 1989 brought a renewed emphasis on the value of family support services, and this approach was later reinforced by government policy on refocusing services. The aim was to shift the focus of attention away from the investigation of abuse, which resulted in the provision of services only to a relatively small group considered 'at risk of significant harm', in favour of providing support to a wider range of families with children assessed as being 'in need' (Department of Health 1995a). One of the principal goals of these family support services is to prevent unnecessary entry to care.

Although there has been an unprecedented expansion of services to support families during the last few years, most of these are aimed at families with younger children (Henricson *et al.* 2001). Yet continuing family problems may bring distress, separation or loss as children grow older. When children reach adolescence, peer groups exert a greater influence on their behaviour, which may be either positive or negative. There is also an increased risk of involvement in drug and alcohol abuse, offending and running away (Graham and Bowling 1995). Mental health problems, uncommon among younger children, also begin to emerge during adolescence (Coleman and Hendry 1999; Meltzer *et al.* 1999).

Indeed, the research evidence suggests that the need for support to families with teenagers may have grown, since over the past 50 years there has been an rise, in real terms, in the prevalence of psychosocial disorders among young people (Rutter and Smith 1995). Rutter and Smith's comprehensive review of the research shows that increasing numbers of young people have conduct disorders, eating disorders, depression or suicidal behaviours or misuse drugs and alcohol. High rates of running away and the problem of youth homelessness are also indicators of family problems for young people, as they are often associated with abuse, neglect and unresolved conflicts between teenagers and their parents (Biehal and Wade 2000; Pleace and Quilgars 1999). Even in the context of preventive services for younger children, support services are still needed for older children in difficulty and their parents.

In the UK, one positive development over the past 15 years or so has been the setting up of specialist support teams to work with adolescents. These have developed rapidly during this period in response to concerns about high rates of admission to care for teenagers and the high costs associated with placement of this group. The majority have been established through the diversion of resources from residential care into an alternative, community-based service, so many of the staff are former residential workers (Brown 1998). The age groups the teams serve and the models they use vary, with some serving only children aged 11 and over while others offer a service to both teenagers and younger children. Specialist teams of this kind go by a variety of names, including 'community support teams', 'adolescent support teams' or 'family support teams'.

Typically, these support teams offer an intensive, short-term preventive service aimed at diverting young people from the care system. Most of their work is targeted at young people considered at high risk of imminent entry to care. A report on the development of these specialist support teams in the north of England found that most claimed to prevent the overwhelming majority of their users from entering the care system (Brown 1998). However, there was no evidence that all of these young people would necessarily have entered care in the absence of the service. This chapter will focus on the small group of studies of these specialist support teams that do exist, and it will also identify other studies relevant to social work with teenagers at risk of family breakdown.

The Nature of the Evidence

The emphasis of most of the research on family support has been on services for younger children at risk of family breakdown primarily targeted at under-11s (for example, Aldgate and Tunstill 1995; Gibbons 1990; McAuley *et al.* 2002; Smith 1996). There is also a wide body of research on vulnerable teenagers which is beyond the scope of this chapter. This includes studies by psychologists and by criminologists (see Coleman and Hendry 1999, for an overview of psychological studies, and Little and Mount 1999, for a summary of the major cohort studies).

Research evidence on *social work* with teenagers in the UK is largely to be found in studies of the care system (for example, Packman and Hall 1998; Sinclair and Gibbs 1998) but there have been few studies which focus specifically on support services to prevent their admission to care. However, in the mid-1990s two studies of social work with teenagers were undertaken, later summarized in a useful overview report (Department of Health 1996a; Sinclair *et al.* 1995; Triseliotis *et al.* 1995b). There have been also been six UK studies of specialist support teams working with teenagers to prevent family breakdown.

Of the two broader studies of work with teenagers one, *Teenagers and Social Work Services*, was a follow-up study of 116 young people aged 13–17 years referred to social work services in Scotland (Triseliotis *et al.* 1995b). Just over half of the sample had just been admitted to care at start of study, so this was a rather mixed group. The other study, *Social Work and Assessment with Adolescents*, was a critical case study of a specialist adolescent assessment service in one London local authority (Sinclair *et al.* 1995). The 75 young people in this study had all experienced a 'transitional event', namely consideration of admission to care, admission to care or placement breakdown, so again the circumstances of this group were rather mixed. Both studies followed up the young people one year later. Only the London study included a comparison group of young people (who received a 'routine' service from area social workers) but in this study outcomes were assessed solely by social workers. Although the Scottish study had no comparison group, outcomes were assessed at follow-up by means of interviews with young people and parents as well as social workers and, unlike the London study, standardized measures of behaviour and self-esteem were used.

It is difficult to draw firm conclusions about effectiveness from these studies since neither was designed with the evaluation of effectiveness as its principal aim. However, both are valuable since they consider social work with teenagers in considerable depth and provide many useful insights into the objectives and the process of social work with teenagers at risk of entry to long-term care.

Most of the research on specialist support services for teenagers has taken the form of small-scale, qualitative studies of single teams. The earliest was an evaluation of the MARS project, a preventive social work team. This study attempted to develop a methodology for evaluating preventive work based on the intensive analysis of 12 cases (Fuller 1989). Few details of the intervention were provided, other than that the team worked intensively with children age ten and over who were at imminent risk of a breakdown in their living or schooling arrangements. The interventions had multiple objectives and the team's staff were asked to rate their success in meeting these. However, the author acknowledged that the lack of any independent assessment of outcomes plus the lack of a control group made it difficult to set much store by the finding that the team was effective in 75 percent of cases.

Shortly afterwards, a more broadly based study of the closure of children's homes in the county of Warwickshire included some discussion of specialist teams set up to offer direct work to (mainly) older children to prevent admission to care (Cliffe with Berridge 1991). Again, the principal focus of the discussion of this service was on process rather than effectiveness, so it is difficult to draw clear conclusions about outcomes.

Towards the end of the 1990s two further small-scale studies of specialist support teams were published. Frost's study of a specialist family support team in the North of England working predominantly with older children and teenagers at risk of placement gathered some descriptive data on 327 families and then examined a sub-sample of 30 cases (Frost 1997). Another small evaluation, with a sample of 16 cases, examined the Adolescent Community Support Team in Stockport. This provided outreach support for children aged 11–15 years and their parents in order to prevent family breakdown (Brodie *et al.* 1998).

The team was based in a small residential unit, which also offered emergency and planned respite care. Again, this was a modest study with a single group design, whose strength lies in its qualitative analysis of process. Like the earlier MARS study, these two studies concluded that the specialist teams were effective in supporting young people at home and so preventing placement but, again, the lack of comparison groups meant that it was unclear what proportion of these young people might actually have been placed in the absence of a service.

Biehal, Clayden and Byford (2000) monitored preventive work undertaken by an adolescent support team with 56 young people and also undertook an intensive study of 20 cases. The focus of this evaluation was on how, why and in what circumstances positive change in child and family functioning occurred rather than on effectiveness in preventing placement. These five small, largely qualitative studies of single teams had modest aims and were not designed to provide robust evidence on the effectiveness of the services they studied. However, they provide much useful description of the young people served and the nature of the interventions.

Only one UK study to date has attempted to evaluate the effectiveness of support teams for teenagers by comparing them with an alternative service. The York University study was a quasi-experimental study of 209 young people aged 11–16 years, which compared outcomes for young people using specialist support teams in six English local authorities with those for a similar group receiving mainstream social work services in three authorities (Biehal 2005). Standardized measures of emotional and behavioural difficulties, family functioning, child well-being and parents' mental health status were completed by young people and parents shortly after referral and at follow-up six months later.

At both points in time data were also gathered from parents, children and professionals on the nature and severity of child difficulties, the nature and intensity of interventions, informal support to families, events such as placement or family change and views of outcomes. Statistical analysis was complemented by qualitative analysis of in-depth interviews undertaken with family members and professionals in a sub-sample of 50 cases.

Evidence of Program Effectiveness

Most of the above studies have focused on providing rich descriptive material on the needs of young people and on the services established to support them and their families. The Scottish study of social work with teenagers characterized the circumstances which bring teenagers to the attention of social services as behaviour in the community (including offending and drug abuse), difficulties in family relationships, school problems and other problems at home such as abuse or parents not coping (Triseliotis *et al.* 1995b). To this list might be added further problems identified in another study: behaviour in the home, violence to parents and others, emotional problems including self-harm, mental health problems, alcohol problems, running away and staying out (Biehal 2005). At the time of referral, professionals were concerned about abuse and/or neglect in relation to over half of this sample. The young people referred to support teams typically have multiple difficulties at referral and high levels of need. A substantial minority have histories of past abuse, neglect or past placement (Biehal 2005; Biehal *et al.* 2000; Brodie *et al.* 1998; Fuller 1989).

For many young people referred to social services, problems have reached an advanced stage by the time they receive a service and a substantial minority have had episodic contact with social services over a number of years (Biehal 2005; Biehal *et al* 2000; Fuller 1989; Triseliotis *et al.* 1995b). Frequent change appears to be a feature of many of their lives as they move backwards and forwards between various addresses (Biehal 2005; Biehal *et al.* 2000; Triseliotis *et al.* 2000). Educational difficulties, in particular high levels of non-attendance and school exclusion, are an additional stress factor for the majority of these young people, and many are in contact with a wide range of services, including health and mental health services, educational psychologists and youth offending teams (Biehal 2005; Biehal *et al.* 2000; Brodie *et al.* 1998; Frost 1997; Sinclair *et al.* 1995; Triseliotis *et al.* 1995b).

Many young people referred to social work services therefore have multiple, severe and often long-term difficulties.

Specialist support teams aim to provide multifaceted interventions to tackle these problems. Their principal objective is to support young people and parents in the community in order to prevent the need for placement. They offer a range of services to parents and young people to improve child and family functioning, including advice on parenting, mediation between parents and children, work on child behaviour and some group work. They may also use sessional staff to befriend vulnerable young people and engage them in activities outside home to alleviate stress (Biehal 2005; Biehal *et al.* 2000; Brodie *et al.* 1998; Cliffe with Berridge 1991). They aim to work in partnership with parents and young people and use a strengths-based approach (Biehal 2005; Biehal *et al.* 2000; Frost 1997). The emphasis is principally on helping parents to develop more consistent and authoritative parenting skills and encouraging young people to change their behaviour. They may also work with young people on relationships, grief and loss, keeping safe, social skills and on building their self-esteem.

The service offered is typically intensive and short term. The York study found that the mean duration of involvement with families was 19 weeks, with 28 per cent of cases closed within three months and 71 per cent within six months (Biehal 2005). In contrast, mainstream services were less intensive but lasted almost twice as long (an average of 36 weeks). Families referred to specialist teams had five times as many hours of face-to-face contact with social work professionals compared to those using mainstream services.

Specialist teams aim to work briefly with families in crisis to calm situations and renegotiate ground rules between young people and parents. After referral, initial meetings are normally held with parents, young people and referring social workers, at which written agreements are drawn up. These agreements are usually reviewed at four- to six-weekly intervals. Support teams are eclectic in their methods and use a range of structured materials including parenting programmes offered individually or in groups, videos on parenting or workbooks on anger management.

The York study found that most support teams did not draw on an explicit theoretical base. Two mentioned that their work was informed by family systems theory, but most described it in more general terms as undertaking 'family work', as well as providing practical and emotional support. The most common approach was solution-focused brief therapy. Although most of the teams did not indicate that they were using any particular theoretical models, the work on anger management that was common to all of them clearly drew on cognitive-behavioural theory and much of the structured work on parenting skills appeared to be informed by social learning theory. Support workers and social workers were often eclectic and some said they were unsure as to what theories informed their work.

Impact on Children's Development, Parenting Capacity and the Prevention of Family Breakdown

Overview

The York study was the only one of the support team studies to report detailed findings on child development and parenting capacity (Biehal 2005). This found that, for the sample as a whole, there was considerable improvement in scores for the number and severity of child problems at six-month follow-up. Between one-third and two-thirds of parents reported improvement on most of the specific difficulties they had reported at referral, including behaviour at home, staying out late, parent–child conflict and communication problems, running away and substance misuse. The greatest improvement was in violence to parents, where parents reported a reduction in 63 per cent of cases.

Standardized measures of child and family functioning also showed that a considerable degree of improvement occurred. The proportion with high scores for emotional and behavioural difficulties, indicating high levels of need, fell from 76 per cent to 55 per cent. This was a substantial improvement but levels of need nevertheless remained high for many of the sample, as scores at this level would only be anticipated for 10 per cent of children in the community (Goodman 1997). Scores on a measure of well-being also showed improvement, rising by ten points or more for 51 per cent of the young people (Huxley *et al.* 2001). A Severity of Difficulties measure designed for the study, which was a scale completed by both parents and children, also showed a significant improvement in mean scores for the severity of child problems.

Results were positive, as the majority of the sample showed improvement in specific difficulties reported at referral, emotional and behavioural problems and general well-being. However, there were no significant differences in scores for the groups using the two types of service, so there was no evidence that the specialist teams were more effective in improving child and family functioning than were mainstream services. Both the York study and the Scottish study found that positive change was more likely to take place in behaviour occurring within the home than outside it, and that there was little improvement in school-related problems and offending (Triseliotis *et al.* 1995).

Parenting Capacity

The York study found considerable improvement in parents' mental health status. At referral, scores for psychological distress were above the threshold for 72 per cent of parents, but by follow-up only 38 per cent scored above this level (Goldberg and Williams 1988). Mean scores for family functioning also improved, indicating positive change in family problem solving, communication, behaviour control, affective involvement and general family functioning (Epstein, Baldwin and Bishop 1983). Yet again, there were no significant differences in scores for those using specialist or mainstream services.

However, although the two groups were equivalent in most respects, a higher proportion of the group referred to specialist teams had severe emotional and behavioural difficulties and they were also more than twice as likely to have chronic difficulties and histories of abuse. It is therefore unclear whether the lack of statistically significant differences between the groups regarding improvement in child and family functioning was due to the fact that specialist and mainstream services were equally effective or due to imperfect matching of the two groups in the study.

Preventing Family Breakdown

Qualitative studies provide some evidence that support teams may help to prevent family breakdown, through mediation with families, negotiation, work on child behaviour and the provision of advice on developing more consistent and authoritative parenting strategies (Biehal *et al.* 2000; Brodie *et al.* 1998). However, any reduction in placement rates cannot be attributed solely to particular social work interventions. Changes in policy and in resources (such as the closure of children's homes) undoubtedly have a major impact on placement rates too, so caution is needed in drawing conclusions on effectiveness from findings on placement prevention (Biehal 2005; Biehal *et al.* 2000; Cliffe with Berridge 1991).

The York study found that, although one quarter of the sample entered care, most of these placements were of brief duration. Only 11 per cent were placed for more than four weeks and in only 8 per cent of cases was placement anticipated to be long term. Where the local authorities did not have support teams, 50 per cent of the young people were placed during the follow-up period, compared to only 25 per cent of those referred to support teams. Perhaps more importantly, in those authorities where only mainstream services were available, young people were significantly more likely to be placed in (what was anticipated to be) long-term care (29%) than those using support teams (6%).

Although the support teams in this study appeared to be particularly successful in reducing placement rates, several studies have questioned social workers' and support workers' preoccupation with avoiding placement at all costs (Biehal 2005; Cliffe with Berridge 1991; Frost 1997; Packman and Hall 1998; Triseliotis *et al.* 1995b). With this age group, it is not uncommon for placement to be used only as a last resort, partly through concerns about its potentially detrimental effects but also due to concern about the costs involved, so that practice becomes resource driven rather than needs led. The emphasis on keeping children at home for too long may lead to episodic intervention which fails to address serious long-term problems and in some cases make problems worse, only delaying a placement that may be in the child's best interests. There is a danger that *any* type of service with the explicit aim of preventing the placement of children may have the unintended consequence of substituting a fixation with avoiding placement in the short term for a more holistic assessment of the child's longer-term needs.

In families experiencing acute stress a planned short-term placement, or occasional brief episodes of respite care over a period of months, might constitute a positive element of a family support service which aims to prevent longer-term family breakdown (see, for example, Aldgate and Bradley 1999). Researchers in both the UK and the US have concluded that the conflation of placement with failure and the concomitant fixation with avoiding placement at all costs may lead to a failure to move beyond short-term crisis-resolution to a consideration of the longer-term needs of children (Biehal 2005; Packman and Hall 1998; Whittaker and Maluccio 2002).

Views of Young People and Their Carers

Although there is only limited research evidence as to the effectiveness of these teams, it is clear that young people and parents value them highly. The York study found that 79 per cent of the young people and 51 per cent of parents felt that the young person's circumstances had improved at six-month follow-up, although there was no significant difference in levels of satisfaction between those receiving specialist and mainstream services (Biehal 2005). The majority felt that support workers, and to a lesser extent social workers, had helped to bring about this positive change. It is difficult to know whether families' more positive evaluations of support workers were due solely to their skills and efforts or to the fact that they had more opportunities for direct work with families than social workers and could therefore build relationships with them.

In undertaking more direct work with families than mainstream social workers, support workers are able to develop specialist skills in working with this age group. The York study found that support workers were highly skilled in engaging young people in working with them, and that this engagement was a crucial factor in bringing about change. Their informal, participative and democratic style of working was valued by both young people and parents, who felt that they were listened to, understood by workers and involved in decision making. Young people's and parents' motivation to change were important factors, and there was some evidence in this study that support workers were particularly skilled at engaging young people who were not initially motivated.

Effectiveness of the Intervention

No studies to date have provided evidence as to the effectiveness of support teams in work with particular subgroups, such as children from ethnic minorities or children with special needs. There is some evidence that these teams may be less successful in work with families where problems were chronic and severe, as their short-term task-centred model may lead to a failure to address underlying long-term problems such as emotional abuse and rejection (Biehal 2005; Biehal *et al.* 2000). This finding is consistent with UK studies of work on child protection, which have found that positive outcomes are harder to achieve with families with multiple, longer-term problems (Cleaver and Freeman 1995; Thoburn *et al.* 2000a). It remains question-able, however, whether positive change for this subgroup in the short term is likely to be sustained without an infrastructure of longer-term, less intensive support services.

Conclusion

High rates of admission to care for older children and teenagers have led both to pro-fessional concerns about outcomes for young people and to managerial concerns about placement costs. These concerns have led to the development of specialist teams to support teenagers at risk of family breakdown, which may offer a valuable means of supporting young people and families in crisis. Since the majority of family support services are targeted at families with younger children, this is clearly an important area of service development; careful appraisal of the effectiveness of these services is needed.

At present there is little robust evidence available on the effectiveness of specialist support teams for teenagers. Nearly all of the existing UK research has been in the form of small, qualitative studies of single teams. These studies have provided rich descriptive material on needs and services, but have not focused on effectiveness. Only one UK study to date has been explicitly designed to assess effectiveness, so the research on outcomes for young people who are referred to specialist teams is in its early stages. Taken together, the evidence from this small group of studies suggests that specialist support teams for older children and teenagers may offer a promising approach in work with teenagers at risk of family breakdown.

The research suggests that young people and families in crisis may show consid-erable improvement in child and family functioning subsequent to the provision of a family support service. However, on the basis of the only study to date which has compared specialist support teams with an alternative 'service as usual', we cannot conclude that these teams are any *more* effective than mainstream services. This study found that many young people who received a support service showed remarkable improvement on a range of measures of child and family functioning, but outcomes were no more likely to be positive for young people receiving a service from a specialist support team than for those receiving a less intensive service from ordinary social workers (Biehal 2005).

In terms of placement prevention, though, the study found that young people referred to specialist teams were both less likely to enter care at all and were less likely to enter long-term care. However, service outcomes of this kind are as likely to be influenced by the local policy and resource context as by the nature of particular interventions. Since the research on these specialist-provided, intensive services is in its early stages, it is too soon to reach firm conclusions regarding their effectiveness.

Although the body of research on social work services for teenagers is small, it nevertheless has important implications for policy and practice.

It is clear from the research that, where no specialist service is available, it is difficult for families with teenagers to obtain *any* family support service until they have reached crisis point. If such a service *is* provided by a mainstream social work team, the demands of case management mean that social workers have fewer opportunities for direct work with families (Biehal 2005; Sinclair *et al.* 1995). The ring-fencing of budgets for support services to families with teenagers through the development of specialist teams may therefore be one means of ensuring that these families do receive a service.

We have seen that many teenagers who come to the attention of social services frequently have multiple difficulties, which bring them into contact with a number of other agencies. Problems in different areas of young people's lives (within the family, at school, in the wider community) may be mutually reinforcing, so risk factors must be addressed in these different domains (Bronfenbrenner 1979). Family support services for teenagers therefore require effective interdisciplinary working. Several studies have argued that family support services for young people need to be coordinated with those provided by other agencies, but this is often difficult to achieve as these other agencies may have different priorities and may respond slowly (Biehal 2005; Sinclair *et al.* 1995; Triseliotis *et al.* 1995).

Although evidence on outcomes in the longer term is not available at present, the fact that many young people in the York University study had had previous episodes of social services involvement suggests that brief interventions may not meet the longer-term needs of young people whose difficulties are chronic and severe (Biehal 2005). Some studies have concluded that, for this group with high levels of need, intensive support services should be located within an infrastructure of less intensive services which can offer advice and support as well as befriending services for young people over a longer period of time (Biehal 2005; Triseliotis *et al.* 1995). Less intensive services of this kind would also be able to offer help to families at an earlier stage before problems became severe, while specialist support teams could target those with the highest levels of need. The research evidence to date suggests that, while specialist support teams may offer a promising approach to work with young people, they should not constitute the only community-based service available to families with teenagers. Instead this short-term, intensive service should be located within a continuum of services, ranging from less intensive support at one end provided by universal services or secondary preventive services, to a range of short-term, respite (and, where necessary, long-term) placement resources at the other.

Further research on support teams for teenagers is needed, both to compare groups with similar levels of difficulty and to explore further which groups of young people, in which circumstances, might benefit most from this type of service. There is also a need for studies which follow-up young people receiving support services over a longer period of time.

CHAPTER 9

Support for Young People and their Families in the Community in the US

Scottye J. Cash and Dawn Anderson-Butcher

Introduction

The emergence of positive youth development programs in the United States has increased the focus nationally on the prevention of problem behaviors and the development of skills and competencies among at-risk youth (Benson 1997; Garmezy and Masten 1991; Lerner 1995). Weissberg, Caplan and Harwood (1991) reported "15–22% of the nation's 63 million children and adolescents have mental health problems severe enough to warrant treatment…[and] fewer than 20% of the young people with mental health problems currently receive appropriate treatment" (pp.830–1). Greenberg and colleagues (2003) reported that "30% of 14- to 17-year-olds engage in multiple high-risk behaviors that jeopardize their potential for life success" (p.467). Given that experiences during youth influence their life course as adults, the need to provide additional support, structure, and engagement to these young people through youth development programs is absolutely critical (Greenberg et al. 2003). As Dryfoos (1990) and Kumpfer and Alvarado (2003) note, the family and the school system are not equipped or supported enough to help transform children into healthy and productive adults. The purpose of this chapter is to provide an overview of youth development programs that target specific behavioral outcomes, have been evaluated using rigorous designs, and offer key strategies that can be implemented in other settings and communities.

Development of Youth Development Programs

In the past, there has been a focus on designing individual and group interventions to target youth displaying single problem behaviors (i.e., substance use, juvenile delinquency, teenage pregnancy, etc.). It was found, however, that being problem-free did not necessarily guarantee youth had the skills and resources needed to succeed in life (Pittman 1991). In response, a shift occurred towards the promotion of healthy development among all youths, particularly those most at risk for engagement in problem behaviors (Catalano *et al.* 2002). Comprehensive, integrated youth development approaches emerged. This trend is the result of research documenting socialization factors at each ecological level (Brofenbrenner 1979) that the community, family, peer, and school systems impact developmental trajectories among youth (Coie *et al.* 1993; Dryfoos 1990; Hawkins, Catalano and Miller 1992; Loeber 1990).

Essentially, research stressed the importance of understanding what turns the tide for at-risk youth. It is now clear that youth problem behaviors co-occur (Benson 1993; Donovan, Jessor and Costa 1988; Jessor and Jessor 1977) and the same factors present within different environmental settings predict multiple problem behaviors (Dryfoos 1990). Exposure to these predictors, also called "risk factors," is related to increased problem behaviors; whereas exposure to increased protective factors (also called "assets") prevents them (Benson 1997; Dryfoos 1990; Hawkins *et al.* 1992; Jessor *et al.* 1997; Rutter 1987a, 1987b; Sameroff and Seifer 1990; Werner and Smith 1982). Table 9.1 highlights examples of these risk and protective factors.

In response, youth development approaches (typically targeting youth ages pre-kindergarten through 19 years old) now focus on developing skills, competencies, and protection, as well as preventing problem behaviors. Reviews and meta-analyses examining outcomes associated with these programs have found that participation is associated with more frequent school attendance, higher academic achievement, less substance use and delinquency, enhanced social competence, and increased mental health (Durlak and Wells 1997; Greenberg, Domitrovich and Bumbarger 2001; Hawkins *et al.* 1999; Roth *et al.* 1998).

Prevalence of Programs and Funding Sources

The number of youth development programs that came into existence in the United States today is unknown. Wandersman and Florin (2003) note that on the whole programs fall into two types of categories: *research-driven* prevention and *community-driven* prevention. Research-driven prevention is usually conducted by universities, where researchers design an intervention, and employ rigorous evaluation methodologies; these programs are fairly expensive and difficult to replicate (Wandersman and Florin 2003). Community-driven prevention involves

Table 9.1: Examining risk and protective factors from an ecosystems perspective

System	Examples of risk factors	Examples of protective factors
Community	Disorganization and mobility Laws inadequately deter and/or may foster problem behaviors Norms promote problem behaviors Drugs, alcohol, and weapons are readily available Media portrays antisocial behaviors Community members feel little attachment/connection to their neighborhood	Multiple opportunities for pro-social involvement through participation in youth organizations, faith-based programs, etc. Rewards are provided for youth's involvement in pro-social activities Presence of caring adults within the neighborhood who are invested in youth and the neighborhood
School	Youth feel little connection with and commitment to school Youth do not enjoy school Youth experience early academic failure School rules are inconsistently implemented Student behaviors are not monitored well Inadequate resources and systems barriers exist	Youth have opportunities for participation in meaningful activities involving service, leadership, extracurricular activities such as sports, classroom activities, etc. Rewards and recognition for pro-social behaviors are provided The school's climate is welcoming and responsive Teachers have high expectations for student achievement
Family	History of conflict and child maltreatment within the family Poor family management and discipline techniques Little supervision and monitoring of children Family has history of problem behaviors	Family members feel connected and attached Positive parent/guardian–child relationships exist Parent/guardian/family members provide reinforcement for pro-social involvement and behaviors Opportunities exist to contribute to the family in meaningful ways
Peer/ individual	Peers/friends are involved in antisocial and/or problem behaviors Youth and their peers have favorable attitudes toward antisocial behaviors and substance use Rewards exist that reinforce antisocial behaviors and substance use Youth are rebellious, alienated, risk taking, and display sensation-seeking behaviors	Youth display social competence through problem solving, decision making, resistance, anger management skills, etc. Youth are involved in religious institutions Youth have high intelligence Youth have high self-esteem, -confidence, and -efficacy Youth display a mild temperament Youth are adaptable/flexible Youth have hope for the future

those programs in place in communities and schools throughout the country; they are created, owned, and provided within the resident community. While there may be an evaluation component or a connection with a university, these programs are not at the same scale as the research-driven programs. Nation and colleagues (2003) summarize the conundrum that exists in trying to replicate research-driven programs: "the difficulty in replicating expensive, science-based prevention models or proprietary commercial products has resulted in many local agencies adapting their own prevention programs with marginal effects" (p.449). Nastasi (2002) and Hallfors and Godette (2002) further identify the complexity of implementing research-driven programs: How do you adapt an evidence-based program to a community or school setting that is different than the program in the experimental evaluation? These community-driven youth development programs have proliferated throughout diverse communities in the US and it is therefore impossible to determine the impact of these programs, with the evaluation and treatment fidelity being key limitations that influence the evaluation findings.

In examining the types of funding sources used for creating and sustaining youth development programs it is necessary to discuss these in terms of research-driven and community-driven programs (Wandersman and Florin 2003). Overall, community-driven programs are generally funded through grant opportunities from the US Department of Education. The Coalition for Evidence-Based Policy (2002) provided the Department of Education with a set of strategies for prioritizing which programs should receive funding. While they argue that it is important to use randomized clinical trials in studying the impact of these programs on youth development, they also recognize that systemic changes will need to be made first (for a detailed discussion see the report). The research-driven programs that are highlighted in this chapter were funded by the Office for Substance Abuse Prevention, the Center for Substance Abuse Prevention, the National Institute on Alcohol Abuse and Alcoholism, the National Institute on Drug Abuse, the Division of Research Resources of the National Institutes of Health, and private foundations. It is evident that government agencies (Department of Health and Human Services and National Institutes of Health) and private foundations provide funding for these large-scale programs and evaluations.

The purpose of this chapter is to provide examples of programs that have sound evaluations and have been implemented among different ecological levels (i.e., one system – school, community; two systems – family and school; three systems – family, school, and community). This chapter is organized around findings from youth development programs that were included in this review. Table 9.2 provides a synopsis of the research methodology and findings from the evaluation. Table 9.3 provides a brief summary of the programs, outcomes targeted, and key strategies. The goal was to tease out individual strategies within these programs shown to work in producing positive outcomes for youth participants. It is believed that a strategy-based approach will help those working with and for this population to adopt specific strategies rather than trying to implement a whole program that may not be specifically geared toward their community.

Evidence of Program Effectiveness

Research-driven (Wandersman and Florin 2003) youth development programs have been evaluated extensively and based on sound and rigorous research methodologies (Catalano *et al.* 1998). The methodologies used in the evaluation of these programs generally used quantitative methods and were large-scale evaluations. Table 9.2 provides the methodology used including sample size, design, and an overview of the outcomes. The programs that were chosen to be included in this chapter are widely representative of the research-driven programs and do not reflect all of the youth development programs. While many schools and communities work to adopt research-based curriculum, the way in which the curriculum is implemented is different than the way it was implemented in the demonstration projects and therefore treatment fidelity is not maintained and transferring the outcomes from one to the other is problematic. Schools and communities, however, are faced with the issue of not providing a program at all or of providing a program that is not appropriate to their school or community. Therefore, based on this issue, we recommend that schools and communities adopt key strategies from these programs rather than trying to implement the entire program. We offer this recommendation with one caveat: when the strategies are implemented, the program should work with the local university faculty to evaluate the program.

A Review of Example Effective Programs

A review of 14 youth development programs is provided in Table 9.2. The programs that are included were selected based on the following criteria: the program influences one or more ecological domains, the program has been evaluated using rigorous methodologies, the program shows positive effects in one or more areas, and has key strategies that can be implemented by others. Each program and methodology is outlined in Table 9.2 and is organized by the number of and type of ecological levels influenced.

Table 9.2: Overview of evaluation findings

Study	Program	Research design	Sample size	Overview of findings
One system				
Botvin *et al.* (1990)	Life Skills Training Program	Experimental design with random assignment. Post-test with one-year follow-up	1185 785 for one year follow-up	A statistically significant difference on knowledge, attitudes, and behaviors was noted between the two intervention groups and the control group. There was more knowledge about substance use, lower cigarette and marijuana smoking, and more knowledge of smoking consequences.
St. Pierre *et al.* (1992)	Stay SMART	Pre-test–post-test non-equivalent groups design, with multiple post-tests	161	Stay SMART program attendees showed programmatic effects on the following outcomes: marijuana-related behavior, cigarette-related behavior, drug-related behavior, and personal and social competence. At the two-year follow-up, the Stay SMART + Boosters group had similar outcomes to the Stay SMART Only group; only significant differences were found with alcohol and marijuana attitudes.
Two systems				
Allen *et al.* (1997)	Teen Outreach	True experimental design	695	The program was successful in reducing school failures, school suspensions, and teenage pregnancy. Additionally, at those sites that promoted student autonomy within a positive social context, the students were more successful.
Allen, Philliber, and Hoggson (1990)	Teen Outreach	Quasi-experimental design with a non-equivalent comparison group	632 in the Teen Outreach Program and 855 comparison students	The more intensive programs with the older students were more effective for reducing problem behaviors. For the younger students, the less intensive program resulted in a greater reduction of problem behaviors.

Study	Design	N	Findings
Hawkins *et al.* (1999)	Quasi-experimental design with comparison groups	643	Students in the experimental condition had stronger attachment to school, and improvement in achievement, and were significantly less involved in school misbehavior than the comparison group. No long-term effects were found between the comparison group and treatment group for the use of alcohol, tobacco, marijuana, or other substances.
Battistich *et al.* (1996)	Quasi-experimental design with comparison groups	2438 in the demonstration group; 2331 in the comparison group (over three separate school years)	For the demonstration group, there was a significant difference for alcohol use; however, no significant difference for marijuana use. Those schools with higher implementation levels did better on the following outcomes: skipping school, carrying weapons, and vehicle thefts.
Kirby *et al.* (1991)	Quasi-experimental design with partial random assignment and comparison groups	758 initially; 722 at six-month follow-up	The experimental groups had a statistically significant increase in their sexual knowledge than the comparison group. The comparison group reported a greater number of their peers/friends having had sexual intercourse than the treatment group. There were no differences in contraceptive practice or use of contraceptives and getting pregnant. At six-months' follow-up there was a statistically significant increase in the number of students in the experimental group who had talked with their parents about sexual activity.

Continued on next page

Table 9.2 cont.

Study	Program	Research design	Sample size	Overview of findings
Three Systems				
LoSciuto *et al.* (1996)	Across Ages	Classic randomized pre-test–post-test control group design	729	Students in the Across Ages group scored significantly higher on the student's attitudes toward school, future, elders, their attitudes toward older people, well-being, reactions to situations involving drug use, and community service than the control group and the group receiving the Positive Youth Development Curriculum. Higher level of involvement between the youth and their mentor produces better outcomes.
Andrews *et al.* (1995)	Adolescent Transitions Program	Experimental pre-test–post-test design	158 high-risk families	Parent and Teen Focus group had higher levels of learning principles, a more significant decrease in the number of negative engagements, and a larger decrease in conflict than the families in the other conditions; they also had the lowest levels of youth aggression.
Pentz *et al.* (1990)	Midwestern Prevention Project	Quasi-experimental, partial randomized control trial with a varied intervention condition	1607 individually tracked over time; 3771 cross-sectionally and randomly sampled by classroom each year	High implementation of the program has a more positive effect impacting use of substances and decreasing the use of cigarettes. The intervention overall had a significant impact on reducing cigarette, marijuana, and alcohol use (measured daily, weekly, and monthly).

LoSciuto et al. (1997)	Woodrock Youth Development Project	Experimental pre-test–post-test with random assignment	367	Results reported for the experimental groups. For the younger sample, there was a significant effect on drug use and relations with and perception of those students who were of a different race than their own; this sample had higher self-esteem, and more positive attitudes toward alcohol and drug use. For the older group, the students in the experimental group reported less levels of drug use over the past month. No other differences between the experimental and control groups were found.
Perry et al. (1996)	Project Northland	Experimental, delayed control group	1901	The students in the Project Northland group had better outcomes than the control group students in the following areas: scored lower on the Tendency to Use Alcohol Scale, used less alcohol and cigarettes, scored lower on the Peer Influence Scale, were more likely to talk with their parents about drinking, and had parents who were more likely to have rules against drinking. Overall, the program was somewhat effective in reducing the onset and prevalence in alcohol use.
Johnson et al. (1996)	Creating Lasting Connections	Outcome evaluation Experimental randomized block design with a comparison group and three repeated measures	217	There were significant differences for the experimental group in the following areas: parents' use of community services, parents' action, parents' perceived helpfulness, youths' service use, youths' action, youths' perceived helpfulness, and parents' communication with their youth. There was a greater increase in parents' knowledge about alcohol and drug (AOD) use than in control, and youths had a higher level of involvement in setting rules about AOD use. There were moderating effects of youth-level involvement.

Key Strategies Implemented within Effective Programs

While the programs reviewed are based on empirical evidence, challenges exist related to incorporating these evidence-based programs into practice. Many organizations continue to choose curricula that have not been evaluated or select programs that are ineffective (Gottfredson and Gottfredson 2001; Rohrbach *et al.* 1996; Tobler and Stratton 1997), and they do not have always the resources to implement research-driven programs with fidelity (Hallfors and Godette 2002; Nation *et al.* 2003).

The challenge still exists in ensuring that evidence-based practices continue, while simultaneously addressing the needs and challenges existing with implementation. In response, Andrews (2003) suggests the diffusion and adoption of best practices or guiding principles within youth development programming, as opposed to the implementation of standardized curricula or evidence-based programs. This would enhance implementation fidelity and assist with the diffusion of best practices into real-life settings. In an effort to promote this best-practice model, we summarize in Table 9.3 key strategies within each of these programs that have been implemented and may be adopted for use within other communities without the issues associated with implementing an entire program. When adopting these strategies, it is imperative that the program implementers continue to evaluate the contribution of these strategies. The present review identifies several emergent best-practice strategies present within these effective programs.

The overall strategy among these effective youth development programs is clear: quality programs that produce outcomes stress a dual focus on risk and protective factors present within the community, family, school, and peer/individual systems. The programs targeted multiple systems in order to reinforce consistent messages across settings, and simultaneously work on reducing risk while enhancing youth competencies, skills, opportunities, and resources. Specifically, these programs utilized a variety of teaching methods, promoted engagement in these activities, and enhanced competencies among youth by teaching life skills such as problem solving, resistance, and decision-making skills. Program strategies also strived to provide opportunities directly to apply these newly learned skills within real-life situations.

Many of the identified programs also adopted social learning perspectives by developing peer relationships and positive norms and interactions. Effective program strategies reinforced pro-social norms through youth leadership, peer mentoring, and role modeling activities. In addition, programs aimed to provide youth with opportunities and rewards through after-school programs, extracurriculars, and special activities. Programs also created meaningful roles for youth through community service, volunteering, and mobilization. These activities aimed to enhance self-esteem, self-efficacy, and social competence.

Table 9.3: Program information and key strategies

Program name	Evaluation authors	Systemic levels	Targeted outcomes	Best practice strategies
Life Skills Training	Botvin et al. (1990)	School	Cigarette, alcohol, and marijuana behaviors	Continued involvement in the program (booster sessions) to reinforce lessons learned and incorporate new ideas Use of peer mentors Use of cognitive behavioral approaches in addition to didactic training
Stay SMART + Boosters; Stay SMART Only	St. Pierre et al. (1992)	Community	Alcohol and drug use, sexual activity	Continued involvement in the program (booster sessions) that incorporates the youth's developmental level Encourage youth to be role models for others
Teen Outreach	Allen et al. (1997) Allen et al. (1990)	School and community	Teen pregnancy and school failure	Create a positive environment that combines classroom and volunteering in community Emphasize autonomy in the context of positive peer relationships Provide different programming structures based on the students' ages
Seattle Social Development Project	Hawkins et al. (1999)	School and family	Crime, teen pregnancy, drug abuse, school failure, drop-out	Resiliency focus which includes training for parents and teachers Use different types of programming based on child's developmental level
Child Development Project	Battistich et al. (1996)	School and family	Alcohol, marijuana, and tobacco use; delinquency	Implement program at all levels of the school system Include the parents to promote a sense of culture and heritage
Reducing the Risk	Kirby et al. (1991)	School and family	Unprotected sexual intercourse	Use exercises where communication with parents is an outcome Try social learning and social inoculation theories to connect and engage students

Continued on next page

Table 9.3 cont.

Program name	Evaluation authors	Systemic levels	Targeted outcomes	Best practice strategies
Across Ages	LoSciuto et al. (1996)	Family, school, and community	Substance abuse	Connect with older adult mentors in the community Reward for higher participation of mentors Provide community service opportunities Incorporate parent involvement activities
Adolescent Transitions Program	Andrews et al. (1995)	Family, school, and community	Substance use	Involve the parents in the intervention Use peer counselors to provide linkages between adults and students
Midwestern Prevention Project	Pentz et al. (1990)	Family, school, and community	Substance use	Continue program from middle school to high school Use community mobilization strategies Examine mass media influences
Woodrock Youth Development Project	LoSciuto et al. (1997)	Family, school, and community	Alcohol, tobacco, and drug use	Create developmentally appropriate curriculum Discuss race relations Use peer mentors Provide linkages between home and school
Project Northland	Perry et al. (1996)	Family, school, and community	Alcohol and other drug use	Use peer-led groups to connect with the students Provide multilevel programming Reinforce parent involvement
Creating Lasting Connections	Johnson et al. (1996)	Family, church, and community	Delay onset and reduce frequency of alcohol and drug use	Have a resiliency focus that promotes social support and family connectedness Capitalize on faith-based community mobilization activities Educate parents regarding substance use Provide early intervention and case management services

Environmental supports were developed within many program strategies. These programs promoted bonding and connections with others and institutions. For instance, programs built positive caring adult–youth relationships through mentoring programs and youth's pro-social behaviors were reinforced through these meaningful relationships. Likewise, school climate and commitment were strengthened through teacher training in consistency management and creating home–school communication networks.

Family level influences were addressed. Effective programs addressed family conflict by enhancing parent management/supervision and monitoring. Family attachment and connections were reinforced through program activities designed to strengthen parent–child interactions and communication.

Finally, effective programs ensured there was a sufficient amount of dosage by encouraging continued involvement over long periods of time (i.e., at least nine months) (Hawkins *et al.* 1999). Additionally, booster sessions were a critical component of successful programs.

In addition, the youth development literature highlights a few additional key strategies. First, it is important to provide programming that is appropriate to participants' age, development (across the age span), and culture (Catalano *et al.* 2002; Nation *et al.* 2003; Weissberg, Kumpfer and Seligman 2003). Second, programming needs to be adapted to local needs and community contexts (Roth *et al.* 1998). Third, there is a need for programs to have well-trained staff and programs support professional development (Nation *et al.* 2003; Weissberg *et al.* 2003).

Conclusion

Youth in the United States face many challenges that cannot be addressed by only the school and/or only the family; they need support. The emergence of quality research documenting outcomes associated with programs has spearheaded policy nationally that encourages youth development practitioners, educators, and others, as well as the organizations they work for, to implement evidence-based programs to meet community needs. Governmental agencies such as the US Department of Education and the Center for Substance Abuse Prevention (CSAP) are now requiring evidence-based programs to ensure accountability and create better outcomes from their investments in youth. This has resulted in an emerging trend in the US toward the use of evidence-based programs and research-based practices (CSAP 2000; Greenberg *et al.* 2003; Weissberg *et al.* 2003). Furthermore, Nastasi (2002) argues that evaluators need to not only discuss those strategies or programs that work, but also discuss what does not work and provide their solutions to overcoming these obstacles. Similarly, there needs to be significant discussion on how can these key strategies be implemented across larger and dynamic systems.

Given the issues of implementation and maintenance of fidelity for these large scale evaluations and programs, we propose adoption and evaluation of a set of strategies that can be implemented within a given community. To evaluate these programs, we suggest creating partnerships between universities and local youth development programs to create a repository and system of dissemination of evaluation findings that would be mutually beneficial to the community and the university (Biglan *et al.* 2003).

In conclusion, much may be learned from the research conducted in the United States documenting positive outcomes associated with participation in youth development programs. Several evidence-based programs and best practice strategies have been described in this chapter. In particular, this information about these identified strategies may be utilized to guide future youth development efforts (from a practice and policy perspective). The targeting of risk and protective factors across multiple systems is critical and youth outcomes will be promoted as a result. Further, the adoption of key strategies or best practices in youth development may further support the diffusion of quality, comprehensive programming for working with at-risk youth and their families in the future.

Therapeutic Interventions with
Children who have Experienced
Neglect and their Families
in the UK

Jenny Gray and Danielle Turney

PART THREE

Evidence on Therapeutic Interventions with Children who have Experienced Abuse or Neglect

Therapeutic Interventions with Children who have Experienced Neglect and their Families in the UK

Karen Tanner and Danielle Turney

Introduction

Our focus in this chapter is on serious and chronic child neglect. Neglect is significantly damaging for those children who experience it and a difficult and complex area of practice for social workers and other childcare professionals. The Department of Health's *Working Together to Safeguard Children* (Department of Health, Department for Education and Employment and Home Office 1999, p.6) offers the following definition:

> Neglect is the persistent failure to meet a child's basic physical and/or psychological needs likely to result in the serious impairment of the child's health or development. It may involve a parent or carer failing to provide adequate food, shelter and clothing, failing to protect a child from physical harm or danger, or the failure to ensure access to appropriate medical care or treatment. It may also include neglect of, or unresponsiveness to, a child's basic emotional needs.

This definition must be satisfied for a child's name to be put on the Child Protection Register (CPR).

While the number of children on CPRs in England has decreased overall in recent years, the proportion registered on grounds of neglect has increased steadily (www.dfes.gov.uk) to the point where neglect has become the highest category of registration. Most recent figures from the Department for Education and Skills (31 March 2004) indicate that of the 26,300 children whose names were included on CPRs in England, 11,000 (i.e. 42%) were registered for neglect. And this is likely to be an underestimate of the problem. Registers will not include children in families where neglect is being addressed through children in need provision (s17 Children Act 1989) rather than the child protection framework.

Not only is neglect significant in terms of numbers, it also raises serious concerns in terms of the range and potential severity of its effects and the difficulties in achieving effective outcomes. So it is perhaps surprising that there is so little UK research to support and inform practice. Neglect has been something of a Cinderella subject for researchers. When it is addressed, it is often linked with physical abuse or subsumed within maltreatment rather than being treated as a subject in its own right, with specific (and possibly quite different) antecedents and consequences. The majority of existing research evidence comes from US studies and reflects that country's political and social welfare context. While there is a small but developing UK literature about neglect, there is still little evidence about effective intervention (Macdonald 2004; Tanner and Turney 2003). We will consider the available evidence in more detail below, but first provide a brief overview of the knowledge base in relation to both the aetiology and the effects of neglect.

Chronic neglect is unlikely to be monocausal and is best understood from an ecological perspective. Ecological approaches identify a number of different levels or interacting systems – the individual or intrapersonal, the interpersonal or family level (microsystem), the social/community levels (the mesosystem), and the societal level (the macro system, which includes the broader cultural values and beliefs) – and look at the way different factors at each level interact, rather than focusing on one dimension (for example, the intrapersonal) and treating it in isolation (Jack 1997b and 2000). This kind of approach allows consideration of 'the balance between stressors and supports, or risks and protective factors' (Jack 1997a, p.105).

Studies of the personal characteristics of parents and the dynamics of family life identify a range of features that contribute to the neglect of children. Much of this research focuses on mothers, reflecting the traditional association between women and caring. Daniel (1998) observes that neglectful mothers often present as powerless and helpless, showing little belief in either their own efficacy or the competence and responsiveness of others. Parents' own experiences of emotionally impoverished and/or abusive childhoods may leave them ill equipped to meet their children's needs. Neglecting parents appear to find it difficult to hold the needs of their children in mind, resulting in an inability to empathize and chaotic and/or unresponsive parenting (Jones and Gupta 1998; Stevenson 1998; Stone 2003). Parental conflict is significantly associated with neglect and/or abuse for children (Bifulco and Moran 1998). Substance-misusing parents may place their children at risk of neglect by being physically or emotionally unavailable to them; they may not be able to offer consistent care or adequate supervision, allowing exposure to unsafe situations, and may buy drugs or alcohol instead of food and other necessities (Bifulco and Moran 1998; Jowitt 2003).

At the social/societal level, there is an association between poverty and neglect although clearly not all poor families are neglectful (Jones and Gupta 1998; Stevenson 1998). Many neglecting families are socially isolated, their key supports being relatives who frequently share their physical and/or emotional impoverishment. The combination of poverty, isolation/dislocation and racism can seriously impact on family functioning, with particular implications for dispersed minority ethnic and asylum-seeking/refugee families.

The Framework for the Assessment of Children in Need and their Families (Department of Health 2000a; Department of Health et al. 2000) identifies seven dimensions of child development: health, education, emotional and behavioural development, identity, family and social relationships, social presentation and self-care skills. The available literature consistently identifies a negative association between neglect and the factors promoting good developmental outcomes for children in each of these dimensions.

At the most basic level of development, persistent neglect may have important neuro-developmental consequences. In America, Perry's research (for example, Perry 2000; Perry and Pollard 1997) has demonstrated the negative impact of trauma and neglect on neurological development. while there is little similar work in the UK, it is important in understanding the impact of neglect on early childhood development (see Rutter 2005). Further, inattentive or unresponsive parenting can have effects on a child's physical well-being. This kind of parenting has been linked to non-organic failure to thrive in babies and young children and to injuries, even fatalities, resulting from lack of supervision (Stevenson 1998; Stone 2003). The literature highlights a significant and enduring connection between neglect and cognitive ability and educational performance (Stevenson 1998). These difficulties may begin in primary school and both persist and deepen in secondary school.

Neglect also affects children's emotional development, identity and relationship capacity: parental apathy and lack of stimulus can result in children developing an internal model of powerlessness and lack of belief in their self-efficacy (Daniel 1998), insecure attachments (Howe et al. 1999) and impaired social competence (Jones and Gupta 1998). Poor self-care skills can lead to social isolation by peers and undermine the social skills required for social integration (Bridge Childcare Consultancy 1995). The social and emotional difficulties experienced by the children may be cumulative and the impact long-lasting, with implications for their own parenting capacity (Bifulco and Moran 1998).

Research into resilience suggests that while some children are more resilient than others, ongoing neglect is likely to affect precisely those factors that promote resilience and provide some protection in adversity, namely, a secure base, good self-esteem and a sense of self-efficacy (Daniel 1998). In the absence of any protective factors, children in neglecting families may experience significant difficulties in forming healthy attachments (Howe *et al.* 1999; Stevenson 1998) with both potential partners and their own children.

Evidence of Programme Effectiveness

While the focus of this chapter is on the UK evidence base, much academic activity in Britain has been informed by American research. For example, many of the UK reviews of the knowledge base (for example, Jowitt 2003; Stevenson 1998) draw on American empirical research (Crittenden 1988, 1993, 1996; Dubowitz 1999; Gaudin 1993a, 1999). However, a number of limitations have been identified in both the UK and US literatures that have an impact on the robustness or quality of the evidence they present.

The first relates to the way the topic is framed. There are continuing problems with child neglect in relation to both the scope and definition of the concept (Stone 1998, p.25). The Department of Health (DH) definition cited earlier is important in practice, but is not necessarily the one that informs research studies. Given the range of definitions used both within and between disciplines, there is potentially a problem in comparing the results of different studies or in extrapolating from one context to another.

Leaving aside the difficulty in finding a workable common definition, there is a paucity of literature specifically on neglect. Much of the literature refers to abuse and neglect almost as if there were no distinction between them, or tends to focus on abuse at the expense of a separate analysis of neglect. It may be that as physical abuse is often easier to identify, such cases attract more research attention, while neglect, with all its definitional complexities, is less amenable to study.

The second area concerns the theoretical base of the work: while many UK researchers agree about the value of an ecological perspective, the theoretical underpinning in much of the literature is not explicitly stated. In addition, there is little *social work* theory on neglect (Stone 1998). The research or theory that addresses neglect comes mainly from psychology, psychiatry, child development, medicine/nursing, etc., rather than from social work itself.

Third, there is a question over the extent to which studies take account of race/ethnicity, gender and class, or otherwise address issues of anti-oppressive practice. It has already been noted, for example, that some of the literature fails to take account of gender, focusing on the role – and often the perceived failings – of women as mothers, without considering the role and contribution of fathers to child neglect (Corby 2000, p.104ff; Featherstone 1999; O'Hagan and Dillenburger 1995; Turney 2004). We are left, therefore, with some concerns about the values underpinning research into child neglect and their implications for the applicability of results.

The last broad area concerns methodological issues. The American research literature shows marked variations in definitions of the problem, sample size and population, and outcome measures, making comparisons difficult. And in the UK there have been very few experimentally based studies, leaving little empirical evidence on effectively working with child neglect.

Given these limitations, it is not possibly to state categorically, on the basis of experimental research, what does or does not work in relation to child neglect. However, it is possible to draw out a number of messages from the existing knowledge base that may assist practitioners working with neglecting families.

The Evidence on Effectiveness

Jowitt (2003, p.6) notes that 'the varied experiences of neglect can be located within a continuum of mild and episodic to severe and chronic physical neglect and emotional abuse'. Different intervention strategies may be appropriate, depending on the nature and chronicity of the neglect and its causation. Macdonald and Winkley (1999) provide a helpful framework for thinking about intervention at different stages. Drawing on what Stevenson (1998) identifies as a medical model of prevention, they analyse a range of interventions that operate at different levels of prevention – primary, secondary and tertiary. Using this framework, the implications of different strategies for understanding and working with neglect can be drawn out.

Primary interventions are broad-based and universal; they are 'aimed at whole communities or populations irrespective of any known particular risk' (Macdonald and Winkley 1999, p.33). These measures promote general well-being; they are usually broadly educational and work on the assumption that prevention is better than cure. Such universal measures, which are all designed to promote resilience in families, may have particular relevance to neglect. For example, measures aimed at tackling social exclusion, poverty, domestic violence (Zero Tolerance) and teenage pregnancy can have a preventative function for potentially neglectful parents. The Sure Start programme is an example of an intervention aimed at a number of the factors associated with social exclusion.

Sure Start is the government's programme to support children, families and communities through the integration of early education, child care, health and family support. Sure Start is committed to delivering the best start in life for every child, better opportunities for parents, affordable, good quality child care and stronger, safer communities (see www.surestart.gov.uk). Although an extensive programme evaluating this initiative is currently under way (see the National Evaluation of Sure Start website www.ness.bbk.ac.uk), the effectiveness of such a radical community programme on the outcomes for disadvantaged children has yet to be demonstrated.

Secondary intervention is aimed at particular groups who have been identified as being at high risk of abuse or neglect. In some families personal and familial characteristics interact with serious social disadvantage and require a more tailored response. Targeting services successfully requires a sound grasp of factors that may predispose individuals towards neglect and a good understanding of the indicators of neglect.

The literature identifies two sorts of intervention – home visiting and parenting programmes – that have been helpful in work with vulnerable parents. However, such programmes typically do not focus specifically on neglect and appear to be aimed at 'abuse and neglect' (without differentiation) or 'maltreatment' more generally. The aims of these interventions, broadly, are to provide early intervention to help develop parenting skills and confidence and improve parent–child interaction. Both home-visiting and parenting programmes may be delivered by different professionals in the voluntary and statutory sectors, paraprofessionals or lay helpers.

Home-visiting programmes have been researched in rather more depth than many of the other interventions referred to in this chapter (Macdonald 2004). Barlow *et al.* (2003, p.174) note that, while 'a recent systematic review showed that it was not possible…to reach any firm conclusions regarding the effectiveness of intensive home visiting programmes in preventing abuse or neglect (due in part to a range of methodological problems such as surveillance bias and non-comparability of measures)', there were nonetheless a number of positive outcomes for target families.

While not specifically aimed at families who neglect, parenting skills programmes, usually delivered in a group setting, may be helpful in addressing some of their difficulties. Evaluation studies (Grimshaw and McGuire 1998; Smith and Pugh 1996) suggest that parenting programmes are generally well received. However, while parenting programmes seem to offer opportunities for positive intervention, Smith and Pugh found some problems with their accessibility, particularly for parents from black and minority ethnic groups, those 'who are not comfortable with the written word', and fathers (Smith and Pugh 1996). In addition, the literature identifies a number of factors – depression, stress, low socio-economic status, lack of a sense of self-efficacy, social isolation, poor relationships, chronicity of problems – that may militate against the success of this form of intervention. These are all factors typically associated with neglectful families. So these parents may need additional individual support to enable them to engage with, and make use of, such programmes. In summary, while there are clearly some indications that parenting programmes could have a place in a broad-based intervention strategy, there is an urgent need for further evaluation of their *effectiveness*.

Perhaps the most difficult challenge for practitioners is effective tertiary intervention to try and halt and then change patterns of chronic and severe neglect. It is not unusual for chronically neglectful parents to come from families characterized by the same difficulties. This transgenerational dimension impoverishes the model of parenting and familial supports available to new parents and, unless effective intervention occurs at an early stage of the new family's life, intractable caring problems are likely to be established. Enduring neglect can also be associated with chronic parental mental health difficulties and/or substance abuse. These difficulties are frequently accompanied by poverty, social marginalization (often, but not always, including familial estrangement) and impaired personal functioning on a number of levels. The long-term combination of these factors can have serious implications for the quality of care available to children. Further, the literature identifies the severity of a family's difficulties as being 'the most powerful predictor of outcome' (Gaudin, cited in Stevenson 1998, p.108).

However, all too frequently the social work response to chronic neglect has failed to acknowledge the complexity of the problem. Intervention has focused on finding solutions to the symptoms of neglect rather than understanding the causes. Such a symptomatic response (the most common example being a focus on the domestic environment alone) is unlikely to be successful if other factors, such as relationship difficulties between parent and child, and the interaction between them, have not been attended to. While there is a lack of robust evidence about effective tertiary intervention, the available research identifies a number of factors that may contribute to an effective strategy for addressing chronic neglect.

Assessment

There is a consensus in the literature that effective intervention depends on a thorough assessment of the specific circumstances of each family and their particular patterns of vulnerability and resilience (Bridge Childcare Consultancy 1995; Stone 2003; Tanner and Turney 2000). Indeed, assessment is in itself a form of intervention, not just an exercise in information gathering (necessary though this is). Assessment provides the first opportunity to engage with the family and to try and gain some understanding of the particular difficulties and strengths in their lives, allowing the worker to map out the interventions and strategies that are going to be needed.

The *Assessment Framework* (Department of Health *et al.* 2000), with its ecological perspective, is an opportunity to improve assessment practice in cases of chronic child neglect (Horwath 2002; Rose 2001; Stone 2003). The framework depicts a triangle of three interrelated domains: the child's developmental needs, parenting capacity, and family and environmental factors. Accurate assessment requires a balanced focus on each domain and consideration of the interconnections between them. However, findings from the studies of the early implementation of the *Assessment Framework* suggest particular difficulties for the assessment of neglect (Cleaver and Walker 2004; Horwath 2002). These include distorted assessments in which some dimensions of the child's world are over- or underemphasized. Jack and Gill (2003) and Cleaver and Walker (2004) noted the failure to appreciate the impact of family and environmental factors on children's well-being. Cleaver and Walker (2004) also identified that an in-depth core assessment is most likely to be carried out when a child is considered at risk of serious harm. Taking these points together, combined with resource constraints and the pervasive belief among social workers that neglect is less harmful than other forms of maltreatment, there is a risk that neglectful families will not reach the threshold of concern required to trigger a detailed assessment.

Given the multifaceted nature of neglect – in terms of its causes, impacts and the range of interventions that may be required – effective assessment requires a coordinated multidisciplinary response. In the first instance, the literature identifies the importance of establishing multi-agency agreement around definitions and thresholds (Stone 2003) so that different agencies have a common framework for recognizing neglect. Information sharing is important (Jowitt 2003) and good assessment will draw on the skills mix provided by the different professionals within the multidisciplinary group (Stevenson 1998). Neglect may manifest in a variety of ways and have a range of effects. Different professionals will 'pick up on' different aspects and build up their own, but inevitably partial, picture of the child and family's circumstances. In this context Horwath (2005) highlights the tendency for social work assessments of neglect to focus on current behaviour and circumstances rather than taking a longitudinal perspective – a worrying situation given that it is the ongoing and cumulative nature of neglect that is most damaging to children. Effective multidisciplinary work provides an opportunity for different perspectives to be brought together and for a more complete view to emerge. Individual elements that are not unduly concerning in themselves, when brought together and considered in the family's historical context, may add up to a much more worrying picture (Munro 1999).

Finally, when considering the relationship between assessment and effective intervention, Thoburn *et al.* (2000a) stress that, without accurate assessment, families may be offered inadequate or inappropriate support and will inevitably then need to be re-referred (the 'revolving door' syndrome). Also, once plans have been developed they need to include clear objectives, time scales and ways of determining whether the required change has taken place.

Working with Parents

'It is very hard to effect change in the behaviour of seriously neglectful caretakers' (Stevenson 1998, p.106). This pessimism is not unwarranted and paradoxically can be a helpful curb where a welfare culture driven by financial imperatives and the desire for short-term outcomes coincides with the 'rule of optimism'. The longstanding, complex problems associated with neglect require longer-term, multidimensional and coordinated intervention (Macdonald and Winkley 1999; Thoburn *et al.* 2000a) involving a blend of concrete and therapeutic services that target the particular issues for the family in each of the framework domains.

The literature identifies a number of different approaches, which may be relevant. However, whatever the approach, the importance of an empowering and empathic relationship between the worker and parent (Daniel 1998; Iwaniec 2004; Jowitt 2003; Turney and Tanner 2001) is underlined. Given the pervasive lack of belief in self-efficacy and the sense of powerlessness found in neglectful parents, a casework relationship that fosters a sense of agency may be a necessary component of any intervention strategy. Paradoxically, while working toward parental competence and empowerment, the casework relationship may require the practitioner to tolerate and work with dependency, particularly in the early stages. Current social work thinking has tended to regard dependency as a bad thing. We would agree, where this has been an unthinking dependency that has arisen almost as a byproduct of intervention. But dependency can have therapeutic uses. So, while it needs to be approached with some caution, in cases of child neglect the concept of dependency may need to be reworked (Daniel 1998). The point here is that an experience of 'managed dependency' in the relationship with the caseworker can offer the parent an alternative model of relating, and perhaps allow him or her to reconfigure previous experiences which will, in turn, affect his or her parenting capacity.

The dysfunctional patterns of relationships and communication difficulties that are found in neglectful families require active intervention (Iwaniec 2004; Stevenson 1998). Iwaniec's 20-year study of a group of 'failure to thrive' children identifies the importance of addressing destructive cycles of parent–child interaction. If these patterns remain unresolved there are negative implications for the child's attachment status, and the likelihood of the difficulties being mirrored in the next generation is increased. At the same time Iwaniec draws attention to the intensive and 'hands on' nature of this work. The entrenched nature of the difficulties and/or lack of confidence experienced by some parents will mean that advice and talking is not enough. Practitioners may need to model the desired behaviours, visit regularly and follow up with supportive telephone calls (Iwaniec 2004). In her study, Iwaniec notes the particular effectiveness of video when working on the parent–child relationship. Parents are able to see for themselves how they are experienced by others and the impact they have upon their child. The power and immediacy of the experience of seeing themselves 'live' can be used as a tool in helping parents get in touch with their own and the child's feelings and recognizing the need for change. Practitioners can then explore with parents different ways of interacting, modelling if necessary, and use the video again to reflect on the impact of changes generated by the different approach. Practitioners may feel such work is the province of more specialist agencies, for example local child and adolescent mental health services. However, particularly in the early stage of work with families, interventions will need to be home-based as parents are unlikely to keep outside appointments.

Parents are also likely to need individual therapeutic intervention (Iwaniec 2004; Iwaniec, Herbert and Sluckin 2002; Iwaniec and Sneddon 2001; Stevenson 1998). This can be achieved by a number of routes and careful assessment is necessary to ensure that the treatment accurately reflects the particular personal need. Parents who have themselves experienced emotionally impoverished and neglected childhoods may benefit from psychodynamic or attachment-based counselling where there is the opportunity to work through earlier experiences and promote personal growth and emotional maturity. However, this is challenging work and parents may need considerable support; faltering beginnings and interruptions may have to be tolerated and worked with. In situations where parents lack insight and/or alcohol or substance abuse is involved, this type of therapy is likely to be inappropriate. However, following detoxification, therapeutic work can help parents to understand why they developed their addiction and support their efforts to avoid relapse.

The assessment may indicate that the parent's personal difficulties are located elsewhere. Parents who neglect their children may have particular difficulty with self-defeating thoughts and the management of stress induced by the difficulties they experience in looking after their children. This is a potent and damaging combination for both the parent and child. In these circumstances parents may benefit from cognitive-based intervention. This approach aims to identify the destructive thought processes, illustrate their impact on the parent's behaviour and help them find different ways of thinking and behaving. This approach will also require modelling, role play and in some situations the support of developmental counselling so that parents can acquire an understanding of child development and a realistic appreciation of their child's developmental capacities. Group work is frequently identified as a potential resource for neglectful parents to address these particular difficulties but, as with parenting programmes, there are indications that some neglecting families may struggle with a group work approach. Again, this highlights the need for careful, individual assessment.

For some families, it may also be necessary to strengthen their social support. The ecological literature suggests that when statutory agencies provide the social support that is missing for neglecting families, the most helpful interventions are thooo which mirror the everyday relationships, and networks that are taken for granted by many families. Developing a network of supportive relationships and services may require moving beyond existing local provision; for example, by linking a more experienced parent with strong local connections with a younger isolated parent, or arranging a weekly outing for a child with a befriender or buddy.

Working with Children

'Children are living the experience and can give a more accurate picture of what life is like in a family than any assessment made by a professional' (Bridge Childcare Consultancy 1995, p.172). Practitioners use considerable time and energy thinking and worrying about children but often spend little time working directly with them. There may be a number of reasons for this, but the literature suggests that this is a serious omission. Children may be in the best position to help professionals understand their situation. Practitioners, therefore, need skills in age-appropriate communication and the confidence to use them routinely as part of the assessment process (Aldgate and Seden 2006; Jones 2003).

In the longer term, while working with parents to bring about change, it is important that children are not marginalized. Positive work can be done to counter the adverse effects of neglect and promote resilience. Protective factors identified by research include achievement at school, the opportunity to develop talents and interests, and the experience of an enduring supportive relationship in which the child feels valued. Practice needs to be informed by an understanding of these protective factors and how they can be incorporated into the child's life (Daniel 1998; Gilligan 2000; Werner 2000).

The value of supplementary care also emerges in the literature. This can range from informal contact with a 'social grandparent', to the involvement of family support workers/family aides, to respite care. Such interventions aim to reduce stress, develop community contact and provide the child with opportunities for a more 'normal' experience. Stevenson (1998) cites research by Aldgate *et al.* (1996), *Respite Accommodation: A Case Study of Partnership Under The Children Act 1989*, as an example of how this provision could assist neglected children, albeit with the proviso of the need for careful negotiation so that low parental self-esteem is not further damaged. However, financial restraints mean that, with the exception of children with disabilities, this service is only available in exceptional circumstances. while it is not a service that should be used to fudge decisions about permanent removal, its value as part of a regularly reviewed package of interventions needs to be revisited.

It should also be noted that in Iwaniec's 20-year follow-up study of children who failed to thrive, those children who were removed from home after unsuccessful intervention had far better long-term outcomes than those who remained at home when there was only limited change (Iwaniec 2004).

while it is hard to offer any conclusive recommendations for action in respect of tertiary intervention, what can be highlighted is the need for professionals to work with a mindset of bringing about change rather than simply offering a static package of concrete resources and surveillance.

Conclusion

At this point, it is probably not very surprising if the first conclusion we draw is that there is a need for more work to be done, as there has to date been little dedicated empirical research of any kind into the *effectiveness* of different interventions focusing on neglect. This is partly because there have been few initiatives that specifically target neglect. While a number of initiatives exist which may help neglecting families, this has not been their guiding objective. So, evaluating them in terms of their effectiveness for these particular children and their families would mean judging them against a criterion that they never sought to address: arguably not a very fair test. The lack of robust research data may also reflect some very real methodological and other difficulties for researchers investigating neglect, for example the uncertainty around definition and thresholds noted at the beginning of this chapter.

However, while there is demonstrably a need for good quality research, the current limitations do not mean that we have no knowledge base. There is a literature providing information about aetiology, discussing family and individual characteristics associated with neglect and outlining the damaging effects of neglect. And in relation to intervention, various themes seem to emerge consistently from the available research and wider literature which we could summarize as follows.

To work effectively with child neglect there is a need for:

- thorough assessment and the formulation of a response that matches treatment to cause rather than symptom/manifestation
- early and sustained intervention within a multidisciplinary framework
- packages of care, involving both therapeutic and practical help and resources, with:
  - direct work with parents both to improve the quality of child care and family functioning and also to increase their levels of self-esteem and self-efficacy. This may include the judicious use of groups – for example, parenting programmes – although home-based interventions will also be important and may be less likely to overwhelm very vulnerable parents

○ direct work with children to ameliorate the damaging effects of persistent neglect and to promote resilience.

For many social workers, these points may seem to be merely an articulation of what they would consider to be good practice – and to some extent, they are. But they seem to be particularly pertinent for the often low-key, long-term work that is required in complex cases of neglect. And in a climate of resource constraint, performance indicators and heavy caseloads, it is important that we should not lose sight of the fundamental tenets of good practice.

CHAPTER 11

Therapeutic Interventions with Children who have Experienced Neglect and their Families in the US

Diane DePanfilis

Introduction

Since child neglect is rooted in multiple and interacting intrapersonal, interpersonal, and environmental factors, no one intervention is expected to be effective in all situations (National Research Council 1993). Early evaluation research suggested greater impacts when programs provided comprehensive services to address both the interpersonal and concrete needs of family members (Cohn and Daro 1987). However, the provision of multimodal interventions makes it difficult to tease out the differential effect of specific service components. Recent reviews of treatment effectiveness studies have emphasized the gaps in our knowledge about the interventions that are most effective for achieving specific results with children, their parents, and/or family systems (Becker *et al.* 1995; Corcoran 2000; DePanfilis 1999; Thomlison 2003; Wolfe 1994; Wolfe and Wekerle 1993).

Federal legislation in the US holds Child Protective Services (CPS) agencies accountable for achieving outcomes of safety, permanency, and child and family well-being (US Department of Health and Human Services (DHHS) 2000). A system of Child and Family Services Reviews measures state compliance with federal requirements in two areas:

1.   outcomes for children and families

2. systemic factors that directly affect the state's capacity to deliver services leading to improved outcomes.

Child welfare agencies provide services to families with indicated reports of child neglect and may also serve families perceived to be at risk of child neglect. To achieve positive outcomes, CPS must engage families to identify and then achieve family-level outcomes that reduce the risk of further maltreatment and ameliorate the effects of maltreatment that have already occurred (DePanfilis and Salus 2003). For calendar year 2003, an estimated 3,353,000 children were referred to CPS agencies for investigation or assessment due to child abuse or neglect concerns (US DHHS 2005). Of those, an estimated 906,000 children were found to be victims, and 60.9 percent of victims experienced neglect. Approximately 1.8 million children received preventive services and another 517,326 children received services following the determination that they were victims of child abuse or neglect. Extrapolating that approximately 60 percent of these children were served due to neglect risk or occurrence, it is estimated that approximately 1,419,296 children and their families received services due to neglect. Services that were provided included both in-home and foster care services.

Scope of the Chapter

The purpose of this chapter is to identify interventions that may be effective with the majority of children and families served by CPS agencies (i.e., neglected children and their families). While consuming the majority of services, there has been far less attention to studying the effects of intervention with neglect compared to physical or sexual abuse. Because neglect and physical abuse are often found together and because much of the available research has not focused exclusively on neglect, interventions were identified in this chapter if study populations included a history of neglect or some combination of neglect and physical abuse. Inclusion criteria were established to narrow the selection of promising or effective interventions. Interventions should be:

1. tested on study populations with "known" neglect or neglect and physical abuse problems

2. geared to address the effects of neglect or reduce the likelihood of the recurrence of neglect

3. evaluated with the use of a comparison or control group.

Interventions were not included if there was insufficient documentation about the nature of the intervention, if the results of the evaluation were not accessible through published reports or papers, if all of the children were living in out-of-home care, or if the intervention's effect on outcomes under study was inconclusive. Interventions were located through prior reviews of intervention effectiveness (Becker *et al.* 1995; Corcoran 2000; DePanfilis 1999; Thomlison 2003; Wolfe 1994; Wolfe and Wekerle 1993) and by searching bibliographic databases for published literature through 2004. Interventions were classified and findings synthesized according to positive outcomes in three domains: child well-being, child safety, and family well-being. Because some programs affected outcomes in multiple domains, brief descriptions of programs are included during the first reference.

Evidence of Program Effectiveness

Prior efforts to systematically review the effectiveness of specific interventions for neglect have been unsuccessful in narrowing the scope to randomly controlled trials since only a few such studies have been conducted. Very few child neglect treatment studies have focused on assessing the differential effect of treatment strategies on children's outcomes. Interventions were selected based on evidence that an intervention may have been effective in helping to reduce the negative effects of child neglect or in helping neglected children achieve other outcomes. Table 11.1 provides a snapshot of identified interventions.

Table 11.1: Effectiveness of interventions on child well-being

Intervention/treatment	References	Target population	Outcomes			
			B	DA	SPR	SC
Home-based family-focused intervention	DePanfilis and Dubowitz (2005)	C, P, F	X			
Multi-family group	Meezan and O'Keefe (1998)	F	X			
Multisystemic therapy (MST)	Brunk, Henggeler and Whelan (1987)	C, P, F	X			
Peer initiation and skills training	Davis and Fantuzzo (1989)	C		X		
Therapeutic day care and counseling	Bradley *et al.* (1986); Culp *et al.* (1987, 1991)	C, P		X	X	X

Key: B: Behavior; DA: Developmental achievement; SPR: Social peer relations; SC: Self-concept; C: Children; P: Parents; F: Family.

Child Behavior

Cognitive behavioral and skill-focused interventions have the most established evidence for significantly affecting child behavior for children of all ages. For example, Resilient Peer Training (20 play sessions for eight weeks with a resilient or pro-social peer guided by trained parent helpers) for pre-school neglected, abused and/or low-income children has demonstrated success in affecting significant pro-social behavior, reduced aggression, and increased positive social behaviors at home and school (Fantuzzo et al. 1996; Fantuzzo, Weiss and Coolahan 1998). Changes in child behavior have also been demonstrated in multiple studies of the effectiveness of the Incredible Years multilevel parenting curriculum delivered to parents or teachers of maltreated elementary school children (Webster-Stratton 1998, 2000; Webster-Stratton and Taylor 2001). The curricula involve interactive play and reinforcement skills with home-based services.

Home-based family focused interventions have also demonstrated benefits in child behavior. Family Connections, a community-based prevention program that served families with and without histories of substantiated child neglect, demonstrated reductions in internalizing and externalizing child behavior between intake, case closure, and six months after case closure for families served for both three and nine months. Children served for nine months demonstrated more significant improvements (DePanfilis and Dubowitz 2005). Similarly, Multisystemic Family Therapy (MST) which uses a range of intervention strategies based on an individualized family assessment demonstrated greater effectiveness than parent training with maltreated children treated by MST exhibiting less passive non-compliance related behavior (Brunk et al. 1987).

Developmental Achievement

A small but promising literature supports the use of therapeutic day care with pre-school neglected children. Most of the time these programs also include counseling services for parents and/or families; therefore the specific benefit of the child-focused therapeutic services separate from these other services has not yet been determined. Goals for therapeutic pre-school programs include the provision of a safe nurturing environment along with increased stimulation to promote cognitive, language and motor development.

Several controlled studies provide support for the positive benefits of therapeutic day-care services on various aspects of development. Pre-school children who received group and individual treatment services along with services for their parents through a therapeutic day-treatment program showed improvement in areas of development related to fine motor, cognitive, gross motor, social/emotional, and language skills (Culp et al. 1987). A later study by Culp and colleagues (1991) also indicated benefits in cognitive, perceptual/fine motor, and social/emotional development, along with increased self-esteem, relative to a control group. Resilient Peer Training (Fantuzzo *et al.* 1996) (described above) and the Incredible Years (Webster-Stratton 2000) programs have also demonstrated improvements in cognitive development and academic skills, respectively.

Self-concept

Child-focused individual and group treatment of pre-school children along with parent services through a therapeutic day-treatment program (previously described) were found to contribute to improving the self-concept of a group of maltreated children, relative to controls (Culp *et al.* 1991).

Social Skills

Consistent with improvements in other aspects of children's behavior, multilevel parenting curricula delivered to parents or teachers of maltreated elementary school children (Webster-Stratton 1998, 2000; Webster-Stratton and Taylor 2001) has been linked to improved social skills and peer relationships. Similarly, withdrawn maltreated children who received Resilient Peer Training demonstrated more positive, pro-social responses and initiations in comparison to controls (Fantuzzo *et al.* 1988; Fantuzzo *et al.* 1996). However, maltreated children who tended to be aggressive did not respond favourably to the same intervention (Davis and Fantuzzo 1989).

Child Safety Outcomes

Even though one of the primary purposes of working with families following an incident of child neglect is to reduce the risk of continuing maltreatment, few treatment outcome studies have used recurrence of maltreatment in the evaluation of interventions (DePanfilis and Zuravin 1998). Despite the limitations of using child maltreatment reports as measures of effectiveness, they are still one of the best indicators of the actual presence of child maltreatment due to validity problems with parental self-reports of maltreatment and reliability problems associated with observations of parenting behavior. Interventions that have used reports as the primary measure of safety have usually included other measures of parent–child interaction and/or family functioning.

Child Abuse and Neglect Reports

Cognitive behavioral strategies, or treatment that incorporates some aspects of these strategies, have been most effective at preventing future incidents of neglect compared to various comparison treatments. In particular, eco-behavioral treatment (Lutzker and Rice 1987) most recently described as Project Safe Care (Lutzker 1994) has been subjected to the most research. The original version of this program, Project 12-Ways (Lutzker and Rice 1984), delivered in-home parent training related to 12 components (e.g., stress reduction, home safety, and money management). Project Safe Care, also designed to improve parenting skills, is delivered with a fewer number of training components (Gershater-Molko, Lutzker and Wesch 2002). Studies of this intervention demonstrated significantly fewer child abuse and neglect reports for families served with eco-behavioral treatment compared to regular child protective services (Lutzker and Rice 1984); however, the differences between groups decreased over time (Lutzker and Rice 1987). A later evaluation (Gershater-Molko et al. 2002) suggested that Project Safe Care was more successful than family preservation services in suppressing future child maltreatment reports, especially when families had high rates of abuse or neglect at baseline.

Numerous clinicians and researchers have suggested that treatment may be most successful when families can be motivated to participate in services (DePanfilis 2000; Miller and Rollnick 1991; Rooney 1992, 2000). One study evaluating a home-based intervention that reached out to maltreating families, attempting to get them to self-refer to child protective services, demonstrated some promising strategies with motivational methods. Once families were engaged in services, the project used an individualized approach to assessment and treatment delivered by a social worker and a parent aide and provided in the home. Confirmed child maltreatment reports were compared between project families and those served with standard protective services with only 1 percent of project clients experiencing a confirmed child maltreatment report within 18 months compared to 14 percent of families served by regular CPS (DePanfilis 1982).

Similar efforts to engage hard-to-reach families following confirmed reports of child abuse or neglect were demonstrated by a center-based program (Laughlin and Weiss 1981). Intervention began with a goal of establishing a relationship with families who were isolated, alone, and fragmented from most community support systems. Some initial home visits were kept to less than ten minutes in an effort to prevent resistance to services. Once family members were in agreement with treatment, transportation was provided to bring families to a family center where they received family and group therapy and were offered opportunities to participate in a craft group. These strategies demonstrated promising results as the program's client engagement rate was 85 percent compared to 25 percent engagement rate of comparison CPS families, and recurrences of abuse or neglect were only 10.8 percent compared to 26.9 percent for comparison CPS families.

In a later experiment (Owen and Fercello 1999) families investigated by CPS but not offered continuing services from CPS were randomly assigned to receive extensive outreach and family support services provided by private agencies or "business as usual" which often involved informal referrals made to community-based agencies. Families in the special project received extensive outreach and were given choices of service providers and vouchers to purchase services such as child care, emergency services, housing services, and legal advocacy services. Families in both the treatment and control condition were identified with very low rates of abuse or neglect within a 12-month follow-up. Non-significant differences between the groups, however, did suggest that the intensive service approach warrants further investigation. For example, 5.4 percent of the treatment group had an open CPS case prior to being assigned to receive family support services, compared to 3.8 percent with an open case within two years of receiving family support services.

While in general, risk assessment and structured decision-making assessment approaches have not demonstrated substantial effects (Doueck *et al.* 1993; Wald and Wolverton 1990), this is partly due to difficulties that agencies have experienced in fully implementing these systems (DePanfilis 1996a). One of the goals of assessing risk is practitioners targeting interventions toward specific risk factors. One study (Luttrell, Hull and Wagner 1995), which compared the impact of Structured Decision Making (SDM) model approaches implemented in selected jurisdictions to comparison CPS families served by counties without structured decision making, indicated lower rates of future substantiated child maltreatment reports among SDM counties. Whereas SDM counties serving 920 families had a 5.2 percent recurrence rate within 12 months, comparison counties serving 866 families had a higher 11.4 percent rate. Isolating the comparison to only open cases, the rate in SDM counties was 6.2 percent compared to 13.2 percent in regular CPS counties. The challenges with implementing these risk assessment or structured decision-making systems for the purposes for which they are intended may account for some of the no-effect results reported in other studies.

A limitation of most of these reported studies is that most often, the specialized treatments were delivered under controled and favorable conditions while not much is known about the comparison group treatment which may or may not have been delivered in any systematic fashion.

Family Outcomes

Interventions that target family outcomes often do so by working to reduce risk factors and enhance protective factors related to child maltreatment (Thomlison 1997). The goal of interventions is to strengthen family functioning so that families will be better able to meet the basic needs of their children. These interventions may be multimodal, focused on family functioning, or more narrowly focused on helping families build social support (see Table 11.2).

Table 11.2. Effectiveness of interventions on family well-being

Intervention/ Treatment	References	Target population	Outcomes							
			EC	AC	PP	SM	CAP	PCI	SS	FC
Anger control group	Barth, Blythe and Schinke (1983)	P		X						
Behavioral stress	Schinke et al. (1986)	P			X	X		X		
Eco-behavioral treatment	Lutzker and Rice (1984, 1987)	P, F	X		X			X		
Home-based family focused intervention	DePanfilis and Dubowitz (2005)	C, P, F	X		X	X			X	
Multi-family group	Meezan and O'Keefe (1998)	F						X		
Multisystemic therapy	Brunk et al. (1987)	C, P, F	X		X	X		X		
Parent training	Brunk et al. (1987); Webster-Stratton (1998); Webster-Stratton and Taylor (2001); Wolfe et al. (1988)	C, P			X	X			X	X
Social support network intervention	Gaudin et al. (1990–1); Lutzker et al. (1998)	P, F			X			X		

Key: EC: Environmental conditions; AC: Anger control; PP: Parenting practices; SM: Stress management; CAP: Child abuse potential; PCI: Parent–child interaction; SS: Social support; FC: Family conflict, cohesion, communication; C: Children; P: Parents; F: Family.

Parenting Practices

Cognitive behavioral interventions delivered in a range of settings have demonstrated effectiveness with enhancing parenting behaviors. Parents who have participated in the Incredible Years (Webster-Stratton 1998, 2000; Webster-Stratton and

Taylor 2001) parenting curriculum have increased their use of positive parenting affect; reduced their use of criticism and negative comments; decreased their use of spanking and harsh discipline; and increased monitoring of their children. Other parent–child training delivered in group settings or in the home has also resulted in improvement of child management skills among parents at risk of child abuse and neglect (Wolfe *et al.* 1988).

Home-based MST demonstrated greater effectiveness than parent training with increasing parental responsiveness to children's needs (Brunk *et al.* 1987). Even though a recent review of MST suggests the need to re-examine the results of some of the early studies of this model (Littell *et al.* 2004), the intervention suggests promise as it is designed for therapists to select from a range of evidence-based strategies tailored to the specific needs of each family. The Family Connections program, a home-based program that uses similar assessments and tailored intervention, also demonstrated improvements in parenting attitudes and satisfaction and physical and psychological care of children. The evaluation also noted reductions in maternal depression and parenting stress for families served for both three and nine months (DePanfilis and Dubowitz 2005).

Eco-behavioral treatment (Lutzker, Wesch and Rice 1984) has also demonstrated efficacy at helping parents improve home safety, health maintenance and nutrition, and positive parent–child relationships. A benefit of this intervention is the use of assessment instruments to both guide the selection of intervention strategies and to measure change over time. For example, the Home Accident Prevention Inventory (HAPI-R) and the Checklist of Living Environments (CLEAN) focus on conditions in the household that could lead to neglect of children's basic needs (Lutzker and Bigelow 2002).

Finally, social support network intervention has also demonstrated effectiveness compared to usual treatment in improving parenting adequacy (Gaudin *et al.* 1990–1).

Family Functioning and Communication

Enhancing family functioning and parent–child communication is one of the goals of several interventions already described. MST (Brunk *et al.* 1987) and parent training (Webster-Stratton and Taylor 2001) have demonstrated improvements in communication and/or parent–child interaction among maltreating families. Anger control training (Barth *et al.* 1983), stress management groups (Schinke *et al.* 1986), and MST (Brunk *et al.* 1987) have also been effective at increasing anger control or decreasing stress which when achieved are hypothesized to improve communication within the family.

Social Support

There is evidence that social support interventions are particularly relevant for families with neglect problems (DePanfilis 1996b). Both individual and group interventions have been tested. Since neglectful caregivers sometimes lack basic verbal/social interaction skills (Gaudin 1993a; Gaudin et al. 1990–1), they may resist group interventions. This was confirmed in the evaluation of Family Connections (DePanfilis and Dubowitz 2005) as, even when extra effort to encourage participation was made (e.g. child care, transportation, refreshments), the program was unsuccessful in encouraging parents to consistently participate in group services. While families who received the home-based component of Family Connections demonstrated positive improvements in perceived social support, poor compliance with group services made it difficult to assess the differential effect of those services. In contrast, Gaudin et al. (1990–1) demonstrated that social support network interventions compared to regular treatment were more effective in strengthening informal networks. Intervention provided between 10 and 23 months included individual and group formats and multiple social support interventions such as family support networking, mutual aid groups, social skills training, and assistance from volunteers and neighbors.

Effectiveness for All Children and Young People

The interventions reviewed here have generally been targeted at convenience samples and very little attention has been paid to the appropriateness of specific interventions for different cultural groups. However, there was some evidence that language barriers and cultural match between parent-group leaders and participants might have been related to the degree of engagement in services (Webster-Stratton and Taylor 2001). The significant effects that motivation to change has on intervention outcomes need to be more often considered as programs evaluate their effectiveness (DePanfilis 2000).

The nature of this review has focused on families with neglect problems and the interventions with some empirical support have targeted both urban and rural populations, early childhood and later childhood, single types of maltreatment problems or multiple problems; in some cases populations have been included with known maltreatment problems as well as those at risk of maltreatment.

The settings for treatment have included home-based interventions (e.g. Brunk et al. 1987; Gaudin et al. 1990–1) as well as center-based interventions (e.g. Fantuzzo et al. 1996). Most interventions were targeted to reduce the risk of future maltreatment; however, some interventions were also focused on ameliorating the effects of child neglect by specifically addressing behavior or developmental achievement of children.

Conclusion

Given that neglected children and their families make up more than half of the families that come to the attention of CPS agencies (US Department of Health and Human Services 2005), it is essential that the field focuses more attention on what works best for responding to this form of child maltreatment. This chapter has identified a small set of interventions that have demonstrated positive impacts on child well-being, child safety, and family well-being outcomes. Across all target populations, cognitive behavioral interventions in particular seem to have the most evidence for positively influencing outcomes for children and families identified with neglect problems. However, the importance of the human ecology and the need for individualized assessment was also established (Gershater-Molko, Lutzker and Sherman 2003).

Multi-family group and home-based intervention targeting families, peer initiation and skills training targeting children, and therapeutic day care with counseling targeting parents and children have demonstrated some effectiveness at helping children achieve outcomes related to:

- behavior
- developmental achievement
- social or peer relations
- self-concept.

Eco-behavioral treatment, outreach and motivational strategies, structured decision-making approaches, and home-based interventions have increased child safety measured by the reduction of future child abuse and neglect reports.

Anger control and behavioral stress management groups, cognitive behavioral treatment, eco-behavioral treatment, family therapy, home-based intervention, MST, parent training, and social support network intervention have demonstrated some effectiveness at helping families achieve outcomes related to:

- environmental conditions
- anger control
- parenting attitudes, practices, and satisfaction
- stress management
- social support
- family communication.

Despite the progress made, particularly in the past ten years, with evaluating the effectiveness of interventions, we are far from understanding what works with whom and under what conditions interventions are more or less effective in helping children and families achieve safety and well-being. In particular, we know very little about how buot to interveni which families have substance abuse and child neglect problems (Donohue 2004) and these families make up a large percentage of the families served by public child welfare agencies in the United States (US Department of Health and Human Services 1999).

What are most needed are studies that replicate interventions that have indicated some effectiveness with some maltreating groups. In particular, further research should be dedicated to studying the effectiveness of cognitive behavioral treatment, MST, home-based intervention, parent training, and social network interventions. And, because there may be greater likelihood for achieving outcomes if families can be reached earlier, we need more studies on prevention strategies designed to reduce the risk of child neglect. The strongest evidence base that supports positive outcomes for children and families emerges from home-based services to prevent abuse and neglect, while promoting maternal and child health and using social support and instructional interventions at all system levels (Thomlison 2003).

CHAPTER 12

Therapeutic Interventions with Children who have Experienced Sexual and Physical Abuse in the UK

Arnon Bentovim

Introduction

Henry Kempe's seminal paper on the Battered Child Syndrome (Kempe *et al.* 1962) initiated international recognition of child abuse as a widespread phenomenon. He described developing waves of recognition in each community: initially serious physical abuse, then neglect of care, emotional abuse, and finally sexual abuse. The effects of abuse have now been described, and approaches to management and treatment pioneered. The notion of 'child protection' has influenced professional practice, and is reflected in UK policy documents such as *Working Together* (Department of Health, Home Office and Department for Education and Employment 1999) which guides professional practice. The Children Act (1989) balances the rights of children to be protected from abuse, with the needs of parents to be supported to maintain family life in contexts of stress.

A review of the management of child protection processes (Department of Health 1996b) indicated that they were reasonably effective. However, providing long-term support and treatment for children and effective support for families was less successful. Sharland *et al.*'s study (1996) of all sexually abused children identified in a UK county demonstrated how few children received specific therapeutic work. Farmer and Pollock's study (1998) of sexually abused children in foster care demonstrated the long-term effects of abuse, including health problems, relationship difficulties, and drifting into prostitution. Limited therapeutic work was offered to these young people. In the UK, protection is offered and alternative arrangements are made to ensure the children do not continue to be abused. However, subsequent interventions remain limited, inconsistent and dependent on local arrangements and facilities. A coherent national approach to intervention is lacking.

Using the definitions of child abuse and neglect in the United Kingdom, Creighton (2002) indicates that between 2.5 and 2.7 children per 1000 are placed on the Child Protection Register each year. However, there are many more children in the community not reported to professionals. Perhaps as many as five or six times the number reported remain unprotected.

Males and females who are exposed to multiple abusive events, including physical abuse and sexual abuse and exposure to violence perpetrated against their mother, are more likely to be involved in interpersonal violence in adult life with women as victims, men as perpetrators. Our cross-sectional and longitudinal research on the origin of sexually abusive behaviour (Salter *et al.* 2003; Skuse *et al.* 1998) demonstrated the deleterious impact of being exposed to a climate of family violence which includes multiple forms of abuse and exposure to abuse against mothers.

The Interventions and their Theoretical Basis

To describe the interventions to ameliorate the ill effects of emotional, physical or sexual abuse requires a model to understand the way that abusive experiences impact on the development of children and young people.

General View of the Process of Abusive Action

Characteristic of all forms of abuse is the negative interlocking aspects of the relationship between parent and child within a social context (Bentovim 1995). A negatively associated, emotionally abusive attitude towards the child is a prerequisite to any form of abuse.

Potential protectors are neutralized, or unavailable. The perpetrator feels overwhelmed by impulses to actions of a physically, sexually or emotionally abusive nature, felt to be beyond his or her control. The cause is attributed to the victim, who, in line with individual, family and cultural expectations, is construed as responsible for the victimizer's feelings and intentions. Actions on the victim's part to avoid abuse are misinterpreted as further cause for violent action or justification for further sexual or emotional abuse.

Silence and dissociation spread to victim and victimizer, and to those who could potentially protect, leading to delayed recognition or the maintenance of secrecy and silence throughout childhood. Both victim and victimizer minimize experiences, dismiss events and blame themselves or others. Because of the repeated nature of violent actions, traumatic stressful effects come to organize the reality and the perceptions of those participating, including potential protectors and professionals. There is a pressure not to see, not to hear or not to speak.

There is a significant intergenerational repetition of abusive patterns. However, there are both risk and protective factors, which mean that not all children and parents are caught up in abusive patterns (Gelles 1987; Gelles and Cornell 1997).

Risk and Protective Factors in Abuse

There are factors which increase the likelihood of abuse occurring, and factors which buffer possible abusive action in high-risk situations. Using the *Framework for the Assessment of Children in Need and their Families* (Department of Health, Department for Education and Employment and Home Office 2000) these can be summarized as below.

THE CHILD'S DIMENSION

The age, sex and developmental stage of the child have an influence. Infants are most vulnerable to physical abuse such as shaking injuries (Creighton 2002); girls are more likely than boys to be abused sexually (Bentovim *et al.* 1988); boys more likely to be victims of harsh punishment (Patterson 1982). Prematurity (Leventhal, Garber and Brady 1989), physical and psychological disability (Knutson 1995), and twin births (Lynch and Roberts 1982) are all risk factors.

Children are more resilient if they have higher levels of intelligence, health and attractiveness, or if they have a supportive parent, sibling or extended family member or adequate support in the community with well-developed universal and targeted services (Browne *et al.* 2002).

THE PARENTING DIMENSION

Risk is associated with youthful parents (Stier *et al.* 1993); poorer levels of education; learning difficulties; living in unstable, transient, conflictual relationships; and a history of poor care and abuse (Belsky and Stratton 2002), associated mental health and personality disorders, substance abuse, alcoholism and associated domestic violence (Cleaver *et al.* 1999). Extended family, community resources and parenting support can reduce risk. A stable partnership and therapeutic work focused on primary parental conditions can also buffer risk effects (Browne *et al.* 2002).

ENVIRONMENTAL CONTEXT

Living in poverty, overcrowding, poor, substandard housing and environment, unemployment, large family size, isolation in the community from wider family, poor community resources and poor primary care are all risk factors (Bergner, Delgado and Graybill 1994; Finkelhor 1980). However, these can be mitigated by targeted interventions at the community level and an integrated services approach which takes a broad view of need.

General Effects on Development

Three major areas of children and young people's development are affected by various forms of abuse (Bentovim 1998) and are the focus for therapeutic work:

1. The regulation of emotional states (Cicchetti and Toth 1995).

2. The development of attachment (Carlson *et al.* 1989).

3. The developments of an adequate sense of self and relationships (Culp *et al.* 1987).

These three areas reinforce each other, and come to underpin the relationship models of the individual child and young person both within the family and within the social context. Overwhelming stress is a characteristic feature of all forms of abuse. Children or young people living in a world invaded by fear and anxieties have their perception of themselves and others coloured and directed by such experiences. More extreme responses will be shown with higher levels of stress.

Responses in each significant area develop as externalizing or internalizing in direction, indicative of the coping mechanisms used; internalizing responses being more avoidant in character, externalizing responses being more active. Disorganized volatile internalizing and externalizing responses will be noted with more severe and multiple forms of abuse (Skuse *et al.* 1998).

An integrated model of intervention is required to counter negative effects. Stages of therapeutic work include the phases of disclosure, treatment in a context of safety, and rehabilitation or move to a new family. Specific interventions are associated with each stage (Bentovim 2002b).

Evidence for Program Effectiveness

The evidence of effectiveness of therapeutic interventions with children who have experienced abuse is well developed in some areas, particularly sexual abuse; physical abuse less so; there is very little evidence in the field of emotional abuse. There are many accounts of treatment with individual cases; however, there are far fewer accounts of research where there is random assignment between two sorts of treatment, or to treatment and no treatment control. The studies which show most evidence of effectiveness are those where the control of treatment in the community 'as usual' is followed, compared to those which take a focused treatment approach. The former group of approaches shows more differences and helps us understand the active ingredients of treatment. Those treatments which compare one active approach to another often show little in the way of difference, perhaps because different active approaches are effective over and above the general factors inherent in all forms of therapeutic work. It is still not possible to indicate with a degree of certainty what the most effective approach is to working with children who have experienced abuse. However, a number of approaches which impact on the areas outlined earlier are helpful.

Useful reviews of studies covering all forms of abuse (Stevenson 1999) or specifically sexual abuse (Finkelhor and Berliner 1995; Ramchandani and Jones 2003) are now available.

Studies of Children who have been Sexually Abused

Tables 12.1 and 12.2 describe the studies carried out in the United Kingdom which focus on the treatment for sexual abuse. In the United Kingdom two randomized designed treatment trials for sexual abuse have been carried out (Monck *et al.* 1994; Trowell *et al.* 2002). Monck *et al.*'s study described a series of children who had been sexually abused, and tested whether the addition of group treatment for family members improved the outcome of a family network approach which strengthened the relationship between a caring parent and an abused child, and modified internalizing and externalizing behavioural patterns. Children felt that their needs were better understood if they had the benefit of group work, and felt more positive about themselves. Their mothers benefited considerably from sharing with others. There was significant improvement on the measures used to evaluate the mental health of the children and young people, but no additional improvement from the addition of group work.

Trowell and colleagues (Trowell *et al.* 2002) randomly assigned 100 girls aged 6 to 14 who had been sexually abused showing symptoms of Post Traumatic Stress Disorder (PTSD). They were allocated to two groups, one receiving up to 30 sessions of individual psychodynamically orientated therapy, modified to ensure traumatic effects were addressed, the other 20 sessions of group therapy. No major differences were found between these two treatment approaches, although individual treatment was more successful at modifying post-traumatic symptoms. The sexually abused girls had higher rates of psychiatric disorder than the general clinic population.

Six UK studies assessed the outcomes of treatment of sexual abuse, looking at the levels of disturbance both before and at the end of a period of treatment. This approach cannot exclude the effect of time, although other studies have demonstrated 'time does not heal'. Four studies (Bentovim *et al.* 1988; Furniss *et al.* 1988; Lindon and Nourse 1994; Nelki and Waters 1988) tested the effectiveness of group treatment. Two studies (Monck and New 1996; Sharland *et al.* 1998) studied the effectiveness of interventions provided by voluntary agencies in the community.

Table 12.1: UK studies of sexually abused children – studies involving random assignment to different treatments

Study	Numbers of children studied	Nature of study	Outcome
Monck *et al.* (1994)	99 children assessed aged 4–16 47 randomly assigned	Standardized family network treatment against effect of adding group therapy	Severity of symptoms related to lack of support rather than severity of abuse
			No differences on objective measures
			Clinical assessments indicate children more positive about selves, felt better understood
			Group work assisted mother
Trowell *et al.* (2002)	100 girls aged 6–14 with symptoms of PTSD	Group 1 had 20 sessions of therapy. Group 2 had 30 individual sessions of therapy	Sexually abused girls have higher rates of psychiatric disorders
	Randomly assigned	General comparison with non-sexually abused girls	PTSD symptoms improve with individual treatment – no other significant differences

Table 12.2: UK studies of sexually abused children – studies involving the follow-up of sexually abused children who had received treatment

Study	Numbers of children studied	Nature of study	Outcome
Bentovim et al. (1988)	180 sexually abused children aged 4–16 compared with 226 sibs group and family treatment	Follow-up assessment of emotional and sexualized behaviour; 6–30 sessions by age	Improvements noted but persisting sexualized symptoms and re-abuse
Furniss, Bingley Miller and Van Elburg (1988)	10 children (female) aged 12–15	Structured group treatment; 12 sessions	Significant improvement in self-esteem and assertiveness
Nelki and Waters (1988)	6 females aged 4–8	Educational/dynamic group; eight sessions	No significant changes
Lindon and Nourse (1994)	6 females aged 13–17	Structured group; 16 sessions	Improvements in self-esteem and relationships
Monck and New (1996)	120 victims and perpetrators of sexual abuse treated by voluntary agencies	Followed up for 12 months	High level of symptoms, depression and sexualized behaviour in victims and history of abuse in victims Follow-up – small numbers, not conclusive
Sharland et al. (1998)	Study of all referrals in a county (220) (aged 5 years +) In-depth interview follow up of 34 children	Assessment of initial symptoms Assessment of improvements 12 months	High levels of persisting depression, behavioural disturbance and PTSD Inconsistent evidence of improvement 2/3 parents felt children had more needs at the end of 12 months
Edwards (in press)	44 males Follow-up 3–6 years of age 12–16 young people offending sexually Residential treatment	Comparison young people completed versus young people dropped out or excluded Assessment of re-offending Psychological functioning re-assessed	Those completing treatment no sexual re-offending Reduction of beliefs and behaviour associated with offending Young people dropping out showed serious conduct disorder

Three of the group treatments showed significant improvement in the area of self-esteem, assertiveness, depression and sexualized behaviour. The more extensive studies of sexually abused children did not demonstrate the general effectiveness of the approaches used compared to more focused approaches. The studies did demonstrate how highly symptomatic children could be at the end of a phase of intervention with the unfolding of traumatic experience triggering extensive depressive symptomatology. Some behavioural sequelae appeared more resistant to treatment efforts, particularly conduct problems including interpersonal sexual behaviour difficulties. These appeared the most resistant to change, and require specific therapeutic approaches.

Anxiety related symptoms, depression, feelings of self-blame associated with traumatic effects did improve in most studies and appeared particularly sensitive to therapeutic work.

Treatment of Young People Who are Sexually Offending

Given the resistance of sexual behaviour to therapeutic work, the risk of developing sexually abusive behaviour amongst young males exposed to physical abuse, and the risk of child violence against a parent (Salter et al. 2003; Skuse et al. 1998), it is important to consider treatment of children and young people who are behaving in a sexually abusive manner against children, peers or adults.

Cognitive behavioural approaches are widely used in young people who are showing extensive sexually abusing externalizing behaviour (Vizard, Monck and Misch 1995) although there are a few randomized trials of effectiveness. Multisystemic Therapy (MST), which includes element of cognitive behaviour and structural family therapy, is now being used extensively in the UK to work with young people who are offending.

Young people who have a higher level of dangerousness and have often been exposed to more extensive abuse and neglect may need assistance in therapeutic community settings providing an extensive programme of treatment focused on all aspects of development. Edwards (in press) demonstrated no recidivism for those who completed a residential therapeutic programme in a three-year follow-up (see Table 12.2). Those young people who did not complete the treatment programme, or whose behaviour was challenging and unmanageable showed much higher levels of recidivism. An effective battery of assessment tools (Beckett 2002) now has been developed and is being used in the UK and Europe to demonstrate the effectiveness of treatment.

Negative Effects of Therapeutic Work in the Sexual Abuse Field

A number of children who complete therapeutic work do show increasing symptoms, become more anxious and show a greater range of post-traumatic anxiety, or aggressive or sexual behavioural difficulties. Such problems may emerge as dissociative mechanisms, which have been effective in reducing psychological distress, are reduced or eliminated. Therapeutic work must provide coping strategies to ensure that traumatized children and young people who are 're-experiencing' the trauma are supported for a long enough period, even if their symptoms temporarily worsen. Negative effects may also emerge as a result of 'cumulative rejection'; for instance, parental denial that abuse occurred and rejection of the child.

Parental support is the strongest family predictor of good outcome for the child who has been sexually abused. Involving a non-abusing parent in the therapy with the children and focusing on the parents' own problems not only improves their parenting skills but also helps parents support their children more effectively. Group work provides parents with considerable support (Monck and New 1996).

Social work support in the community is an important element so that a treatment network effect is established linking the therapeutic team, the family and the care system. Social workers were crucial in supporting children between therapeutic sessions in the Tavistock Clinic study (Trowell *et al.* 2002). Lack of support for treatment services is often cited as the reason children do not receive therapeutic services.

A variety of approaches can reduce the intensity of symptoms: education, modelling body and safety skills, gradual exposure, encouraging children to confront abuse-related thoughts and situations *within a safe environment* – all with the aim of diminishing avoidance and anxiety. Parents need to be involved and taught about PTSD, reducing the same fears and avoidance which they may experience themselves.

Jones and Ramchandani (1999) and Ramchandani and Jones (2003) conclude that all children who have been sexually abused, whether or not symptomatic, require basic education concerning sexuality, sexual roles and the nature of abuse and mal-treatment which is adapted to their age and developmental stage. Symptomatic treatment requiring a specialized treatment focus will need to be integrated with the general care and family system.

Therapeutic Work with Physical Abuse

There are two basic approaches to studies of treatment of physical abuse: studies which focus directly on ameliorating the impact of abuse on the children themselves, and those which focus on modifying punitive parenting, improving parenting skills and providing safe care.

One recent randomized controlled trial study in the UK focused on parenting (see Table 12.3). Nicol and his colleagues (1988) compared therapeutic work focused on the family as a whole to therapeutic work with the child individually. A focus on the family resulted in improved interaction and reduction of abusive action did result giving an indication of the effectiveness of working with the family as a whole to improve the child's state. It is essential for parents to acknowledge their responsibility to abuse, and a second UK study (Healey *et al.* 1991) (see Table 12.3) demonstrated that when families were admitted to a therapeutic hospital, taking responsibility for abusive action was a key factor in achieving successful outcome for therapeutic work to change family relationship patterns.

Table 12.3: UK studies of physically abused children

Study	Numbers of children studied	Nature of study	Outcome
Nicol *et al.* (1988)	30 physically abused children randomly assigned to assess impact of treatment on family relationships	15 children assigned to play therapy 15 children and families assigned to focused case work	Family interaction improved significantly as a result of focused case work
Healey *et al.* (1991)	27 physically abused children and families treated in residential psychodynamic hospital	Assessment of success of intervention	Level of improvement was greater when family members acknowledged responsibility for abusive action

There is limited evidence from which one can conclude which form of treatment is most effective, but it is essential that children are adequately protected and that parents undertake training or therapeutic work to improve their interpersonal affective skills and find alternatives to inappropriate punitive modes of controlling children. Anger management is likely to be an important factor in helping parents to understand the nature and origin of coercive behaviour, teaching positive communication skills and developing problem solving without violence.

Which Families, under Which Circumstances, Might Benefit from the Intervention?

It is helpful to consider the issue of the prognosis for effective intervention and which families under which circumstances might benefit from intervention. Assessing the degree of protectiveness and the capacity of parents to change is essential if they are to support children and young people who are suffering the consequences of physical, emotional or sexual abuse. These are key elements of contributing to good therapeutic outcome. It is important to evaluate the prognostic factors (Bentovim, Elton and Tranter 1987) we will now discuss, using the *Framework for Assessment of Children in Need and their Families* (Department of Health *et al.* 2000).

Prognostic Factors

CHILD DIMENSION

- The level of abuse perpetrated and the extensiveness of traumatic damage caused to the child's physical and emotional health.
- The level of care the child will require to recover.
- The specific therapeutic work required.
- The level of parental skill required meeting the child's needs within their time frame.

PARENTAL DIMENSION

- The degree of responsibility for the state of the child taken by the parents, from initial denial through contemplation to acknowledgement (Bentovim 2003).
- The level of parental psychopathology and the motivation the parent has to undertake the necessary therapeutic work to reverse the personal attributes which have contributed to creating an abusive context.
- Issues such as parental drug addiction, mental health problems, and parental domestic violence, amenability to treatment and likelihood of modification within the child's time frame.
- The general attitude of the parents to the professional networks – whether there is a prospect of a reasonable collaborative approach, or whether the parents take a negative stance of denial and grievance.
- The availability of a supportive family network.

ENVIRONMENTAL DIMENSION

- The availability of an integrated community approach to ensure a broad-based approach to include environmental factors as well as the child and parents (Bentovim *et al.* 1987)
- The availability of settings for therapeutic work, whether on an out-patient, day or residential basis.

Requirements for a Hopeful Prognosis

CHILDREN'S DIMENSION

- The child's state: the child's emotional state, attachments and sense of self are modifiable within the family context, given the child's time frame (i.e. how long it is appropriate to delay, given the child's need for security).

PARENTING DIMENSION

- Parents take adequate responsibility for abusive action where appropriate.

- There is a protective capacity within the family or family network, for example a non-abusive parent who recognizes that his or her partner has abused the child and who is prepared to protect the child over and above his or her own relationship with the partner, and/or extended family who acknowledge abuse and will act protectively.

- The possibility of a capacity for change in parents who have been abusive, a willingness to work reasonably cooperatively with child-care professionals, a willingness to accept the need for change even if it is with the motivation of maintaining children within the family context.

- There needs to be the potential for the development of a reasonable attachment and relationship between the parents and children, and a reasonable degree of flexibility in family functioning.

ENVIRONMENTAL DIMENSION

- Appropriate therapeutic settings need to be available, whether on an out-patient basis, in a day-care setting or as residential resources, depending on the severity of abuse and the nature of family strengths and difficulties.

- Environmental factors are modifiable within the children's and families' time frames.

Prognostic Issues

The prognosis is much less hopeful when none of these criteria are fulfilled; for example, there is a severe physical or mental state in the child, rejection of the child or a failure of parents to take responsibility for the state of the child, the needs of parents take primacy over the needs of the children or the parents take a combative oppositional stance to professionals. Severe psychopathology may become evident in a parent once a more in-depth understanding of the family has been achieved.

Progress is doubtful where professionals are not yet clear from the original work with the family whether the situation is hopeful or hopeless. In such a situation the professional may be uncertain about the nature of the child's state and as to whether the parents are taking adequate responsibility, whether parental pathology is changeable, whether parents will be willing to work with care authorities and therapeutic agencies, or whether resources will be available to meet the extensiveness of the problem. Further therapeutic work with parents or children needs to be suggested to help professionals clarify the needs of the child and the capacity of the parents to provide adequate care.

The prognostic model of hopefulness, doubt and hopelessness was tested using an attributional approach (Sylvester *et al.* 1995). A similar set of factors associated with outcome was noted by Jones (1998); for example, poor prognosis was associated with parents who had a variety of serious mental health problems, delusional beliefs involving children, serious learning disorders or prior serious injury; it was also associated with parents who were substance abusers or who frequently abused their child. Court-ordered therapy was more successful for those cases of greater concern.

Dale and his colleagues (1986 and 2002) and The Marlborough Family Unit (Asen *et al.* 1989) found that a period of intensive assessment of parents' capacity to change was helpful in making a decision when serious abuse occurred. Asen *et al.* (1989) noted 30 per cent of severe physical abuse situations could not be recommended for longer-term treatment.

Bentovim *et al.* (1988), Monck *et al.* (1994) and Sharland *et al.* (1998) described the proportion of children who could be rehabilitated to families or required longer-term care. Jones and Newbold (2001) have used residential settings to assess the capacity of parents to work with therapeutic agencies in general situations and in Munchausen by Proxy.

Effectiveness for All Children and Young People

There are general factors which are present in all forms of therapeutic work which are essential to effective work with children being physically, sexually and emotionally abused. The general factors are all concerned with meeting the attachment needs through reliability, availability and consistency of the therapists' response. Children need to live in a context of protection, a context where they are supported and emotionally and physically protected. If the child becomes more open about their experiences, rather than dissociated, there is a risk of provocation to an abusive parent, and more serious abuse may result.

Parallel work needs to be provided for members of their family. In the sexual abuse field therapeutic work with the child is more effective if a parent is involved. Effective interventions with physical abuse require intervention focused on the parent and the family as well to ameliorate the abusive effect on the child. If a child is placed in an alternative family, intensive supportive work is required for those caring for the abused child so that they can manage provocative, challenging behaviour that the child may exhibit and avoid re-creating abusive situations.

The child needs to be helped to share his or her experiences of abuse, physical, sexual or emotional, in a context of safety, either in a group or with an individual. Exposure to such experiences is a way of processing traumatic experiences so they no longer influence current thinking and feeling. Children need help to re-learn ways of relating safely, and to be helped to understand the nature of abusive parenting.

Not all children who have been sexually, emotionally or physically abused are symptomatic. Considering the different developmental needs of children at different ages, and the multiplicity of factors associated with abusive action, one approach to treatment may not cover the needs of all children and family members. Children of different age or particular groupings of symptoms often require a particular focus of therapeutic work, or decision about when and how to involve in therapeutic work, particularly where younger children are concerned.

There are few studies which have focused on children with disability or children from particular ethnic backgrounds. There is a concern that children may drop out from treatment for any form of abuse when coming from impoverished socio-economic backgrounds. A failure to address environmental risk factors can lead to the failure of what would be effective forms of intervention.

Conclusion

A significant number of children and young people experience sexual and physical abuse during childhood. Only a limited number of these young people come to the attention of authorities, and an even smaller number will have had any effective therapeutic intervention. As a result some may seek help in adult life or when they have difficulties in parenting their own children. This may be one way to avoid per-petuating the intergenerational transmission of family violence.

The evidence of effectiveness of intervention is patchy, inconsistent, better developed in some areas such as sexual abuse, less developed for physical abuse and least for emotional abuse. However, there are consistent messages which have emerged from the best-conducted research.

We can conclude that all forms of abuse have a potentially traumatic impact on children and young people. The effect varies depending on the particular form of abuse and whether there are multiple forms of abuse which result in the child/young person living in a climate of violence and abuse. Therapeutic work is effective provided that the child is protected, that there is a specific focus on the traumatic effect of the abuse and that help is offered. The help should attempt to repair the attachments of the child, modify their negative effects on the child's emotional life and provide a better perspective for him or her in the future. Work in parallel with family members enhances the impact of the therapeutic work. Assessments should ensure that work is offered to family members who can benefit. Alternative care needs to be found for those children whose parents cannot protect them to ensure that therapeutic work is successful.

Whenever abuse is recognized, there needs to be an extensive assessment of the needs of the child based on an understanding of the impact of abusive experiences on their development. The child's safety must be assured. Therapeutic services need to be provided by both statutory and voluntary agencies, providing focused, effective, evidence-based approaches to therapeutic work.

Although we have knowledge about general factors and specific recommendations about therapeutic work approaches which are effective, there is a good deal that remains to be learnt about effective therapeutic work for children. We have good information about what is effective in the field of sexual abuse, and reasonable understanding of effective interventions with physical abuse. If this knowledge were applied to all children who have been abused it would significantly reduce the negative effect of being abused on the life of a child and young person. There is evidence that the general rate of sexual abuse and physical abuse is dropping. It is a goal for the future to ensure that those children who are being abused are less affected and do not carry the effects through their lives.

CHAPTER 13

Therapeutic Interventions with Children who have Experienced Sexual and Physical Abuse in the US

Jacqueline Corcoran

Introduction

Federal concern in the US with child abuse and neglect was mainly enacted through the Child Abuse Prevention and Treatment Act, which was originally passed in 1974 and reauthorized through the Keeping Children and Families Safe Act of 2003 (National Clearinghouse on Child Abuse and Neglect Information 2004). Prevalence rates of both sexual abuse and physical abuse, the focus of this chapter, have been found to be high. Sexual abuse in childhood occurs to 13 percent of males and to between 30 and 40 percent of females (Bolen and Scannapieco 1999). A recent national survey has paralleled these findings, indicating that 14.2 percent of men surveyed and 32.3 percent of women had been sexually abused as children (Briere and Elliott 2003). A host of serious effects resulting from sexual abuse include Post Traumatic Stress Disorder (PTSD), behavior problems, sexual acting out, low self-esteem, depression, and anxiety (Kendall-Tackett, Williams and Finkelhor 1993; Paolucci, Genuis and Violato 2001). The impact of sexual abuse has also been found to extend into adulthood (Jumper 1995; Nelson *et al.* 2002; Neumann *et al.* 1996).

Physical abuse, too, occurs to a significant proportion of the population and has both short- and long-term consequences. According to statistics compiled by the United States Department of Health and Human Services (2003), out of 903,000 children victimized in 2001, 18.6 percent were physically abused. Briere and Elliott's national survey (2003) of adults found childhood rates of physical victimization among 22 percent of men and 20 percent of women. Short-term consequences of physical abuse include aggression, impaired social competence, reduced empathy, poor impulse control, academic and behavioral problems, and internalizing problems, such as depression and low self-esteem (Azar, Barnes and Twentyman 1988; Conaway and Hansen 1989; Graziano and Mills 1992; Malinosky-Rummell and Hansen 1993; Mueller and Silverman 1989; Toth, Manly and Cicchetti 1992). Long-term consequences are also found for physical abuse suffered in childhood (Briere and Elliott 2003). For adults, violence against others – their partners, children, and people outside the home – is high (Malinosky-Rummell and Hansen 1993). Internalizing problems have also been reported in women physically abused as children (Malinosky-Rummell and Hansen 1993). Because the prevalence of physical and sexual abuse is high and the consequences of maltreatment potentially harmful, effective treatment is critical. This chapter will summarize the treatment outcome research in these areas. (For a more complete discussion of studies, see Corcoran 2000a, 2004; James and Mennen 2001; Saunders, Berliner, and Hanson 2003].

The Interventions and their Theoretical Bases

Parental involvement in treatment for child abuse is critical. For sexual abuse, maternal support[1] assumes a central role in the child's immediate and long-term adjustment (Conte and Schuerman 1987; Edwards and Alexander 1992; Everson *et al.* 1989; Gold 1986; Nash *et al.* 1993; Paredes, Leifer and Kilbane 2001; Peters 1988; Tufts New England Medical Center 1984; Wind and Silvern 1994). Intervention can help caregivers recognize and react sensitively to their child's symptoms, and respond appropriately to questions and concerns about the abuse. Caregivers generally experience a number of distressing emotions of their own upon learning of their child's sexual abuse (see Corcoran 1998 for a review). Treatment may be necessary for mothers to help them negotiate and cope with the stressors associated with disclosure.

In cases of physical abuse, parents are usually the perpetrators (Petit and Curtis 1997). Such parents lack more effective and appropriate discipline methods than physical punishment. They may attribute negative intentions to their children's behavior (Azar *et al.* 1988). They may have higher expectations for their children's behavior than the child's developmental level would warrant. Moreover, they may lack problem-solving skills, so when overwhelmed by stress – often from poverty and social isolation – they may not see or be able to implement options, leading to frustration and possible loss of control (Azar *et al.* 1988).

For both sexual and physical abuse, cognitive-behavioral therapy has dominated as the treatment with the most empirical validation.

Cognitive behavioral treatment for sexual abuse involves the provision of psycho-education on sexual abuse, attribution retraining, building coping skills, and parent training (Cohen and Mannarino 1993; Deblinger and Heflin 1996). Deblinger and Heflin's (1996) work focuses on PTSD; therefore, their cognitive-behavioral package emphasizes exposure techniques. Interventions have typically been brief, ranging from 8 to 12 sessions. Cognitive-behavioral treatment has been offered in both individual (e.g., Cohen and Mannarino 1996) and group (e.g., Deblinger et al. 2001) modalities, and for both pre-school (e.g., Cohen and Mannarino 1996; Deblinger et al. 2001) and school-age (e.g., Cohen and Mannarino 1998; Deblinger et al. 1996) children and their parents.

For physical abuse, cognitive-behavioral treatment models have been represented among the strongest studies. Parent training – in which parents are taught how to behaviorally specify goals for change, to track target behaviors, to positively reinforce pro-social conduct, and to punish or ignore their children's aversive behaviors (Kolko 1996; Schinke et al. 1986; Wolfe et al. 1988) – have also been expanded to include coping skills (Kolko 1996; Wolfe et al. 1988), self-control skills (Kolko 1996; Schinke et al. 1986), communication skills training (Schinke et al. 1986), and psycho-education (Kolko 1996). Schinke et al. (1986) focused on parents of children with developmental disabilities who are considered to be at high risk for abuse because of the challenges they pose for parenting (Kolko 1993). Wolfe et al. (1988)'s intervention with the parents of pre-school children also included a component on helping parents promote their children's language competencies and social interaction skills given the impact of child abuse on these domains. Kolko (1996) further offered a parallel cognitive-behavioral intervention to children that involved social skills training and building social support. (See Kolko and Swenson 2002 for treatment manual.) Interventions have been brief – 6 to 19 sessions – and offered in individual and group modalities. Parent training and other cognitive-behavioral interventions have also been shown effective with the treatment of conduct problems (Saunders et al. 2003). Families in which physical abuse and child behavior problems occur share similar characteristics (Gelardo and Sanford 1987; Wolfe et al. 1985), and conduct problems in children are one potential consequence of physical maltreatment (Malinosky-Rummell and Hansen 1993). Therefore, knowledge of the treatment of children with conduct problems may be transferable to children who have been physically abused. At the same time, it is recognized that certain factors associated with lack of treatment response, including high levels of negativity toward the child, maternal problems (e.g., substance-use problems, depression), negative life events, social isolation, and low socio-economic status, are often present in parents who have physically abused their children (Fonagy and Kurtz 2002). Parent training must be accordingly adapted to the needs of these parents (see Corcoran 2004 for an example).

A major thrust in the child maltreatment field has been the use of family preservation programs, which are characterized by three central characteristics (Nelson and Landsman 1992; Nelson, Landsman and Deutelbaum 1990; Stroul and Goldman 1990). The first is an emphasis on having children remain in their own homes with caretakers to whom they are attached. A second emphasis is on the whole family rather than on just individual members. Third is the provision of and linkage with comprehensive services in the community so that families' concrete needs are met with treatment.

Some interventions have been developed specifically for children who have been physically abused. These include peer training, a school-based intervention that uses pro-social peers to help children who are withdrawn develop social skills (Fantuzzo *et al.* 1996). For very young children, between birth and five years of age, a therapeutic child development program has been developed to provide an intensive milieu of services, such as nutrition, health care, developmental therapies, case management, provided by responsive adults (Moore, Armsden and Gogerty 1998).

Group treatment has been a typical modality of intervention for sexual abuse given its potential to reduce stigma and for its cost effectiveness. The theoretical orientations of group therapy have varied widely and include most commonly eclectic treatment models comprising various combinations of the following components: "psychoeducation regarding sexual abuse and sexual abuse prevention, exploration of the abuse experience, exploration of feelings, art therapy, play therapy, role plays, problem solving, puppet work, writing exercises, and behavior management" (Reeker, Ensing and Elliott 1997, p.674).

Promising Interventions

Because maternal support often becomes entrenched, intervention that takes place during the crisis of disclosure may be particularly needed. Jinich and Litrownik (1999) proposed an alternative intervention with the non-offending caregivers of school-aged sexually abused children. Their intervention occurred when the child and parent were being interviewed about the sexual abuse and consisted of a 20-minute videotape based on social learning theory, teaching parents to convey appropriate support to their children.

A promising intervention for child physical abuse involves Multisystemic Therapy (MST) (Henggeler *et al.* 2002). MST, delivered intensively in the home, goes beyond family therapy in that it emphasizes individual cognitive variables, as well as broader system influences beyond the family that play a role in maintaining problems (Brunk *et al.* 1987). MST also shares elements with family preservation in that services are delivered in the home; however, treatment is manualized and requires supervision to ensure fidelity to the model. Although only one study has been conducted on the use of multisystemic treatment with child abuse (Brunk et al. 1987), an extensive body of knowledge supports its use for the treatment of juvenile offending behavior (Henggeler et al. 2002). However, MST is more structured and relies on manualized treatment. In addition, a recent systematic review of MST has questioned some of the positive findings previous reviews have found (Littell, Popa and Forsythe 2005).

Evidence on Program Effectiveness

Sexual Abuse

CHILD OUTCOMES

- For pre-school-aged participants, parent and child cognitive-behavioral therapy improved sexualized acting out (Cohen and Mannarino 1996; Deblinger et al. 2001; Stauffer and Deblinger 1996). These findings are particularly important, since onset of sexual abuse at a young age is the strongest predictor of inappropriate sexual behavior (Wolfe 1998).

- Deblinger et al. (1996) found that parental involvement in cognitive-behavioral treatment impacts child externalizing problems and child depression, which were not affected by child treatment alone.

- Cognitive-behavioral treatment with the child is needed to impact child PTSD symptoms (Deblinger et al. 1996; King et al. 2000).

- In the 20-minute videotape intervention following disclosure children reported significantly less distress regarding parental unsupportive behaviors on the Child Perception Questionnaire than those whose parents watched the control video (Jinich and Litrownik 1999).

- In the meta-analysis of 15 group treatments for sexually abused children, the mean effect size for studies was 0.79, which indicates a strong effect of treatment[2] (Reeker et al. 1997). The average impact on internalizing symptoms was 0.84 according to parent reports and 0.46 according to child reports. The average impact on externalizing symptoms was 0.74 according to parent reports and sexualized behavior was 0.83. The average child's report of their self-esteem was 0.71. It appears that group sexual abuse treatment might produce impacts on various domains of child functioning.

PARENT OUTCOMES

Studies mainly focus on child outcomes, but a few studies report outcomes for parents as well. In their videotape intervention, while parents did not perceive themselves as being more supportive, behavioral observations that day showed they acted more supportively with their children than did the control group parents after viewing the videotape (Jinich and Litrownik 1999). Deblinger *et al.* (2001) also reported on parent outcomes and found that mothers had greater reductions in their intrusive thoughts and their negative reactions regarding the sexual abuse when they were part of the cognitive-behavioral treatment in comparison to supportive non-directive therapy. These post-test advantages were maintained at three-month follow-up. Because of the importance of maternal support, these findings show promise for children's future adjustment.

Physical Abuse

CHILD OUTCOMES

- Pre-test, post-test studies of family preservation programs report prevention of child out-of-home placements rates, ranging from 55 (Bribitzer and Verdieck 1988) to nearly 99 percent (Bath *et al.* 1992) at case termination and from 65 (Fraser, Pecora and Haapala 1991) to 83 percent (Bath *et al.* 1992; Yuan and Struckman-Johnson 1991) at follow-up.

- In quasi-experimental studies, family preservation programs have higher prevention of child placement rates (Feldman 1991; Schwartz, AuClaire and Harris 1991; Walton 1996; Wood, Barton and Schroeder 1988) than control groups. However, for the Feldman (1991) study, significant differences between groups dissipated after nine months. In Schuerman, Rzepnicki and Littell (1994), the family preservation group was actually more likely to experience a placement than the casework-as-usual comparison group.

- Children who are socially withdrawn as a result of physical abuse develop improved social skills as a result of being matched with pro-social peers (Fantuzzo *et al.* 1996). However, children who are aggressive rather than socially withdrawn may not benefit from the peer treatment program (Fantuzzo *et al.* 1988).

PARENT OUTCOMES

- Parent training for parents with pre-school children was more effective than simply providing such information to families through handouts (Wolfe *et al.* 1988).

- Cognitive-behavioral therapy showed advantages over eclectic family therapy on aggression and use of physical discipline (Kolko 1996).

- MST was more effective than parent training in improving parent–child relationships and in helping physically abusing parents gain better control over their children's behavior (Brunk et al. 1987). Parent training delivered in groups was more effective in relieving parents' social isolation.

- A six-week cognitive-behavioral package consisting of cognitive restructuring, relaxation techniques, and problem-solving training was more effective than its individual components or regular agency services (Whiteman et al. 1987).

For family preservation,[3] some studies have focused on the outcome of repeat parent maltreatment. Schuerman, Rzepnicki and Littell (1994) failed to find cost savings or reduced child maltreatment referrals when comparing family preservation to services-as-usual. Lutzker and Rice (1987) also looked at maltreatment referrals and found recidivism rates for the in-home services group of 21.3 percent compared to a rate of 28.5 percent for the Child Protective Services group. Although these differences were statistically significant, they tended to decrease over time.

A recent evaluation of family preservation and family support services comprising 1601 clients found that those services targeting families' basic concrete needs, or those providing parents with a support person, were found to be more effective than other service models, including parent education and family preservation (Chaffin et al. 2001). Office-based services, in comparison to home-based services, although involved with higher-risk families, were associated with lower recidivism rates.

Effectiveness for All Children and Young People

For predictors of outcome for parent-involved cognitive-behavioral treatment of sexual abuse, social support to the non-offending parents has a role in predicting positive response of children to treatment (Cohen and Mannarino 2000). Therefore, group treatment may be preferable for mothers, as they may gain social support from other members who understand their situation. Alternatively, treatment might need to center on how mothers can build naturally occurring support networks.

Although gender and ethnicity have not tended to impact treatment outcome in the few studies examining these variables, there may be some need to focus on referring, recruiting, and engaging children and families from minority groups (Cohen et al. 2001). Celano et al. (1996) worked with a primarily African-American sample using a culturally relevant version of Finkelhor and Brown's (1985) traumagenic model. The traumagenic model compared to treatment-as-usual did not, however, always provide differential gains in areas presumed to be affected by sexual abuse. Epidemiological studies have shown no difference between the prevalence rates of child sexual abuse in African-American and Caucasian populations. However, Hispanic females appear to be at greater risk for sexual abuse (see Wolfe 1998) and possibly also for higher symptoms levels as a result (Cohen *et al.* 2001). Unfortunately, Hispanic populations remain under-represented in the available literature.

At the same time, it could be that cultural factors may be less important than other cross-cutting issues, such as:

> the type of treatment provided, the child's abuse-related cognitions, parental emotional distress related to the child's abuse, and parental support for the child predict treatment response more strongly than race, gender, socioeconomic status, or even abuse-related factors such as the number of abusive episodes, the type of sexual abuse, or the identity of the perpetrator. (Cohen *et al.* 2001, p.153)

For family preservation, predictors of placement have been examined in various studies. Tentatively, it appears that parental cooperation with and utilization of services (Nelson 1991; Schwartz *et al.* 1991) and severity of problems at intake (Berry 1991, 1992, 1995; Nelson *et al.* 1988) might influence placement rates. Presenting problems that posed difficulty in the avoidance of prevention of placement involved parents' substance abuse (Nelson 1991), parental mental health problems (Nelson *et al.* 1988), and neglect (Bath *et al.* 1992; Berry 1991, 1992; Yuan and Struckman-Johnson 1991).

Evidence of Program Effectiveness

The sexual abuse literature has been marked by an over-reliance on pre-test/post-test designs. For example, the meta-analysis on group treatment was comprised mainly of pre-test/post-test designs (Reeker *et al.* 1997). Treatments have also typically not been driven by theory. For example, most of the studies in the meta-analysis comprised "integrated treatment," which involved an eclectic mix of techniques.

The parent- and child-involved cognitive-behavioral intervention research (Cohen and Mannarino 1996, 1997, 1998, 2000; Deblinger *et al.* 1996, 2001; Deblinger, Steer and Lippmann 1999) is exemplary in its methodology with randomization to alternate conditions, use of follow-up assessments, adequate sample size, and examination of outcome predictors. Abuse-specific cognitive-behavioral treatment was the only intervention out of a comprehensive review of both published and unpublished studies conducted by the National Crime Victims Research and Treatment Center (Saunders *et al.* 2003) to receive the highest rating of a "well-supported, efficacious treatment."

However, concerns remain about low sample sizes, particularly given the use of multiple tests to examine treatment effects. Another shortcoming of this literature is that parent and child treatment are often confounded. Differential parent-involved and child-only treatment conditions were examined in only two of the studies reviewed (Deblinger *et al.* 1996, King *et al.* 2000). As a result, it is difficult to know the type and level of parental involvement necessary to treat sexual abuse. Also since treatments have been delivered as a cognitive-behavioral package, it is not understood how well each component, such as psycho-education, acts on its own.

In the physical abuse arena, overall, what is most striking is the dearth of empirically and theoretically sound evaluation studies on treatment despite the fact that child abuse is regarded as a central social issue. For instance, in the National Crime Victims Research and Treatment Center review (Saunders *et al.* 2003), none of the physical abuse interventions earned a rating of a "well-supported, efficacious treatment," or the next best category, a "supported and probably efficacious treatment." Instead, many of them received the rating of "supported and acceptable," including family preservation.

It also should be noted that a majority of the studies have been conducted in the 1980s with very few in recent years. The child maltreatment outcome research has been marked by an over-reliance on single subject (e.g., Dawson *et al.* 1986; Fantuzzo *et al.* 1986); post-test only (e.g., Ferleger *et al.* 1988; Rivara 1985); and pre-test/post-test (e.g., Acton and During 1992; Golub *et al.* 1987; McLaren 1988) designs (e.g., Kaufman and Rudy 1991; Mash and Wolfe 1991), although some improvements have been made with both quasi-experimental (e.g., Brunk *et al.* 1987; Elmer 1986; Gaudin *et al.* 1990–1; Irueste-Montes and Montes 1988; Kolko 1996; Nicol *et al.* 1988; Schinke *et al.* 1986; Szykula and Fleischman 1985; Wolfe *et al.* 1988) and experimental (e.g., Whiteman *et al.* 1987) designs. However, even when comparison groups have been employed, they have not always been equivalent, thus rendering reported positive results suspect.

A further flaw in evaluative research has been the lack of follow-up in studies (e.g., Acton and During 1992; Golub *et al.* 1987; Irueste-Montes and Montes 1988; McLaren 1988; Meezan and O'Keefe 1998; Whiteman *et al.* 1987). An additional problem is that studies often combine families referred for abuse as well as for neglect and fail to report outcome(s) separately for these maltreatment groups. Another problem with the treatment outcome research is the tendency of child maltreatment programs to involve combinations of services (Azar 1986). Composite services appear to be a response to the multi-problem nature of child maltreatment families. However, the essential components of interventions need to be tested and applied in a more systematic way. Further, a decision-making process must be formulated so that clients with particular characteristics and circumstances undergo the appropriate type and course of treatment. At the same time, a recent five-year study tracking 434 families in the Child Protective Services system found that out of all service variables, only participation in services predicted lack of maltreatment recidivism (DePanfilis and Zuravin 2002). More specifically, if families attended services, they were 33 percent less likely to have another incident of maltreatment. Therefore, perhaps simple engagement in intervention is sufficient to have impact. Overall, compliance in physical abuse cases is low. For example, in examining parents of young children mandated for services, Rivara (1985) found that only one-third complied with recommendations to treatment, despite Child Protective Services Supervision.

Specific to family preservation programs and the use of placement as the main outcome criterion, there is a lack of conceptual clarity for how out-of-home placement is defined. Some authors fail to define placement at all, while others offer varying definitions based on the duration of placement, the formality of placement in terms of licensing and payment from the state, and the involvement of relatives (Schuerman, Rzepnicki and Littell 1991; Wells and Biegel 1992).

Further, the reliability of placement data is influenced by the source of information. If information is only gleaned from case records or just practitioners, the number of placements is likely to be underestimated (Pecora *et al.* 1992). Parental self-reports of children running away or informal neighbor or relative placements might need to supplement official records in order to obtain accurate results. In addition, agency data may not capture psychiatric hospitalizations, in-patient substance-abuse treatment, and juvenile justice institutional stays. Hence, multiple indicators are needed in order to obtain precise information on placement (Fraser 1990).

Another critique of placement outcome is the assumption that remaining in the home is always desirable for children. In some cases, substitute care or intensive treatment outside the home represents an optimal outcome (Bath and Haapala 1994; Rossi 1992; Wells 1995). Prevention of unnecessary placements while keeping children safe within their own homes embodies a more appropriate goal for family preservation programs (Tracey 1991). A further goal is that functioning of families and living conditions are improved.

Implications for Children's Services Policy, Practice, and Service Delivery

Certain implications for service delivery can be advanced from the present review. First, the importance of maternal support for the recovery from sexual abuse is critical; therefore, parents need to be involved in interventions that increase their supportive attitudes and behaviors. The studies in this review point to the benefits of parents, as well as their children, receiving abuse-specific, cognitive-behavioral treatment. Of note is that the non-directive treatments, which translated into play therapy for pre-schoolers (e.g., Cohen and Mannarino 1996), were not as effective, and this has also been reflected in a study of play therapy with children who had been maltreated (Reams and Friedrich 1994). These findings are important because non-directive play therapy is a commonly used intervention for maltreated children (James and Mennen 2001).

Another service delivery implication involves the fact that sexual abuse victims do not typically display a similar symptom constellation as a result of maltreatment. Therefore, individual symptoms need to be targeted with the appropriate parent and child components. The research to date indicates that child PTSD symptoms can be treated through child-only treatment, but parent-involved treatment may offer certain benefits when addressing other symptoms, such as child behavioral problems and depression.

For child physical abuse, certain service delivery recommendations can also be presented. Considering the evidence from the treatment outcome research with child physical abuse, as well as child conduct problems, parent training and coping skills training show promise for the treatment of parents who have physically abused their children. Child Protective Services agencies are urged to train their workers, as well as having contracted therapists, to provide these skills-based services.

Conclusion

Because the prevalence of physical and sexual abuse is high and the consequences of maltreatment potentially harmful, effective treatment is critical. However, research on effective treatments has been limited. Based on the limited evidence, cognitive-behavioral interventions seem to show promise for both sexual and physical abuse, although treatment is obviously manifested in different ways depending on the type of abuse suffered.

A policy implication from the available research is the need for educating child welfare administrative and treatment personnel on evidence-based approaches, such as cognitive-behavioral treatment, over types of interventions that are popular in practice, such as non-directive play therapy and supportive counseling. In addition, more methodologically strong research is needed in the area of maltreatment; such research should involve randomization to control/comparison groups, sufficient sample sizes, standardized measures, and follow-up periods. Multiple outcomes might be necessary, including recidivism, family functioning, and child adjustment. A policy implication is the partnering of universities and child welfare agencies so that the necessary evaluation of services will be conducted.

Notes

1.   The term "maternal support" is used because most non-offending parents involved in intervention are mothers; however, it is recognized that not all non-offending parents are mothers.

2.   Using Cohen's (1988) categorizations of small (0.00–0.29), medium (0.30–0.50), and high (0.6–1.00). It is also recognized that pre–post designs, which comprised the majority of studies in the meta-analysis, have a tendency to inflate effect sizes.

3.   Family preservation programs typically involve families in which neglect and/or physical abuse has occurred; therefore, outcomes for family preservation programs are not specific to physical abuse alone.

PART FOUR

Evidence on Foster Care, Adoption and Transitions for Children and Young People

CHAPTER 14

Foster Family Care in the UK

Kate Wilson

Introduction

This chapter is about foster care in the UK and what we know about its effectiveness as a service for looked-after children and young people.[1] Most children and young people separated from their families and who are looked after by local authorities live in foster families. It dominates provision for younger children but offers a service for children of all ages. A foster placement can be for a single weekend to relieve a crisis; it may provide a permanent home for a child who cannot live with her or his birth family. Its importance as a service provision for children, the majority of whom will have experienced difficult and potentially damaging situations in their own families, therefore cannot be underestimated.

In caring for these often troubled children, foster care consumes considerable resources (an estimated 22% of social service department expenditure on all children). The priorities implicit in this financial distribution partly reflect the awesome responsibility of looking after other people's children. It remains, however, a relatively cheap service and considerable challenges are placed on departments to provide sufficient resources to enable the service to address the needs of a diverse range of children and young people.

The Legal and Policy Context

The increasing recognition of the challenges posed by foster care has led during the 1990s to an unprecedented focus on children's services in general and fostering in particular. The legal basis of fostering is laid down in the Children Act 1989 in England and Wales, which provides the general legal framework for children and young people at home, in care and for those leaving care. Subsequent key policy and legislative developments include the Quality Protects and Choice Protects initiatives;

the Performance Assessment Framework, setting out indicators of performance for local authorities (e.g., stability of placements, educational qualifications of care leavers); the Government Objectives for Social Services and the UK national standards for foster care; the Children (Leaving Care) Act 2000 and the Adoption and Children Act 2002. Standards are buttressed by guidance, such as the *Guidance on the Education of Young People in Care* (DfEE/DH 2000), and the looked after children assessment and action records developed with funding from the Department of Health. The latter are intended to measure whether the day-to-day needs (on five dimensions: health, education, identity, family relationships and social presentation) of these children are being met. (See Ward 1995.)

Current Figures on Foster Placements

Government statistical information on looked after children and young people is published annually. Table 14.1 sets out figures for the different placements in the UK, although, since figures are collated differently in the four countries, comparable figures are not always easy to reproduce (see for example footnotes to Table 14.1).

The extent of foster children's contact with the system varies greatly. A majority of those who enter the system spend little time there – just under 25,000 children entered the care system in the year ending March 2002, and a similar number left, with under a third having spent less than eight weeks and a bare majority (54%) less than a year (Department of Health 2002c). After a year in the care system, the chance of leaving drops rapidly and those who stay on make up the great majority of those looked after at any one time. In the year ending March 2002 57 per cent of children in England had been looked after for over six months; of these children, 12 per cent had been looked after for five years or more (Department of Health 2002c). Thus, of the roughly 30,000 children in non-relative foster care on 31 March 2002, around a third have been in foster care for over four years.[3]

Who are the Children?

Fostering offers an important service for young people and children of all ages: over five out of every ten foster children in England and Wales are aged ten or over.[4] Of children in placement in the UK at 31 March 2004, just under half were female. In England, disability was the principal reason for just 3 per cent of all children starting to be looked after in 2001/02, which contrasts sharply with those children starting to be looked after under a series of short-term placements, where disability was the recorded need code for roughly seven in ten of the cases (Department for Education and Skills 2002f). UK research suggests that approximately 18 per cent of looked after children are 'black', a figure which conceals wide variations between authorities and across regions and countries.[5]

Table 14 1· Children looked after in the UK – by country and by placement as of 1 March, 2004[2]

	England		Wales		Scotland		N. Ireland		UK	
	No.	%	No.	%	No.	%	No.	%	No	%
Foster placements[a]	41,600	68	3075	71	3461	30	1529	61	49,665	62
Children's homes (LA, vol, or private)	7000	11	277	6	787	7	325	13	8369	10
Placed with parents, friends, family[b]	5900	10	–	–	6408	55	561	22	12,840	16
Placed for adoption/adopted from care	3300	5	237	5	147	1	–	–	3684	5
Other[c] e.g. living independently, schools, secure accommodation, homes and hostels	3400	5	963	22	873	7	95	4	5331	7
Totals	61,200		4315		11,675		2510		79,889	

a   The figures for those in foster placements in England and Wales include those fostered with relatives and friends. The same figures for Northern Ireland include those fostered with relatives (although friends are not mentioned in the Northern Ireland classification). In Scotland the figure does not include 'kinship' foster placements.

b   In England, Wales and Northern Ireland these figures refer to children placed on a care order with adults who have parental responsibility for them. In Scotland they include children on supervision orders.

c   Includes Youth Treatment Centres, Young Offenders Institutions and various other categories in England and secure and other residential accommodation in Scotland.

Key: LA: Local authority; vol: Voluntary; –: data for a particular category were not available (e.g. children placed for adoption are not included in the returns for Northern Ireland); percentages may not equal 100 due to rounding.

Sources: Department for Education and Skills (2005a), Welsh Assembly (2005), Scottish Executive (2004), NIDHSSPS (2004).

Compared to the early 1980s, children now are much less likely to enter 'care' because of truancy, delinquency or parental difficulty, and the care system has become increasingly concentrated on maltreated children. Child abuse and neglect are the main reasons for approximately half of the admissions to the looked after system while, on the latest figures, around 45 per cent of children in the UK excepting Northern Ireland, for which figures are not given) are said to be suffering from a childhood mental disorder (Department for Education and Skills 2005a; National Statistics 2005). Challenges to the foster care service, too, have been increased by changes in residential care, where numbers have dropped dramatically over the same period, with many of those who would previously been served by residential care now being fostered.

Classifying Foster Care

There is a wide variety of different kinds of foster care. Broadly it can be classified by length of stay (e.g., short term), purpose (e.g., bridging) or provider (relatives, local authority or non-governmental including private, independent, and voluntary organizations). These different classifications overlap. For example, different providers may care for all age groups for a variety of purposes. Some short-stay care may simply be to provide a break for a mother admitted to hospital, while other short-stay care may be 'remand' placements. One general classification adapted from Rowe and her colleagues (1989) which still appears useable distinguishes between the following types:

- short term – emergency, assessment, roof over head, remand
- shared care – regular short breaks
- medium term (task-centred) – professional/treatment, bridging placements preparation for independence
- long term – upbringing.

The outcomes to be expected from these different kinds of foster care are clearly different. It is not to be expected that short-term care will *of itself* radically change a child's education, mental health or behaviour. The plan for a child admitted to short-term foster care may for example be to ensure that s/he can return home. The degree to which this is speedily and satisfactorily achieved is likely to depend heavily on the system of which it is part, for example on the effectiveness of subsequent care in the community. For these reasons most research and official writing on the outcomes of foster care has focused on those that might be expected of medium- or longer-term fostering (e.g., Quality Protects, Choice Protects, Looking After Children: Good Parenting – Good Outcomes).

Evidence of Program Effectiveness

'Effectiveness' in this context we understand to mean the achievement of outcomes which one policy discussion paper defines as the 'desired end result and intended improvement after a specific period…the impact, effect or consequence of a particular service intervention' (Utting, Rose and Pugh 2001, p.16). Thus, effectiveness in foster care means the achievement of changes which are desired and would not have occurred but for this experience.

Three issues confront any attempt to evaluate the effectiveness of foster care as a service intervention. First, there is the limited quality of the research evidence available. Although there are many kinds of writing about foster care, research on its effectiveness is much less frequent than might be expected, not rich in comparisons and less fertile in different kinds of outcome measures than might be expected. Second, the different purposes and different kinds of foster care argue for the need for different outcome criteria. As argued above, most of those who enter foster care do so for a brief period – less than six months. It is not intended that this experience would radically improve their educational performance, nor in most cases has it any chance of doing so. By contrast there is an expectation that children who spend a relatively long time in foster care should benefit educationally. So in dealing with effectiveness we need to consider the kinds and purposes of foster care, and hence the different criteria by which outcomes should be judged.

Third, it is difficult to demonstrate that what happens to foster children is the result of being in foster care, and not merely something which happens as a consequence of predetermined characteristics of those entering the looked after system. Their often severe difficulties make it unsurprising that the rate of emotional, social, behavioural and educational problems found in children in foster care is substantially higher than in the general population. This is not to say that foster care should not do more to improve these problems; merely that they pre-exist for most children and should not necessarily be seen as evidence of a lack of effectiveness or the failures of the state to be a good parent.

The Evidence for Effectiveness

Against this background, we shall consider first process issues such as the evidence of satisfaction on the part of the main consumers: in this case most importantly the children. Next we consider the evidence of outcomes of different kinds of foster care: short-term, specialist and longer-term foster care; we then consider what may be termed 'final outcomes' (i.e., what happens to those leaving care) and finally, whether any other factors (e.g., matching carers/children, or type of placement) identified by researchers, policymakers and practitioners seem to improve outcomes.

Children's Views of Foster Care

Official guidance and reports have emphasized the importance of setting up adequate systems for listening to looked after children as a means of ensuring children's safety from abuse as well as their more general well-being (Department of Health 1998c; Welsh Office 1996). This emphasis has been matched by a growth in research studies which directly involve children (see Hill 1997 for a review of different approaches, and McAuley 1998 for an overview of some of the ethical and methodological issues in children's participation in a longitudinal study of long-term foster placements). Studies of children's views are frequently hampered by problems of poor response rates, and the underrepresentation of young children and those who spend brief periods in the care system. The key issues are sensitive, and children may not always feel free to express negative views. Different samples, for example those selected because they are teenagers (Triseliotis *et al.* 1995b), reveal different perceptions.

Despite these difficulties there are some reasons for confidence in the findings. These are: the development of child-centred and ethically sound approaches to consulting children (McAuley 1996; Schofield *et al.* 2000), the consistency with which the same themes are repeated in the literature, the degree to which they seem to be natural in the context, and – in the rare occasions when this comparison has been possible – the lack of evidence that respondents differ from non-respondents in ways likely to bias the results (Sinclair *et al.* 2001).

The foster children in the studies do not all want the same things. Nevertheless they have some common needs, which include:

- a normal family life
- progress and encouragement to succeed
- respect for their individuality, values and culture
- basic information about their rights and entitlements
- adequate educational provision
- choice over the amount and type of contact with their own families
- (for most) a say in their careers in care.

(Sinclair *et al.* 2001; Sinclair, Wilson and Gibbs 2005b).

Being looked after was considered to have made a difference to educational progress by most of a sample interviewed about their educational experiences and, for the majority, this was seen as a positive change, with a large number of children describing positive educational experiences. Overall (and with some exceptions, e.g., Morris and Wheatley 1994) foster children are positive about their care (Baldry and Kemmis

1998; Colton 1988; Lynes and Goddard 1997; McAuley 2005, in press; Shaw 1998; Sinclair *et al.* 2001; Sinclair 2003).

Short-stay Foster Care

Short-stay foster care caters for a greater number of children than any other. Social workers see short-stay foster care as serving a variety of ends – to cool an inflamed situation, to support parents at the end of their tether, to manage a temporary crisis or to allow a risky situation to be managed and assessed (Packman and Hall 1998). In general the evidence suggests that foster care is valuable and valued. The great majority (over 85%) of placements in one study were perceived as meeting their aims in most respects or fully (Rowe *et al.* 1989).

The issue is how far short-term care can be used as part of a package in which social work and other community care is an essential element. Non-comparative British studies suggest that purposeful, committed social work can make successful rehabilitation more likely (Aldgate and Bradley 1999; Bullock *et al.* 1993a). Such practice promotes good contact between the birth parents, foster carers and the child, supports the foster carers and the birth parents and coordinates a multi-agency approach to treatment of the child and parents before, during and after placement. Key aspects of this work by social workers probably include the identification of specific problems which the family needs to resolve, and helping the birth family to keep a place at home for the child. However, there is little evidence on the longer-term outcomes of these children – except for the sizeable number who have multiple attempts at rehabilitation, and then become part of the looked after system on a more or less permanent basis.

Specialized or Professional Foster Care

Some fostering schemes are singled out as providing specialized, therapeutic or professional foster care. These schemes are likely to be marked out by a number of features, not all of which are necessarily present in each scheme. The features include:

- an above-average level of support, training and remuneration for carers
- a theoretical model of the aims and approach needed in foster care
- a difficult (often teenage) clientele
- a restricted length of stay.

Early British research showed that more difficult young people could be successfully included in these schemes than had hitherto been thought possible. This lesson has recently been reinforced by a Scottish study which explicitly targeted a population who would otherwise be in secure accommodation (Walker, Hill and Triseliotis 2002).

However, British studies that use relatively rigorous methods of evaluation suggest that schemes which train carers in listening or managing behaviour and do no more than this do not have a significant impact on outcomes (Macdonald and Kakarelakis 2004; Minnis and Devine 2001; Pithouse, Lowe and Hill Tout 2002) There is as yet no British evidence which replicates the findings of American schemes which offer both foster carers and birth parents training in the same parenting skills, ensuring consistency of approach and outcome, and which have been positively evaluated (Chamberlain 1988; Chamberlain and Reid 1991).

Medium- to Long-term Foster Care

Foster care provides upbringing for some (although not all) of the children involved with it. Longer-term placements should be judged by a variety of criteria, including the effects on development, educational performance, achievement of close relationships and a sense of identity. Such criteria also need to take account of whether on the evidence the alternatives to foster care offer better outcomes. Evidence relevant to all these includes the following:

- *Health and disability.* Foster children tend to be somewhat less physically healthy than their peers: although acute illness is treated, chronic conditions are often overlooked and dental care neglected and they may be without anyone who has an overview of their health needs and history (Jackson 2002; Ward 1995; Williams, Jackson and Maddocks 2001). A significant minority have some physical disability and a sizeable proportion, perhaps approximately 25 per cent, have a learning disability, in a minority of cases a serious one, although there are difficulties in providing precise degrees of impairment (Morris 1998; Sinclair *et al.* 2005b).

  Most disabled foster children are looked after not because of their disability, although this may be a contributing factor, but for the same reason as for others – the existence or risk of abuse (Farmer, Moyers and Lipscombe 2004; Sinclair *et al.* 2005b). In some cases, poor health seems to reflect previous treatment by birth families. In these cases, children in foster care may do better than those remaining at home (King and Taitz 1985). Gibbons and her colleagues (1995) found that in her sample of children on the 'at risk' register (the then-equivalent of the Child Protection Register) those removed from home did better on purely physical criteria than those remaining with their families.

- *Mental health and emotional/behavioural problems.* The proportions of foster children identified as having serious problems of this kind vary with the sample studied, the measure used and, possibly, the date of study. A recent survey by the Office of National Statistics (ONS) suggested rates of mental disorder among about 45 per cent of looked after children in England (Meltzer et al. 2003). Comparable rates were produced by the ONS for the Welsh Assembly 2004, and Scottish Executive Department 2004.

- *Educational achievement.* Children in the care system have consistently been found to have a lower level of academic achievement than their peers (Brooks and Barth 1998; Colton, Drury and Williams 1995; Department of Health 1991; Heath, Colton and Aldgate 1994; Jackson and Martin 1998; Stein 1997; Zima et al. 2000.) They are far less likely to achieve General Certificates of Education (a UK examination taken normally after five years of secondary education, the number and choice of subjects being based on individual selection), any A-levels (advanced level examination usually involving between one and four subjects after seven years of secondary education) or go to university than their peers (Blome 1997; SSI/Ofsted 1995, as cited in Broad 1998). On recent figures, 5 per cent of children in foster care gained five or more GCSEs at grades A to C, and 41 per cent one GCSE (Department of Health 2002a). Comparable figures were collected for the first time in Scotland in 2001/2002, and showed that 40 per cent of 16- and 17-year-old care-leavers attained a qualification (Scottish Executive 2002). During the same year in Wales, 33 per cent of children leaving care obtained a GCSE or GNVQ (Welsh Assembly 2003).[6] When further data are collected in these countries it will be possible to chart trends over time.

- *Obtaining a qualification.* The percentage of care-leavers in England with at least one qualification has risen steadily from 1999/2000 to 2001/2002, with girls performing consistently better than boys (Department of Health 2002a). High educational achievement amongst care-leavers is associated with placement stability and having a parent or carer who values education (Jackson and Martin 1998). So it does seem as if improvement in educational performance in foster care is possible. It does not seem that fostered children do worse than if they had remained at home. Comparative longitudinal studies of children in the care system suggest that their educational problems antedate their arrival. The care system may not do enough to ameliorate their difficulties. Arguably it does not, however, cause them harm either (Aldgate et al. 1992; Essen, Lambert and Head 1976).

- *Achievement of close relationships and achieving a positive identity.* The disturbed backgrounds of foster children and the frequency of their moves make such criteria highly relevant. There is, however, no agreement on how these criteria can be measured and so no agreed measure of the degree to which they are met.

- *Do either of the two alternatives to foster care (adoption and residential care) offer better outcomes for children?* The evidence is complex and space does not allow a comprehensive review. On balance, however, the evidence on the general effects of adoption is favourable, although later adoptions prove more problematic. One review concluded that other things being equal, adoption was to be preferred to long-term foster care since it offered a greater emotional security, sense of well-being and belonging (Triseliotis 2002). Sellick and Thoburn (1996) conclude, however, that when age at placement was held constant breakdown rates were not dissimilar between adoption and foster care.

Because of changes in policy and practice, comparisons between residential and foster care are problematic. However, residential care is usually seen as a less benign and less safe environment than foster care. Although some formerly fostered residents in children's homes say that they prefer residential care (Sinclair and Gibbs 1998) foster children almost universally prefer to be fostered (Colton 1988).

Longer-term Outcomes

A key question concerns the outcomes in adult life for those who have been fostered. As discussed above, distinguishing the impact of foster care itself is not easy, both because of factors which predate foster care, and due to the time scales involved. As Thoburn reasonably comments "stability", i.e., did the child find a family for life, can only be measured when the young person, possibly placed at 6 weeks, is in his or her mid 20's' (Thoburn *et al.* 2000a, p.103).

Care-leavers are clearly vulnerable. On average, foster children move to independent living at an earlier age than their peers, for reasons which may include the potential loss of fostering allowances by carers, a perception on the part of professionals, carers and young people that it is time to move on, placement breakdown and the placement being needed by the local authority for another child.

Changes in practice over the years make it very difficult to give general statements about the long-term outcomes of foster care. In general evidence over time suggests that:

- Those who graduate out of the care system commonly have to cope on their own at a much earlier age than their peers. Typically they face difficulties over loneliness, unemployment, debt, and generally settling down (Biehal *et al.* 1995; Broad 1998; Sinclair *et al.* 2005; Stein and Carey 1986).

- Disabled young people are more likely than others to remain with their carers after reaching the age of 18.

- Surveys of young people in serious difficulty (e.g., homeless young people, young prisoners, the unemployed, those in difficulty over parenting and relationships with partners, and those with mental health difficulties) commonly find young people who have been at some time in the care system over-represented (Broad 1998; Lyon *et al.* 2000; Triseliotis *et al.* 1995b; Wade *et al.* 1998).

- Longer-term follow-ups also find care-leavers more likely to have problems with mental health, personal relationships (including parenting) and social integration (Buchanan 1995; Cook-Fong 2000).

- A substantial minority – perhaps around 30 percent – get into serious difficulties in the long term (Dumaret *et al.* 1997; Fanshel *et al.* 1990; Quinton and Rutter 1988; Thoburn *et al.* 2000b).

Nevertheless longer-term follow-ups into early/middle adulthood suggest that many of those in difficulty immediately on leaving the care system are subsequently able to settle down, even re-establishing friendly contact with foster families after breakdown (Schofield 2003; Thoburn *et al.* 2000).

Factors which may make a Difference to the Effectiveness of Foster Care

The outcomes of foster care could be determined by a number of factors which researchers have variously tried to identify. These include the type of provider, the degree to which the child and placement are matched, the birth parents and contact with them. We look at these factors below:

- *Types of provider.* Providers include kinship or relative carers, local authority, independent/voluntary providers and the private sector. There is evidence of substantial differences between providers, but as yet no firm evidence that one type of provider is more effective than another. One early study of relative placements suggested that they were less liable to breakdown (Rowe *et al.* 1984). More recent research (Sykes *et al.* 2002) has failed to confirm this, perhaps because they are now used more frequently and therefore cater for a wider and more difficult population.

- *Matching.* In terms of practice there has been a search for 'rules of thumb' – that children should be placed with siblings, placed where there are no children of the foster carers close in age, placed with relatives or situated in placements with carers of the same ethnicity. The evidence on the relationship between outcomes and these placement choices is either conflicting (e.g., on placements with siblings) (Quinton *et al.* 1998; Rushton *et al.* 2001; Sinclair *et al.* 2005b) or ambiguous (e.g., the major British study of ethnicity found that ethnic minority children placed with carers from ethnic minorities were no more or less likely to have a placement breakdown than similar children placed with a white British family but the researchers stress that qualitative data make clear the importance of ethnicity to the black and Asian children and the extra difficulties that white carers have in bringing them up) (Thoburn *et al.* 2000b).

- *Flexibility in applying 'rules'.* The evidence does suggest that the rules relate to key issues (e.g. that the attitude of carers' children to the child is important but this can work for good or ill). In most cases there is a moral presumption in favour of the 'rules' (e.g., that children should be placed with siblings or in 'same race' placements). This has to be backed by careful attention to what the children want and to particular factors in the situation (e.g. a child's extreme jealousy of a sibling).

- *The impact of foster carer characteristics on placement success.* Researchers have identified a number of parent characteristics which may be related to outcomes. These include:

  ○ *'Specific family characteristics.'* Studies have variously identified the age of the carer, the existence of birth children in the family and the age of these birth children relative to the child. There is not yet a clear consensus on what, if any, these key variables are.

  ○ *Parenting characteristics.* Carers who are responsive, child oriented, warm, firm, clear, understanding, and not easily put out are all likely to have better than expected outcomes (Sinclair *et al.* 2005a, b).

  ○ *Previous performance.* There is some evidence that carers who have experienced allegations or a higher than expected number of previous disruptions do less well with subsequent foster children than other carers.

  ○ *Ability to handle disturbed behaviour.* Carers who are able to tolerate a particular child's difficult behaviour may prevent the latter from leading to placement breakdown. Qualitative studies suggest that a key factor is the carer's ability to handle disturbed attachment behaviour and to control the child without making her or him feel rejected (Schofield *et al.* 2000; Wilson, Petrie and Sinclair 2003).

- *Contact with birth families.* A key issue for almost all placements is the relationship between children and their birth families. Research prior to the Children Act reported a desire on the part of children for more contact, difficulties in providing it, and an association between contact and return home. More recent research shows an increase in contact and ito continuing importance to foster children. While the moral case for it remains unimpaired there is now doubt that it produces all of the outcomes claimed for it (Quinton et al. 1997; Wilson and Sinclair 2004). Moreover there is evidence that it can be distressing to children or foster carers. One study showed that prohibitions on contact with at least one individual were associated with better outcomes when the child had been abused (Sinclair et al. 2004).

- *The influence of school.* School has been identified as a key factor in success. Happiness at school can produce better behaviour and adjustment and help prevent placement breakdown. Educational supports, and the encouragement of carers and other children committed to educational achievement can contribute to success and enhance self-esteem and resilience (Farmer et al. 2004; Sinclair et al. 2004; Thoburn et al. 2000b; Sinclair 2005).

Children's Characteristics and Foster Care Outcomes

Generally it is difficult to identify the different impact of foster care on different groups of children because of some of the complexities of provision identified above. Evidence of effectiveness for groups such as children with disabilities or children of minority ethnic origin is problematic because of the diverse needs and purposes of the foster care provision.

In practice the children's characteristics clearly have an important effect on what happens. For example, up until the age of 15, the older a child is the more likely he or she is to suffer a placement breakdown (Sinclair et al. 2005a). Children who have had previous placement breakdowns are more likely to have subsequent ones. Those youth who show more difficult behaviour, or who do not wish to be in foster care, are more likely to have placement breakdowns (Biehal et al. 1995; Sinclair et al. 2005b). Equally, age is a major factor in whether or not children are adopted. The likelihood of adoption drops rapidly with age. Children who are first looked after when aged five to ten are much less likely to be adopted than those who are first looked after before age five; children who are first looked after when aged 11 and over are very unlikely to be adopted. Few of them will spend very prolonged periods in the care system (see above for factors affecting the achievement of 'permanence'). The use of treatment foster care, or implementation of policies which provide alternatives to residential care or secure provision or policies which seek to ensure that these young people have a realistic base for independent living, may be particularly relevant to them (Sinclair 2005).

Conclusion

In considering the evidence of the effectiveness of the service, we are confronted with the difficulty of evaluating different kinds of foster care and its different purposes, the difficulty of deciding what should be seen as evidence of the intervention itself rather than merely something which happens after foster care and over what period of time it should be judged, and the often equivocal nature of the research evidence.

Overall, however, the evidence suggests that foster care provides a positive service to many children. Often it is both valued and, as far as research has been able to assess, valuable. Nonetheless, more could be done to improve its effectiveness. On balance it mitigates the ill effects of damaging environments but does not as yet do enough to reverse them. Efforts to improve the situation need to target:

- the making of placements (providing a range of placements to meet the varieties of need)

- the quality of placements (including training for foster carers and birth parents, expanding the provision of genuine long-term foster care, support for foster carers e.g. in managing difficult behaviour, contact)

- the arrangements for moving children out of the foster care system, including greater determination in facilitating the transition into adulthood

- the supply and support of foster carers.

Although we now know at a general level a good deal about what is needed, there are considerable gaps in the evidence of how to achieve this: more research (e.g., longitudinal large cohort alongside cross sectional-studies, qualitative and mixed-method studies) and/or innovatory practice is needed on the benefits of different kinds of provider (e.g., kinship versus stranger foster care, independent providers), the efficacy of different kinds of foster care/birth parent training, contact with birth parents from multiple perspectives, promoting the opportunities for children to grow and change in foster care, and how to improve the transitions out of foster care.

Notes

1. Over half the looked after population in foster care in the UK is over the age of ten. However, for ease of communication, we shall refer to both children and young people in this chapter as 'children', unless we are specifically addressing issues relating to older groups, such as care leavers.

2. Children looked after for an agreed series of short breaks are not included in this table.

3. These figures suggest a certain stability. This, however, is misleading, reflecting the fact that in a cross-sectional survey a child who spends a year in foster care is much more likely to be 'in care' on 31 March than one who spends one week.

4. Figures on ages are collated differently in Scotland and Northern Ireland.

5. It is now mandatory to collect data on ethnic origins for looked after children, but accurate statistics do not yet exist and differences in definitions of ethnicity make establishing proportions of children from minority ethnic groups difficult.

6. We were unable to find comparable data for Northern Ireland on the topic of education, although we are aware that such data are currently being collated.

CHAPTER 15

Foster Family Care in the US

Anthony N. Maluccio and Peter J. Pecora

Introduction

Overview

Following a review of family foster care statistics, program evolution, its definition and its functions, we describe the conceptual perspectives that guide social work intervention. The effectiveness of foster care programs in attaining key outcome areas is then presented, along with some important evaluation challenges. We conclude with selected suggestions for research that may provide better data for rational program planning as well as further studies.

Numbers and Characteristics of Children in Foster Care

In 2003, nearly three million US children were reported as abused and neglected, with 906,000 confirmed victims (US Department of Health and Human Services (US DHHS), Administration for Children and Families, Children Bureau, National Clearinghouse on Child Abuse and Neglect Information 2005a, pp.5, 21). Only one-fifth of child maltreatment victims are placed in out-of-home care by US government officials as a result of a protective services investigation. But these actions have substantial effects when new entries, failed reunifications, and children continuing in foster care from one year to another are aggregated – about 800,000 children are placed in foster care in family and non-family settings every year (US DHHS, 2005b). A little less than 1 percent of children in America are in out-of-home care at any one point in time. The numbers of children in foster care have risen substantially since 1980 and are only now just decreasing.[1]

Characteristics of Children in Family Settings in Foster Care

Aggressive adoption programs (Stein 1998; Testa 2002) and family reunification programs (e.g., Pine, Healy and Maluccio 2002; Walton *et al.* 1993), are reducing the numbers of children spending long periods of time in substitute care. But even though the child welfare industry strongly emphasizes *preventing* child placement, many children will spend a substantial amount of their childhood in foster care homes.

For example, of those children still in family settings in foster care as of September 30, 2002, mean length of stay was 31.1 months and median length of stay was 18.0 months. Of those leaving care in federal fiscal year 2002, mean length of stay was 22.7 months and median length of stay was 13.3 months. Put another way, nearly half of children who are placed in family settings in foster care will remain there for a year or longer. For example, of those leaving family settings during fiscal year 2002, 53.2% had been in care one year or more, and 20% had been there for three years or more (US DHHS, Administration for Children and Families, Children's Bureau 2005d).

Just over half (61.5%) of children remaining in family settings in foster care in 2002 were aged 0–10. The length of time that children are spending in foster care has diminished during the last few decades, but remains a concern.[2] (See Tables 15.1 to 15.6 for summary statistics of the children exiting and those remaining in family and non-family care in the US in 2002.) These estimates are based on the federal Adoption and Foster Care Analysis and Reporting System (AFCARS) – national data from 45 state and other jurisdictions, including Washington DC and Puerto Rico. The best data, however, are not from "point in time" snapshot studies, but from cohort or administrative database studies that follow children over time to pick up the dynamics of change. With these data, for example, we are able to determine that infants and adolescents spent longer periods in care in certain states (Wulczyn, Harden, and Goerge 1997).

Historical and Current Context of Family Foster Care

Family foster care in the US began in the 19th century as a method of rescuing children from their "inadequate" or "bad" parents. Toward the middle of the 20th century, it evolved into a temporary service aimed at providing a secure and loving home with the birth family or relatives. More recently, it has been regarded (at least in theory) as a treatment-oriented service intended to promote the optimal development of young people into adulthood. Currently, foster care practice and programs are governed by an intricate—and not necessarily coherent—set of polices and laws at the federal, state, and local levels (see Chapter 3 in this volume; Pecora, Whittaker, Maluccio and Barth 2000).[3]

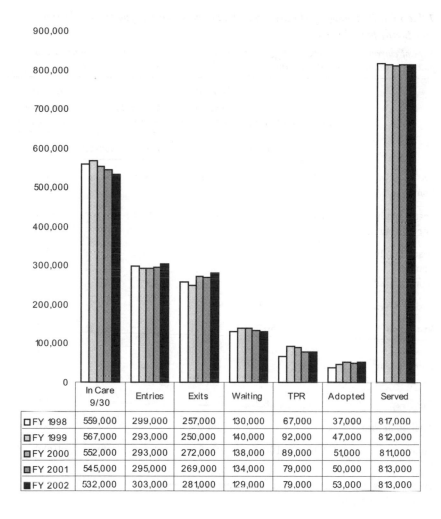

	In Care 9/30	Entries	Exits	Waiting	TPR	Adopted	Served
☐ FY 1998	559,000	299,000	257,000	130,000	67,000	37,000	817,000
☐ FY 1999	567,000	293,000	250,000	140,000	92,000	47,000	812,000
▨ FY 2000	552,000	293,000	272,000	138,000	89,000	51,000	811,000
▨ FY 2001	545,000	295,000	269,000	134,000	79,000	50,000	813,000
■ FY 2002	532,000	303,000	281,000	129,000	79,000	53,000	813,000

Figure 15.1 Trends in foster care and adoption

Source: www.acf.hhs.gov/programs/cb/did/afcars/publications/afcars.htm. Estimates are based on data submitted by states as of 1 March 2004. Some states may submit revised data at a later date.

Table 15.1: Percentage of children in each placement setting type for family and non-family placed children

Type of current placement setting	Children exiting foster care during fiscal year 2002			Children still in foster care as of September 30, 2002		
	Last placement setting		% of all placement setting types	Current placement setting		% of all placement setting types
	Fam.	Non-fam.		Fam.	Non-fam.	
Pre-adoptive home	17.2		13.1	6.1		4.7
Foster family home (relative)	24.9		18.9	30.2		23.6
Foster family home (non-relative)	41.3		31.4	59.2		46.3
Group home		35.0	8.4		39.5	8.6
Institution		50.2	12.1		47.3	10.4
Supervised independent living		6.1			4.9	1.1
Runaway		8.7			8.2	1.8
Trial home visit	16.6		4.6	4.6		3.6
Total	100.0	100.0	100.0	100.0	100.0	100.0

Key: Fam.: Family placement; Non-Fam.: Non-family placement.
Source: US DHHS (2004a)

Table 15.2: Percentage of children in each placement setting type by length of stay for children exiting foster care during fiscal year 2002

Length of stay from entry to exit	Last placement setting		Total
	Family placement	Non-family placement	
0–11 months	46.8	63.4	50.8
12–23 months	21.3	14.6	19.7
24–35 months	11.9	6.4	10.6
36–47 months	7.0	4.1	6.3
48+ months	13.0	11.6	12.7
Total	100.0	100.0	100.0

Source: US DHHS (2004a)

Table 15.3: Average exit age and length of stay for family and non-family placements for children exiting foster care during fiscal year 2002

Last placement setting		Age at entry in years	Age at exit in years	Length of stay in months
Family placement	Mean	6.72	8.59	22.69
	Median	5.82	7.97	13.34
Non-family placement	Mean	13.14	14.65	18.87
	Median	14.62	16.06	6.34

Source: US DHHS (2004a)

Table 15.4: Gender distribution of family and non-family placed children in foster care on September 30, 2002

Gender	Current placement setting		Total
	Family placement (%)	Non-family placement (%)	
Male	50.2	60.6	52.5
Female	49.8	39.4	47.5
Total	100.0	100.0	100.0

Source: US DHHS (2004a)

Table 15.5: Race/ethnicity for family and non-family placed children in foster care on September 30, 2002

Race/ethnicity	Current placement setting		Total
	Family placement (%)	Non-family placement (%)	
Black	37.2	34.8	36.7
Hispanic	17.1	16.0	16.8
White	37.5	42.5	38.6
Other	8.3	6.7	7.9
Total	100.0	100.0	100.0

Source: US DHHS (2004a)

Table 15.6: Current age groups for family and non-family placed children in foster care on September 30, 2002

Age groups as of Sep 30, 2002	Current placement setting		Total
	Family placement (%)	Non-family placement (%)	
Ages 0–10	61.5	12.6	50.9
Ages 11–20	38.5	87.4	49.1
Total	100.0	100.0	100.0

Source: US DHHS (2004a)

Definition and Functions of Family Foster Care

"Foster care" is generally used as a term encompassing not only family foster care but also placement of children and youths in group homes and residential settings. "Family foster care" itself has been defined as:

> the provision of planned, time-limited, substitute family care for children who cannot be adequately maintained at home, and the simultaneous provision of social services to these children and their families to help resolve the problems that led to the need for placement. (Blumenthal 1983, p.296)

The above definition reflects various principles that are increasingly accepted in the field of child welfare, as exemplified by the CWLA *Standards of Excellence for Family Foster Care* (Child Welfare League of America 1995). First, family foster care is conceptualized as a comprehensive family support service, and the family is regarded as the central focus of attention. Second, family foster care is carefully planned, in order to maximize its potential as a vehicle for helping families and children. In other words, the central purpose is not simply to provide substitute care—as in the past; it is to provide services and opportunities that can help families to become rehabilitated and children to grow up and develop. Third, it is meant to be time limited for all but a small number of children, in order to avoid children drifting in care, and to promote permanency planning for each child.

The major functions of family foster care include emergency protection, crisis intervention, assessment and case planning, reunification, preparation for adoption, and preparation for independent living. To implement such functions, diverse forms of foster care are required, including emergency foster care, kinship foster care, placement with unrelated foster families, treatment foster care, foster care for medically fragile children, shared family foster care, and family group homes. Also, long-term foster care is an option for a small number of youths for whom family reunification, kinship care, or adoption are not viable permanency planning options.

In addition, there are indications that family foster care is at another turning point in its history and that its direction is changing "from a largely custodial system to one that is essentially treatment oriented" (Woolf 1990, p.75). In response, we are seeing the development of specialized family foster care programs—particularly treatment foster care—for children and youths with special needs in such areas as emotional disturbance, behavioral problems, and educational underachievement (e.g., Chamberlain 2003). Family foster care is provided as a multifaceted service, including specialized or therapeutic services for some children, temporary placements for children in "emergency" homes, and supports to relatives raising children through kinship care (Maluccio, Pine, and Tracy 2002).

It should also be noted that there is a tendency to lump children needing family foster care into one category; there is, therefore, an urgent need to clarify the different types of family foster care appropriate for different children on the basis of such factors as nature of problem, age of child, reason for referral, situation of parents, and intensity and length of service required. In the past, calls for foster parenting focused on the importance of providing loving care for needy children and appealed to the altruistic feelings of adults. Today's youngsters with special needs and problems require different types of foster care, such as diagnostic placement to assess a child's needs, interim or respite care, pre-adoption placement, specialized care, therapeutic care, guardianship homes, long-term care, and kinship care.

In addition to the question of the different types, we observe that different "permanency status" types of outcomes are possible in family foster care, including reunification, foster parent adoption, adoption by other families, and preparation for independent living. These are in addition to desired emotional, physical and education-related developmental outcomes—such as reduction in emotional trauma of child maltreatment; healthy physical development because of regular check-ups and adequate medical, dental and vision care; avoidance of teen pregnancy; life skills development; and high school graduation.

Given the diverse needs and goals of children and families, it is vital to define each type of foster care precisely and to delineate the differential purposes and components of each. This is an ongoing task for the profession and the field of child welfare. In the US nearly half of children placed return home within one year. A small group of children, however, may need high-quality long-term family foster care (Fanshel, Finch and Grundy 1990), while other children can benefit from a two to six month stay in a therapeutic foster home (Hudson and Galaway 1995). In regard to all children in foster care as well as those being *considered* for foster care, a key question should be: What qualities of foster families and what mix of services do they need in order to promote their development in such areas as their social skills and preparation for adulthood?

Foster Care Intervention and its Conceptual Base

Overview – Conceptual and Theoretical Perspectives

What are the theoretical perspectives that guide social work intervention with children and youths in foster care and their families?[4] Various foster care programs have been informed by models of evaluating services that consider a range of child, family, community, foster home and other factors in explaining the service effects on children and the functioning of alumni as they leave foster care and create a new life for themselves.

Ecological and Risk-based Developmental Models

In examining life outcomes and mental health functioning of children in foster care as well as alumni, it is important to note that child characteristics interact with the experience of child maltreatment (risk) and foster care (protection) to produce outcomes. These characteristics include genetic factors, risk factors such as poverty, racism and dangerous living environments, and family of origin characteristics and functioning (Cicchetti and Lynch 1993; Fraser 2004). In addition, foster family char-acteristics and functioning, other child/family supports, the quality and nature of services provided by various community agencies, and other factors interact with the experiences of child maltreatment and foster care to produce certain outcomes.

According to an ecological perspective delineated by Cicchetti and Lynch (1993, pp.102–103), foster families can act as a powerful microsystem intervention that can have important protective and ameliorative functions for the youth. In terms of outcome areas, it is important to assess a range of domains, including mental and physical health, adaptive functioning, cognitive functioning, and social functioning.

Five theoretical approaches related to developmental theory are especially relevant to informing foster care practice. First, *attachment theory* addresses relationships and traumas occurring prior to age two (e.g., Ainsworth 1989; Weinfield, Ogawa and Sroufe 1997). Second, *trauma theory*, as researched by Briere (1992) and others regarding the effects of abuse and neglect, offers explanations for variations in the types and impact of abuse and for the impacts of immediate or delayed intervention. Third, *the ecological perspective* offers useful concepts addressing the relative importance of individual, familial, and societal contexts (e.g., Bronfenbrenner and Morris 1998; Garbarino 1992; Pecora *et al.* 2000). Fourth, *risk and protective factor frameworks* have descriptive utility for explaining resiliency in children and youths and for identifying predictors of adult outcomes. Protective factors can be personal (e.g., social competence) and environmental assets (e.g., supportive parents or other relatives) that buffer or suppress risk (Catalano and Hawkins 1996; Fraser 2004; Rutter 1989). Fifth, Erikson's *developmental theory* is useful in understanding and predicting child adjustment sequelae (Erikson 1985).[5]

Social Learning and Social Support Theory

Chamberlain (2003) and her colleagues have implemented one of the most successful lines of evidence-based research regarding a particular model of treatment foster care that is based on various theoretical perspectives, particularly social learning theory. The latter emphasizes the complex nature of social situations and holds that human behavior occurs within a complex social context.

Social support theory is just beginning to be recognized as important, as we document with even firmer data that placement disruptions and school dislocation result in poor adult outcomes, in direct contrast to what we know about the buffering effects of a positive social support system (Maluccio *et al.* 2002; Pecora *et al.* 2003a). Such a perspective stresses the importance of providing consistent supports to children, birth parents and foster families.

Evidence of Program Effectiveness

Overview

In Box 15.1 we present a cross-section of recent research studies on outcomes in foster care conducted in the United States in two major areas:

- progress and outcomes of children while in foster care
- follow-up studies on youth status and functioning after discharge from foster care.

Box 15.1 A Cross-section of Foster Care Outcome Data[6]

Studies have demonstrated that after leaving foster care, many alumni are coping well with the effects of child maltreatment. But a substantial proportion of alumni are struggling. The field needs to pay attention to the many alumni success stories while learning from areas where services were less effective. Outcome data also need to be viewed within the context of the length of stay in foster care and the type of program (e.g., shelter care, short-term foster care, treatment foster care, long-term foster care). This table presents a cross-section of data from short-term programs and for children who had longer stays in care.

Selected During-care Outcome areas

Education

- About one-third of alumni lack a high school diploma or GED (graduate equivalency degree examination) at discharge. Too many alumni complete high school via GEDs.[7]

- Life skills for independent living need to be taught more intensively and earlier in a child's life.[8]

Health and Safety

- Protection from child maltreatment has been inconsistent.[9]

- Teen pregnancy while in foster care has been too high,[10] but there are signs that this rate may be decreasing in certain agencies.

Permanence

- Placing children with relatives or other kin has increased in recent years, but could be higher.

- More siblings could be placed together, and agencies are increasing their focus on this aspect of practice.[11]

- Evidence is growing that placement stability is linked with short- and long-term youth outcomes and therefore must be maximized.[12]

- Adoption delays are decreasing but are still too long for some children.[13]

Post-discharge Outcomes

Education

- According to studies of 19–22-year-old foster care alumni, about one-third lack a high school diploma at discharge and many never complete their degree.[14] However, studies that have followed youth farther after leaving care have found higher rates of high school completion.[15]

- Few alumni attend, and even fewer complete, a four-year college degree, but longer-term alumni studies have found that even at the age of 30 over 12 percent of alumni were still in school of some kind. So vocational training and college completion rates may actually be higher.[16]

Transition Services and Preparation for Independent Living

- A substantial number of alumni report not being prepared sufficiently to emancipate successfully.[17]

- Twelve to forty-four percent of foster care alumni have experienced homelessness after discharge—with rates varying by study sample and definition.[18]

Employment and Self-sufficiency

- Some alumni have difficulty finding employment, with rates generally lower than the general population.[19]

- Disproportionately high numbers of alumni receive public assistance,[20] are struggling to earn a living wage and/or do not have health-care benefits.[21]

Criminal Justice Involvement

- A significant proportion of alumni have spent time in jail.[22]

Mental Health, Parenting and Relationships

- Over one-third of alumni have at least one serious mental health treatment condition or have experienced emotional problems after leaving foster care.

- Few alumni have had their own children placed in foster care, but the rate is higher than the general population.[23]

- Community involvement and volunteer rates are substantial, but are rarely tracked.[24] Good citizenship in the form of voter registration and voting, however, has been measured in a few studies.[25]

In-care Findings

Most studies of foster care have focused on the needs, behaviors and outcomes of the children while they are in care, using cross-sectional surveys and qualitative case studies. There have been relatively few studies that employed experimental designs. Until recently, this research has been limited by the poor agency management information systems that have been in place, poor staff training, inconsistent recording of data, and a growing but slow realization that there are key functional or developmental outcomes that should be tracked in addition to various "status" outcomes such as permanency status, and living situation restrictiveness. There are pockets of positive findings, however – especially among the programs with higher quality services.

Post-discharge Findings

As described in Box 15.1, some key large-scale follow-up studies have been conducted that have used quantitative research approaches to measure the post-discharge functioning of youth who had been placed in foster care. Some of these follow-up studies have been limited by a lack of agency funding, as well as staff time and expertise to conduct these evaluations. Until recently, little consensus existed about what aspects of alumni functioning to measure and when to measure it. These results have been sobering reminders of the agencies' need to do more regarding preparation for independent living skills, employment training, relationship formation, and mental health counseling. More studies using multiple time points and longer-term follow-ups are needed.

Wider Reflections on Foster Care Outcomes

Practice experiences, research findings from landmark studies such as those of Fanshel and Shinn (1978), Maas and Engler (1959), and more recent critiques of foster care have underscored a number of points:[27]

- Some children still experience too many placement changes, as the latest federal outcome data document shows, but permanency planning has reduced this problem.[28]

- Early on children were inappropriately moved out of their homes—with little effort to help the parents to care for them. If anything, the system encouraged parents to abandon their children, which is less the case now—especially with the emphasis upon kinship care by relatives if the birth parents are unable or unwilling to care for the child adequately. However, there are disturbing reports that a new wave of child relinquishments is emerging due to the more restrictive Temporary Assistance to Need Families (TANF) public assistance program five-year lifetime limits, and the Adoption and Safe Families Act of 1997 18-month time limits for parent rehabilitation before termination of parental rights (personal communication, Raymond Kirk, June 15, 2004).

- Children from minority families—especially black, Hispanic, and Native American—are disproportionately represented in foster care, and many have had less positive service outcomes (Hill 2001; see www.racemattersconsortium.org).

- There has been relative little attention directed toward gender differences in foster care services or outcomes.

- Most of the children placed in foster care came from poor families—often families that were barely managing to survive on limited income from public assistance programs.

- Although some children were effectively helped through placement in foster care, for others the experience of separation from their families had adverse aspects, including losing track of siblings, feelings of inadequacy, unplanned school changes, mental health problems, and disrupted relationships.

As a result of these and other findings, as well as the rapid increase in the numbers of children going into foster care that has only recently slowed, questions have been raised about the effectiveness of the child welfare system. One partial response has been the development of more evidence-based treatment foster care models (e.g., Chamberlain 2003; Meadowcroft, Thomlison and Chamberlain 1994; and Pressley Ridge Schools as described by Meadowcroft and Trout 1990) and more explicit foster care practice philosophies and guidelines (e.g., Casey Family Programs 2000, 2003a). The need for treatment fidelity measurement is being more widely recognized. In both areas of research that we reviewed earlier, there are many research gaps and areas where the evaluations could be strengthened. Suggested refinements are presented in the next section.

Future Research Directions

As in other areas of the human services, rigorous research on outcome of family foster care is limited, due to such factors as insufficient financial resources as well as the complexities of the problems under study. It is critical that this important gap in research be closed in order to provide data that can be used for rational program planning. For this reason, we offer a few suggestions:

1. Implement new studies of youth outcomes during and after care for all types of substitute care populations.

2. Use standardized diagnostic measures that assess behavior, educational functioning, satisfaction, self-esteem, and other central dependent variables.

3. Involve more youths in care, caregivers, alumni, and front-line staff in study design and data interpretation to help ensure that researchers gather meaningful information in respectful ways.

4. Conduct longitudinal research aimed at evaluating model foster care programs. This will enhance efforts to delineate program components that should be required of service contractors or incorporated into revised state models of foster care.

5. Conduct experimental or quasi-experimental program studies to evaluate different models of family foster care or interventions to help children.

6. Add to the few studies that have examined mental health disorders other than drug and alcohol use or depression.

7. Provide comparisons with the general population of youths of similar age, gender, or ethnicity, along with the use of benchmarking data from similar programs and service populations. For example, we could explore the proposition that placement in family foster care, in conjunction with mental health, education, tutoring and other services, may have a protective mediating effect upon the sequelae of child maltreatment.

8. For more efficient collection of certain kinds of outcome data, use administrative databases, such as those on employment (Goerge *et al.* 2002).

9. Involve young people more actively and consistently in planning foster care (see Sinclair 1998; www.Casey.org).

10. Conduct further research on the impact of post-permanency services (Freundlich and Wright 2003).

Conclusion

The scope of family foster care is extensive in the US, with over 800,000 children served each year, some as a result of failed reunifications or adoptions. Considerable amounts of money are invested to care for these children and the data suggest that we have achieved mixed results, some of which is no doubt due to the early childhood adversities experienced by these children (Pecora *et al.* forthcoming).

There are a huge number of areas that need to be more extensively explored, such as assessment methods to help place children in the most appropriate foster homes, interventions to help stabilize youth while in care, strategies for achieving permanency, methods to help youth reach key developmental milestones and gain life skills, and which life skills development approaches will help youth make a successful transition from foster care to living on their own. Our research evidence base is thin in most of these areas and has few national studies, as most research has been based on limited geographic areas. Consequently, the field lacks a firm empirical foundation upon which to base policies and practice guidelines. Fortunately, the sophistication of the research is growing, more cohort studies are being conducted, agency management information systems are improving, and there is more consistency in some of the variables being used. As mentioned above, there are a variety of research efforts that could be launched that would build on this foundation. Given current fiscal constraints, these studies most likely will need to be true collaborations with mixed methods evaluations and blended/pooled funding.

Acknowledgements

Special thanks to Alice-Lynn Ryssman and John Hargrove of the US Department of Health and Human Services, Children's Bureau, Administration on Children, Youth and Families for providing data from a special set analyses of the Adoption and Foster Care Analysis and Reporting System (AFCARS).

Notes

1. The 1 percent in foster care figure is derived using the following statistics: 523,000 divided by total number of youth aged 18 and under in the US population in 2003 (72,634,422= 0.72% or a little under 1%). For US national foster care data, see www.acf.hhs.gov/programs /cb/publications/afcars/report8.pdf, pp. 1-2. The best data, however, are not from point- in- time snapshot studies, but from cohort or administrative data base studies that follow children over time to measure the dynamics of change. With these data, infants and adolescents were the two groups spending longer periods in care (Wulczyn, Harden, & Goerge, 1997).
2. Wulczyn and Brunner (2001).
3. For further details, see Curtis, Dale and Kendall (1999)
4. Adapted from Pecora *et al.* (forthcoming).
5. For a more thorough description of the application of Erikson's theory to foster care research, see Downs and Pecora (2004).
6. Adapted from Pecora *et al.* (2003b).
7. For educational achievement data see Barth (1990); Blome (1997); Brandford (2004); Cook (1992); Cook, Fleishman and Grimes (1991); and Reilly (2003).
8. Brandford (2004); Leibold and Downs (2002b).
9. Reliable data about rates of child abuse or neglect in the general foster care population are sparse, so it is difficult to gauge agency performance in this area.
10. Cook *et al.* (1991); Pecora *et al.* (2003a), p.23.

11. Casey National Resource Center for Family Support (2003) p.1. For more resources see: www.caseyfamilyprograms.org/cnc/policy_issues/siblings.htm; Child Welfare Watch (2002) p.35.

12. See federal outcomes and case reviews, at www.acf.hhs.gov/programs/cb/cwrp/2002cfsrresults.htm; James, Landsverk and Slymen (in press); Rubin *et al.* (2004); Ryan and Testa (2004).

13. Federal outcomes and case reviews, at www.acf.hhs.gov/programs/cb/cwrp/2002cfsrresults.htm

14. Casey Family Services (1999) pp.13, 26; Courtney *et al.* (2001), pp.705–706. The "non-extended foster youth" are those who left Casey foster care before they reached age 19. Their experiences more closely resembled standard foster care experience and had much lower high school completion rates.

15. See Courtney *et al.* (2001) and Pecora *et al.* (2003a, forthcoming).

16. See: Festinger (1983), p.151; Jones and Moses (1984), p.62; Pecora *et al.* (2005).

17. Brandford (2004); Courtney, Terao and Bost (2004).

18. Courtney *et al.* (2001); Pecora *et al* (2003a), p.25.

19. For employment-related outcomes see Alexander and Huberty (1993), p.22; Barth (1990), p.424; Courtney *et al.* (2001), p.710; Pecora *et al* (2003a), pp.35–7.

20. See Courtney *et al.* (2001); Festinger (1983); and Pecora *et al.* (2003a, forthcoming).

21. Goerge *et al.* (2002); Pecora *et al* (2003a).

22. Cook *et al.* (1991), pp.1-2 to 1-6, 4-1 to 4-29; Widom and Ames (1994), pp.307, 310.

23. Barth (1990), p.428; Courtney *et al.* (2001, 2004); Pecora *et al.* (2005). But note that over 50 percent of adults in America have had some form of mental illness sometime during growing up (Kessler and Magee 1993).

24. Festinger (1983); Zimmerman (1982); Pecora *et al.* (forthcoming).

25. One exceptional study that tracked this outcome is Casey Family Services (1999), p.14.

26. See Thompson *et al.* (forthcoming).

27. This review draws from Maluccio, Ainsworth and Thoburn (2000); McDonald *et al.* (1996); Pecora *et al.* (in press); and Whittaker and Maluccio (2002).

28. The most relevant federal goal focuses on "no more than two placements for children in care for 12 months or less." The current performance goal level: 81 percent have two or fewer placements in less than 12 months of care. In terms of actual performance, the national median for 2000 was 84 percent—with a range of 58–100 percent. Source: www.acf.hhs.gov/ programs/cb/cwrp/2002cfsrresults.htm. More recent federal reviews have found continued wide variations in state performance (McDonald *et al.* 2004, p.7).

CHAPTER 16

Residential Care in the UK

Ian Sinclair

Introduction

In recent years the amount of residential care provided for children in the English care system has shrunk dramatically. This decline has affected the institutional descendants of both 'orphanages' and 'reformatories'. In the early 1950s, around half the children in care who were under five were in residential homes (Parker 1991). By 31 March 1996 there were only 50 children under the age of five in community homes (some no doubt babies with their mothers) and only 380 who were under the age of ten. In 1912 residential schools for the delinquent catered for over 25,000 young people. By 1991 their successors housed just over 1000 (Department of Health 1993; Hyland 1993). As the numbers in residential care have fallen so the difficulties presented by their residents have, on average, increased (Berridge 1985; Berridge and Brodie 1998).

This chapter is about the community homes that now provide all residential care in the care system. Other systems also provide residential care for young people away from their parents. These include prisons, boarding schools for children whose emotional or behavioural difficulties have produced problems in their other schools, health establishments for sick children and children with psychiatric difficulties, and establishments for young people in the services. By far the largest amount of accommodation in this field is provided by the independent boarding schools.

There is probably a substantial overlap between the kinds of children and young people in these different systems. However, the children in community homes are set apart from the others by the legal basis on which they are admitted. Basically, they enter the homes because of abuse or because family relationships have broken down. In these circumstances the Children Act 1989 allows for them to be looked after by local authorities either compulsorily under a variety of court orders or voluntarily because they or their parents have asked for this.

Against this background the chapter considers

- the role the homes play
- their current difficulties (and implicitly the reasons for their numerical decline)
- what English research has to say about the characteristics of effective homes
- how these homes might be produced.

This in turn will allow us to consider whether the homes are playing a needed role whose difficulties can be overcome or whether they are form of provision which has effectively had its day.

The Role of English Residential Care

At the latest count there were 8320 children and young people in residential homes in England. These children were looked after in small establishments – six residents is a common number but it is even possible for a home to have no more than one. A small number of homes are 'secure' and some have education on the premises. Most, however, are open institutions and the young people are expected to attend local schools.

The homes are marked by:

- high staffing levels – one study reported a variation of from 24 hours per resident per week to 142 with a median of 56 (Sinclair and Gibbs 1998)
- high costs – on average in excess of £61,000
- high turnover in many (not all homes) – one study (Sinclair and Gibbs 1998) found that slightly over three times as many residents were resident at some time in a home in any one year as were resident at the end of it
- a difficult clientele with high levels of behaviour problems.

What are the homes supposed to do? Two reports or enquiries into English residential care (House of Commons 1984; Utting 1991) have seen them as appropriate for those who:

- prefer them to fostering
- are unable to cope with the pressures of family life
- cannot be contained elsewhere
- would otherwise be accommodated apart from their siblings.

Essentially these criteria provide reasons against fostering rather than for residential care. However, it is also thought that residential care can provide:

- specialist services to the rest of the system (preparation for fostering or independence, observation and assessment, respite care, juvenile justice projects, etc.)

- expert multidisciplinary help with social and personal problems, some of it perhaps in conditions of security (Utting 1991).

Empirical evidence suggests that the preferences of residents do play a part in their selection for residential care. Those in residential care are more likely to express a preference for it than are those in foster care. None if any of the latter say they want it. Some of its residents say they do (Colton 1988; Sinclair and Gibbs 1998). Undoubtedly, however, the main reason for using residential care is that it is believed that the residents cannot be managed in other ways. In keeping with this evidence young people in residential care are difficult. They differ from those in foster care in educational performance (Biehal *et al.* 1995), measures of psychiatric ill health (McCann *et al.* 1996), delinquency (Colton 1988) and the likelihood of having 'serious problems' (Rowe *et al.* 1989).

One study (Sinclair and Gibbs 1998) described an apparently representative sample of 223 residents in local authority community homes in the early 1990s. According to their social workers less than one in six of the residents had families where both natural parents were living together. Seven out of ten had been excluded from school or frequently truanted; six out of ten had had at least some involvement in delinquency; sizeable proportions (four out of ten or more) had been violent to adults, violent to other children, run away from their own homes, run away from care and put themselves or others at risk through sexual behaviour; roughly a third had attempted to commit suicide or had harmed themselves. Generally they had entered 'care' for the first time as teenagers – only a third had done so before the age of 11 – and in the great majority of cases this was because they could not get on with their parents. They had been seen as too difficult to be fostered or as unwilling to be fostered. Roughly six out of ten had had previous experience of foster care and a similar proportion had experienced residential care. They were clearly not easy to contain in any form of accommodation.

The concentration on 'difficulty' as a criterion of placement is in conflict with the perceived need (Utting 1991) for residential homes to provide a specialist function. Sinclair and Gibbs (1998) found that some homes sought to define their role in terms of the young people served, the length of care provided and the kind of treatment given. In practice, however, most homes played most roles. Roughly three in ten of their residents were there for short-term purposes (temporary care, providing a 'roof', remand or assessment). Five in ten were there for treatment or preparation for independence of another placement and two in ten were there for upbringing. In these ways the homes could be seen in three different ways:

1. as forming part of tertiary prevention – receiving the walking wounded of family warfare and returning them quickly to the front line

2. as a method of 'career management' – receiving children under emergency situations and enabling them to be assessed and held so that sensible plans could be developed and implemented

3. as a source of specialized treatment designed to prepare the young people – for reintroduction to family, for a new placement or for independence – and as a long-term shelter in which a minority of residents are brought up.

Sinclair and Gibbs were studying homes provided by the local authority. Typically these served local children and did not have specialist roles. Since then there has been a growth in the number of homes in the independent sector. Typically, these take young people from a wider catchment area. They do not have to perform any role for any child who happens to live within a certain distance of them. As a result they are able to specialize. They can, for example, set out to provide a service for adolescent girls who have been sexually abused. As will be seen, this may make it easier for them to provide an ordered regime. Certainly it means that the system of residential care is now likely to be more specialized than was the case when it was last widely studied in the mid-1990s.

Evidence of Programme Effectiveness

There has been considerable English research into kinds of residential care that no longer exist. This stream of research came to an end in the early 1970s. There was then a small flurry of research in the middle 1990s. Since the year 2000 there have been few studies in this area. Methodologically the previous research has included a mix of qualitative description, statistical description and – a distinctively English approach – cross-institutional designs which try to relate the outcomes of different establishments to their varying characteristics after allowing for the different characteristics of their clientele. Randomized controlled trials are very rare and are problematic where found. Conclusions have to be based on putting together this rather motley array of evidence and making of it what sense one can.

The Problems of Residential Care

English residential care has been undermined by scandals, variously reflecting the harsh discipline exercised by staff (Levy and Kahan 1991), sexual abuse by staff

(Hughes 1985) and the suicidal behaviour of residents (Williams and Macreadie 1992). More fundamental difficulties are the lack of belief in residential care, the lack of theoretical basis for it, the difficulties in achieving clear roles and reasonable order, and the high costs. The context of the attack on residential homes is that many people no longer believe in them (Bullock, Little and Millham 1991, 1993a; Parker 1991).

Residential care has typically flourished as a method of inculcating social values and skills. Public schools, progressive boarding schools, monasteries, the Israeli Kibbutzim and the boarding schools set up in Soviet Russia differed dramatically from each other but each set out to create a world where a particular ethos or system of values permeated all aspects of everyday life (see e.g. Wolins 1974). There was a time when the values and ideas that underpinned English residential care attracted passionate commitment. All this has now changed. Private boarding schools more commonly mix full boarding with weekly boarding and day provision, therapeutic communities are no longer uncritically accepted and the strong religious convictions that animated much of residential care are increasingly suspect in a society that prides itself on treating equally the children of all faiths and none.

This decline in the belief in residential care corresponded with an increasing disparity between theories of residential care and the nature of current provision. Small, local children's homes do not fit ideas developed from the public school. They do not provide high class education on site and they do not provide work training or training based on a vigorous outdoor programme. They do not possess the small, stable staff group committed to bringing up children from an early age on which the former orphanages were based. They do not isolate their children from their parents as Bettelheim recommended. They do not have the trained staff, which would seem a pre-requisite for homes which seek to use the interactions of everyday life as the material for therapy. In two notorious cases (Kirkwood 1993; Levy and Kahan 1991) highly abusive practices were accepted as good practice, a situation which highlighted the lack of any adequate theory of what good residential care is. The distinctive feature of residential care – that it is a group experience – is undermined by the rapid turnover of residents and their decreasing size. Some homes now cater for only one child.

This lack of a theoretical basis is one of a number of factors leading to a lack of clear roles. Other factors include frequent reorganizations, the rundown in the number of homes and the expectation that children are placed close to their families. The small number of homes means that there is little choice. The emphasis on geographical choice further restricts what choice there is. Staff and heads of homes routinely complain of the unsatisfactory and explosive mix of children with which they have to cope (Whitaker, Archer and Hicks 1998). Official reports and inspections (Fraser 1993; Utting 1991, 1997; Warner 1992) have consistently argued for greater clarity of purpose at the level of the individual home and of the service as a whole.

The lack of a clear, theoretically grounded purpose for homes has been accompanied by a lack of evidence for the success of homes with delinquents (Cornish and Clarke 1975), attacks on the quality of care provided by homes with young children (most now very dated) (Bowlby 1951), evidence of the negative effects of even benign residential nurseries (Tizard 1977), and popular versions of Goffman's (1961) attack on total institutions.

Difficulties over control are also widespread. A number of recent studies have identified homes where order has effectively broken down (Berridge and Brodie 1998; Brown et al. 1998; Sinclair and Gibbs 1998). Delinquency and despair are widespread. In one study (Sinclair and Gibbs 1998), 40 per cent of those who entered the homes with no previous convictions and stayed for at least six months were convicted or cautioned while in the home. The comparable figure for those with previous convictions was three out of four. In this study five out of ten residents said that someone had tried to either bully them or sexually harass them since arrival. Those reporting these experiences were significantly more likely to be among the 40 per cent who said they had thought of killing themselves in the previous month. Farmer and Pollock (1998) give detailed descriptions of bullying, sexual involvements between residents and prostitution among residents.

These difficult experiences do not come cheaply. According to a 1997 study the total costs attributable to children in residential care (including social work costs) was almost exactly a third of all social services expenditure on children, 44 per cent greater than the total costs of foster care and roughly three-quarters of all the expenditure on children who were 'on the books' of the local authority but not looked after (Carr-Hill et al. 1997).

What Constitutes an Effective Residential Home?

Effective residential homes provide reasonable and preferably enjoyable places in which children and young people can live. They should also enable success in the next stage in the young people's careers. It seems likely that success in creating a 'good environment' will be influenced by factors similar to those which are important in schools and families. Successful schools are characterized by strong leadership. They involve both pupils and parents in the life of the school. They pursue instrumental goals with high expectations and an emphasis on achievement which they monitor. They deal with pupils consistently with an appropriate mix of incentives and punishments. Successful families are not so different from successful schools. The parents in these effective schools avoid parental discord or disagreement, and hostile as opposed to warm parenting; the also avoid discipline that might be characterized as ineffective or indifferent which includes among other aspects unclear expectations and a failure to encourage pro-social behaviour (Rutter, Giller and Hagell 1998).

These requirements are consistent with what we know from interviews with young people who are or have been in the care system. These suggest that the young people want to be cared for, to be free from bullying and sexual harassment, to have their needs and wishes taken into account, to be subject to reasonable expectations, and to receive encouragement to fulfil those expectations. Such messages imply the need for a coherent approach by carers, adults who are warm and prepared to listen and a constructive approach to the development of useful and valued skills.

An early theory of residential care which is consistent with these requirements was provided by Lambert, Millham and their colleagues (Lambert, Millham and Bullock 1970; Millham, Bullock and Cherrett 1975). They emphasized the need for institutions to find an appropriate balance between organizational goals (keeping themselves going), expressive goals (e.g. the creation of warm relationships) and instrumental goals (e.g. achieving at school or work). These goals needed to be pursued through adult support for residents and an emphasis on reasonable expectations to which the residents could be committed. These broad theoretical explanations can be applied to the wide variations in delinquent and criminal behaviour which have consistently been found between residential establishments and which are not apparently fully explained by intake (Berridge and Brodie 1998; Clarke and Martin 1971; Dunlop 1975; Heal, Sinclair and Troop 1973; Millham *et al.* 1975; Sinclair 1971, 1975; Sinclair and Clarke 1973; Sinclair and Gibbs 1998).

An early empirically based analysis of the reasons for these variations was provided by Sinclair's (1971) study of probation hostels. He found that the proportion of residents leaving the hostels as a result of absconding or offence varied from 14 to 78 per cent. Case studies of hostels with low rates showed that they were characterized by strong discipline, agreement between the wardens and matrons jointly responsible for the hostel, and a warm atmosphere. Case studies of hostels with very high rates showed patterns which deviated from this: there was a high degree of discord between warden and matron, there had been a major breakdown of discipline, or there was a harsh and repressive regime. A statistical study showed that high failure rates were correlated with a measure of warmth on attitude questionnaire completed by the warden, and a measure of consistency based on the number of times the warden and matron disagreed when filling in the questionnaire independently. These studies focused on delinquency.

More recent research has suggested that low delinquency rates can also indicate that other goals are being met. Sinclair and Gibbs (1998) measured the degree to which residents in a home were running away or getting into trouble with the police more frequently than would have been expected given their backgrounds. This measure correlated strongly with other apparently desirable features of a home staff morale, resident perceptions of the degree to which the home was a worthwhile and friendly place in which to be, resident satisfaction with the regime and an independent rating of the warmth of staff–resident relationships. Residents in homes which scored low on such indicators were more likely to report attempted bullying and those residents became happier when they left that form of care. By contrast, those in more benign institutions were less likely to report attempted bullying and on average became more unhappy when they left.

Similar evidence that good characteristics cluster was also produced by Brown and her colleagues (1998) in a study of nine homes. Characteristics in the homes which clustered included the children's feelings that they were cared for, the apparent warmth of the staff, the welcome accorded to visitors, the pride of the staff in their work, and more objective measures such as sickness rates, and rates of running away. Berridge and Brodie (1998) rated 12 homes on 13 separate dimensions covering among other things quality of relationships between staff and residents, control problems and external relationships of various kinds. They report the correlation between these individual ratings and an overall summary score, finding in all but two cases a high correlation (0.64 to 0.97).

How far does success in providing such regimes lead to success in the longer term? Early evidence suggested that the influence of homes was powerful but short. The major variations in delinquency between probation hostels were not translated into similar variations after the period in these hostels was over. Young delinquents from 'unsatisfactory families' did indeed do better than other residents while in the hostel. Subsequently they did worse (Sinclair 1971). Young women returning to dis-harmonious families did worse on a number of criteria than other young women in residential care (Quinton and Rutter 1988).

Despite this there is some evidence of a long-term influence for residential care. Some of this may be negative. Absconding – a form of behaviour strongly influenced by institutional environment (Clarke and Martin 1971; Sinclair 1971) – did lead to further convictions (Clarke and Martin 1971; Sinclair 1971; Sinclair and Clarke 1973). Residential establishments that emphasized training for work had, after allowing for intake, lower reconviction rates than those which did not (Dunlop 1975; Millham *et al.* 1975).

It is likely that these influences persist, if they do, at least partly through their impact on the way a young person sees him- or herself. The influence of absconding on re-absconding seemed to depend on the reactions of the staff towards it (Sinclair 1971). Those who run away from homes may acquire not only this habit but also the friends, skills and way of thinking of themselves that are required to survive on the streets (Wade *et al.* 1998). It was not trade (employment) training per se which led to success – as that was often of poor quality within individual establishments and did not have a particularly good impact on those exposed to it (Dunlop 1975; Millham *et al.* 1975). Rather the establishments which emphasized trade training also emphasized 'responsibility' (Dunlop 1975) and their residents came to see themselves as more responsible (Millham *et al.* 1975).

The influence of trade training may also depend on both the wider and more immediate social contexts. Trade training is unlikely to be valued if it is not seen as leading to work. Its value (and the value of educational skills) will also depend on the new context to which the young person moves. If their immediate future is pregnancy or a financial situation in which the need to earn is paramount, the young people may not be able to use their educational skills in a way which promotes their well-being. A key issue in this new environment is relationships with family. As argued above, a 'disharmonious family' can undermine the good work of the best institution. Some English evidence suggests that work with families is possible from an institutional base and leads both to improved family relationships and better long-term adjustment (Gibbs and Sinclair 1998b; Sinclair and Gibbs 1998).

Overall, therefore, long-term effects of residential homes are likely to depend on:

- the control of absconding, offending and other negative behaviour

- an emphasis on the acquisition of 'pro-social skills' in education or work

- the development of a culture which values these skills and so builds self-esteem

- effective work on the relationship between young people and their families

- after-care which enables the young people to use the skills they have acquired.

These hypotheses are far from confirmed by English research. They are, however, in keeping with it as well as with the results of longitudinal studies which emphasize the role of families, education and work in escape from disadvantage (Sampson and Laub 1993; Schweinhart *et al.* 1993; Werner 1989).

How Effective Homes can be Produced

If these are the characteristics of effective homes, how can they be produced?

On this matter official reports have much to stay. Specification of the roles of particular establishments will avoid an unsuitable mix of children or functions. In particular young people with very challenging behaviours may need to be separated from their more malleable peers. Adequate choice of placement is therefore crucial (Utting 1997). The homes should be small – certainly with fewer than 12 beds (Utting 1991). Staff should be trained. The resulting system should be reinforced by strong management, clear procedures, including particularly procedures for complaints, care planning, inspection and appropriate staff selection, training and development (see for example, Utting 1991, 1997; Warner 1992). Other recommendations are intended to deter unsuitable people from applying for residential posts, for detecting them if they do, and for empowering staff and residents so that unsatisfactory staff who do get through are safely and confidentially identified (Utting 1997; Warner 1992).

In general research suggests that treatment effectiveness is more likely where:

- heads of home have a clear remit and adequate autonomy to pursue it
- the heads themselves have clear, appropriate ideas on how the home should run
- the staff are in agreement both with the head and with each other on how the home should run.

One study (Sinclair and Gibbs 1998) suggests that these conditions are easier to bring about in small homes. Other studies (e.g. Berridge and Brodie 1998) have not found this association.

The Roles and Autonomy of the Homes

Brown and her colleagues (1998) suggest that in successful homes there is a congruence between the official goals set by the department and the goals explicitly and implicitly pursued by the head. Berridge and Brodie (1998) found that their measure of good quality was positively associated with the ability of the head of home to state specific objectives for the home (with a substantial correlation of $r=0.64$). It was even more strongly associated with the heads of homes' ability to articulate a clear theoretical/therapeutic orientation or specific method of work for caring for children. Sinclair and Gibbs' study (1998) found that 'clarity of remit' (as rated by the head of home) was associated with a feeling of autonomy. Homes were less turbulent when the heads felt that the aims of the home were clear and compatible and that within this context they themselves had adequate autonomy.

Head of Home

The influence of the head is constrained by the characteristics of the organization and by staff. Heads with little autonomy, or those faced by entrenched bodies of hostile staff, have less influence. 'Runs of trouble' may also infect the most stable establishment. Nevertheless, there is little doubt that heads are usually key to what occurs. Sinclair (1971) studied the outcomes of 4000 young men (aged 15 to 21) in probation hostels. Under different wardens the proportion of probationers leaving hostels as a result of an absconding or offence varied from 14 per cent to 78 per cent. These variations were not explained by differences in intake or by any feature which was characteristic of the hostels themselves (e.g. their committees, localities or buildings, or the age range of the youth served). Differences in the failure rates of successive wardens in the same hostel were as great as the differences between wardens in different hostels.

Staff Unity

Clearly staff agreement or coherence on its own is not a guarantee of a successful outcome. It is possible to imagine a coherent but oppressive or cruel regime. Nevertheless, Brown and her colleagues (1998) make coherence the key to their analysis of the differences between successful children's homes and others. They argue that there is a need for consistency between the goals which the establishment is supposed to pursue, those which the head of home espouses both officially and in her or his behaviour and those which the staff embody in their approach to particular events or incidents. In their three successful homes (where success was measured in accordance with the criteria outlined above) staff adopted a common approach which was less apparent in their three less successful homes and missing in their three unsuccessful ones.

Two other recent studies support the general direction of Brown and her colleagues' work. Sinclair and Gibbs (1998) measured staff unity in two different ways (one emphasizing staff relationships with each other and the other the success of the head in uniting staff around a particular approach). They found both measures were significantly correlated with a measure reflecting the absence of delinquent behaviour in a home and positive accounts of the home from staff and residents. Berridge and Brodie (1998) found that their measure of quality was correlated with low staff turnover. They interpreted these results as showing among other things the need to develop staff teamwork and a common ethos.

Effectiveness for All Children

There is very little evidence on the effectiveness of residential care for minority groups. Some establishments are specifically designated for children and young people with impairments. According to Berridge and Brodie (1998) they tend to be characterized by good practice. Ethnic minority children can be subject to racist abuse. There is no evidence that they are more likely to be bullied than others. They may, however, have other difficulties. In particular they may find it more difficult to get close friends and may find the food alien and unfamiliar (Sinclair and Gibbs 1998). In mixed establishments young women are more likely to be subject to sexual harassment than young men and some of them express a preference for being in single-sex homes.

Other Possible Conditions for Effectiveness

Very few studies have looked at the statistical effects of building or location. There is no evidence that the kinds of buildings have a large impact on outcome. Locality, however, may be an important influence. Qualitative evidence suggests that it can be difficult to run homes in delinquent neighbourhoods from which the young people come – although those doing so may still think the experiment worthwhile. Individual young people may benefit from a relocation that breaks links with prostitution (Farmer and Pollock 1998) or delinquency (Cliffe and Berridge 1991). Young people attending homes in the private sector, typically some distance from their homes, report less pressure to take drugs than before – a contrast with young people in the local authority sector (Gibbs and Sinclair 1998a). Independent homes seem to be better ordered than local authority homes, despite taking more difficult residents. However, the young people themselves seem to prefer local authority homes, arguably because they are closer to their families.

Contrary to what might be expected there is little evidence that either staffing ratios or staff qualifications are related to outcomes. Neither Berridge and Brodie (1998) nor Sinclair and Gibbs (1998) found an association between their measures of outcome and staffing ratios. (Sinclair and Gibbs found that, regardless of size, the more generously staffed the home was, the more turbulent the result.) Neither group of researchers found that qualified heads had better results than unqualified ones. Sinclair and Gibbs found no association between the proportion of qualified staff and outcomes. As Berridge and Brodie point out, however, it cannot be assumed that training of itself will affect outcomes. What is required is knowledge of what kind of training produces what kind of staff behaviour in what circumstances.

Conclusion

Residential care is by far the most expensive resource in the English care system. For this, among other reasons, it is essential to appraise residential care carefully. There is at present a lack of comparative evidence which would suggest that this form of care is more or less effective than other comparable provisions. There is however evidence on which cases for and against residential care can be made.

The case *for* residential care is, essentially, that some children want it and others cannot be managed in any other way. It is also possible, if unproven, that homes are a potential means for delivering effective treatment.

The case *against* the current homes is strong. They are unstable, and prone to scandal and disorder. They lack a coherent theoretical justification. Their most notable difference from foster care – the existence of a resident group – is commonly seen as a threat rather than asset. Their outcomes are, if not demonstrably worse than would be the case for similar young people in foster care, certainly discouraging.

They are very expensive. The costs make it impossible to keep young people in them as long as they would often like. They divert resources from former residents and other needy young people alike.

In terms of practical implications it may be that if the homes are to survive they are likely to play four roles:

1. They may be needed to hold difficult adolescents in emergency until they are either returned to their families or moved on within the care system. The disadvantage of putting adolescents together is that they can lead each other astray. However, it is difficult to find foster carers who can do this job and this form of residential care may be a practical necessity.

2. Residential care is needed to provide 'treatment' in conditions of 'security'. Public opinion will not allow some young people, for example those who have murdered, to live in open conditions. At present there is a growing trend for such young people to be in prisons. For practical reasons they need to be in closed accommodation. For moral reasons they should be provided with a regime which allows them to change.

3. Residential care may be a 'treatment of choice'. If so, it needs to be shown that the potential advantages of forming a group of young people outweighs the obvious risks. The likely key ingredients of effective treatment are education and work with birth families. These can be provided through other means – foster care, residential schools or, if necessary, a combination of foster care and day schooling. The costs of residential care mean that there is always pressure to move young people on. There is no evidence that current residential care easily provides the stable, positive group experience which might lead to long-term change.

4. Residential care may be needed for those who prefer it as a place to grow up. It has to be shown that what they want is residential care and not, for example, a form of foster care which does not threaten their bonds with their family or tantalize them by offering a closeness it cannot really provide. This form of residential care must also be less lavishly staffed. There is no evidence that high staffing ratios buy good order, nor perhaps is it necessary that long-term homes need to have two staff on duty at all times or even be staffed at all hours. These assumptions are not made for foster care. Why are they made for residential homes? Unless these homes become cheaper, it is unlikely that they can survive as providers of upbringing.

All these forms of residential care need to take account of the conditions of effectiveness. So they need to have clear aims, effective heads and staff who are agreed on what they are trying to bring about. The crucial importance of staff cannot be stressed too much. In my personal opinion, it would be better if there were fewer staff and they were paid and valued a great deal more.

As for research priorities, these uses of and forms of residential care need to be tested. And research should also concentrate on the potential of foster care and intensive provision of services to children and families in their own homes to determine if those forms of service can provide effective substitutes for residential care. In this field the more expensive provisions are not necessarily the best.

CHAPTER 17

Residential Care in the US

James K. Whittaker

Introduction

A reading of Chapter 16 on residential care research in the UK by Ian Sinclair, while suggesting many areas of commonality, underscores the cross-national differences that exist with respect to group residential care's place in the overall service continuum. Although with respect to general acceptance of legitimacy, the gap appears to be narrowing. Citing Roger Bullock and Roy Parker, Sinclair notes: "The context of the attack on residential homes is that many people no longer believe in them" (see p. 207). And so it is in the US At least as measured by a sampling of recent expert opinion in child welfare and child mental health, the prospects for residential care and treatment range from extremely cautious to bleak:

> Group care is expensive and restrictive and should be used only when there is clear and convincing evidence that the outcomes will be superior to those of foster care and other community-based services... this review indicates that there is virtually no evidence to indicate that group care enhances the accomplishment of any of the goals of child welfare services: it is not more safe, or better at promoting development, it is not more stable, it does not achieve better long term outcomes, and it is not more efficient as the cost is far in excess of other forms of care. (Barth 2002, p.31)

There appear to be severe risks associated with residential treatment, including the learning of antisocial or bizarre behavior from exposure to deviant peers, failure to learn behavior needed in the community, possibility of trauma associated with separation from the family, difficulty returning to the family, and victimization in residential treatment centers (Barker 1998; English 2002, p.309).

Currently, no conclusive evidence exists to support the effectiveness of residential treatment over other service types (Kutash and Robbins Rivera 1996, p.121). These sentiments echo the concerns raised by Burns, Hoagwood and Mrazek in the section on 'effective treatments for children and adolescents' prepared for the most recent US Surgeon General's Report on Mental Health: "Given the limitations of current research, it is risky to reach any strong conclusions about the effectiveness of residential treatment for adolescents" (1998, p.18).

Prospects for a rejuvenated residential service for juvenile offenders appear rather dim at present. This is partly due to concerns about the potential for institutional abuse and the unintentional promotion of deviant behavior through modeling and imitation. Additionally, there is an increasingly negative consensus about the continued reliance on residential care and treatment as a major child mental health service, or as an alternative to foster care (Dishion, McCord and Poulin 1999; Poulin, Dishion and Burraston 2001). Yet, serious attention including both theoretical and empirical analysis must be directed to the purposes, change theories, treatment protocols, expected outcomes, comparative advantages and organizational requisites for residential treatment if it is to retain its legitimacy as a viable service option for troubled children and their families. Perhaps, it is simply the culmination of factors afflicting residential care, in any of its forms, described graphically by Martin Wolins in 1974:

> Group care of normal children was, for all intents and purposes, off the professional's agenda either as a solution to some types of problems or even as a theoretical concern. Like Lamarckian genetics or the demon theory of mental illness, it had been laid to rest. (Quoted in Pecora *et al.* 2000, p.406)

As one small step toward identifying a possible future course for residential care research, this chapter will do three things:

1.   Provide a brief summary of what might be taken as the current "conventional wisdom" with respect to residential treatment in North America and address some of the attendant causes and consequences of this thinking.

2.   Offer a very brief "sketch" of demographics, service trends, and outcome research in residential treatment.

3.   Identify three key domains of critical problem solving for residential treatment and touch briefly on each:

     •   the "definition and purpose" of residential care and treatment in an overall continuum of child and family service

- questions of "intake": What youth are best served by residential placement?

- questions of "outcome" indicators: What are reasonable outcomes for the multiple forms of residential care and treatment that presently exist?

The chapter concludes with several brief recommendations for innovations in residential care research and practice and future evaluation challenges.

The Nature of the Evidence on Residential Care

As noted, more often than not, residential care is seen as a service that one uses as a last resort. Often, residential care is viewed more as part of the problem than as part of the solution. In part, this is owing to an absence of clear and compelling empirical evidence of effectiveness, and other reasons having to do with perceptions of the service, uneven theoretical development and concerns about costs and the potential for abuse. For example:

1. *Lack of diagnostic indicators.* The identification of a scientifically based diagnostic criteria for residential placement continues to elude us.

2. *A presumed preference within some service systems for placement without first attempting some less radical community- and family-based interventions.* An argument strengthened by the fact that "intensity" of treatment, once thought the sine qua non of residential treatment, may now be found in equal measure in less restrictive, community- and family-centered alternatives such as "treatment foster care" and "wraparound services" (Kutash and Robbins Rivera 1996, p.120).

3. *A presumption of "intrusiveness" and concerns about attachment for children placed.* A set of concerns voiced, in particular, where very young children are involved (Berrick *et al.* 1997).

4. *Fear of abuse and neglect within residential settings.* A story that will not go away, either in recently voiced concerns about past practices including some highly regarded treatment settings, or in current exposés of institutional abuse in sectarian group care settings here and abroad.

5. *Questionable effectiveness of residential treatment.* Virtually every review of residential treatment research begins with a comment about the unevenness of the research corpus, with virtually none of the benefit of the doubt given as it is to, say, newer interventions which fit more closely with the value base of systems of care thinking.

6. *A lack of consensus on critical intervention components.* As noted in the US General Accounting Office study (1994) cited later in this chapter, while various lists of intervention components exist, there is little indication of which are necessary and which are sufficient ingredients in a quality residential treatment program.

7. *A lack of residential treatment theory development, particularly in recent years.* It is telling that recent reviews in child mental health (Burns and Hoagwood 2002; US Department of Health and Human Services (US DHHS) 1999b) must reach back to a model from the 1960s (Hobb's Project Re-ED) to muster even the most muted enthusiasm for any form of residential care and treatment.

8. *Cost of care.* A first order argument for system reform is that 70 percent of service dollars continue to be spent on residential provision when lower cost, community-centered alternatives are available (Duchnowski, Kutash and Friedman 2002, p.30).

9. *A continuing familialist bias in service selection.* Since at the least the first decade of this century, there exists a presumption that residential care if used at all ought to be seen as a "last resort" (i.e., when all other options are exhausted). This is particularly so when child dependency is the primary issue. Preference should go to foster family care, adoption, guardianship or other alternatives. In child mental health, this translates to viewing treatment foster care as a more desirable alternative to residential treatment.

For out-of-home placement as a whole, the single most stable trend line in child welfare over the last 75 or so years of the 20th century was the shifting ratio of children in foster family vs. residential care as a proportion of the total number of children in out-of-home care. As Kadushin (1980) notes, from approximately the early 1930s to the mid 1970s, the percentage of children in residential care declined from 57 percent to 15 percent, while the percentage in family foster care increased from 43 percent to 85 percent for the total population of children served in out-of-home care. Thus, despite an increase in the rate of placement and in the ratio of children out-of-home to those served in-home, the proportions of children in residential vs. foster family care options have remained relatively constant.

Since then, government policy (in child welfare) has been even more supportive of family-based alternatives (e.g., adoption incentives) for children for whom there is little hope of return to parents of origin. At the level of individual states, "family group conferencing" originating in New Zealand has replaced intensive family preservation service as the "cutting edge" of practice innovation (Connolly and McKenzie

1999). Serious discussions of group care options for long-term care occur only at the margins of policy and practice debate; for example, in the interest sparked by the Pew Memorial Trust, San Diego County, and others in "residential academies."

For these and related reasons, residential treatment as a subset of group child-care programs begins from a position of weakness when it is advanced as a treatment of choice within an overall system of care.

Evidence of Program Effectiveness and Implications for Program Design

A Brief Overview of Contemporary Residential Care in the US

The previously mentioned lack of interest in residential care is reflected in administrative data gathering as well. Despite several exciting initiatives in federal and state data gathering in children's services (e.g., US DHHS, Children's Bureau 1997), it is still difficult to compile an up-to-date and accurate picture of group care. From our latest census data and other sources (Pecora *et al.* 2000), we do know the following:

1. While the numbers of children residing in substitute care are small in proportion to the total child population (less than 1%), they are increasingly troubled and present multiple problems at intake.

2. Anywhere between 15 percent and 30 percent of the out-of-home care population resides in residential as opposed to foster family care.

3. We have more residential facilities, albeit with smaller-sized living units.

4. Lengths of stay are shorter and children are, on average, older at intake.

5. In certain sectors, we are seeing more proprietary agencies (e.g., children's psychiatric facilities) and more specialized facilities (e.g., those serving youth with substance-abuse problems, and problems related to sexual offending).

6. Among residential centers (many of which are voluntary), we are seeing more mergers, more closures, and less stability with respect to funding.

7. There is a growing emphasis on specification of standardized child and family outcomes and, not surprisingly, more emphasis on specification of treatment and care protocols. In large measure this influence is positive, though in certain types of residential facilities, some have used the term "medicalization" to describe what is happening to residential programs as they strive to meet criteria for psychiatric reimbursement.

At the level of actual residential practice, the clinical equivalent of the "holy wars" (e.g., between psychoanalytic, psycho-educational, behavioral, and positive peer culture approaches) has receded into the background. There is instead a much more eclectic, non-dogmatic, perhaps atomistic approach to practice, as programs struggle to meet the highly prescriptive outcome and procedural requirements of their contracts. The resultant aggregation of program components — each targeted to a particular youth problem — often yields a structure that, in my judgment, lacks coherence as a total milieu: Much of current residential treatment in the States, in my opinion, is being built "brick by brick" without a blueprint (I am reminded here of the observation of one of my favorite historians of science, the late Steven Jay Gould of Harvard, who described an exclusive reliance on inductive processes in science as akin to constructing a building, brick by brick, without a blueprint!).

Evidence of Program Effectiveness

Let us turn now to the question of outcome research and what is "known" about residential care. I will offer only the briefest overview (see Curry 1991 for a more complete review) here, and only from a US context. For European perspectives, please see Hellinckx *et al.* (1991) and the excellent UK review authored by Roger Bullock, Michael Little and Spencer Millham for the Dartington group (1993b). Whittaker and Pfeiffer's (1994) earlier critique of the residential research base remains largely accurate: studies that do exist tend to focus on a single setting, lack control or comparison conditions, suffer from lack of specificity of treatment variables and absence of randomization.

Perhaps a good place to begin from an American perspective is with the mid-1990s report of the US Government Accounting Office (1994), the office charged with answering questions posed by members of Congress on a wide variety of policy-related topics. Typically their reports involve synthesis of existing research as well as conducting original studies. Here is a statement from their executive summary:

> Not enough is known about residential care programs to provide a clear picture of which kinds of treatment approaches work best or about the effectiveness of the treatment over the long term. Further, no consensus exists on which youths are best served by residential care…or how residential care should be combined with community based care to best serve at risk youths over time. (p.4)

This report identifies 11 characteristics which appear to be related to success:

1. developing individual treatment plans

2. participation of a caring adult

3. self-esteem building

4. planning for post-program living

5. teaching social, coping, and living skills

6. coordination of services

7. involving the family

8. positive peer influence

9. enforcing a strict code of discipline

10. post-program support

11. providing a family-like atmosphere.

While these are socially significant as indicators of presumed "best practices," not all share the same degree of empirical validation. Among those that do appear to be supported by outcome studies are:

1. involving a parent or other concerned adult in the client's care

2. planning adequate supports for the youth's return to the community after completing the program.

Support for these findings is noted in several earlier reviews of residential care research (Curry 1991, 1993; Whittaker and Pfeiffer 1994) and underscore the importance of contact and involvement with family during the placement period and, more generally, on the importance of supports in the post-discharge environment. For example, a follow-up study by Wells (Wells, Wyatt and Hobfoll 1991), formerly the research director at Bellefaire — a well-known residential treatment center in Cleveland, Ohio — repeats the classic follow-up research conducted in that same agency in the 1960s (Allerhand, Weber and Haug 1966). Dr. Wells concludes as follows:

> A failure to respond in some way to the conditions in the environments in which youths were discharged may well undo the hard won gains youths make in treatment... We need...the reconceptualization of residential treatment as a family support system and to identify the potential stressors and stability of the environments to which youth are returned. (Wells *et al.* 1991, p.214)

As Curry notes in an insightful review paper, we are learning more about the various domains of social support and their relationship to adaptive outcomes for youth:

> Results [of the Wells *et al.* study, 1991] showed that measures of adaptation were positively intercorrelated, but measures of social support were not. Thus, while a youngster tending to function well in one area was likely to function well in others, sources of support were not necessarily correlated. Support from family members was most strongly related to psychological adaptation. (1993, p.13)

Curry concludes by affirming the importance of increasing family support in the post-discharge period and suggests that alternative sources of support may not fully compensate for lack of family support. So what can be said at this point from the existing research base with respect to residential care? A recent review suggests three things:

1. Regardless of a youth's status at discharge, the quality of supports available in the post-discharge environment appears to be associated with subsequent community adjustment.

2. Continuing contact and involvement with family appears to be positively correlated with post-placement success.

3. Youths with supportive community networks are more likely to maintain their treatment gains than those who lack such supports (Pecora *et al.* 2000, p.421).

I am hopeful because a number of imaginative residential practitioners and innovative agencies have created some interesting options in the last several years for engaging families more fully while providing support for youth. A recent publication by the Child Welfare League of America documents some of these efforts for those who might be interested in further detail (Whittaker 2000).

Future Challenges for Research and Development in Residential Care: Shedding Light on the Residential Family Connection

As residential programs move forward to adopt and adapt many of the family-focused practice innovations from these and related projects, it is critical that these be accompanied by rigorous evaluations to insure their relationship to the ultimate outcomes of interest: Community adjustment and integration for youths returning from care (Whittaker and Savas 1999). Researchers and practitioners alike will face several critical challenges in providing empirical validation for family–agency partnerships. These include, but are not limited to:

1. developing protocols for family practice

2. developing rapid assessment/brief intervention models for family work

3. developing family work that is effective with special populations and which reflects appropriate cultural and ethnic variation

4. documenting the link between family support intervention and youth outcomes.

While the existing corpus of residential outcome research leads us ineluctably to work on improving agency–family partnerships, it remains to be documented how increasing familial support actually improves and enhances youth outcomes. With the growing trend towards outcome-based contracting, it is critical that we increase our understanding of the mechanisms by which a supportive (and well-supported) family serves to buffer the adverse effects of the otherwise stark community environments to which youth must all too often return following residential placement.

I believe our greatest challenge in these and in all other areas of residential research is that we take care to match theory-based and well-crafted and innovative residential practice with the appropriate choice of our increasingly diverse evaluative research methods. Otherwise, we run the risk of subjecting what is essentially the "best of the past" (in residential practice) to research analysis characterized by increasing rigor and sophistication.

Conclusions

I end this brief chapter with a few specific prescriptions for innovation in residential treatment identified in an earlier review essay by the present author and Anthony Maluccio (Whittaker and Maluccio 2002). These remedies are partial and to a certain degree idiosyncratic and I have no illusion that they constitute a panacea. However, I believe that collectively they will increase the likelihood of finding answers to many of the questions I have posed regarding residential care.

First and foremost, I believe we need to design a new service continuum that softens the differences and blurs the boundaries between in-home and out-of-home options such as shared care, respite care, and partial placements (for a fuller discussion of the "placement" issue, see Whittaker and Maluccio 2002). Kinship care may be a step in that direction. Moreover, it is critical that those who believe residential care and treatment has a niche to fill in the overall service spectrum make the case based on analysis buttressed by empirical outcome data in ways that allow us to see the *relative* contributions and best uses of wraparound treatment, foster care, multisystemic treatment, and residential treatment in an overall system of care.

Some other suggestions that would be helpful include:

- redoubling our efforts at parent involvement
- expanding residential respite options
- developing more creative short-term residential treatment
- focusing on child well-being and family functioning as outcome measures
- studying honestly the limits as well as the potential of family-centered service delivery

- developing models of whole family care, for example by combining respite with holiday time and skill building for families

- working to personalize residential care settings and reinforce primary caregivers

- examining the potential for the co-location of services: for example family support and residential care

- seeking partners and being able to locate our residential programs in an overall service network

- conducting longitudinal research to study of developmental outcomes for youth in shared care and those temporarily placed

- re-designing some group care settings for permanent living and re-examining communal alternatives (e.g., Israeli cluster foster care, i.e. proximal siting of foster care homes with a common support base).

The New York City AIDS Orphan Project (Levine, Brandt and Whittaker 1998) reached the tentative conclusion that group residential care ought to be at least *one* option open to children made orphans by the disease. Such group care settings, it was argued, ought to meet five basic criteria:

1. Continuity of developmentally appropriate caregiving, with stable caregivers.

2. Maintenance of stability of sibling groups.

3. Provision of a structured and predictable environment.

4. Maintenance of meaningful connections with "family."

5. Continuity with community and culture.

While I am not particularly optimistic about achieving even a few of these modest changes in the absence of a more focused and thoughtful discussion on substitute care as a whole, my strong sense is that we need to bring the worlds of policy, research, and practice in residential and foster care into much closer proximity so that we can assess what the challenges and strengths are in each domain and then chart a course of action for renewal. To do this, we sorely need fresh conceptual thinking on milieu treatment as well as empirical research. International perspectives such as those provided in this present volume on the issue of the proper place of residential care and treatment in an overall service continuum will be helpful as well in broadening and stimulating our limited and, typically, parochial discussions in the states. I hope that the present volume and the considerable research and program expertise reflected in its numerous contributors will serve as a catalyst for addressing some of the issues concerning residential care and treatment raised here. It is a task long overdue.

Acknowledgements

Earlier versions of this chapter appeared as "The re-invention of residential treatment: An agenda for research and practice" in B. Leventhal (ed.) *Child and Adolescent Psychiatric Clinics of North America 13* (special issue) 2267–278 (2004, Elsevier Science) and "Reinventing residential childcare: An agenda for research and practice" in *Residential Treatment for Children and Youth 18* (special issue) 13–31 (2000, Haworth Press). Portions of the chapter were presented originally at several professional symposia, including The Sixth Congress of the European Scientific Society for Residential and Foster Care for Children and Adolescents [EUSARF], September 23–26 1998, University of Paris-X Nanterre; The Duke Symposium on Group Care, April 10–11 1997, East Carolina University, School of Social Work, and a working conference of The New York City Aids Orphan Project: Planning and Placement: Expanding the Options for Orphans of the HIV Epidemic, Fund for the City of New York, October 17–18 1996.

CHAPTER 18

Support for Young People Leaving Care in the UK

Jim Wade

Introduction

Each year more than 6000 young people leave care in England, most to establish an independent life in the community as young adults.[1] In doing so, they are expected to make a series of complex and difficult transitions. Some manage these quite successfully, while others encounter serious difficulties. It is only since the early 1980s in the UK that the testimony of care-experienced young people, allied to growing academic and professional concern, have placed leaving care higher on the research and policy agenda. As a result, our knowledge of how young people may be most effectively assisted through the transition to adulthood is at a relatively early stage.

However, there has been considerable evidence of the need for improved support. Throughout the 1980s and 1990s, research has consistently highlighted the relatively poor life chances of young people leaving care, including poor levels of educational attainment and a heightened risk of unemployment and homelessness when compared to the general population of young people (Biehal *et al.* 1995; Broad 1998; Jackson 1994; Stein and Carey 1986). Despite the emergence of specialist leaving care projects over this period, there were large and continuing variations in the support provided to care-leavers across different local authorities (Broad 1998; Department of Health 1997). It was in response to this pattern of poor outcomes and of inconsistencies in the framework of services that new legislation governing leaving care was introduced in England and Wales in 2001.[2]

The implementation of the Children (Leaving Care) Act 2000 (CLCA) and linked initiatives such as Quality Protects (England) and Children First (Wales) are intended to bring about a seismic shift in the landscape of leaving care. The explicit purpose of the CLCA is to delay transitions from care; improve preparation, planning and consistency of support for young people; and strengthen arrangements for financial assistance. At its heart are new duties to assess and meet needs, provide personal advisors and develop pathway planning for young people up to the age of 21 (or beyond if they are continuing in education). Regulations and guidance have spelt out the core areas of young people's lives that should be addressed through pathway planning (Department of Health 2001c).

Given this new framework for thinking about leaving care services, the substantive part of this chapter will review what we currently know about what may help to improve services and outcomes for young people. However, it is first necessary to consider the status of the evidence available.

The Nature of the Evidence

The development of an 'evidence-based' approach to inform services has been emphasized by the UK government as part of a modernizing agenda for health and social care (Department of Health 2000b). Within applied social research, debates about what counts as evidence of 'effectiveness' remain contentious and have sometimes been narrowly drawn. While some researchers assert the primacy of experimental design, involving the use of matched trial and control groups to assess particular interventions, others advocate broader evaluation methodologies with greater emphasis on an understanding of process and context in shaping outcomes (Lewis 1998; Macdonald, Sheldon and Gillespie 1992; Newman and Roberts 1997; Pawson and Tilley 1994).

From an experimental perspective, we would be able to say very little about what works in leaving care, since these studies have simply not been done in the UK (Stein 1997). However, careful consideration of the messages that emanate from research, inspections and guidance in the leaving care field can tell us much about the kinds of policies and services that appear helpful to young people when negotiating major changes in their lives.

From the late 1970s, a number of mostly small-scale exploratory studies emerged that helped to raise the profile of leaving care and shape the course of future research (Bonnerjea 1990; Godek 1976; Kahan 1979; Lupton 1985; Morgan-Klein 1985; Stein and Carey 1986; Triseliotis 1980). These studies alerted us to the diversity amongst young people leaving care in terms of their past experiences and their experiences upon leaving. They also highlighted the risks that many young people encountered, including further movement and disruption, unemployment, homelessness (Randall 1989), a heightened risk of custody (Prison Reform Trust 1991), and pointed to the uncertainty that could exist for black young people who had become separated from family and community (First Key 1987). While these descriptive studies gave voice to young people's views, identified a range of needs and highlighted service issues, their findings for practice were inevitably limited in scope. Small-scale exploratory studies continue to open up new areas for further investigation – for example, in relation to health (Saunders and Broad 1997) and disability (Rabiee, Priestley and Knowles 2001).

Research undertaken since 1990 provides a broader range of evidence. These have included larger-scale surveys of care-leavers (for example, Biehal *et al.* 1992; Garnett 1992) that, although unable to address the question of service effectiveness, did begin to map more systematically the characteristics of care-leavers and the patterns and outcomes associated with leaving care. Descriptive surveys of care providers (Fry 1992) and of specialist leaving care services have also been undertaken (Broad 1994, 1998; Stein and Wade 2000), providing some evidence about the role of foster carers and of issues associated with providing specialist services. In addition, findings from single and multi-site evaluations of leaving care projects can provide a useful source of information (for example, Smith 1994; Stone 1990). However, some caution must be exercised when considering the robustness of findings from project evaluations in the leaving care field. These evaluations have rarely adopted a 'before and after' methodology designed to assess change in participants and to relate starting points to outcomes. They have tended to be partly descriptive, describing services provided, models of delivery and work undertaken, and partly evaluative, assessing costs, user destinations and client satisfaction with services (Stein 1997, 2002).

Very few studies have adopted an explicit comparative design. Biehal *et al.*'s (1995) study of leaving schemes compared a group of young people receiving scheme services with a naturally occurring group of care-leavers who were not in touch with these specialist schemes. The study represented an early attempt to grapple with the outcomes achieved by specialist services. Another study drew on cohort data from the National Child Development Study (NCDS) to compare educational and employment outcomes in adulthood for those within the cohort who had experienced care with those who had not, and provided evidence of a long-term negative legacy of care (Cheung and Heath 1994). More studies of this kind will be needed if we are to improve our understanding of outcomes for young people leaving public care and of the effectiveness of services designed to help them.

Finally, information can be drawn from more 'official' sources of data. These include inspections of leaving care services (Department of Health 1997), thematic reviews of local authority data submitted to government (Department of Health 2000c; Robbins 2001) and from guidance and regulations associated with the Children Act 1989 (Department of Health 1991) and the new Children (Leaving Care) Act 2000 (Department of Health 2001c). The interpretation of this type of information requires caution, since it inevitably carries the imprimatur of government and the accuracy of data provided by local authorities are uncertain. However, it can be used to help gauge service developments and major service issues and forms part of the mix through which we can assess the current state of policy and practice in leaving care.

Evidence of Programme Effectiveness

The provision of support for young people leaving care rests on an extension of the principles of corporate parenting enshrined in the Children Act 1989. As such, it should approximate the care and attention given to young people approaching the transition to adulthood by their families. The review of evidence that follows will focus on five core areas essential to a successful transition – transition planning, accommodation, education and employment, health and social support.

Transition Planning

Young people leave care at a much earlier age than young people in the wider population leave home (Biehal *et al.* 1992; Garnett 1992). A majority will move to independent living before the age of 18 compared to fewer than one in ten of their peers (Jones 1995). Why this should be is not fully understood. However, Biehal *et al.* (1995) found that, while some young people were attracted to the freedom of independent living, factors such as placement breakdown, lack of alternative placements, challenging behaviour from young people and staff expectations often led to accelerated departures.

In addition to leaving early, the main elements of the transition to adulthood tend to be compressed. While youth transitions have generally become more extended (Furlong and Cartmel 1997; Jones 1995), for young people leaving care, learning to manage a new home or starting a career or their own family tend to overlap soon after leaving. The high level of parenthood amongst care-leavers has been consistently highlighted in the literature and links to patterns of early family formation (Biehal *et al.* 1992; Corlyon and McGuire 1997; Dixon and Stein 2002; Garnett 1992). Young people leaving care are therefore expected to shoulder a broader range of responsibilities far earlier than is common for their peers.

The preparation that young people have received to equip them for this journey has tended to be variable in quality and unsystematic (Clayden and Stein 1996; Stein and Carey 1986). In addition, leaving care planning has not always been consistent or, in some circumstances, possible. For example, in one study, placement breakdown precipitated an accelerated departure for around one third of those who left care before the age of 18 (Biehal *et al.* 1995). Furthermore, a small-scale study has highlighted the planning blight that can create uncertainty and confusion for disabled care-leavers, the authors concluding that 'It is not uncommon for looked after disabled young people, including those with the most complex impairments and health needs, to reach the age of 18 without the completion of any formal planning for adult services' (Rabiee *et al.* 2001, p.61).

Few studies have focused on what makes for effective preparation. Evidence from research and evaluations of practice suggest that preparation for adult life may be best achieved in the environment of a stable placement, allowing for the gradual development of skills, negotiation and appropriate risk taking, where there is continuity in important links and relationships, where educational progress is encouraged and where it is formally integrated into child-care planning (Clayden and Stein 1996; Stein and Wade 2000). There is also evidence that specialist leaving care schemes can contribute at the preparation stage and offer valuable life skills support once young people have moved on (Clayden and Stein 1996).

Interpersonal skills and identity issues have often been overlooked in preparation (Stein 1997). Helping young people to develop relationships and build self-esteem through knowledge of their personal histories and that of their families, cultures and communities – an area where black young people have experienced particular disadvantage when links have been allowed to erode (First Key 1987; Ince 1999) – are as vital as acquiring practical and financial skills (Department of Health 2001c).

New duties in the CLCA to assess and meet the needs of young people should help to ensure that a full audit is undertaken of young people's skills and abilities before leaving care and pathway planning is intended to improve the consistency and coordination of subsequent support. Evidence from research and practice review suggests that it is helpful for leaving care planning to start early and proceed at the young person's pace, for it to assess the young person's needs in a rounded way and in the context of their lives and for it to ensure that the young person is clearly signposted to future sources of support and how to access them (Biehal *et al.* 1995; Stein and Wade 2000). Early planning for disabled young people aimed at removing disabling barriers to independent living is both required and, in the light of evidence, particularly necessary (Rabiee *et al.* 2001).

Accommodation

Studies across the UK have pointed to the high mobility of young people after leaving care and to a heightened risk of homelessness (Biehal *et al.* 1995; Dixon and Stein 2002; Pinkerton and McCrea 1999). Surveys of young homeless people using hostels have also highlighted the overrepresentation of young people with experience of care in their samples (Smith *et al.* 1996; Strathdee and Johnson 1994).

Concern at the vulnerability of care-leavers has been reflected in recent homelessness legislation by including them amongst groups deemed in priority need. In addition, the Quality Protects initiative requires local authorities to maximize the number of care-leavers in good quality accommodation. However, and despite these concerns, it is important to remember that care-leavers form a heterogeneous population whose accommodation needs are likely to differ according to their past experiences, current wishes and abilities.

Specialist leaving care schemes have been shown to be successful in developing a broad range of supported and independent accommodation options for young people and in providing continuing support to help young people maintain their homes (Biehal and Wade 1999; Broad 1998; Stein 1990; Stone 1990). However, it is also the case that difficulties in the supply of accommodation, and problems with the quality of that which is available and with providing suitable specialist accommodation for young people with particular needs, are a continuing source of frustration for local authorities (Broad 1998; Department of Health 2000c).

Although evaluation evidence is limited, what there is suggests that it is helpful to avoid moving young people who are settled (including where they are in settled foster placements) and to avoid unplanned moves. Planning for accommodation is also helped where there is a careful assessment of a young person's needs, time to prepare, where there is some choice in the type and location of accommodation and a clear financial and support plan (Hutson 1995, 1997). Young people's adjustment may be helped where they are housed close to important family, community or cultural supports (Biehal *et al.* 1995) and careful planning is necessary for young disabled people to maximize opportunities for independent living or to prevent an abrupt transfer from children's to adult services (Rabiee *et al.* 2001). Pathway plans should also include contingency arrangements in the event that young people experience a crisis in their ability to manage and should include an option to return to more sheltered accommodation where necessary (Department of Health 2001c).

Education and Employment

A depressingly consistent finding from the literature on leaving care concerns the poor educational attainment and economic participation of formerly looked-after young people (Aldgate *et al.* 1993; Biehal *et al.* 1992; Broad 1998; Cook 1994; Festinger 1983; Jackson 1994; Pinkerton and McCrea 1999; Raychuba 1987; Stein and Carey 1986). Government statistics for the year 2000/2001 in England suggest that 63 per cent of young people left care with no qualifications at GCSE/GNVQ level (General Certificate of Secondary Education and General National Vocational Qualification) and just 5 per cent left with five or more GCSEs at grades A–C (Department of Health 2001b).[3] In the same year only around one half (47%) of care-leavers were known to be in education, work or training at age 19 (Department of Health 2002d). Raising the educational attainment and economic performance of looked-after young people is a key objective for Quality Protects and these statistics point to the scale of the challenge that lies ahead.

There is also evidence of a long-lasting legacy from care into adulthood. Cheung and Heath (1994) used data from the NCDS cohort study of 17,000 children born in 1958 (and regularly followed up) to compare those adults with past experience of care to those within the cohort who had never been in care. They found that those with care experience had lower educational attainment and, even where they did have qualifications, these tended to be at a lower level. In relation to economic activity, they were more likely to be unemployed and, if not, were more likely to be in semi-skilled or unskilled employment. Even when they controlled for social origin (economic disadvantage), the distinct disadvantage of those with a care background remained.

Our understanding of why educational attainment is so poor is less certain. Evidence points to the effects of poor early family experiences, of disorientation, movement and disruption, of school non-attendance and exclusion and of the low social work priority given to education. There is some evidence that those who do better educationally tend to be female, to have been looked after longer, most often in foster settings, to have had fairly settled care careers and active encouragement from those around them (Biehal et al. 1995; Robbins 2001). Providing young people with a stable and positive experience while they are looked after, one that can provide a foundation for educational progress, is therefore likely to be very influential for effective careers planning at the leaving care stage.

Findings from research and inspections have found that initiatives to promote education, training and employment opportunities for care-leavers have, until recently, been limited (Biehal et al. 1995; Broad 1998; Department of Health 1997). However, recent reviews of practice developments are more encouraging, even though most have not as yet been evaluated to assess their effectiveness. Initiatives include the creation of specialist education posts and secondments within social work teams, multi-agency steering groups to coordinate access, support and to monitor outcomes, formal partnerships to develop education and/or work experience projects, mentoring and financial support and incentives schemes (Department of Health 2000c; Stein and Wade 2000).

At the leaving care stage, many young people will lack skills and confidence. They will need help to identify their strengths and weaknesses and to prepare them for education, work or training. Continuing contact and support can provide encouragement, help with motivation and provide a channel for financial assistance to those who may wish to return to education some time after leaving care (Smith 1994).

Health

Until recently, the health needs of young people leaving care have been neglected in research and practice (Stein and Wade 2000). However, there is growing evidence of need. Studies have pointed to the high incidence of emotional and behavioural disturbance amongst young people referred to social services (Sinclair *et al.* 1995a; Triseliotis *et al.* 1995b) and, in comparison with non-care peers, to far higher levels of recognized psychiatric disorders amongst looked-after children (McCann *et al.* 1996). The response to these health needs has been at best patchy. There has been evidence of a low take-up of statutory medical examinations (Mather, Humphrey and Robson 1997), of poor health record-keeping (Department of Health 1997) and, especially in relation to children's homes, of limited opportunities for young people to access counselling or other specialist health services (Berridge and Brodie 1998; Farmer and Pollock 1998).

Surveys of care-leavers, though mostly small in scale, have found high levels of smoking, drug and alcohol use, chronic physical conditions and mental health problems, including self-harming and attempted suicides (Saunders and Broad 1997; Smith 1998). The tendency for early parenthood also points to needs around sexual relationships and sexual health and there is evidence that young people may be deterred from active pursuit of leisure interests due to the costs involved (Broad 1999; Department of Health 1997).

Given the relative neglect of health and lifestyle issues, the evidence base necessary to guide practice is limited. Guidance to the CLCA states that pathway plans should become a vehicle for assessing and monitoring health needs and for promoting healthy lifestyles (Department of Health 2001c). However, there is some evidence that this may not work unless young people's own health concerns are listened to more carefully, they are more fully involved in health planning, their rights to confidentiality are more readily respected and access to primary and specialist health services can become more flexible and user friendly (Broad 1999; Farmer and Pollock 1998; Mather *et al.* 1997).

Evidence from best practice points to the value of partnerships with health professionals to provide and deliver accessible information on leisure, sexual health, sexuality, the needs of learning disabled and physically disabled young people and on the health, cultural and dietary needs of young people from minority ethnic communities (Stein and Wade 2000). Recent reviews of Quality Protects management action plans, while drawing attention to the low starting point of many authorities, especially with regard to disability and mental health services, point to recent developments that may be helpful. These include the emergence of multidisciplinary health and social work teams or secondments, formal partnerships with Health Promotions teams, peer education schemes and initiatives around sexual health and teenage pregnancy (Department of Health 2000c; Robbins 2001).

Social Support

The accelerated transition to adulthood experienced by young people leaving care and the disadvantages they face suggest that many will not make a successful journey without a strong network of social support from social workers, family and friends. Yet studies carried out during the 1990s consistently found a tendency for planned social work support to fall away soon after young people left care (Biehal *et al.* 1992; Garnett 1992; Pinkerton and McCrea 1999).

Quality Protects and the CLCA require local authorities to stay in touch with those leaving their care and personal advisors have responsibility for coordinating networks of support to assist these young people. Pathway planning should explore all sources of potential support for young people, including that from family, friends, past carers, social workers, specialist schemes and from other professionals (Department of Health 2001c). If undertaken thoroughly, this may help to provide continuity for young people, assist staying in touch and reduce the risk of social isolation.

Further attention should be paid to exploiting the potential of family support. While leaving care is a time when young people often actively attempt to renegotiate family relationships and seek renewed support, family mediation has rarely been a priority for social work activity at that stage (Biehal and Wade 1996). Leaving care planning has also tended to exclude the potential from extended family members. Research has found that many young people are aware of being part of an extended family network, are quite realistic about the support that might be available from its different components and often identify members beyond the immediate family as their key kin (Marsh and Peel 1999). Social workers, however, are often unaware of key kin and fail to include them when planning support.

The potential for support from past foster carers and residential workers has also been under-utilized. Relatively few young people are able to continue living with foster carers after leaving care and only around one in three have continued to receive support after moving on (Fry 1992; Wade 1997). Where foster carers have continued to provide support, they have often had to do so in their own time. Given the importance of stability and continuity, the provision of modest funding could help to ensure a larger role for foster carers and residential workers in the leaving care process.

Inspections and reviews have also found that authorities that have invested in specialist leaving care schemes tend to have more comprehensive, effective and age-appropriate services for care-leavers (Department of Health 1997, 2000c). Specialist schemes can help young people to form new links and relationships. Provision of social groups and drop-ins, guidance on social and relationship skills and links with youth and leisure provision can help care-leavers combat isolation and strengthen their resistance to exploitation by others (Biehal *et al.* 1995). The informality of schemes is valued by young people and may therefore assist them to stay in touch or return for help when it is needed.

From the early 1980s, growing awareness of the problems faced by young people led to the steady growth of leaving care schemes (Bonnerjea 1990; Stone 1990). Evidence from research and inspections suggests that specialist services tend to make a helpful contribution to the coordination of leaving care policies and services, to the provision of direct support to young people and to the development of wider resources to assist them (Biehal *et al.* 1995; Broad 1998; Department of Health 1997). Specialist schemes can also help to improve outcomes for young people – one study finding that, in overall terms, three-quarters of scheme users over a period of 18–24 months had made positive progress relative to their starting points (Biehal *et al.* 1995).

Effectiveness for all Children and Young People

Very little is currently known about what makes for effective support services for particular groups of young people leaving care. As yet studies of sufficient rigour have not been completed. With respect to gender, what little evidence there is suggests that there are more similarities than differences in their experiences of leaving care, although females may do slightly better in areas such as education and life skills (Biehal *et al.* 1995). Although isolated, relatively small-scale studies have been completed on black youth (First Key 1987; Ince 1999), young parents (Corlyon and McGuire 1997) and on young disabled people (Rabiee *et al.* 2001), which have opened up their needs for further investigation; these need to be followed up more systematically. The needs of young people with mental health issues and, more recently, of young people who arrived as unaccompanied minors, have also been neglected in research terms. Generic studies of leaving care, even when they have attempted over-sampling (Biehal *et al.* 1995), have tended to have little to say about the experiences of specific groups and it is unlikely that practice guidance can be developed without more targeted research.

Conclusion

It should be apparent from this review of leaving care research in the UK that, at least at present, we know far more about the problems and risks young people may face and, in this sense, about what does not work well, than we do about what forms of support are effective in helping young people through the transition to adulthood. The consistency of these findings over time and in different countries gives them persuasive force.

Research on effective interventions is undoubtedly at an early stage. It is only in the past decade that we have begun to develop an understanding of outcomes in child care and of strategies that can be used to assess them (Parker *et al* 1991; Ward 1995). As we have seen, there have been very few studies in the UK that have adopted a comparative or quasi-experimental design in an attempt to disentangle the relationship between experiences, support and outcomes, and there have been no experimental studies in this field. It is also the case that studies have seldom been replicated, or adopted similar sampling, in order to test the rigour of earlier findings. Furthermore, our reading of earlier findings must be tempered by an awareness that services change over time, perhaps never more so than in the current context, and that findings generated in one era may be less applicable in another.

While these considerations suggest a need for caution when linking research to practice, it is also the case that evidence from research and practice evaluations have generated some consistent themes that, in themselves, present significant challenges to the resources and organization of the looked-after system, many of which have been picked up in the new legislation and guidance. First, this body of work has highlighted the early age at which young people leave care and the complex and demanding responsibilities that are placed on them, many of whom are ill equipped to cope. Can this be realistic? Whether it is or not, how best can young people be helped? This evidence points to the importance of delaying transitions until young people are ready to leave, which has significant implications for resourcing placements, of providing a range of intermediate supported options and of improving the consistency and quality of preparation for adult life that takes place. The absence of research with a specific focus on preparation has hindered an understanding of 'what works' in this regard.

Second, by connecting leaving care careers to young people's careers while looked-after, research has reinforced the value of a stable and positive looked-after experience. Stability, positive attachments and educational experiences, providing continuity in important links and relationships with carers, social workers, family and friends should be, in many respects, the foundation for all that follows. Third, it has identified the value of well-planned and supported transitions that can help to reduce the incidence of abrupt or accelerated departures and provide longer-term support. It is to be hoped that the introduction of pathway planning will provide a vehicle for ensuring greater consistency and quality of support. Finally, there is evidence of the contribution that can be made by specialist leaving care services. This suggests that their accumulated expertise, flexible style of working and ability to engage with disaffected young people can be of particular value and may encourage young people who reject initial help to return when they need it.

However, there is undoubtedly need for a more robust evidence base to support policy and practice in leaving care. We need to know more about what types of support appear to work for particular groups of young people in different contexts. While experimental designs based on random allocation may not be appropriate on grounds of ethics and feasibility, it should be possible to exploit naturally occurring groups of young people to develop systematic and comparative evaluations of services. It should also be possible to take forward comparisons of outcome utilizing matched samples of young people who have not been looked after. For example, it would be valuable to know whether and in what ways outcomes for young people who have been 'in need' but not looked after differ from those who have. Studies of this kind would help us to isolate more clearly the extent of a care effect and how it might be remedied. Most follow-up studies have also tended to be relatively short term and, in consequence, miss out on factors associated with adjustment in later adulthood. Longitudinal studies, perhaps utilizing existing data sets, would help us to understand more about the factors that appear to make a difference when comparing those who do well with those who do not.

There is a need to focus more clearly on particular areas of need that have been under-researched, such as health, and, as indicated above, to focus on particular groups of young people leaving care who have been relatively invisible in research terms. Finally, given its intended scope and impact, the operation of the new legislation will require careful monitoring. Although some assessment has been made of the first one or two years of implementation (Broad 2003; Hai and Williams 2004), longer-term follow-up will be necessary to evaluate the extent to which it does help to improve outcomes, generate greater consistency in the support arrangements for young people leaving care and the degree to which it is able to match the ambitions that young people leaving care have for themselves.

Notes

1. During the year ending 31 March 2003 6500 young people aged 16 or over formally ceased to be looked after. One half were aged 16 or 17 and 49 per cent were formally discharged on their 18th birthday (Department for Education and Skills 2004a).

2. Scotland and Northern Ireland represent separate jurisdictions within the UK. Although similar leaving care legislation has been implemented in these countries, it will not be considered here.

3. General Certificate of Secondary Education and General National Vocational Qualification. This level of attainment compares very unfavourably with government data on national attainment for 2000 for pupils aged 15 – just 5.5 per cent failed to attain a pass at GCSE/GNVQ level in that year and 50 per cent attained five or more (Department for Education and Skills 2001).

CHAPTER 19

Support for Young People Leaving Care in the US

Kimberly A. Nollan

Introduction

Between 18,000 and 20,000 youths ages 16 and older transition from foster care (family foster homes, group homes, residential care, emergency shelters, child-care institutions, and pre-adoptive homes) in the United States each year. In general, the findings of several outcome studies indicate youths placed in foster care do less well than their peers in the general population in such areas as high school completion rates (Barth 1990; Cook 1994; Cook *et al.* 1991; Courtney and Dworsky 2005; Dworsky and Courtney 2000; Festinger 1983; Jones and Moses 1984; McMillen and Tucker 1999; Pecora *et al.* 2003a, 2005; Zimmerman 1982), and employment (Cook 1994; Cook, McLean and Ansell 1989; Goerge *et al.* 2002; McMillen and Tucker 1999; Pecora *et al.* 2005; Triseliotis and Russell 1984), and experience higher incidences of homelessness than their peers (Susser *et al.* 1991).

The disruptions and traumas often suffered by youth in out-of-home care may result in delays or interruptions in the development of life skills needed for successful transition to independent living from out-of-home care. Additionally, inadequate and ineffective life skills training hinders youth preparedness for independence.[1] However, we expect these youths to live without system support at age 18, earlier than their counterparts in the general population who grow up with their families.

In 1999, the John Chafee Foster Care Independence Act of 1999 (P.L. 106-169) doubled from $70 million to $140 million the funds available for Independent Living programs and expanded state flexibility in the use of funds for living and medical expenses and mentoring. Outcome measures to assess state performance in areas like educational attainment, employment, avoidance of dependency and homelessness are being developed and will be required of care providers. The new law also requires that young people enrolled in Independent Living programs directly participate in the design of their own program goals and activities. Finally, it is required that performance measurement and rigorous evaluation of independent living programs be conducted (National Foster Care Awareness Project 2000).

Supportive Interventions

From research and theoretical literature, four effective and related strategies recommended in preparing youths for self-sufficiency emerge:

1. systematic skills assessment

2. independent living skills training (including education and employment)

3. involvement of youth and caregivers in the planning and implementation of the training

4. developing birth family and other community connections (Muskie School of Public Service 1998; Sheehy *et al.* 2002).[2]

Systematic Skills Assessment

Recognition of the importance of identifying gaps in youths' learning and youths' strengths through systematic skills assessment is growing. One study found that, depending on the skills tested, anywhere from one fifth to one third of youths placed in out-of-home care were in serious need of specialized services, independent living planning, follow-up, and/or aftercare (Hahn 1994). The former and current Independent Living laws and the Council on Accreditation Standard S23.7.05 recommend systematic skills assessment to document the competency levels of youths. Systematic skills assessment helps with development of a specific plan based on the individual's strengths and deficits and involves foster parents, youths and birth parents (if available) in the assessment and teaching processes.

There are a variety of instruments designed to measure life skills. Many were developed to use with youths with disabilities (e.g., *The Scales of Independent Behavior*, Bruininks *et al.* 1984). Others do not have known psychometric properties. A promising assessment is the Ansell–Casey Life Skills Assessment (ACLSA) (see Nollan *et al.* 2002a and www.caseylifeskills.org).

The ACLSA is a brief, developmental (for children aged eight and older) measure of life skills acquisition across several domains, available in youth self-report and caregiver report formats. The ACSLA has good psychometric properties and is useful as a research tool. It was originally designed as a practice tool to provide a snapshot of youth ability and knowledge, and start a conversation between the youth and appropriate caregivers. Thirty-eight states either require or prefer the ACLSA as part of their work in transition services. The assessments are designed as the *first step* in preparing youth for living on their own. Other steps include goal setting, action planning, instruction, learning, and application, followed again by assessment to measure progress.

Independent Living Skills Training

After assessment, focused skills training can occur, which is the second strategy in preparing youths for self-sufficiency. Training is recommended to better prepare youths for adulthood and is positively related to job maintenance, adequate health care, economic independence, and general satisfaction with life (Austin and Johnston 1995; Cook 1994; English, Kouidou-Giles and Plocke 1994; McMillen *et al.* 1997; McMillen and Tucker 1999; Muskie School of Public Service 1998; Scannapieco, Schagrin and Scannapieco 1995).

One example of a training tool is the *Life Skills Guidebook* (Guidebook), used for goal setting and action planning, as well as teaching, learning and applying of skills. The Guidebook provides Learning Goals (competencies), Expectations (behavioral indicators of the Learning Goals), and Activities that youths and parents, teachers or social workers can use to further explore youths' readiness to live on their own, set goals and develop plans. The Guidebook incorporates the Continuum of Independent Living Preparation as described by Cook *et al.* (1989): informal learning, formal learning, supervised practice living, and self-sufficiency.

Involving Youths and Caregivers

Youths and caregivers are more invested in the life skills learning process when they are involved in all aspects of it, which is the third strategy effective in preparing youths to live on their own (Nollan *et al.* 2002). It is critical to involve youths in the development and implementation of their Independent Living plans. Involving the youth and caregiver as integral players can have far-reaching effects on preparing youths for living on their own, and models the belief that young people can make good decisions for themselves. Not only is the relationship between the caregiver and youth strengthened, but youths will have a more realistic picture of what they need to know before living on their own (Nollan *et al.* 2000; Taber and Proch 1988).

A caregiver or other significant adult in the youth's life can offer skills training formally as part of an independent living group or program and also informally, utilizing strategies like "teachable moments" (Wolf, Copeland and Nollan 1998), which is the third recommended intervention. Social support networks for youths are often disrupted by placement (and events leading to placement) and need to be rebuilt. Caregivers can often be a vital part of a young person's support network because many youths stay in contact with their foster parents after leaving care (Courtney *et al.* 2001; English *et al.* 1994; Jones and Moses 1984).

In addition, youths reported that foster parents eased the transition out of care (McMillen *et al.* 1997). The Foster Care Independence Act of 1999 (P.L. 106-169), requires states to use Title IV-E training funds to train adoptive and foster parents, which is critical for them to be effective teachers of life skills, as are awareness of the range of life skills that promote independence, and being able to measure these life skills (Wolf *et al.* 1998). There are a variety of advantages of using caregivers as the primary life skills teachers (Mech and Fung 1999). For example, caregivers can coach and model appropriate behaviors in real situations; skills can be taught incrementally and can be tailored to the youth's unique strengths and needs; skills can be practiced in a safe environment; and progress can be regularly reinforced (Ryan *et al.* 1988).

Developing Community Connections

In addition to connections with foster parents, the development of other community connections is needed to help young people as they support themselves economically. Community connections help replace the youth's reliance on the agency for support, as well as help them address and resolve feelings of grief, loss, and rejection (Ryan *et al.* 1988). Community contacts are also needed for securing jobs and receiving support in retaining them. The risk and resiliency literature as well as some foster care research show that having a positive strong relationship with an adult in and after care is related to positive outcomes and is important to aftercare success (Cook 1994; Mallon 1998; Muskie School of Public Service 1998; Nollan 1996; Pecora *et al.* 2003a, 2003c; Sheehy *et al.* 2002; Werner 1989). In particular, connections to the birth family are also important to consider during life skills assessment and training because youths tend to turn to their birth families for support once they leave care (Courtney *et al.* 2001; Jones and Moses 1984; Zimmerman 1982). In addition, even when youths grow up in high risk environments, they are more likely to have positive outcomes when they experience a relationship with a caring adult (Werner 1989).

Theory Base

The recommended areas of intervention (assessment, teaching, youth and caregiver involvement, and community connections) are based on Erikson's developmental theory (e.g., Erikson 1968), attachment theory (e.g., McMillen 1992), the risk and resiliency literature (e.g., Rutter 1987a; Werner 1989), positive youth development literature, and the ecological perspective (Bronfenbrenner 1979). (See Table 19.1, Nollan 1996, and Collins 2001 for a more detailed summary.) Human development theory offers a framework for understanding some of the barriers that youths face when working to resolve issues of past stages. It suggests that variables like age and gender, as well as different risk factors (e.g., removal from the birth family) affect identity achievement and future development. In addition, this theory guides the appropriateness of different life skills to be learned at different ages.

Table 19.1: Theoretical underpinnings of recommended interventions for helping older youth

Intervention	Attachment theory	Risk and protective factor	Positive youth development	Developmental theory	Ecological perspective
Assessment			X	X	X
Independent living skills training			X	X	X
Caregiver involvement	X	X			X
Community connections	X	X			X

Attachment theory offers a framework for understanding the different emotions and issues facing youths as they prepare for self-sufficiency. It points to the need for involving caregivers and birth family, as well as helping youths develop a social support system. Additionally, it suggests that certain protective factors (such as bonds between birth parents and the youth) may moderate attachments and life skills. The risk and protective factor literature further clarifies some of the different factors which may influence interdependent living (see Glantz and Johnson 1999; Nollan et al. 2002). Promotion of these protective factors (identified through assessment) is important.

The ecological perspective focuses assessment to take into account factors at different levels (e.g., microsystem, mesosystem) of the youth's environment and suggests the inclusion of multiple people in the assessment, goal setting, and plan development and implementation. The ecological perspective supports the need for assessment of not only the youth's individualized skills, but also of potential micro- and meso-level protective factors like quality of family relationships. In addition, the suggested interventions rely on the literature around Positive Youth Development which recommends youths taking increasing responsibility for their lives as they grow older.

Evidence of Program Effectiveness

Much of the evidence base about service delivery effectiveness is derived from follow-up outcomes studies. It is limited due to small sample sizes, lack of standardized measures, lack of comparison groups, non-random assignment and few rigorous qualitative studies. The majority of studies providing intervention evidence occur at discharge or shortly thereafter.

The research falls generally into two categories: those that seek to establish a correlational or non-causal relationship between receipt of services and outcomes (e.g., Cook *et al.* 1991; Lindsey and Ahmend 1999; Mech, Ludy-Dobson and Hulseman 1994); and those which evaluate a particular program or approach to providing independent living services (e.g., Mallon 1998; Scannapieco *et al.* 1995; Waldinger and Furman 1994).

Until more robust studies are completed, practitioners, policymakers, and caregivers will rely on summarized promising approaches, practice wisdom, and the few outcomes studies that currently exist. The overall implication of this is that more rigorous studies are needed to identify and validate different practice approaches and interventions. Specifically, it is recommended that evaluation efforts document services, costs, and short- and long-term outcomes, and that they use a comparison or control group (randomly assigned when possible), larger sample sizes and standard measures. These studies will inform practitioners, policymakers, and youths and caregivers. Next, specific evidence addressing intervention effectiveness is reviewed.

The Evidence on Effectiveness

There is some emerging consensus about what approaches to practice best prepare youths for living on their own. Preliminary studies suggest the four interventions of assessment, life skill instruction, youth and caregiver involvement, and community connections have a positive impact, especially when the focus of them is education, employment, housing, and life skills development. While the long-term impact of many of these strategies is not yet known, generally, higher levels of educational achievement and independent living training were related to employment success, greater housing stability, lower levels of public assistance usage, and greater ability of the youth to take care of themselves (Cook *et al.* 1991; Dworsky and Courtney 2000; Iglehart 1994; Lindsey and Ahmed 1999; Mech 1994; Pecora *et al.* 2003a). For a more thorough review of the foster care outcomes literature see for example McDonald *et al.* (1996), Nollan (1996), or Pecora *et al.* (2003a).

Box 19.1 summarizes several studies which suggest support for the different interventions. A few studies documented the use of assessment as an intervention (e.g., Hoge and Idalski 1999; Leibold and Downs 2002a, 2002b). Most studies focused on receipt of some type of independent living services or participation in an independent living program and the effect on educational attainment, employment and being a cost to the community at discharge or within a short time thereafter. None of the studies reviewed lent empirical evidence to the effectiveness of involving youths and caregivers in the independent living preparation process, although practice wisdom supports this intervention. The studies supporting birth family and community connections suggest mentoring or connection to a caring adult is positively related to living successfully as an adult.

Box 19.1 Summary of the Effectiveness of Different Types of interventions

Assessment

1. *Supervised Independent Living Program at Boysville* (Hoge and Idalski 1999)

    Design: Assessment at discharge, three- and twelve-month follow-up.

    Intervention: assessment, placement, treatment plan, independent living skills instruction (along with opportunities to practice), supervision, and community relations.

    Results: At three months 87 percent lived at home, 29 percent were enrolled in school, 55 percent were either full- or part-time employed, and 95 percent lived law-abiding lifestyles. At 12 months 90 percent lived at home, 19 percent were enrolled in school, 77 percent were employed full- or part-time, and 87 percent lived legal lifestyle.

2. *San Antonio Preparation for Adult Living, Casey Family Programs* (Leibold and Downs 2002a)

    Design: ACLSA administered as a pre- and post-test to youth (N =101) enrolled in PAL classes.

    Intervention: Life Skills training focused on personal and interpersonal skills, housing and transportation, planning for the future, job skills, personal health care, and money management.

    Results: Life Skills mastery scores on the ACLSA increased after youths completed the PAL program, indicating that the life skills training program was effective.

---

3.   *Stepping Stones Life Skills Program, Casey Family Programs, Rapid City, SC* (Leibold and Downs 2002b)

Design: Pre- and post-assessment (N=197).

Intervention: Life skills classes, independent living experience, scattered site housing, individual services and assessment.

Results: Assessment scores increased significantly after completion of life skills classes, 61 percent were regularly employed, and 87 percent were enrolled in school or completed a degree.

4.   *Green Chimneys* (Mallon 1998)

Design: Data collected at intake, discharge and follow-up (six months or more post-discharge) (N=46).

Intervention: Assessment, weekly counseling, weekly participation in a life skills course using a structure life skills curriculum.

Results: 75 percent completed high school or equivalent; 72 percent had full-time employment at discharge; 78 percent had employment by follow-up; 65 percent had savings at discharge and 39 percent had savings at follow-up. Life skills scores increased from intake to discharge; 96 percent had at least one person who provided a strong close relationship suggesting those who have supportive relationships after discharge are more likely to be functioning well after care than those who don't. Supports include family, relatives, friends, community resources and agency/program services.

5.   *The Independent Living Program, Maryland* (Scannapieco *et al.* 1995)

Design: Case record review of youths ages 16 and older who participated in Independent Living Programs (N=44) and were compared to youths who did not (N=46).

Intervention: A range of individual, group and family services; independent living plan based on assessment; personal counseling; advocacy; resource referral; life skills instruction and practice.

Results: Participants were more likely to complete high school, have employment history, be employed at discharge, and were more likely to be self-supporting at case closure than non-participants.

Independent Living Skills Instruction

6.   *The Work Appreciation for Youth Scholarship Program at Children's Village in Dobbs Ferry, New York* (Baker, Olson and Mincer 2000)

     Design: Outcomes comparison between youths who remained in the program, those who left early, a comparison group, and national comparison samples (N=93 participants and N=76 comparison).

     Intervention: Educational advocacy and tutoring, work experiences and work ethics training, group activities and workshops, financial incentives to help youth save, and counseling and mentoring.

     Results: Program completers had higher educational achievement than comparison group youths and as good or better achievement than various populations' generated from US Census data (including Black, Hispanic and special education in New York city, and children in poverty in the US).

7.   *Title IV-E Independent Living Programs for Youth in Foster Care* (Cook *et al.* 1991; Hoge and Idalski 1999)

     Design: Retrospective; youths aged 18 to 24 were interviewed 2.5 to 4 years after discharge from care (N= 810).

     Intervention: Receipt of Title IV-E monies and general foster care services.

     Results: When life skill training in the areas of money management, credit, consumer, education, and employment were provided in combination, they had positive effects on youths' overall ability to maintain a job for at least one year, obtain health care, not be a cost to the community; youths had a greater overall satisfaction with life.

8.   *Youth Emancipation Services (YES), San Diego, CA (Jones 2001)*

     Design: Data were collected pre- and post-treatment for treatment (N=28) and comparison (N=27) youths.

     Intervention: Independent living skills training, mentoring, case management, and employment internship.

     Results: Treatment youths at post-test had more mature work and study habits, were more optimistic about the future, and had more independent living skills than the comparison group. Three months' post-program completion, 95 percent were in school, working or both.

9. *Powerhouse, Casey Family Programs Collaborative, Portland, OR* (Lehman and O'Dell 2002; Leibold and Downs 2002a, 2002b)

   Design: Process and outcome evaluation of the community-based, collaborative effort to support the transition of youths from foster care to independent living (N=46).

   Intervention: Collaborative service coordination, continuum of housing, financial resources, community resource volunteer, establishment and maintenance of collaborative relationships.

   Results: Difficult to interpret because many youths were not located 6 and 12 months after discharge. Of those that were contacted (N=22), most had stable housing and half had stable employment.

10. *North Carolina Independent Living Program* (Lindsey and Ahmed 1999; Mallon 1998)

   Design: Stratified sampling, comparison of post-discharge outcomes between participants (N=44) and non-participants (N=32).

   Intervention: Independent living services beyond the federal required initial assessment.

   Results: Service participants were more likely to be living on their own, to complete high school or equivalent, to use public assistance, and sometimes to have difficulty paying bills (but fewer had these problems often) than non-participants.

11. *Missouri Division of Family Services* (McMillen and Tucker 1999)

   Design: Case record review from a randomly selected sample of youths (N=252).

   Intervention: Non-specific.

   Results: Most youths left without a job (62%) or high school diploma (61%). The most common living arrangement at the time of exit was with relatives. The number of placements and the completion of high school predicted employment status. High school completion was associated with age and history of inpatient psychiatric care, running away and mental disability.

12. *Casey Family Programs Alumni* (Pecora *et al.* 2003a; Scannapieco *et al.* 1995)

   Design: Case record review (N=1609) and interviews (N=1087) about the life experiences, educational achievements and current functioning of alumni.

Intervention: Range of counseling and other services over a long period of time, depending on the unique needs of the child.

Results: Life skills/independent living training and participation in clubs or organizations while in care were found to be some of the major predictors associated with adult success. Providing independent living training and a positive relationship between the child and foster parents was associated with high school completion.

Youth and Caregiver Involvement

13. *Child Trends* (2002) research brief reported that teens who have positive relationships with adults outside their families are more social and less depressed and have better relationships with their parents.

14. *The Fanshel, Finch and Grundy Study of Casey Alumni* (Fanshel *et al.* 1990)

    Design: Interviews of a non-random sample of 106 young adults who had been placed in Casey foster homes.

    Intervention: Individual, group and family services based on assessed need of the youth.

    Results: Most respondents (66%) were wage-earners, with 10 percent receiving public assistance. One third regarded their finances as inadequate. Of those working, about 83 percent were somewhat or very satisfied with their current jobs. Two-thirds still maintained contact with foster families. Achieving emancipation at case closure was negatively correlated with criminal activity. Connections to birth family and others in the community are important associations, because this is where youths tend to turn for support once they leave care and these resources can help youths address and resolve feelings of grief, loss, and rejection.

15. *Foster Care Youth United* (Baker *et al.* 2000; Pecora *et al.* 2003a) Children placed in foster care need a sense of their future and some role in decision making.

Community Connections

16. (Fein, Maluccio, and Kluger 1990; Hoge and Idalski 1999; Jones 2001; Mallon 1998) Maintaining some connection with birth families, as children are better able to modify their relationships with parents if they are not denied these relationships or expected to abandon them completely.

Future Directions

Practice

There are several service delivery ingredients recommended to effectively prepare youths for living on their own. First, youth strengths and weaknesses need to be accurately assessed by both the youth and a known caregiver. Second, life skills instruction and learning need to be offered using a complimentary set of competencies and activities that are compatible with assessment results. Third, youths need to be involved and empowered to set their own goals and achieve them as they consider living on their own and face the challenges associated with that. In addition, youths and caregivers need to be involved in teaching life skills. Fourth, relationships with others in the community need to be nurtured so the youth has a viable support system when they leave care.

Research

More work is needed to document the effectiveness of the interventions of assessment, youth and caregiver involvement and community connections, as well as to clarify which aspects of independent living training are particularly important for success. The Foster Care Independence Act of 1999 (P. L. 106-169) mandates evaluation of services for all states receiving federal independent living funds. There is evidence about the poor outcomes of youths emancipating from out-of-home care (e.g., lack of housing, low employment rates, poor academic success), but little is known about what services contribute to positive outcomes or youth strengths. Program evaluations need to measure immediate, short-term (6–12 months) and long-term (over a year) outcomes after program completion in a more uniform manner, nationally. Programs are encouraged to develop a common language to define the services provided and create uniformity of reporting (via, e.g., standardized reporting and assessment tools), document their activities, document costs, and utilize comparison groups.

Policy

Policy supporting more uniformity in data collection and reporting is needed. Outcomes research and service delivery effectiveness research are critical to policy formation. The lack of a national, uniform data collection system limits comparison between service delivery systems. This in turn results in policy based on non-representative samples. The Chafee Independent Living Evaluation Project may provide some of the rigor that is needed, by identifying programs that can be rigorously evaluated and developing evaluation designs that meet the requirements of authorization legislation. The effects of independent living programs should be assessed via both process (e.g., what and how services are delivered) and outcomes (e.g., educational attainment, employment rates, interpersonal and relational skills, non-married pregnancy rates, and delinquency and crime rates).

Conclusion

We are all dependent on one another for our survival and successful living in our world. Youths who spend time in the out-of-home care system are more likely to have weaker support systems and lower levels of preparedness for living on their own. This can result in lower education levels achieved, less stable work histories, greater reliance on public assistance, more incidences of homelessness, and many other undesirable life outcomes. In addition, youths who emancipate from out-of-home care frequently do so at often younger ages than their counterparts in the general population.

This chapter described four strategies for preparing youths for interdependent living that especially address the areas of housing, education, employment and life skill training:

1. systematic skills assessment

2. independent living skills training

3. involving caregivers and youths

4. developing birth family and other community connections. The theoretical underpinnings for these strategies stem from attachment theory, ecological perspective, risk and protective factor literature, positive youth development literature, and developmental theory. While the life skills intervention research literature for child welfare is in an early stage of development, it is building, useful evaluation instruments are being developed, and the wealth of research in education, vocational development, employment and other fields can be used to advance this work.

Notes

1. While it is recognized that no one truly lives "independently," the terms "independent living" or "self-sufficiency" are referred to as the ability to provide economically for oneself. *Interdependent* living is a more accurate description of a person's state of living on their own.

2. A system that incorporates the first three is free and online at www.caseylifeskills.org. The skills learned in this system will help in forming social support networks. This collection of tools and a description of how to use them will be covered briefly in this chapter. The reader is encouraged to visit the website to gather more complete information.

CHAPTER 20

Adoption in the UK

David Quinton and Julie Selwyn

Introduction

A chapter on effective interventions in adoption presents something of a challenge. In England, adoption involves the complete legal transference of parental responsibility from one set of parents to another. For the child it provides full legal membership of a family other than the one into which he/she was born. Up until very recently adoption in the UK has *itself* been seen as the intervention, with little attention paid to helping and support; for this reason alone there is remarkably little research in the UK about supporting adoptive families. Recent policy changes are designed to make a radical difference to this picture but, as yet, these policies have not been evaluated.

The Legislative and Policy Context

The use in the UK of adoption as a solution to the needs of children unlikely to return to their birth parents has changed dramatically since the mid-1970s, partly in response to changes from adoptions of 'illegitimate' babies to children adopted out of care, usually after infancy (Department of Health, Home Office and Department for Education and Employment 1999). In 1975 only 7 per cent of *all* adoptions were of children from the care system ('looked-after children'). By 2000, more than half of all children adopted had been looked after by local authorities prior to adoption, but this still represented only 5 per cent of the looked after population (Department of Health 2001a).

During this time the regard with which adoption has been held as a solution to meeting these children's needs has been subject to contradictory influences. During the 1970s and 1980s the two most important of these were the Children Act 1989 and the permanency movement. The Act emphasized the importance of keeping children with their birth families and reuniting them as soon as possible if receptions into public care occurred (Department of Health 2002a). The permanence movement stressed the other side of the picture; that to develop satisfactorily children needed stable permanent families and that this might need cessation of contact with their birth parents (Goldstein, Freud and Solnit 1980).

Perhaps for these reasons, the number of children adopted out of care declined between 1992 and 1996. At the same time there were concerns about the length of time some children were remaining looked after, their poor outcomes (Department of Health 2000d), the quality of adoption services (Social Services Inspectorate (SSI) 1996, 2000), the priority given to adoption, and wide variations in its use. As a response to this, a Department of Health circular to local authorities insisted that adoption should be in the mainstream of children's services and given a higher priority (Department of Health 1998c). The impact of the circular was almost immediate. The numbers of children adopted out of care began to rise and adoption became firmly established as a policy issue.

These changes were given formal weight in the Adoption and Children Bill, which passed into law in 2002, but with a phased introduction of certain provisions, together with National Standards, an Adoption Register to link children with prospective adopters and an Adoption and Permanency Taskforce, which works with authorities to improve standards. Public Sector Agreement (PSA) targets were set to encourage the use of adoption and speed up decision making.

Current Use of Adoption

There are signs that an increase in the use of adoption is happening. There has been a rise in the numbers of children adopted out of care from 2200 in 1998–1999 to 3800 in the year ending 31 March 2005 (Department for Education and Skills 2005c). A Department of Health (2002b) analysis of the trends concluded that decisions were being taken more speedily and that the average age of children placed for adoption was going down.

WHO GETS ADOPTED NOW?

Very few babies are now adopted from care. Only about 7 per cent are under the age of one, compared with 75 per cent in the 1960s. The majority are aged between one and four (60%), with 28 per cent aged five to nine and only 5 per cent aged ten or over. Since government intervention, the rise in the number of adoptions is largely of children in the one to four age group, which has seen a 25 per cent increase since 1996/97 (Department of Health 2002b).

The potential benefits from these policy changes need to be seen in the context of the poor experiences of the children now being adopted. When the Performance and Innovation Unit reported in 2000, these children were on average 4.4 years of age, had spent several years in care, were more likely to have been abused and neglected than the rest of the child-care population, had generally entered care early in their lives, and were unlikely to return home, but often experienced many placement moves before a decision for adoption was made (PIU 2000).

HOW MANY CHILDREN ARE WAITING FOR ADOPTION?

'Waiting' figures depend on when you start counting. The National Standards state that permanency plans have to be in place within four months of a child becoming looked after. If the plan is not for return home, then adoption should always be considered. As yet, there are no national statistics on 'waiting' children. Over a two-year period up to March 2003, 3200 children were entered on the register (Adoption Register 2003), mostly boys over age six, sibling groups, *all* children with special needs, and black and mixed parentage children. These data reinforce what is known about children who are harder to place (Collier, Hutchinson and Pearmain 2000).

The Nature of the Evidence

As pointed out earlier, there has, until recently, been an almost total lack of data, even in the short term, on the outcomes for children now being placed for adoption in the UK. Consequently, there is also a lack of systematic data on the effectiveness of support services or therapeutic interventions, or the effects of other changes, such at the increase in contact. Earlier follow-up studies of children adopted in infancy (reviewed below) show advantageous outcomes for the adopted over disadvantaged children who remain with their birth families, but these studies are not informative on outcomes from the adoptions now being made.

There are some recent well-sampled studies with a short-term prospective element and measurement of outcomes that have followed families over the first year of placement (Quinton *et al.* 1998; Rushton *et al.* 2001). These have good checks or representativeness but lack a true comparison with alternative kinds of placement. There are also some valuable retrospective studies with volunteer samples, but with the uncertainties inherent in such sampling methods and long-term recall (Howe 1997). The study by Selwyn and her colleagues is the first we know of to allow a comparison, using a catch-up prospective design, of outcomes from adoption and long-term foster care of children with similar experiential backgrounds (Selwyn *et al.* 2006).

Robustness of the Evidence

Before reviewing what these studies show, it is important to decide what we mean by 'outcomes', and with whom these are to be compared. The word 'outcome' is best used to mean where people have 'got to' in their lives in things like educational attainment or good personal relationships. Assessing this depends on whether we are interested in how close these outcomes are to some general population average, to the *degree of change* within a group or within individuals, or *in comparison* with people with similar adversities but different kinds of placement.

The obvious comparison with long-term foster care is problematic because, unlike adoptions, 'permanent' foster placements are seldom planned, so identifying a true comparison sample is very difficult. Long-term foster placements are also a rarity (Sinclair, Wilson and Gibbs 2000). For this reason children whose placements survive long term are likely to be atypical, a difference from adoption that will be increased if adoption holds on to children with problems more successfully. Finally, children in foster and adoptive placements may be different in the kind or severity of their needs but, at present, adequate systematic assessments are lacking. All UK studies that we know of rely on data gleaned from case files or the BAAF Form E – a commonly used tool to collect children's histories, developmental progress and placement needs.

For all these reasons, despite a few assertions to the contrary (Eeklaar 2003), there is no evidence on which to judge the comparative outcomes of planned long-term foster and adoptive placements, apart from studies of disruption rates, which show some advantages in favour of adoption (Triseliotis 2002).

Evidence on Program Effectiveness

The Structure of the Review

As we have pointed out, the evidence for the effectiveness of adoption as the intervention for children needing long-term substitute family care is very limited. Evidence on the effectiveness of other aspects of the intervention – such as contact – or specific supports and interventions is even sparser. This review deals first with what is known about the effectiveness of adoption itself as the intervention. We deal first with adoptions made in infancy and then with the adoption of older children, first as regards disruption and then on psychosocial outcomes. Following this we summarize current approaches to service interventions and supports and conclude with an account of the factors that do influence outcomes, as a guide to the development of service provision.

Outcomes of Adoption in Early Childhood

Most of our knowledge on the long-term effectiveness of adoption is based on studies of children adopted under the age of two and with less severe genetic and experiential vulnerabilities than those currently being placed. Nevertheless, these studies provide important information on how well adoption *can* work and on outcomes in adulthood, and – because placements were made before the contact movement developed – on long-term outcomes from early closed adoptions.

Most of this research is based on large national cohort or register samples and thus has the advantage of large and representative samples. These studies have consistently shown that psychosocial outcomes in adulthood are good (Bohman and Sigvardsson 1980). Not only do the adopted children do better on educational attainment, stability of relationships, self-esteem, mental health and substance misuse than children from similar socio-economic backgrounds, they also compare favourably with the general population (Collinshaw, Maughan and Pickles 1998; Maughan, Collishaw and Pickles 1998). The majority of those adopted as infants and their adoptive parents rate their experience of adoption as satisfactory and disrupted placements are rare, with disruption rates around 1 per cent (Bohman and Sigvardsson 1990; Holloway 1997).

Adopted infants are slightly more likely to show behavioural difficulties than children in birth families during adolescence (Fergusson, Lynskey and Horwood 1995; Maughan and Pickles 1990), although in most studies this excess is temporary. Adopted children are also somewhat overrepresented in psychiatric clinics (Hersov 1990; Howe and Hinings 1987; Warren 1992), but this seems to be because adopted children are more readily referred to mental health settings for minor problems (Brodzinsky 1993).

Variability of Outcomes from Infant Adoptions in Early Childhood

It is important to stress the large individual differences in recovery from apparently similar experiences. For example, children adopted from Romanian orphanages, mostly before the age of two, show remarkable physical and cognitive catch-up (Rutter and ERA study team 1998). On the other hand, at age six some of these children had difficulties in making relationships, were inattentive and impulsive, displayed autistic-like behaviours and had lower cognitive levels. The main risks to social development seemed to be a marked lack of early play and social interaction with caregivers. Even so, three-fifths of the children taken from the orphanages *after* the age of two were free of pervasive problems and over a fifth had no problems in *any* of seven assessed domains. The strongest predictor was the overall duration of institutional privation, a finding supported in other studies (Barth and Miller 2000; Verhulst, Althaus and Versluis-den-Bieman 1992), but none suggested a time when intervention is too late.

Outcomes of Adoptions Later in Childhood

DISRUPTION

There are very few UK studies of the effectiveness of adoption for children who now comprise the great majority adopted out of care. Before the late 1990s the majority of what studies there were focused on breakdown and disruption rather than on developmental and behavioural outcomes (Howe 1997), but even this outcome is often not measured from the same point in the adoption process. Some studies only include disruptions occurring after placement, whilst others include those occurring during matching as well. Follow-up periods, and thus the period at risk of disruption, also vary. Given this, it is not surprising that disruption estimates vary widely. If disruption is considered at any time during the adoption process (e.g. Seglow, Pringle and Wedge 1972) the figure lies between 1 percent and 50 percent, with the higher figure usually explained by placements in adolescence, and a commonly quoted average of about 25–30 percent.

Disruption is a crude measure of 'success' since placements may continue although children and adoptive parents are unhappy. Rushton and Dance (2004) noted that about a third of children still in placement at their six-year follow-up had problematic placements. Howe (1998) combined disruption rates, developmental measures and adopter satisfaction to produce a crude measure that suggested that 50–60 per cent of later adoptions are 'successful'. Of course, these estimates need to be set against the potential outcomes from other kinds of intervention.

PSYCHOSOCIAL OUTCOMES

Children adopted past infancy generally do worse on psychosocial measures than children in the general population or those adopted as babies (Hodges and Tizard 1989a, 1989b) but do better than those who remain in residential care, foster care or returned to their birth families (Hodges and Tizard 1989b; Thoburn 1990; Triseliotis 2002; Triseliotis and Hill 1990).

Prospective studies since the 1990s show that later-placed children's problem can persist for many years; a corrective to the over-optimism of the 1960s and 70s that a loving family could usually undo earlier bad experiences (Rosenthal and Groze 1992; Rushton *et al.* 2003). The problems that persist include difficulties in peer relationships, over-activity and poor concentration, and forming attached relationships with adopters. Nevertheless, it should be stressed that the majority of adoptive children and their new parents stay together and that no more than one third of these remain very problematic (Selwyn *et al.* 2006). On this basis the outcomes from adoption should be seen as a success, especially given the children's difficulties at the time of placement and the lack of support given to the families.

Service Supports and Interventions

POST-ADOPTION SUPPORT

The acceptance that adoption often needs ongoing support has only very recently become part of policy (Department of Health 2003b). For this reason there are, to our knowledge, few studies evaluating different models of support. Indeed, there is little good information on what adopters and children find helpful or on what works for them (Rushton and Dance 2002). Lowe and his colleagues (Lowe, Murch and Thomas 1999) concluded that: 'good quality adoption services were a lottery' and a SSI report (SSI 2000) found post-adoption support to be underdeveloped and poorly advertised. Rushton and Monck's current randomized control trial (RCT) of adoption support services is, to our knowledge, the first systematic comparison of this kind in the UK. For all these reasons what follows is an overview of what is being tried out, not of what appears successful.

There is some evidence that high quality support does make a difference (Barth and Berry 1988; Lowe *et al.* 1999). An inspection of adoption agencies (SSI 2000) showed that one agency with a high level of services had had no disruptions in the previous three years.

LOCAL AUTHORITY SERVICES

Rushton and Dance's (2002) survey indicated a recent increase in specialist placement and permanency teams, although mostly to increase the recruitment of adopter and to organize up to the time of the adoption order. Forty per cent of authorities had post-adoption services (usually a single worker). These were mostly concerned with managing letterbox contact, training adopters, maintain support groups and researching the need for local services. Casework with adopters was rare. Adopters were most likely to get support after the adoption if their problems were already recognized when the order was made. If problems arose later parents had to recontact social services or make their own approaches to mainstream or specialist provision.

SPECIALIST SERVICES

There are many independent schemes that address emotional and behavioural problems, handle contact, help with 'attachment' issues and meet educational needs. These began with Parent to Parent Information on Adoption Services (PPIAS), which was set up in 1971 and changed its name in 1999 to Adoption UK; it is a self-help network that organizes local support groups and offers training workshops and resource and information packs. The Post Adoption Centre, set up in 1986, was the first of its kind in the UK. Howe's (1990) evaluation of it highlighted the need for help with children's behavioural difficulties and with adopters' need to deal with their own complex feelings, including guilt and anger. Other centres have been set up to deal with contact issues (Beek 1999; Magee and Thoday 1995) or post-adoption support more generally. Parents for Children, The Children's Society and Coram Family have appointed post-adoption workers. Other initiatives include After

Adoption, Keys Attachment Centre and Family Futures in London. The Talk Adoption helpline was set up especially for adopted children and young people.

It is clear that these practice and support developments point to a serious need for help, support and information for adoptive parents and adopted children. It is also clear that the need for both ongoing help and a rapid response to crises is needed for many years. Unfortunately, support is not obviously given to the families who need it most nor when they need it (Rushton 2003; Selwyn *et al.* 2006).

Research on this issue needs first to look at whether support is related to needs and how good the assessments of needs are – the evidence so far suggests that these are seldom systematic (Department of Health 2000a). It is essential that such developments continue and that their programmes are clearly described and their effectiveness independently evaluated. Evaluations should go well beyond assessing the satisfaction of users. They should test the effectiveness of a favoured approach against other interventions. If this is not done we shall not learn what works and for whom. Rushton and Dance (2002) list only four RCTs with any reference to adoptive placements.

Programmes and Interventions

ATTACHMENT-BASED APPROACHES

Many programmes derive their theoretical basis from attachment theory, rather than through the 'grief and mourning' model that was influential in the 1980s (Fahlberg 1988). Some try to improve the relationship between the child and his or her carers generally, whilst others try to modify the child's 'internal working models' of attachment figures. The most interesting UK research on this topic is the Coram Family Study, which looked at changes in children's representations over time using story completion techniques. One purpose was to see whether changes in children's representations were related to adopters' parenting styles and to their representations of their own childhood attachment figures (Hodges *et al.* 2000).

This recent emphasis on 'attachment' is welcome, since the failure of affectionate relationships is one of the key predictors of placement disruption. On the other hand, the conclusion that representations of disturbed early attachments *underlie* a host of other problems is not yet warranted. Even if it were, this would not necessarily lead to the conclusion that these problems are best dealt with through therapies working with representations (Rutter and O'Connor 1999).

Of course, working on the child's internal world does not have to follow these theoretical perspectives. Roberts (1996) has described her use of cognitive behavioural therapy in trying to alter negative patterns of thought and to teach more adaptive strategies.

OTHER APPROACHES

We can finally mention a number of other approaches, some of which are promising, although none has been evaluated and not all have been applied to adoption. The first – holding therapy – has claimed success with adopted children (Myeroff, Mertlich and Gross 1999) but many variables could have influenced outcomes. Its use is controversial, since it involves close physical and eye contact between the child and the therapists, and it has been linked with serious child injuries. It is presented as based on attachment theory, but this claim has been denied by those working in the attachment field (O'Connor and Zeahah 2003).

FAMILY THERAPY

Family therapy has attractions because it works with the whole family – or at least with the child and the new parents – but it developed in clinical work with birth families, not with newly created and unrelated ones. Its usefulness may lie, as Hart and Thomas (2000) suggest, in providing a 'secure base' in which adopters and adoptees can explore what concerns them.

PARENT TRAINING

Parent training potentially provides what adopters often say they are desperate for: help with and techniques for dealing with oppositional and challenging behaviour. It has been shown to be effective with behavioural problems in birth families (Webster-Stratton 1985). Parent training has the virtue that it can be tailored to the specific concerns of adopters and to the sometimes unusual behaviours and responses of adoptees. They also provide a basis for group support and discussion. Adoption UK offers a time-limited group support and parenting strategy approach through eight sessions led by trained adopters (Adoption UK 2000) but, as with all other interventions, parenting approaches remain to be formally evaluated.

MULTISYSTEMIC THERAPY

MST was developed in the US in work with persistent juvenile offenders and substance misusers. It argues that to address such persistent problems it is necessary to work simultaneously with all the subsystems within the young person's social ecology – family, friends, school, neighbourhood, work etc. (Henggeler *et al.* 1996). It requires intensive (and expensive) coordination of interventions. In addition, very good training and quality conditions have to be met (Kazdin 1997). This approach is now being tried in the UK with young people with persistent antisocial behaviour but, again, has not been evaluated, nor has it yet found its way into adoption interventions.

For Whom is Adoption an Effective Intervention?

In this final section we review what is known from the UK literature on the factors that influence the success or otherwise of adoption as an intervention. As we pointed out earlier, adoptions made in infancy are notably successful both with respect to the stability of placements and on psychosocial outcomes right through into adulthood. The evidence on adoption made after infancy – the majority of placements now made in the UK – is much less secure, because there are very few well-sampled studies of these children and because there is generally a lack of appropriate comparisons with other forms of intervention for children with similar characteristics and problems. We review what is known, as this provides the basis for the development of interventions.

Age and Delay

Nearly all studies show age at placement to be a major influence on the likelihood of disruption, with rates rising with age, probably because of a longer exposure to adverse parenting and frequent moves in care, leading to an entrenched pattern of maladjustment, as well as complex feelings due to child's memories of and contact with his or her birth family. However, although adoption is more likely to be successful the earlier it is made, the converse is not necessarily true: that adoptions later in childhood or in adolescence are not worth considering. Rather, the assessment of needs, careful matching and focused support are more important than the application of a rigid rule. Nevertheless, earlier placements have a lower risk of disruption, increase children's chance of developmental recovery and make it easier to find families for them. For these reasons it is important to address delay. Children's time scales are not the same as those of adults. A wait of one year encompasses a fifth or more of the life experience of a pre-school child and delay creates uncertainty and insecurities. Moreover, as Selwyn et al. (2006) found, the odds against being adopted increased 1.8-fold for every year of delay.

Social services decision-making is by no means the only delaying factor. Court processes have a major role in this (Lowe, Murch and Borkowski 1993), as are children's guardians' requests for further assessments, and problems of contested adoption – which the majority now are. Nevertheless, perhaps as a consequence of PSA targets, the time taken for children on Care Orders to be adopted has dropped from three years four months to three years two months (Department of Health 2002b).

Child Factors

Many characteristics of the child are not related to increased psychosocial problems or to disruption. These include gender, sibling placements, ethnicity, ethnic matching and physical or intellectual disability – indeed, placements of disabled children in adoption and foster care are, if anything, more stable. On the other hand, problems in emotions, behaviour and attachment are a major influence on placement success. Over half of the five- to nine-year-olds in Quinton *et al*.'s. (1998) study had mental health problems according to standard criteria, and about one third had not developed attached relationships with their new parents by the end of their first year in placement.

Many of these problems proved persistent – especially overactive and restless behaviour and relationship problems – sometimes as much as eight years after placement, and were predictive of disruption (Rushton and Dance 2004). Genetic and neurodevelopmental factors clearly play a part in these problems, although the broad conclusion from genetic studies is that, although adopted children are often at greater risk for genetically based psychosocial difficulties, their early rearing environment and quality of subsequent adoptive family life has a major impact on whether these genetic vulnerabilities are expressed (Cadoret 1990). There has also been much recent interest in the impact on early brain development of pre- and post-natal trauma; parental substance abuse, particularly alcohol (Fisher *et al*. 2000; Perry 1995); and inadequate environments for the development of emotional regulation and attachment. These are important new considerations, but their implications for intervention and support are not yet clear.

The most clearly established predictor of poorer outcomes is the lack of the development of any positive relationship or attachment between the child and the new parents. Adopters seem able to cope with quite high levels of emotional and behavioural challenge as long as they feel they are getting something back in the way of affection and connection (Quinton *et al*. 1998), a finding also true for foster care (Sinclair *et al*. 2000).

Adoptive Family Characteristics

Many features of adoptive families bear *no* relationship to placement success. These include adoptions by single parents (Owen 1999), parental income, education and age. The placement of siblings together into a home without birth children does not increase disruption rates and may lower them (Groze 1996; Quinton *et al*. 1998; Rushton *et al*. 2001). However, placement with adopters who have birth children at home appears to increases the risk of disruption, regardless of whether the adopted children are the youngest in the family or not (Rushton *et al*. 2003).

Parenting Styles

Most studies show the often astonishing tenacity and dedication of adopters (Quinton *et al*. 1998; Rutter and ERA Study Team 1998) and that the majority of parents report high levels of satisfaction with their experience as adopters (Rushton

2000; Selwyn et al. 2003). Nevertheless, parenting styles have a measurable influence on outcomes, the following qualities especially: warmth and positive regard, sensitivity to the children's feelings and needs, setting clear boundaries, providing positive experiences and exercising discipline in a non-aggressive way that makes the messages clear and helps the child learn to control his or her own behaviour (Quinton 2004).

Contact

Finally, it is necessary to touch on the issue of contact with birth parents, since this is often argued to be a positive influence on outcomes and is therefore a kind of intervention itself, even though the evidence on positive effects on placement stability and outcomes is equivocal (Quinton et al. 1997). Arguments for contact on the basis of rights have been less in evidence until recently (Eeklaar 2003).

Earlier research by Barth and Berry (1988) reflects a conclusion from many of the studies that contact enhances the success of straightforward adoptions but can disturb higher risk placements, a finding that applies to foster care as well (Farmer, Moyers and Lipscombe 2001). The conclusion must be that major studies on the psychosocial consequences of contact in modern UK adoptive samples remain to be done. There are no studies to compare with the sophisticated measurement of outcome used in the prospective study in America by Grotevant and his colleagues (e.g. Grotevant et al. 1999) of a sample of adoptions of infants. Unfortunately, the characteristics of this sample were very dissimilar from those of the later-placed samples usual in the UK.

A recent review by Neil (2003) points up the need for much greater refinement in the research, including with whom contact is established (sibling contact is generally less problematic), children's wishes to see some people but not others and differences according to whether the child remembers the birth relatives or not.

Conclusion

The Relevance of Adoption as an Intervention

Adoption is the most radical attempt permanently to change a child's rearing environment for the better and is thus an intervention of major interest.

Outcomes

We have stressed the great change in the characteristics of adopted children in the UK, the persistence of their difficulties, the policy promise of better and better-evidenced support and the striking lack of data on longer-term outcomes and on 'what works'. Evidence does point to the greater stability of adoption over long-term foster care, a difference likely to increase when it is possible to take into account the advantages that adopted children have in the way of support into and through adulthood.

Support

The evidence on effective support is likely to change over the next few years, but some comments on what existing studies of later adoptions point to are in order. First, there is a striking need for adoption support that addresses the needs of adopters and adoptees. Second, this support should be proactive rather than a piecemeal response to crises. Third, support should take the concerns and experiences of the adopters as their starting point and treat adopters as capable and responsible (Kaniuk 1992). At present even fairly basis elements in this – like providing adequate information on and to the children, working on good links between adopters and the education system or listening to children's wishes and feelings in a spirit of dialogue – are often not met. Finally, it should be taken for granted that adoption support should be an ongoing process. Many problems will be long-standing, and shorter interventions, like parenting courses or MST, while helpful, are likely to deal with immediate issues but not anticipate new ones.

Research

The need for all kinds of research is obvious, but amongst the most pressing needs are for well-sampled and well-measured longer-term outcome studies comparing children with similar characteristics who take different career paths through adoption or care. Then there need to be well-designed comparative studies – ideally RCTs – comparing different shorter-term interventions, such as attachment or other ways of helping adopters and their new children.

CHAPTER 21

Adoption in the US

Ruth G. McRoy

Introduction

Adoption, a form of family building, provides an opportunity for children who have been orphaned, abandoned, voluntarily or involuntarily relinquished by their birth parents, to have a permanent family. According to Costin (1972):

> in western culture, adoption is a social and legal process whereby a parent–child relationship is established between persons not so related by birth. By this means, a child born to one set of parents becomes, legally and socially, the child of other parents, a member of another family, and assumes the same rights and duties as those that obtain between children and their biological parents. (p.359)

In recent years, the shift from confidential adoptions, in which there is no post-placement contact between birth and adoptive parents, to post-placement contact between these parties has led some to redefine adoption. It is now considered as:

> a means of providing some children the security and meeting their developmental needs by legally transferring ongoing parental responsibilities from their birth parents to their adoptive parents; recognizing that in so doing we have created a new kinship network that forever links those two families together through the child, who is shared by both. (Reitz and Watson 1992, p.11)

Regardless of type of adoption, this method of building a family has for years been considered to be "the best solution" (p.157) for both infertile couples and single, pregnant women (Melosh 2002). Families are carefully selected by agencies and/or, in the case of independent adoptions, have approved home studies which suggest that they are able to assume the responsibility of parenting. Adoption benefits birth parents who are then relieved of the responsibility of parenting to enable them to complete their education or get on with their lives. Most relinquishing parents feel at the time of the placement that they are not in a position to assume parental responsibility and wish to have the child raised by a stable two-parent family (Pecora *et al.* 2000).

Adoption also provides children whose birth families are unable or unwilling to care for them another opportunity for a family. Birth families which have been abusive or neglectful, often due to parental substance abuse and sometimes parental incarceration, sometimes have their children removed and placed in foster care, and in some cases termination of parental rights occurs. The children are often given another opportunity for an "adequate family life" (Pecora *et al.* 2000, p.363) through adoption with relatives, Native American clan members, or non-relatives.

The adoption of older children who have been permanently removed from their birth parents due to parental abuse, neglect or abandonment, is referred to as "special needs" adoptions. These placements are typically handled through public child welfare agencies. According to the AFCARS report, as of September 30, 2002, there were 126,000 children waiting to be adopted in the public child welfare system. Many are members of a sibling group, members of a minority group, are older, or have an emotional, physical or developmental disability (P.L. 96–272 1980), and many have experienced several moves while in the foster care system prior to adoption.

Statistics suggest that about 2 percent of all US children or 1.5 million US children are adopted (Fields 2001). Children voluntarily relinquished typically are born to unmarried mothers, often teenagers, who make adoption plans for their children to enable the child to have a two-parent home. These infants are generally adopted by infertile couples. About 500,000 currently or formerly married women between 18 and 44 were seeking to adopt a child in 1995 (Chandra *et al.* 1999).

US domestic infant adoptions have been declining since the mid-1960s. At that time, about 31.7 percent of unmarried teen mothers placed children for adoption (Cartoof and Klerman 1982). By the early 1970s, about 19.3 percent of children born to unmarried Caucasian women were placed for adoption and now only about 1.7 percent of children born to unmarried Caucasian women are being placed through voluntary relinquishments. The percentages of African-American women choosing to place children for adoption have always been significantly lower, ranging from 1.5 to 2 percent (Bachrach, Stolley and London 1992; Chandra *et al.* 1999; Donnelly and Voydanoff 1991).

Children who are voluntarily relinquished for adoption may be placed through private agencies or by independent or private means. Independent adoptions occur when "parents place children directly with adoptive families without the use of an agency as an intermediary" (Pecora *et al.* 2000, p.362).

Another form of adoption, "stepparent adoption," refers to the adoption of a child of a spouse, typically a child already in the home. About 40 percent of all adoptions are stepparent placements (Flango and Flango 1995). More recently, adoption is also occurring among related persons, generally referred to as "kinship adoptions." These adoptions often involve grandparents or other relatives taking permanent legal responsibility of children who are blood related, but whose parents have had their rights terminated.

Partly due to the decline in the availability of US healthy Caucasian infants for adoption, many families consider adopting children from other countries, generally referred to as "intercountry" or "international" adoption. Currently, 45 percent of children internationally adopted are under one year old and 43 percent are between one and four. Sixty-four percent of these children are female (Immigration and Naturalization Service 2000). The numbers of immigrant visas issued for orphaned children nearly tripled from 1990 to 2001. In 1990 there were about 7000 international adoptions and by 2001 that number had increased to more than 19,000 (US State Dept. 1990, 2001). Almost half of these children came from Russia and China (National Adoption Information Clearinghouse 2000).

This chapter will provide a brief discussion of research findings on outcomes of adoption for young and older children in the United States, with an emphasis on infant, special needs, transracial and intercountry placements. Limitations of the research as well as implications for policy, practice and future research will be presented.

Evidence of Program Effectiveness

Over the years, numerous US studies have been conducted on the impact of adoption on children adopted at young and older ages as well as on birth and adoptive families and the wider community. Most research on infant adoption outcomes has explored to what extent adoption is a risk factor for children's adjustment (Brodzinsky and Pinderhughes 2002) by examining such issues as the incidence of adopted children in mental health settings; academic, behavioral and emotional adjustment problems; temperament; mother–infant attachment; mental and motor functioning; adoptive identity; children's cognitive understanding of adoption; and how children's understanding may vary developmentally and in situations of post-adoption contact with birth families. Family issues, such as motivation for adoption, perceptions about adoption, adoptive family life cycle, parenting and talking with children about adoption, have also been explored.

Adoption has also been studied to determine to what extent it serves as a protective factor (Brodzinsky and Pinderhughes 2002), for older children who otherwise might be living in stressful traumatic environments with birth families or in institutional or foster care settings. Some studies have focused on adoption outcomes for children who have had varying pre-placement experiences such as prenatal drug exposure, sexual abuse, multiple foster placements, disruptions and dissolutions, attachment issues, and separation from siblings. Factors influencing outcomes for families such as parental satisfaction, use of pre- and post-adoptive services, family adjustment, stressors, expectations, and children's behavior problems, among others have been addressed.

There is much variety in the types of published research on adoptions. Although the majority of studies have used quantitative methods, there is a growing emphasis upon using qualitative data or using mixed methods. Research on outcomes in infant placements has been largely theory driven. While the majority are cross-sectional in nature, others are longitudinal. Sample sizes vary from small convenience samples to very large nationwide outcome studies. A few have included comparison groups such as clinical and non-clinical samples of adoptees and non-adoptees in in-patient and out-patient populations, transracial and inracial adoptees, intercountry adoptees, and comparisons between adopted children in varying openness arrangements (children in confidential, mediated and fully disclosed adoptions). Data collection methods for these studies have included case record reviews, epidemiological data, surveys and interviews. While a number of studies have examined the impact of adoption from the perspective of children as well as parents, only a few have examined the impact of adoption on all parties involved: birthparents, adoptive parents, adopted children, and adoption agencies.

The following summary of key findings from the research includes selected studies related to outcomes for children placed as infants and as older children. Priority was given to include studies on outcomes for varying types of adoption.

Outcomes for Children Placed as Infants

Numerous outcome studies have been conducted over the years to examine whether adoption increases the risk of adjustment disorders for children. A review of clinical literature suggests that adopted children are overrepresented in out-patient settings and even more overrepresented in in-patient populations (Haugaard 1998). Yet a closer look at these studies reveals conflicting results when clinical and non-clinical populations are compared. Haugaard (1998) found that, in clinically based studies, adoption may be a negative risk factor on a child's development, yet non-clinical samples suggest very little or no risk associated with being adopted.

More clarity on these disparate outcomes comes from longitudinal studies of non-clinical populations. These studies suggest that there may be an increased risk of problems for some adopted children at certain ages, "but that this risk is neither high nor widespread" (Haugaard 1998, p.59). Moreover, both genetic and environmental factors may contribute to the overrepresentation of adopted children in child psychiatric populations. It is also possible that adopted children are more likely to be referred to mental health treatment settings than non-adopted children presenting similar problems (Kim *et al.* 1988).

Wierzbicki (1993), in his meta-analysis of 66 published studies on the psychological adjustment of adoptees and non-adoptees, found that although most adoptees do not experience psychological problems, adoptees had higher levels of externalizing disorders and academic problems than non-adoptees. Ingersoll (1997) suggested that outcomes may be impacted on by factors such as:

> pre-adoption events (prenatal and peri-natal factors); quality of care and attachment during pre-adoption period) and post adoption events, such as the quality of the adoptive parent–child relationship and the identity struggles with which the adopted child must contend (p.63)

Loss of personal identity, family identity, cultural identity, may all occur as a result of the adoption. The outcome of the child's adjustment to this loss is influenced by the child's cognitive appraisal of the meaning of his/her adoption as well as the child's coping efforts in response to the perceived stress of adoption (Brodzinsky 1990, p.10).

Most of the research addressing loss in adoption has focused on children placed in traditional confidential adoptions, in which the adoptee had no further contact with the birth family once the adoption has been finalized. Early studies which examined the impact on birth mothers who placed children in confidential adoptions revealed that they often experienced "prolonged feelings of loss, anxiety, and in some instances psychological impairment" (Millen and Roll 1985; Sorosky *et al.* 1978; Winkler and Van Keppel 1984).

Since the mid-1980s, Grotevant and McRoy (1998) have been studying longitudinal outcomes of more open adoptions in which birth families and adoptive families can have an opportunity to exchange pictures and non-identifying information, and have face-to-face meetings and ongoing direct contact between birth and adoptive parents. Grotevant and McRoy (1998) have reported benefits and satisfactions with openness for birth mothers, adoptive parents and adopted children placed as infants. Birth parents in fully disclosed open adoptions experienced less grief, better post-placement adjustment, and less guilt and regret than those in confidential adoptions. Adopted children in open adoptions expressed a greater understanding of adoption than those in confidential adoptions and no significant adverse effects have been identified (Grotevant 2000). However, these researchers caution that levels of openness should be decided on an individual basis as each type of adoption has benefits as well as challenges. In general infant adoptions, regardless of type of adoption, are considered to be very successful.

Outcomes of Older Child Placements

Unlike infants who are adopted, children placed when older have typically experienced abuse or neglect and some have emotional and behavioral problems, physical or developmental disabilities, intellectual disability, and/or chronic medical conditions. Many have attachment issues due to experiencing multiple foster placements, and separation from their family of origin. Although placement disruption rates can range from 10 to 20 percent (Rosenthal 1993), most of these adoptions are successful with reports of satisfaction by parents and children (Pinderhughes 1998). Factors that seem to lead to success are good matches between children and families, realistic parental expectations, parental commitment, willingness to utilize post-placement services, parental flexibility, prior parenting experiences, availability of subsidies, and availability of informal and formal supports such as extended family and friends and other adoptive families (Barth and Berry 1988; McRoy 1999).

Unlike families who adopt infants, special needs adoptive families are much more likely to be single and older, have lower income and education, and to adopt older, often troubled children. In some cases, these adoptive families have fostered the children prior to the adoption. However, according to several empirical studies, special needs adoptive families are not at increased risk of disruption, perhaps due to their having more realistic expectations of the children and greater tolerance (Barth and Berry 1988; Brodzinsky and Pinderhughes 2002).

Another option being considered for some older children needing adoption is kinship placement. In recent years, the number of children in out-of-home care has increased and the number of licensed foster parents has decreased. Many states are developing relative caregiver or kinship care programs as well as promoting kinship adoptions. The majority of kinship care providers in most states are African-American. Recent research suggests that children placed with relatives are more likely to be placed with siblings, to move less frequently and to have more stability while in care (Duerr-Berrick and Barth 1994). However, other research suggests that many children in kinshipcare homes do not receive adequate medical and mental health services (Dubowitz, Feigelman and Zuravin 1993). Leslie *et al.* (2000) has called for more longitudinal studies which examine the diverse experiences and placement histories of children in kinship care. As kinship providers increasingly adopt children in their care, research is needed to examine roles and relationships, and boundary issues, as well as long-term outcomes.

Outcomes of Intercountry and Transracial Adoptions

A number of factors tend to influence outcomes of intercountry adoptions including age at time of placement, pre-placement experiences such as time in orphanage and type of care received, preparation of family for intercountry adoption, fluency in the language of the adopted country, and parental attitudes and willingness to provide information about the child's birth country and culture. A review of the research on outcomes yields mixed results; although most studies show that intercountry adoptees appear to have adapted well, others have evidence on more psychological and behavioral problems among these children (Brodzinsky and Pinderhughes 2002). Groze and Illeana (1996) found that US adoptive parents of 462 Romanian children reported parent–child relations were good and that there were few behavioral problems with children except with those children from institutions. Eighty-six percent of 34 families of pre-school (54% Asian) international adoptees in Trolley, Wallin and Hansen's (1995) study reported that birth culture was relevant to their child's identity and 90.5 percent expressed concern that their child might worry about their background.

A study of 29 Asian adults, primarily Korean, who had been adopted by Caucasian US families, revealed that most adoptees lived in Caucasian neighborhoods, had Caucasian best friends and dated Caucasians. The researchers noted that these adoptees did not feel that having a different ethnic background from their families was an important factor in their lives (Altstein et al. 1994).

These same issues related to ethnic background and identity have also been studied in relation to transracial adoptions—the adoption of children from one racial background by families of a different racial background. The majority of research on this topic has looked at outcomes for African-American children adopted by Caucasian families. Issues such as racial identity, self-esteem, satisfaction, and social adjustment have been examined by researchers over the years (i.e. McRoy and Zurcher 1983; Shireman and Johnson 1988; Simon and Altstein 1994) and many others have reported findings that suggest that transracial adoptees are well adjusted. However, findings on racial attitudes and racial identity of transracially adopted children yield varying results and some suggest that racial identity formation is more complicated in transracial adoptive families (DeBerry, Scarr and Weinberg 1996; Hollingsworth 1997; McRoy and Zurcher 1983; Shireman and Johnson 1988). Families who recognize the complexities involved in racial socialization in the US, and who seek opportunities for children to interact with others of the same racial and ethnic background to facilitate the development of a strong positive racial identity, tend to have children who have a more secure sense of their racial background and more positive racial self-perceptions.

The aforementioned studies provide a brief glimpse at the type of research that is under way in the US examining the impact of adoption on children and families. There are a number of adoption practices which have been reported as successful, but have not received a great deal of empirical attention. These will be described in the next section.

Promising Approaches

Forty percent of the 119,000 children in public child welfare settings who need adoptive placement are African-American. Much more focus is needed on identifying and evaluating African-American recruitment and retention programs. For example, One Church One Child, Black Homes for Black Children, and the Institute for Black Parenting are often identified as model programs for successfully recruiting hundreds of African-American adoptive families (McRoy, Oglesby and Grape 1997).

Other less-known but very promising service delivery models include the Bennett Chapel Project in Possum Trot, Texas. In this very small, rural community, over 70 African-American older children have been adopted by about 26 African-American families. These children were placed by the state and have been adopted by both single- and two-parent families in a community in which the average income is less than $20,000. These adoptions have been spearheaded by Reverend Martin and his wife, Donna, who call this the "Saving a Generation Ministry." These unique approaches must be replicated in other communities to begin to find new resources for children in care (McRoy 2005).

Conclusion

Society benefits from the practice of adoption, as children are key to our future and, if they are without a stable home life, they as well as wider society are at risk. Adoption becomes, therefore, a "substitute" form of parenting to insure that children have an opportunity to be properly cared for and raised in family environments.

Numerous changes have occurred in adoptions practice and policies within the US over time. Since 1851, when adoption laws were first enacted to permanently sever relationships between birth and adoptive families, and the passage of the first sealed record laws in 1917 in Minnesota, adoptions have changed dramatically. From a focus on confidential, same-race infant placements, there is now an array of adoption possibilities which include intercountry adoptions, transracial adoptions, foster parent adoptions, older child adoptions, kinship adoptions, and open adoptions. The face of adoption has changed from primarily focusing on finding white infants for childless couples to focusing on finding permanent homes for a growing number of older and often minority children in the nation's child welfare system.

The empirical and theoretical literature has also been expanding to include these new forms of adoption and our knowledge of the impact of adoption on the child and family has broadened. Much more attention has been placed on the development of adoptive identity, psychological adjustment and children's understanding of adoption, and factors associated with successful adoptive parenting of older children.

The research generally suggests positive outcomes and satisfactions for both infant and older child adoptions.

It is obvious there is a great need for US families to adopt children in the foster care system. In fiscal year 2002, 53,000 children were adopted from the public foster care system, the average age of these placed children was 6.9 years and it took an average of 16 months from termination to adoption. Sixty-one percent (30,969) of the placed children were adopted by foster parents. Long-term studies with comparison groups are needed to assess how these foster parent placements are working. Policy and practice research is needed to determine "process variables" which may be leading to the 16-month placement delays between termination and adoption.

Additional research is needed on many topics, including the impact of age at adoption on psychological adjustment, maintaining family boundaries in open adoptions with older children, issues in post-adoption services, preparing children for adoption, matching children and families, openness in special needs adoptions, successful African-American foster and adoptive family recruitment, and outcomes of kinship care and kinship adoptions. More research is needed on single-parent adoptive families, gay and lesbian adoptive families, and racial and ethnic minority families. Although much theoretical attention has been given to the long-term adjustment of children adopted as infants, more longitudinal studies are needed on family relationships, dynamics, boundary issues and attachment in older child adoptive families. Moreover, research is needed to examine how children, placed when older in open, foster parent, or kinship adoptions, view their adoptive identity and how this may affect long-term outcomes.

Finally, since national legislation including the Multiethnic Placement Act and Interethnic Provisions have precluded race matching in adoption in order to promote transracial adoption, research is needed to assess the impact this legislation has had on transracial placements. As many agencies are no longer assessing or preparing families specifically for transracial adoptions, outcomes for these children and families may vary. Longitudinal research on outcomes for children and families who who have been assessed and prepared and those who have not will yield very important information for future practice and policy decisions in transracial adoptions.

PART FIVE

Innovative Approaches in Schools and Community Programmes

CHAPTER 22

Interventions in Schools in the UK

Gillian Pugh and June Statham

Introduction

Schools have a potentially critical role to play in enabling children to fully enjoy childhood, get the best out of life and realize their full potential. Children spend nearly half their waking time at school, and the significant impact that schools have on many aspects of children's development has been well documented (Rutter *et al.* 1979). An ecological approach to children's well-being builds on the interrelationship between children, their families and the communities in which they live. For almost all children, a central part of this community is the school.

The importance of strong home–school links has long been acknowledged (Pugh *et al.* 1994), and over the years there have been various initiatives in the UK to extend the role of the school, for example through Educational Priority Areas in the 1960s and 1970s (Halsey 1972) and the development of 'community schools' in some authorities around the same time. The introduction of the National Curriculum in 1988 and the subsequent emphasis on educational standards, testing and league tables, have tended to limit schools' capacity to take on a broader community role. But while the standards agenda remains, the emphasis is now beginning to change. Concerns over the large number of children and young people who are socially excluded have led to a growing interest in how schools can contribute to the renewal of disadvantaged neighbourhoods (Department for Education and Employment 1999a).

A considerable number of initiatives or interventions intended to promote children's well-being more widely are now fairly commonplace in schools. Home–school link programmes and family literacy programmes, for example, are now widespread, as are a range of health-related initiatives – the Healthy Schools Programme and subsequent National Healthy Schools Standard (Rivers *et al.* 2000);

Health Action Zones; personal, social and health education (PSHE) and citizenship; drug education and sex education programmes. Many of the projects supported through the Children's Fund, a government-funded initiative to provide preventive services for children between the ages of 5 and 13 who are at risk of social exclusion, are school based (Ofsted and Audit Commission 2003).

About 2000 schools described themselves in 2002 as community schools, and a review of the relationship between schools and communities illustrates the wide range of ways in which schools are supporting families and communities (Ball 1998). A more concerted attempt to develop 'full-service schools', offering a range of health and social services to families as well as education, is currently underway in Scotland (Sammons *et al.* 2002), and a similar initiative on 'extended schools' is now established in England (Wilkin *et al.* 2003). The Education Act 2002 encourages all schools to extend their role within the community through providing child care and other facilities. The central role of schools in coordinating a wide range of services and support for children has been further reinforced by the government Green Paper *Every Child Matters* (Cm.5760 2003), the subsequent publication *Every Child Matters: Change for Children* (HM Government 2004b) and the Children Act 2004. Schools and children's centres are seen as key to delivering the 'joined up' services that the new Children's Trusts are required to put in place, and there is an expectation that professionals from teaching, health, social care and youth justice sectors should be encouraged to work in multidisciplinary teams based in and around schools and children's centres. The five-year strategy published by the HM Government (2004a) sees the 'welfare agenda' as embodied in *Every Child Matters* as key to contributing to the continuing drive to improve standards in schools.

The Nature of the Evidence

An 'intervention' is usually interpreted as an additional input over and above what is available to all children as part of mainstream provision. Since school-based initiatives to support children's wider well-being are becoming increasingly prevalent, it has not been easy to decide what should count as an intervention. We have focused in this chapter on initiatives to promote positive mental and physical health, reduce exclusion and prevent re-offending. Against a backdrop of consider-able small-scale activity, much of it developed through the voluntary sector, we have endeavoured to identify those initiatives that have been found to be effective.

There is, however, very little robust evidence for the effectiveness of school-based programmes in the UK. Many studies have small samples or are working in single settings. A number of reports are unpublished or are published in-house by the organization providing the programme, so have not been subject to peer review. Some evaluations have no comparison or control group, so it is not possible to say whether any improvements might have occurred without the programme or it is unclear if the comparison group is well matched. It is common for studies to use feedback from participants or teachers, and while this is important, it cannot be objective. Users will generally say that they find interventions helpful but, where more objective measures are used, evaluations have rarely found convincing evidence of a significant impact.

Reviews (Ball 1998; Department for Education and Employment 2001; Dyson and Robson 1999; Weare and Gray 2003) have found no shortage of short-term initiatives, but very little evidence of systematic evaluation or of longer-term outcomes. If strict methodological criteria were adopted, there would be very few studies left to include. For example, a systematic review of universal approaches to mental health promotion in schools (Wells, Barlow and Stewart-Brown 2003) found only 17 studies meeting their inclusion criteria of controlled trials involving more than 100 pupils in at least four classes or schools, which demonstrated similarity of control and intervention groups, and used validated outcome measures. None of the 14 interventions covered by these studies was in the UK.

This chapter therefore does not aim to provide a systematic review of effectiveness. Many of the interventions we discuss can best be described as 'promising approaches' rather than being of proven effectiveness, although we have tried to indicate where the evidence is less robust. The interventions can be classified in a number of ways, illustrating as they do a huge variety of overall aims, content, and approach. Some interventions are primarily concerned with promoting emotional well-being and mental health; some with reducing school exclusion and offending behaviour; some with improving literacy and academic achievement; some with health promotion; and some – more broadly – with supporting families, often using the school as a focus for multi-agency support. Within these broad areas, many of them overlapping, three main approaches can be identified: whole school or class approaches, working with small groups, and individual one-to-one work. These classifications can be further divided into those which involve parents and those which do not, and into those which operate within primary schools, and those within secondary schools.[1]

The divisions between groups are not clear cut, but Table 22.1 provides a framework for presenting evidence on some of the main school-based intervention programmes currently operating in the UK, for which published data/evaluations are available. Limitations of space mean it is not possible to discuss all these interventions, but key references are given for all those that we list. Further details on some of the projects for younger children are also provided in the publication *Intervening Early* (Department for Education and Skills/Coram Family 2002).

Table 22.1: Examples of school-based programmes

Overall aim	Main focus		
	Whole school approach	*Group approach*	*One-to-one*
Promoting emotional well-being and mental health	Circle Time (P) *Family Links Nurturing Programme (P)* *Taking Care Project* Sheffield anti-bullying programme (P/S)	Nurture Groups (P) Pyramid System (P) Action Groupskills Intervention (P)	*The Place2 Be (P)* *A Quiet Place (P)* Peer support schemes (P/S)
Reducing school exclusion and offending behaviour	Programmes to promote emotional well-being and mental health (above) often also aim to reduce school exclusion and offending behaviour.	*SPOKES Project (P)* Programmes to promote emotional well-being and mental health (above) often also aim to reduce school exclusion and offending behaviour.	*Matrix Project*[a] *(P)* Project Chance (P) Big Brothers/Big Sisters (P/S) Dalston Youth Project (S) *Dorset Healthy Alliance Project*[a] *(P/S)* xl Network (S) *Home–school support workers project*[a] *(S)*
Health promotion	Project Charlie (P) Bodyzone Programme (S) Healthy Schools Programmes (P/S)		
Supporting families	*Community Schools*[a] *(P/S)* *Home–school link programmes (P)*	*SPOKES Project (P)*	*East London Schools Fund*[a] *(P/S)* *Matrix* and *Dorset Healthy Alliance* (as above)

a   Programme uses school as a focus for multi-agency support

Key: P: primary school (4–10 years); S: Secondary school (11–18 years).
Programmes in italics also work with parents

Evidence of Programme Effectiveness: Whole School Approaches to Supporting Children's Well-being

These interventions are available to all children in a school, and therefore have the potential to benefit all children and not just those who have been identified as being 'in need' or 'at risk'. Whole school approaches are not targeted on individual needs, but on developing an ethos throughout the school which is conducive to harmonious relationships between children and adults, and between children themselves. By providing a set of principles across the whole school, particular interventions focused on more needy children (see below) may be more effective. Whole school approaches are common in the field of health promotion, and characterize some of the programmes to promote children's mental health, reduce offending and improve academic achievement. Underpinning many is a focus on 'emotional competence' or 'emotional literacy' – the social and relationship skills that enable children to make and sustain relationships and become responsible citizens.

Promoting Positive Mental Health and Reducing School Exclusion

Whole school approaches combine positive behaviour methods (including care and respect for others, and listening skills), with appropriate expectations, empathy and high self-awareness and self-esteem. The most widely used is Circle Time, where whole classes of primary school children meet together for a 'special time' each week (Mosley 1993). Each child is encouraged to speak about his or her feelings, and success is celebrated and rewarded. All school staff, including lunchtime supervisors, sign up to the approach. An intervention used in a number of Oxfordshire schools, the Family Links Nurturing Programme, combines Circle Time methods with a ten-week parent-training programme. Schools generally report noticeable improvements in children's behaviour, self-esteem and learning after introducing Circle Time, as well as in the general ethos of the school (Cooper 2001), and an evaluation of the Family Links Nurturing Programme in one school found that children involved in the programme were significantly more assertive, socially aware and less aggressive than a control group of 30 children in a similar school without the programme (Layton 1996). The evidence is not robust, and there appears to be considerable diversity in how Circle Time is implemented in schools (Taylor 2003), but reports are consistently positive and are supported by anecdotal accounts of the impact of such programmes.

Bullying is increasingly recognized as one of the most widespread threats to children's well-being within schools, and a number of initiatives have attempted to tackle this. The Sheffield Anti-bullying Initiative, which ran for three years in 23 primary and secondary schools in Sheffield, is one of the best-evaluated. It included establishing clear school policies and procedures, better playground supervision, improvements to the school environment and individual work with bullies and victims. An evaluation showed the scheme had had a positive impact by comparison to a control group (Smith and Sharp 1994).

Health Promotion

Health promotion is part of the PSHE (personal, social and health education) strand of the National Curriculum although, with the current emphasis on standards in numeracy and literacy, there is some concern at the amount of time available for this broader aspect of children's learning and development. The National Healthy Schools Standard (Department for Education and Employment 1999a) is part of a broader government initiative to improve aspects of school not directly linked to academic achievement. An evaluation of the National Healthy Schools Programme showed that the programme was providing a structure for schools to develop health promotion work. It found some improvement in measures such as misuse of drugs, fear of bullying and pupils' self-esteem in schools that were actively engaged with the programme, although it was difficult to definitely attribute these improvements to the impact of the Healthy Schools projects (Aggleton *et al.* 2004).

With regard to drug and alcohol education, there are a number of innovative programmes using, for example, peer tutors, theatre workshops and outside professionals as well as or instead of teachers. However, there is little consensus on what approaches are most effective (Ives and Clements 1996). Conclusions from a number of research reviews have been that there are too few methodologically sound studies to support the effectiveness of either drug or alcohol prevention programmes (e.g. Canning *et al.* 2004), although some evidence that peer-led and interactive programmes which foster the development of interpersonal skills work better than other programmes (Waller, Naidoo and Thorn 2002). One such example is Project Charlie, a drug education project in primary schools, using a life skills model, aiming to develop children's self-esteem and help them resist social pressure, as well as provide them with education about drugs. Evaluations at the time and four years later found that the intervention group was significantly more able to resist peer pressure, had more negative attitudes towards drugs and was less likely to have smoked cigarettes or used illegal drugs – or so the children told the researchers (Hurry, Lloyd and McGurk 2000; Hurry and McGurk 1997).

A review of school-based sex education, mostly in the US, concluded that it can be effective in reducing teenage pregnancy, especially when linked to access to contraceptive services (NHS 1997). Again, however, there is little sound evidence from the UK on which programmes work best, although pupils appear to prefer peer-led sex education (Stephenson *et al.* 2004). One innovative project in Oxfordshire secondary schools, the Bodyzone Programme, operates a confidential drop-in health and advice service for young people on school premises, staffed on a multi-agency basis. Although most students welcomed the service, an external evaluation could find no objective evidence of increased awareness of health issues or greater use of contraceptives compared to a control school (Carlson and Peckham 2001). There is, however, reasonably good agreement from a number of studies on the factors that influence the use of such services by young people, including good advertising, easy accessibility outside school hours, informality, confidentiality and staff who are trained to work with young people.

Evidence of Effectiveness: Group Approaches to Supporting Children's Well-being

Small group interventions are those in which children experiencing difficulties can spend all or part of the school day, or a period of time after school, in a specific group. A survey of local authorities conducted as part of the Coram project cited above (Department for Education and Skills/Coram Family 2002) found that this approach was the most common, although there are considerable variations in the size of the group, the activities within it, the adults who run it, the ratios of adults to children and the length of time the children remain in it. For children who are not able to cope with the demands of a large class, a small group offers better ratios and the chance of establishing closer relationships with both staff and other children. Children who need support can be identified and targeted and the type of support offered can be more easily tailor-made to each child.

Promoting Positive Mental Health and Reducing School Exclusion

Nurture groups are the longest-established of the small group approaches and are experiencing a resurgence of popularity. They are small classes in primary schools, where children with emotional and behavioural difficulties may remain for a year or so before rejoining mainstream classes. Staff aim to create a warm, caring environment with clear rules and structures to help children feel secure and thus able to learn (Boxall 2002). Evaluations show that most children are able to return to mainstream classes without further support (Iszatt and Wasileska 1997), and one study found that nurture group children made significantly better progress after a year than a matched sample (Cooper, Arnold and Byford 2001). Qualitative data from both parents and teachers support these findings.

There is also some evidence for the effectiveness of the Pyramid Scheme – after-school clubs run by trained volunteers for up to ten children, where they engage in activities designed to give them a sense of belonging, security and enjoyment. The scheme also includes screening of all children in the class for emotional difficulties, and interdisciplinary meetings to discuss additional support that might be needed by children or their parents. The programme is delivered through partnerships which appoint a local coordinator. There have been a number of research studies which have produced positive results, although most have been small scale. Outcomes have included improvements in self-esteem, social skills and relationships with peers and adults (Skinner *et al.* 1996), in locus of control and mathematical achievement (Headlam-Wells 2001). Anecdotal evidence from parents, teachers and children also suggests that the clubs have a beneficial effect, at least in the short term (Makins 1997).

Drama group therapy is another approach that has also had some success with children with emotional and behavioural difficulties. The Action Groupskills Intervention uses psychodrama approaches such as role play to reduce disaffection and the risk of school exclusion. Small groups of children from a deprived estate in the north of England met weekly with a trained teacher/therapist for an hour a week for 12 weeks. A randomized controlled trial found that the drama therapy group showed significant improvements, and that these were maintained a year later (McArdle *et al.* 2002). A similar approach – the Taking Care Project – in seven Sheffield primary schools, using drama and Circle Time techniques on a whole class basis, found significant increases in children's ability to understand and express feelings and in their feeling able to ask for help, and teachers noticed improvements in class behaviour among some of the children (Day 2002).

Finally, in this section on small group approaches, the SPOKES (Supporting Parents on Kids Education) project is unusual in that it was devised to help parents (and teachers) rather than children, with the two areas of difficulty in which the project leaders felt they most often sought help: behaviour and learning. The SPOKES project was offered to parents of five- and six-year-olds in eight schools in south London. The intervention involved a parenting course, a reading workshop for parents and a combined course in the third term. Strong evidence for the effectiveness of this approach comes from a study which randomly allocated parents of children at risk of behavioural problems to either the SPOKES programme or a telephone helpline. The programme improved not only children's social behaviour but also their reading ability, and parent satisfaction was very high (Scott and Sylva, forthcoming). Having a reading element appeared to make the programme more acceptable to parents, since it was not perceived as being about their children's 'bad' behaviour.

Evidence of Effectiveness: One-to-one Approaches to Supporting Children's Well-being

Having a special and trusted friend who can help them through difficult times is one of the main protective factors for children as it is for adults. Two main approaches are considered in this final section: an individual who is trained to support children, based in the school so that children can access him or her either when they wish or at fixed times; and a mechanism for finding, training and matching individual adults (often volunteers) to individual children so that they can spend periods of time together, either in or out of school. This approach can be targeted on the most needy children, and can be concentrated and intense. It may also provide mediation between the family and the school where relationships have been damaged. Many of the methods used by whole school and group approaches, outlined above, can also be applied in programmes that are delivered to individual children.

Therapy

The Place2Be is a preventive mental health service for children based on therapeutic counselling (Baxter 2000). Volunteer therapists, supervised by qualified clinicians, work in primary schools with children assessed as being in need of therapeutic support, either on an individual basis or in small groups. The programme also works with parents, teachers and the whole school to encourage the creation of mentally healthy environments. There is no published evidence of effectiveness, although Ofsted reports of some schools using the programme have been very positive. In addition, internal reports note that there has been a reduction in exclusions, unauthorized absences and numbers of children with special needs in schools using the programme, as well as improvements in teachers' ratings of children's behaviour.

A Quiet Place offers a six-week intervention programme to children identified as having emotional or behavioural difficulties, based on a holistic educational therapeutics approach. Children attend three sessions a week, in a room with a warm, relaxing environment, for psychotherapy, massage and relaxation training. The project also works on stress management and behavioural techniques with parents and teachers. One evaluative study has been carried out which showed significant improvement in children's self-esteem and behaviour, although the effect was less marked for children referred for poor self-esteem than for those with behavioural problems (Renwick and Spalding 2002; Spalding 2000).

Peer Support

There is increasing interest in peer support schemes, where pupils support each other, usually under the guidance of a teacher or other adult. These schemes may focus on emotional, social, physical or cognitive functioning, and commonly address issues such as bullying. The Mental Health Foundation (MHF) funded seven demonstration peer support projects in London schools between 1998 and 2000, aiming to demonstrate the importance of schools promoting positive health and building a positive school atmosphere. The projects developed different forms of peer support, including one-to-one work, a playground listening service, peer-led assertiveness skills workshops, homework and lunchtime clubs, information and a website about mental health issues. All schools had a high proportion of minority ethnic pupils and were able to recruit peer supporters from these groups, but experienced difficulties in getting boys involved. The evaluation, based on self-reporting rather than more objective measures, showed benefits to those providing the support, such as increased self-confidence, as well as to those being supported (MHF 2002). Staff also reported a positive impact on the school as a whole, reflected in reduced incidence of bullying, better communication and the enhancement of the school as a caring community.

A survey of over 2000 pupils and teachers in secondary schools with peer support systems in place, which also relied on the perceptions of participants, found that in general the schemes were effective in reducing the negative effects of bullying. They also provided benefits for the peer supporters and for the school as a whole (Naylor and Cowie 1999). A follow-up study showed continuing strong support for the schemes (Cowie *et al.* 2002) but also highlighted the difficulty of involving young adolescent boys in mixed-sex schools, and the potential ridicule and sabotage of male peer supporters. It is suggested that this could be overcome by raising peer support to the status of a whole school issue.

Mentoring

Mentoring is in principle similar to peer support, but involves an older volunteer acting to befriend and provide a role model for someone younger or less experienced; often the younger person is having particular difficulties at school or at home or is in trouble with the police. Mentors are usually matched by a scheme organizer with their 'mentee' and spend several hours each week with them engaged in shared activities, including hobbies, sports and help with school work. Children and young people who could benefit from mentoring are often identified by the school, but activities usually take place outside school. Examples include Project Charlie for primary-aged children. Evidence for the effectiveness of mentoring programmes in improving poor or undesirable outcomes (such as reducing school exclusions and offending behaviour) is not strong, although they do appear to help young people to build a relationship with a responsible adult (Barnardo's Evidence Network 2002; St James-Roberts and Singh 2001; Tarling, Davison and Clarke 2004).

Support from Home–School Workers and Social Workers Based in Schools

Almost all schools will have a home–school liaison policy, and many will have specific members of staff, perhaps a deputy head, with particular responsibility for establishing good relationships with both parents and the local community. But there are a number of specific projects where home–school liaison is a particular focus, such the East London Schools Fund, which places staff in schools to support individual children and their families, and the Home–school support workers project which operated in selected secondary schools in Yorkshire (Webb and Vulliamy 2004). Both provide targeted assistance such as befriending, extra-curricular activities, home visits, liaison with other agencies and support for parents, and are viewed positively by participants. However, hard evidence of effectiveness, as in other areas covered by this review, is hard to come by.

As the government develops its preventive strategy as outlined in the Green Paper *Every Child Matters* (DfES 2004a), the role of schools in coordinating support for children and families within communities is likely to increase. There is some evidence to support the effectiveness of multi-agency interventions, such as social workers based in schools. The Matrix Project, a three-year programme in a small number of Scottish schools, reported 'promising' results (McIvor and Moodie 2002). It aimed to reduce anti social behaviour amongst children aged 8–11 through taking a 'whole family' approach, and linking families into other services such as mental health, debt and advice services. In England, an evaluation of the Dorset Healthy Alliance Project (which provided a school-based child and family social work service in a primary and linked secondary school in an area with a high number of exclusions) found significantly better outcomes in the project schools than in comparable schools, with a halving of the truancy rate, a reduction in delinquency and an improvement in teachers' morale and pupils' educational achievement (Pritchard and Williams 2001).

The school base of such projects appears to enable them to meet the needs of troubled and vulnerable children and families in a non-stigmatizing environment. They work with parents to strengthen their aspirations for their children and their own sense of worth, and contribute to the ethos of the schools as supportive and caring environments.

Effectiveness for all Children and Young People

It is difficult to say whether school-based programmes are likely to work better with some children than others, because few evaluations mention differential impact for different groups. Interventions to promote children's mental health seem to be more effective in improving outcomes for children who are withdrawn or have low self-esteem than for children with behavioural problems, although this could reflect the outcome measures used: reductions in school exclusions are probably less easy to achieve than self-reported improvements in self-esteem. Many of the interventions we describe have been carried out in areas of relatively high disadvantage, with children from lower-income families, and it is not clear whether the same results would be found with children from different circumstances. Few studies also differentiate between those who engage in the intervention and those who do not. A randomized controlled trial of a home–school support project found positive results only when the children and families in the intervention group who were 'non-compliant' were removed from the analysis (Panayiotopoulos and Kerfoot 2004).

Some studies report gender differences, such as the difficulty in involving young men in some of these programmes, particularly mentoring projects, and the resistance of boys to discussing feelings. We could find little specific evidence on the effectiveness of programmes with different ethnic groups, with the exception of a descriptive overview of whole school approaches to raising the achievement of African-Caribbean youth (Weekes and Wright 1998), which highlighted the importance of individual support from a key adult.

Interventions have the potential to be not just positive or neutral, but actually damaging to some children's well-being. Negative results are rarely reported, though this does not necessarily mean that they do not exist. For example, the consequences of failed mentoring or peer support relationships for vulnerable children are rarely considered systematically, nor the impact on other pupils of support for selected classmates. In one study, withdrawing some pupils for Circle Time was found to have an unsettling effect on the rest of the class (Kelly 1999).

There is some evidence to suggest that interventions need to be sustained if they are to have a lasting impact. A number of follow-up studies found that effects tended to fade with time, in areas as diverse as improving reading ability (Hurry and Sylva 1998) and reducing bullying (Eslea and Smith 1998). There is also a question mark over how far effects generalize to out-of-school behaviour. Several studies have found that teachers tend to report greater impacts on children's behaviour than the children do, and parents report the fewest changes.

Conclusion

Schools have a significant role to play in enhancing children's well-being and in working more closely with parents to support all areas of children's development. The range of interventions described in this chapter is increasing in number and this growth is likely to continue following the government's Green Paper *Every Child Matters* and the Children Act 2004. There has, however, been little systematic evaluation or evidence of longer-term outcomes, and most interventions can best be described as 'promising approaches'.

With this caveat in mind, an analysis of the mechanisms by which many of these school-based interventions support children's well-being suggests that they work by:

- increasing pupils' self-esteem, self-awareness and self-confidence
- reducing fear of failure
- promoting attachment and developmental catch-up
- improving relationships and peer acceptance
- improving educational attainment
- focusing attention on the needs of vulnerable children.

They can also support parents in:

* managing stress and difficult behaviour
* understanding children better and understanding how to support their development
* improving self-esteem and confidence.

Schools can also play a valuable role in providing a base for multi-agency support for families within local communities.

Many successful interventions target different levels. They may work with individual children, but also address whole school issues, and vice versa. For this reason, and the diversity of the interventions described above, it is difficult to identify which factors lead to success. However, the studies point in general to the value of a broad, holistic approach. A whole school approach, which improves the emotional climate of the school and builds on relationships with families, is more likely to promote the well-being of all children and to form a sound basis for more structured and sustained intervention for those children with particular needs. A number of programmes also point to the value of working with parents and children, both together and separately. The degree of overlap between the aims of the programmes (promoting mental health and well-being, reducing behavioural problems and social exclusion, supporting families) suggests that a holistic approach should be adopted in planning such interventions. There is also a strong case for more rigorous long-term evaluation of interventions, and a greater sharing of experience of what works between those involved in such programmes.

At a policy level there clearly is a potential role for schools to increase their involvement in supporting children's well-being, but this does raise a number of questions. To what extent can schools, as autonomous agencies, deliver the government's 'prevention' agenda, and what balance should there be between their responsibilities for individual children and for building capacity within local communities? Is it realistic to expect schools to play a key role in local multi-agency teams and what training and additional support do they need to do so? Is there a potential downside to this expanded role of schools in children's lives, as Moss and Petrie (2002) have argued? But above all, our conclusion would be that special programmes and interventions, if they work, should be incorporated into everyday practice in schools. Time-limited initiatives are no substitute for mainstream services supported by adequate funding to support the well-being of all children.

Note

1.   We have not included projects operating in early childhood settings, as this is the focus of another chapter.

CHAPTER 23

Interventions in Schools in the US

Joy G. Dryfoos and Helen Nissani

Introduction

In the United States, a new social movement has been reshaped out of an old concept under the rubric "full-service community schools" (Dryfoos and Maguire 2003). Its history and form are not dissimilar to those of the British experience, but the operations differ markedly. In Britain, the school remains the major actor in the planning and implementation processes, both at the local level and the national level. In the US, the local school is matched with a local partner (or several partners) to form a collaborative relationship, while the federal government has only played a minimal role in these events. This chapter explores the basic concepts of comprehensive school-based programs and their effectiveness. An extended discussion of family resource centers located in schools provides a detailed view of an essential aspect of this movement.

A full service community school is one that is open most of the time (before and after school, evenings, weekends, summers) and offers a wide range of educational enhancement, social and health support programs for children and families, and community enrichment. (See Table 23.1 for a list of key components.) Why are such schools necessary in the US?

The status of children in the US is not unlike in the UK although the prevalence of problem behaviors and neglect may be higher in the inner cities of America. Children from low-income and minority families often start school at a great disadvantage, not having attended pre-school and often not ready to learn. In addition newcomers whose children do not speak English are enrolling children in our schools in increasing numbers. Many children suffer from poor health, stress, neglect, violence, and isolation, preventing them from fully engaging in opportunities to learn. Families have difficulty responding to children's needs because they are beset

Table 23.1: Components of full-service community schools

Component	Description	Outcomes for children	Outcomes for parents, school, community
Comprehensive community school (Childrens' Aid model)	Open extended hours, health clinic, parent resource center, after school integrated with class work, community orientation	Higher achievement, better attendance, access to health services, enjoy school more	Improved parent involvement, lower mobility, high satisfaction, improved teacher attendance, community improvement
Family resource center	Support services, educational opportunities, basic food and clothing, help with parenting, outreach/home visiting	Reduced abuse and neglect, improved achievement	Improved parenting practices, gained education and access to needed services, socialization
School-based clinics	Primary health care, mental health counseling, dentistry	Improved attendance, children feel better	High parent consent and approval
After-school programs	Homework, enhanced instruction, sports, arts, mentoring	Improved achievement, better behavior	Increased ability to work

with other problems, such as lack of housing, food, jobs, medical care and language skills. Many poor disenfranchised parents are unable to access needed services to stabilize and strengthen the family unit so that their children can come to school ready to learn.

The school systems in the US (15,000 separate independent units) are experiencing growing difficulties trying to adhere to the No Child Left Behind law, promulgated by President Bush and his administration, to bolster school performance (Dillon 2003). Schools are required to use standardized tests to account for progress within several years or the students can transfer out to a better school (assuming the spaces are available).

Thus, in recent years, great emphasis has been placed on school achievement, with little recognition within the political establishment that children cannot learn when they are confronted with so many barriers. And teachers are frustrated because they find it difficult to teach children who present so many problems in the classroom. Parents need increased access to services that will help them strengthen their family unit and support their children.

The full-service community school movement has emerged as one response to all of these issues. The basic concept is comprehensive, including early intervention, access to health and mental health services on site, family resource and support centers on site, extended hours, and community enhancement.

We do not yet have a count of the number of schools that meet the criteria for being called a community school. It has been estimated that 2000–5000 schools may have these attributes (out of a total of 85,000 public schools). A Coalition for Community Schools has been organized by the Washington-based Institute for Educational Leadership. This group is currently devising a census that will attempt to enumerate and categorize full-service community schools at various stages of school/community partnerships (see www.communityschools.org).

Evidence of Program Effectiveness

Impacts of Community Schools: The Available Evidence

Because of the national fixation on educational achievement, one cannot discuss the efficacy of community schools without focusing on educational outcomes. The question immediately arises – does achievement improve after traditional schools are transformed into community schools? Does it really improve test scores if a whole array of services and programs are made available in the school building to children and their families? A recent publication, *Making the Difference*, reviewed 20 evaluations of major community school initiatives and came up with a strong affirmation of success: "Community school students show significant and widely evident gains in academic achievement and in essential areas of nonacademic development" (Blank, Melaville and Shah 2003, p.33).

Almost all of the initiatives had positive results in regard to improved grades and many showed improved attendance, reduced discipline problems in school, reduced drop-out rate, increased sense of attachment, and better social behavior. In 11 of the 20 studies, family outcomes were measured. Families were shown to have improved communication with the schools, were more likely to have their basic needs met, and could work longer hours. Most of the initiatives showed increased community use of the school building improved safety in the neighborhood, reduced mobility (fewer families moved out of the neighborhood), and strengthened community pride and engagement.

An Exemplary Community School

The Salome Urena Middle Academy (Intermediate School 218, referred to as IS218), operated jointly by the New York City School System and the Children's Aid Society (CAS), is one example of a full-service community school that has been evaluated (Dryfoos 1990). CAS's approach to community schools is to provide a "seamless" learning and developmental experience for children, families, and communities. IS218, located in a new building in the disadvantaged area of Washington Heights in NYC, was designed to be a community school, with air-conditioning for summer programs, outside lights on the playground, and an unusually attractive setting indicative of a different kind of school. It offers students a choice of four self-contained "academies"—Business, Community Service, Expressive Arts, and Mathematics, Science, and Technology. The school opens at 7:00 a.m. and stays open after school for educational enrichment, mentoring, sports, computer lab, music, arts, trips, and entrepreneurial workshops. In the evening, teenagers are welcome to use the sports and arts facilities and take classes along with adults who come for English, computer work, parenting skills, and other workshops.

A family resource center provides social services to parents including immigration, employment, and housing consultations and trains parents to become family advocates. A primary health, vision, and dental clinic is on site. These facilities, arrayed around the attractive lobby of the school, are open to the whole community. School-supported and CAS-supported social workers and mental health counselors work together to serve students and families. The school stays open weekends and summers, offering the Dominican community many opportunities for cultural enrichment and family participation.

IS218, along with Elementary School 5(PS5), CAS's pilot schools, were the subject of a six-year process and outcome evaluation conducted by researchers from Fordham University. The elementary school also offers an array of services in a new building designed to be a community school. It houses a complete medical and dental clinic as well as a parent resource center, an extended-day program, summer camp, Head Start and Early Head Start, parent involvement, mental health and social services. Partners include the Manhattan Theatre Institute and Boy and Girl Scouts.

The Fordham University evaluation focused primarily on formative issues during the first three years and selected outcomes in the subsequent three years. The earliest evaluation of IS218 in 1993 showed encouraging results: Highest attendance rates in the district, improved reading and math scores, and no serious incidence of violence (despite the school's location within the highest crime rate area in the city).

A formative evaluation of PS 5 conducted in 1995 by Ellen Brickman of Fordham University described the various aspects of the program and also raised a number of questions about the scope of a community school, space constraints, and integration of the academic program with the support program (Brickman 1996). The report also documents significant improvements in both reading and math achievement. Tracking the class that entered in third grade in 1993, 10 percent were reading at grade level then, 16 percent by grade four and 35 percent by grade five. Scores for math increased from 23 percent to 56 percent during the same three-year period.

A three-year evaluation report of both schools issued in 1999 contrasted the CAS schools with matched schools in the neighborhood (Cancelli *et al.* 1999). Three sets of outcomes were examined: psychosocial, parent involvement and academic for students in grades three and six when the research started. In regard to psychosocial findings, students in the community schools appeared to have a more positive sense of self-worth, and to like their teachers and schools more than the students in the comparison schools. Regarding parental involvement, the research found high, consistent, and meaningful involvement in the community schools, more so than in the other schools.

Academic achievement over the years improved in both sites, although the rate of increase leveled off or decreased after the initial major gains were recorded. At PS 5, the percentage of children reading at grade level rose from 28 percent when they were in grade four to 42 percent by the time they reached grade six. The same cohort math scores moved from 43 percent at grade level in grade four up to 50 percent by grade six. The progress matched the improvement rate at comparison schools although the PS 5 children had lower scores at baseline. The researchers also found a significant positive correlation between attendance at extended day programs and reading scores.

At IS218, the research team found a clear pattern of steady though less dramatic improvement over time. Some 39 percent of students performed at grade level in reading at grade six, rising to 45 percent by the time they were in grade eight. For math, the levels went from 49 percent to 52 percent.

Finally, the research concluded that, seven years after the establishment of the community schools, many of the goals had been reached. The buildings were full of people throughout the day and evening, engaged in a wide array of activities. Children were receiving high quality medical and dental care, and had access to on-site mental health services. Parents were involved in the schools and felt a strong sense of responsibility for their children's education, particularly new immigrants. In regard to psychosocial development, the students had more positive attitudes toward school experiences.

Summing up the decade of experience, Philip Coltoff, CAS Executive Director, stated that CAS operated 13 community schools locally, now serving more than 12,000 students in New York City and more than 150 adaptations across the country. CAS's technical assistance center has assisted in the development of community schools in ten other countries. "We initiate and sustain those programs and services because they are what children and families need and want – and in the case of community schools, they make good sense" (Coltoff 1999, p.11).

Other Community School Models

Many different models in addition to the CAS initiative have been promulgated that encompass some or all of these community school concepts. Another approach, University-Assisted Community Schools, involves university professors and students in direct relationships with school teachers and administrators in devising educational interventions such as new curricula for the classroom, and enrichment experiences and service in the community (Walsh *et al.* 2000). University students help the teachers implement the classroom work, and spend time with the students at all hours of the day and night in creative projects in the school and the community.

United Way's Bridges to Success is oriented toward encouraging United Way's constituent community agencies to move into school spaces. A city-wide representative council oversees the program and places coordinators in schools to make sure that the services are integrated. Beacons, initially in New York, and now a national model, gives community-based organizations the funds to "light up" the school-houses and keep them open for an array of youth development activities during extended hours. Communities-in-Schools creates local councils that raise funds to relocate social workers and other youth workers into schools to work on case management and other issues.

Perhaps the least documented model of full-service community schools is "principal initiated." The principal invites partners into the school to extend the day and provide what are perceived in that school as essential child and family services and enrichment programs. The Molly Stark Community School is one such site where the principal established relationships with 40 different community partners to keep her school open all the time and address the human factors that couldn't be taken care of by the school system (such as, among other factors, early child care and dentistry) (Dryfoos and Maguire 2003).

Who Benefits Most from School-based Interventions?

Most of the emerging full-service community schools are located in very needy communities. In middle-class suburban communities many of the components, such as after-school enrichment, parent involvement, and use of the school as a community hub, are already in place. Practitioners and advocates have been more interested in providing services to disadvantaged communities. No statistics are available on the racial and ethnic make-up of students who attend community schools, but a general observation can be made that most of these schools are primarily populated by African-American or Hispanic children. In community schools with strong family resource centers, families can gain access to programs that meet their basic needs for food and clothing.

Another concept that emerges from these school/community partnerships is a strong emphasis on cultural awareness. At the Quitman Community School in Newark, New Jersey, children and families spend time together celebrating African-American rites and festivals (Dryfoos 2003). In that school, one can observe very high levels of parental participation. Parents whose children are enrolled in the after-school program are required to spend six volunteer hours per month helping at the school. At least a dozen parents are hired each year as classroom aides. The Community School Room is always full of parents visiting with each other and the teaching staff, enjoying refreshments, and using the computer. In the community schools where surveys have been promulgated, parent satisfaction is high, and teachers and administrators like having the partners in the school to relieve them of some of the responsibility.

Family Resource Centers and other School-based Family Support Initiatives

Full-service community schools, as described in this chapter, offer a wide range of activities and services that enhance the capacity of the school to meet the academic needs of its students better. Some of these same activities and services are offered by family resources centers and other school-based family support initiatives who may not self-define their initiatives as community schools initiatives but take a holistic approach to strengthening families in order to reduce risk factors that lead to poor educational outcomes.

In the course of collecting data on family support programs nationally, Family Support America, a non-profit organization based in Chicago, has discovered that currently the majority of such programs are in fact school based or school linked. The principles of family support promulgated by this organization are based on ecological research describing the importance of relationships not only within families but between families and other community institutions, such as schools, in positive child outcomes (Bronfenbrenner 1979).

School-based family support initiatives can range from general efforts to reach out better to parents about their children's education to the development of comprehensive family resources centers. Comprehensive centers offer parents the opportunity to develop skills and obtain information in a manner that is flexible, respectful, and culturally responsive while building community. They assist families to identify their strengths and challenges and help them to locate and access local and regional services. Family-supportive efforts in schools might include an independently administered parent resource room in the school building, the integration of multiple services and programs into the school's programming, increasing parent involvement broadly, and changing the school's culture to reflect a better understanding of the needs, strengths, mores, and cultures of local families. While the goal of some school-based family support efforts is to enhance parent participation in children's education, others seek to prevent juvenile delinquency, teen pregnancy, or other negative outcomes.

Family Support Initiatives in School – Evidence of Program Effectiveness

In their attempts to describe and categorize family support initiatives in schools, researchers have been frustrated by the lack of consistent definitions of terms such as parent involvement, community involvement, and community-based family support programming. According to the Southwest Educational Research Laboratory's recent publication *Emerging Issues in School, Family and Community Connections* (Henderson and Mapp 2002), clarifying these concepts and their potential outcomes is necessary in order for it to become possible to evaluate the impact of these initiatives.

The few evaluations that have been carried out concentrate on programs offered to young parents in pre-kindergarten or early elementary schools settings. A longitudinal study of Chicago public schools' Child–Parent Centers (Reynolds *et al.* 2001) shows that family support services and programs did more than strengthen parenting skills: They cut the rate at which enrolled children were subsequently abused or neglected, enhanced parent–child interactions and parent–child appreciation for school, and increased parents' social support networks, increasing the likelihood of sustaining these results.

The state of Washington conducts a biennial study of its Readiness to Learn Program for each session of its legislature. These 24 school-based family support programs meet the needs of communities statewide through outreach to difficult-to-engage families, links to community services and supports for families, parenting classes, tutoring. The report conducted by RMC Research Corporation (2001) indicates that children grades K–12 whose families received services and who were referred to these services due to student academic problems improve their grade point average by 23 percent. This two-year study also indicated a reduction of 72 percent in student detentions and an 89 percent decrease in the number of days students were suspended from school. It can be inferred that these findings document student success as a result of the interventions; however, the dosage amounts and specific programs provided are not identical from one community to the next, as each is tailored to the needs of local families. Long-term research with controlled interventions is needed.

Kentucky also administers state-funded family support programs based in schools. The goal of the Kentucky Family Resource and Youth Service Centers is to help families and children find local solutions to the non-academic barriers to student success. Health services and referrals are the most common service provided. There are 358 family resource centers, 208 youth service centers, and 144 combined centers, totaling 710 centers in the state (Southern Regional Education Board, no date). Between 1992 and 1998, the state contracted with a private research group to evaluate the program. While the results did not measure family outcomes, teachers reported improvements in students' homework and class work completion, compliance with school rules, and interactions with teachers and peers after the school-based services began to be provided to families. As with Washington state, the variation from center to center, while necessary to meet local families' needs and build on their strengths, has made it difficult to draw system-wide conclusions regarding impact.

Educational researchers (Henderson and Mapp 2002) have pointed out the great need for research into school-based family support initiatives. Such research is necessary to unearth information that is needed to ensure successful programming in schools, including strategies for:

- working with families of all cultures in all languages

- helping families support their students, with provision of such facilities as homework help, support during critical transitions, and promotion of safety

- working with families whose children are of a variety of ages, in a developmentally appropriate way

- connecting with families of children in all grades, elementary through high school

- engaging parents in decision-making and leadership roles in education

- providing preparatory education to teachers that equips them to work with families and make community connections.

Researchers must recognize that family support programs operate from a unique and local perspective. Evaluation approaches therefore must be innovative and based on customized processes that embrace the principles of family support while investigating the family and student outcomes that these programs strive to achieve. Evaluations can be designed to be:

- participatory – involving multiple stakeholders, including parents, students, community partners, school staff, and other key decision makers

- focused on promotional indicators, which highlight positive development, growth, and capacities in children and families

- based on adherence to family support principles—understanding that how staff interact with participants and how participants engage with the program and each other affect family and student outcomes

- specific – addressing local models and indicating which and how many (dosage) interventions are best suited to strengthening families

- creative – developing links between specific interventions and their outcomes with respect to student success (Family Support America's Evidence Along the Way Project 2003).

Family support programs in schools and in the communities are characterized by adherence to a set of principles, notably that families have strengths; parents are critical to child development; parent engagement is crucial to program, school, and community success; and programs have the role of encouraging and building family strengths and capacities. Evaluation of family resource centers and other school-based family support initiatives is likely to lead to improved collaboration efforts involving schools; as such research unearths the positive impact of school-based efforts centered on the principles of family support.

Finally, in terms of other challenges to the robustness of the body of evidence, researchers observed that as the program matured, new challenges were arising regarding the logistics of managing growth such as setting up information systems that could track all the traffic, getting teachers to "buy in" to the concept, negotiating the competition for space, firming up the relationship between classroom instruction and extended day programs, and translating the programs and services into demonstrable improvement in academic outcomes (Coltoff 1999).

Conclusion

Schools in the United States are in trouble. They are being pressured to raise the test scores of millions of children who are not prepared to meet the demands. Young children start school unprepared to tackle even the simplest lessons. Older children come to school stressed out and with low expectations that they will be able to succeed. In this difficult period of our educational history, one concept has become very clear: Schools cannot do it alone.

Fortunately, they don't have to. Community agencies of every description are willing to form partnerships with schools and bring needed programs and services into school buildings creating what we call "community schools." Social workers, mental health specialists, nurse practitioners, youth development specialists, parent organizers, and others are all being relocated into schools to work with school personnel to alleviate the enormous pressures.

We report growing evidence that these interventions make a difference, especially when they are integrated with what goes on in the classroom. We can see great reductions in stress, better behavior in school, more parent satisfaction, and more community involvement. Improvement in achievement, the most important outcome in this domain, is harder to prove, given the high mobility of the population targeted and the tremendous challenge in improving what goes on in the classroom. Nevertheless, a number of community schools can show that their transformation has led to better outcomes including in reading and math. We cannot say that all community schools will succeed. In some, the problems are still overwhelming; in others, collaboration is weak. Some schools are heavily utilized by parents; in others, parents are still loath to come to what they perceive as an hostile place. Researchers are beginning to track more closely what practices can overcome these problems.

A wholly new area of research is opening up with regard to "going to scale." Various cities (Chicago, Portland, Oregon, Boston) have started to create community schools system-wide, quite a different methodology from doing it one school at a time. We are looking at the influence of mayors and the body politic on planning and implementing new initiatives.

We do know that the community school movement is growing rapidly in the United States and around the world. Legislation is currently being introduced which, if supported by federal government, would give this movement visibility and some funding. Practitioners across disciplines are enthusiastic about coming together with a goal of improving the lives of children.

CHAPTER 24

Community Programmes in the UK

Gordon Jack

Introduction

At the outset it is important to clarify what is meant by 'community programmes' here, distinguishing them from the community-based interventions that are discussed elsewhere in this volume. For the purposes of this chapter, therefore, 'community programmes' will be defined as those directed at geographical communities, using community development methods to work with disadvantaged people, and designed to achieve improvements in community functioning and outcomes for children and families.

Four broad groups of interventions have been identified for examination, aimed respectively at neighbourhood regeneration, community development with young people, the 'prevention' of child abuse and neglect, and the reduction of youth crime. The theoretical and research background to each type of programme is considered, followed by a discussion of the methods used and what is known about their impact on children, families, and the wider community. The concluding section considers the implications of the evidence presented for children's services.

The Nature of the Evidence

Although community programmes are currently very popular, evidence of their effectiveness in the UK is surprisingly thin. Much of the available evidence is drawn from abroad, particularly the US, where there is a longer history of implementing such programmes and evaluating their impact. However, assumptions cannot safely be made about the transferability of programmes between different political, cultural and social policy contexts. Although most community programmes now being implemented in the UK involve an evaluation component, their longer-term impact will not be known for some years to come.

There are, in addition, some inherent difficulties involved in the evaluation of community programmes which limit the strength and reliability of any judgments about effectiveness that can be reached (Lewis and Utting 2001; Newburn 2001). while studies using experimental and quasi-experimental research designs, involving 'intervention' and 'control' groups, normally provide the best sources of evidence about effects and causal processes, these approaches are often not considered to be either ethical or practical in the social welfare field (Ghate 2001). By their very nature, community programmes are complex phenomena to evaluate because they involve so many different individuals, groups and organizations, each subject to an array of potential influences within changing social, economic and political contexts (Coote, Allen and Woodhead 2004). What is to be measured and how it is to be measured are also often highly contested, with many outcomes subject to differing interpretations (Hughes and Traynor 2000; Pawson and Tilley 1997).

Evidence of Programme Effectiveness: Neighbourhood Regeneration

All community programmes are based on an understanding of the way that people living in the same geographical location interact with each other and their local environment, and the influences that these interactions have upon their behaviour and attitudes. This requires an ecological approach to understanding human development, in which the mutual influences between individuals, families, groups, organizations, communities, and wider society, are all fully considered (Bronfenbrenner 1979; Department of Health 2000b; Jack 2000).

More specifically, neighbourhood regeneration programmes are based on a theoretical understanding of the multiple and interconnected problems that are experienced in disadvantaged areas. Not only does the UK exhibit high levels of relative poverty, but there are also significant geographical variations in the distribution of that poverty (Department for Work and Pensions 2004). These variations in poverty are closely matched by other inequalities, relating to issues such as housing, education and health. The term 'social exclusion' is now widely used to capture the connections between different aspects of inequality, concentrated amongst particular groups or in particular locations. However, as the majority of disadvantaged *individuals* do not actually live in the most disadvantaged *areas* (Gordon 2000), community programmes need to sit alongside other policies and interventions (some of which are covered elsewhere in this volume) able to reach disadvantaged people wherever they happen to live. So what can research tell us about how effective neighbourhood regeneration programmes are likely to be? To begin to answer this question, we need to consider that *where* people live can have major effects upon them.

The research evidence indicates that neighbourhoods do exert an influence on their residents, but that these effects tend to be smaller than those resulting from a combination of wider inequalities in society and individual characteristics (Ellen and Turner 1997; Shouls, Congdon and Curtis 1996). For example, a recent study of area effects on parenting found that living in disadvantaged communities in the UK contributes additional stresses to parenting, independent of individual characteristics (Ghate and Hazel 2002). International research into spatial differences in rates of crime, child abuse and neglect, and various aspects of children's behaviour and development also confirms that, while compositional factors explain much of the variation, area effects also play a significant role (Bottoms and Wiles 1997; Coulton *et al.* 1995; Garbarino and Kostelny 1992; Sampson, Raudenbush and Earls 1997; Vinson *et al.* 1996). The important message carried by this body of research is that appropriately designed community programmes should be able to achieve some improvements in children's lives but that, on their own, they are unlikely to be able to overcome the stronger influences of structural inequalities and individual characteristics.

So, what is it about different geographical locations that might influence the health and well-being of the people who live there? This is where the concept of social capital is helpful. There is a growing consensus that it provides an important means of understanding how individuals are influenced by the formal and informal interactions and norms of trust and reciprocity within different communities and societies (Cote and Healy 2001; Portes 1998). Social capital thrives in societies and communities that are equal, open and fair, but it is undermined by inequalities, divisions and exclusions that act as barriers to trustful and cooperative interactions (Jack and Jordan 1999).

Researchers have identified two main forms of social capital in recent years. 'Bridging' social capital connects people from diverse backgrounds, helping to link disadvantaged communities with external resources and information, while 'bonding' social capital tends to reinforce existing social identities, protecting disadvantaged groups from the negative effects of living in adverse circumstances (Putnam 2000). It is not difficult to see why social capital is now attracting so much attention. There is increasing evidence that higher levels of social capital are correlated with a wide range of desirable social policy goals, including lower crime and child abuse rates, better health and educational attainment, longer life and improved economic performance (Harper 2001).

The concept of social capital provides a way of capturing important aspects of the social interactions that occur in different communities. General population surveys in the UK reveal that most people have regular contact with a fairly wide circle of relatives and friends, some of whom may live a considerable distance away (Park and Roberts 2002). However, research with more disadvantaged groups, such as lone parents, parents of children with disabilities and ethnic minority members, reveals that they tend to have smaller social networks, being more reliant on relatives living nearby (Brassard 1982; Cross 1990; Dunst, Trivette and Jodry 1997; Gill, Tanner and Bland 2000). Social networks that provide reliable sources of support have consistently been found to be associated with positive influences on families (Jack 2000). Conversely, social isolation has been identified as potentially harmful to satisfactory parenting, with a number of research studies demonstrating an association between social isolation and child abuse and neglect (Coohey 1996; Thompson 1995), as well as poorer health (Blaxter 1990). However, personal social networks are not automatically beneficial. Unreliable, critical or conflictual network relationships can seriously undermine well-being, especially for those who are dependent on more restricted networks to begin with. Unfortunately, those who are likely to be in the greatest need of the benefits of social support also tend to have access to more restricted, unreliable or unsatisfying social relationships (Jack and Gill 2003). This tendency, along with the other features and functions of social capital and social networks highlighted above, have obvious implications for the design of community programmes intended to improve the lives of children and parents living in disadvantaged areas, as we will now go on to consider.

Until recently, the main source of support for neighbourhood regeneration programmes in England was the Single Regeneration Budget (SRB), which supports over 1000 separate schemes in the most disadvantaged communities, using a partnership approach involving the local authority, residents, the business community, voluntary organizations and community groups. The main targets for improvement are the employment prospects, education and skills of local people, as well as housing, community safety and overall quality of life. Funding is used to employ staff, develop local community groups and improve local facilities, including the housing stock. In this way, neighbourhood regeneration programmes aim to tackle some of the structural inequalities that affect people living in disadvantaged areas, as well as to improve the levels of social capital.

Researchers at Cambridge University who are evaluating the SRB programme have identified effective partnership working as the key to success. Problems have arisen where key partners have been excluded, where the right calibre of staff has not been recruited or where insufficient support and training have been provided to facilitate the full participation of local people. However, although it is too early to draw firm conclusions about the overall impact of the SRB programme, the initial findings appear to be rather disappointing. Although it has been successful in targeting social need and deprivation and has encouraged more effective community participation (with some private sector involvement), significant beneficial changes in outcomes have been more difficult to identify. For example, although SRB programmes are associated with some movement from welfare to work, this is only apparent amongst younger age groups, and there was no evidence of improved health outcome amongst residents in three early case study areas. Other small improvements within SRB areas have tended to mirror similar changes for England as a whole (Rhodes *et al.* 2002).

Two more recent government-supported neighbourhood regeneration programmes, the New Deal for Communities (NDC) and the Neighbourhood Renewal Fund (NRF), are also in the process of being evaluated. The NDC is providing substantial funds for 39 of the most deprived neighbourhoods in England, to set up *community-led* partnerships, delivering multifaceted regeneration initiatives over a ten-year period, targeted at improvements in employment, health, crime and educational achievement. Once again, partnership working appears to be of central importance, with several schemes experiencing conflicts between local residents, community representatives and other partnership members. The 'formidable obstacles to effective partnership working' that have been identified tend to be exacerbated by the top-down nature of these programmes, with budgets and targets dictated largely by Whitehall (Painter and Clarence 2001, p.1229). Many NDC schemes also report being over-burdened by government red tape, with the Treasury apparently anxious about having put responsibility for so much money into the hands of local people, yet at the same time criticizing them if they fail to allocate it on time. In future, the government is unlikely to set up regeneration programmes with local people in the lead role. For example, the Neighbourhood Renewal Fund (NRF), targeted at a further 88 deprived areas in England, is being delivered through Local Strategic Partnerships led by local authority chief executives.

Within neighbourhood regeneration programmes there is also increasing interest in the role that schools can play. For several years, education policy has focused almost exclusively on raising standards *within* schools. However, there is now a growing realization that there are limits to what can be achieved by schools serving very deprived areas if they do not also work with their local communities. This is the idea behind 'extended schools' that are open beyond normal hours to provide a wider range of services for the local communities in which they are situated, including adult education, sports and arts facilities, child care, parenting support, ICT access and on-site health and social services. The government has provided funding to support 240 extended school projects over a three-year period from 2003, with the aim of establishing at least one extended school in every local authority area by 2006 (Ashton 2003). Researchers at Newcastle University are currently studying two such schools in contrasting local education authorities, to evaluate their contribution to neighbourhood regeneration. Preliminary analysis has not revealed evidence of differential effectiveness between the local authorities, but some familiar difficulties have already emerged in relation to partnership working, as well as concerns about the limited impact of other initiatives to relieve deep-seated deprivation in their catchment areas (Dyson, Millward and Cummings 2003).

Evidence of Programme Effectiveness: Community Development with Young People

Although community development and user-participation strategies are common to all community programmes, the particular issues involved in working with children and young people make it worth dealing with this topic separately here. In broad terms, community development involves working with people (usually disadvantaged groups), who are helped to identify and organize effective ways of expressing and meeting their needs, through a combination of self-help, mutual aid, social networking, community participation, advocacy, and campaigning initiatives (Craig 2002; Popple 1995). The participation of children and young people in decisions that affect their lives is now firmly enshrined in national and international legislation, such as the Children Act 1989 and the United Nations Convention on the Rights of the Child. However, there is a growing recognition that it can also provide benefits for the development and delivery of services overall.

A small but growing number of UK publications are beginning to provide insights into some of the issues involved in achieving the participation of children and young people in community programmes (Cairns 2001; Henderson 1995; Lewis and Lindsay 2000; Prout 2002; Wellard, Bartley and Gleave 1997). For instance, one study found that young people were enthusiastic about participation in local government in relation to specific issues, such as crime and safety, education, and leisure. However, the research revealed that success often depended on developing innovative approaches that challenged the capacity and established practice of staff and organizations (Combe 2002). Other studies and reviews provide insights into the issues raised when involving young people in community safety projects (Kitchin 2000; McGee 2001) and neighbourhood regeneration in general (Fitzpatrick, Hastings and Kintrea 1998; Speak 2000), including their participation through youth forums and councils (Matthews *et al.* 1998).

Unfortunately, firm evidence about the actual effectiveness of community development work with young people, from a UK perspective, is rather more limited, with many programmes either reporting at a purely descriptive level or awaiting the outcome of evaluations that are currently in their early stages. What little evaluative research has been conducted tends to focus on process rather than outcome issues. In particular, a number of studies have looked at the ability of outreach schemes to engage with 'hard-to-reach' groups of young people, such as those who live in isolated locations, or belong to socially excluded groups, such as disabled or homeless young people, or those excluded from school (Doy, Gilbert and Aitland

2001; Pain *et al.* 2002). while they help to identify important components in strategies to effectively consult with socially excluded young people and to involve them in decision making and service development, most of them have yet to produce meaningful evidence about the lasting impact of different approaches with different groups.

Evidence of Programme Effectiveness: Preventing Child Abuse and Neglect

There are a number of reasons why community approaches to the prevention of child abuse and neglect ought to be able to make a significant contribution to the range of different strategies for tackling this issue. First of all, rates of officially reported child abuse vary from area to area and some of this variation remains after controlling for local agency policies and resources, and the individual characteristics of residents (Baldwin and Carruthers 1998; Cotterill 1988; Coulton *et al.* 1995; Garbarino and Kostelny 1992; Vinson *et al.* 1996). Second, there is considerable evidence to show that physical child abuse and neglect, and the stresses experienced by parents, are associated with *community* levels of poverty and other forms of inequality (Ghate and Hazel 2002; Graham *et al.* 1998; Macdonald 1999; Putnam 2000; Wilkinson 1996). Third, the cultural attitudes and beliefs that exist at community levels also influence levels of child abuse (Belsky 1993).

Any strategy to prevent child abuse and neglect is heavily dependent on their official definitions. It is well documented that, historically, the UK has developed rather narrow definitions of child abuse that have focused on individual 'cases', with responsibility usually laid at the door of specific 'perpetrators' (Parton 1991, 1997; Wattam 1999). As a result, attempts to prevent the problem have concentrated on identifying the adults responsible and designing intervention strategies directed at 'high-risk' families. Wider issues in society that are also damaging to children's well-being, such as poverty, exclusion from mainstream services, and racial discrimination, which highlight the need for more fundamental social, political and cultural changes, have hitherto been largely excluded from the agenda.

Advocates of community approaches to the prevention of child abuse and neglect point to the fact that children officially categorized as having been abused, as well as the families they come from, are not inherently different from many other children and families (Cawson 2002). Furthermore, epidemiological evidence indicates that the number of children identified as having been abused, in any society, is likely to be strongly correlated with the general conditions in which children are being raised in that society. The best way of preventing or reducing the problem might, therefore, lie in achieving moderate levels of change in the circumstances of all children and families, rather than focusing exclusively on 'high-risk' groups (Rose

1992). Without achieving such change, people successfully removed from a high-risk category are likely to be quickly replaced by others from the general population, a pattern all too familiar to child protection workers in the UK.

In recent years, attempts have been made to broaden the definition of child abuse used in the UK, notably by the National Commission of Inquiry into the Prevention of Child Abuse (NCIPCA), set up in 1994 by the NSPCC. Their definition included: 'anything which individuals, institutions or processes do or fail to do which directly or indirectly harms children...' (NCIPCA 1996, p.4). The report provoked a generally hostile political and media reaction when it was published. However, more recently, a number of the commission's broader recommendations are being introduced, including the development of Children's Trusts, bringing together social, health and education services for children, and the appointment of an independent Children's Commissioner for England, to match similar appointments in the other parts of the UK. The government has also committed itself to ending child poverty and has funded community-based programmes like Sure Start and the Children's Fund, as well as requiring local authorities to develop preventive strategies for children and young people, most recently under the Children Act 2004.

The neighbourhood regeneration programmes that have been considered already in this chapter share some of the features that the research suggests need to be included in community approaches to the prevention of child physical abuse and neglect. Common features include community surveys to identify local needs, services and patterns of social support, and goals to alleviate the stressful effects of community-level poverty and other inequalities, to build the capacity of the community through improved training and employment opportunities and to enhance social capital through the development of trusting and reciprocal social networks and participation in community organizations and activities (Gill *et al.* 2000; Jack 2004; Nelson and Baldwin 2002, 2004).

Although most community programmes do not explicitly identify the reduction or prevention of child abuse amongst their stated goals, one programme that did aim to do this was developed on the Canklow estate in Rotherham. Here, the local authority set up a small team of community social workers to develop the social support networks of local families. They used community development methods to establish and support a wide range of community groups, including pre-school playgroups, youth clubs, women's groups and adult education classes. An evaluation of the project, after a five-year period, revealed significant reductions in children placed on the child protection register and children 'looked after' by the local authority or supervised within their own homes (Eastham 1990). Unfortunately, the culture within mainstream child welfare agencies in the UK, with its emphasis on individual approaches to safeguarding children, in the context of high profile public inquiries into child abuse deaths such as that of Victoria Climbié (Cm.5730 2003), means that initiatives of this kind have proved difficult to maintain in the long term (Davies 2004; Jordan 1997).

Since sexual abuse tends not to show the same associations with poverty and deprivation as other forms of child abuse, community programmes designed to prevent child sexual abuse have adopted more universal approaches, often involving education strategies. Nearly all of the programmes whose outcomes have been evaluated have dealt with the education of children, usually in school settings. The general conclusion that emerges from these evaluations is that education programmes, usually combining verbal instruction with some form of skills training, are effective in increasing children's knowledge and skills in the classroom. However, these benefits fade over time and their effectiveness in preventing actual incidents of sexual abuse is not known (MacMillan *et al.* 1994; Rispens, Aleman and Gourdena 1997).

Another important aspect of community responses to child sexual abuse has been the growth of self-help groups, particularly women's groups and those for adults and children who have either experienced sexual abuse themselves, or who are non-abusing parents (Lloyd 1993; Smith 1994). When considered individually, groups of this nature could not be classified as coming within the definition of community programmes used in this chapter. However, when viewed as part of the social capital of the community, providing opportunities for individuals to extend their social networks and influencing community beliefs and attitudes about sexual abuse, they clearly play a role. In a similar way, parenting groups, as well as a wide range of child care and educational facilities in an area, can all help to enhance the level of social cohesion and interaction within a community, breaking down barriers and potentially developing both bonding and bridging social capital. These sort of developments may also have an important role to play in combating organized sexual abuse in particular communities, although this is not something that has been investigated in any systematic way so far (Gallagher 1998).

Evidence of Programme Effectiveness: Reducing Youth Crime

As with the other social problems that have been considered so far in this chapter, the research evidence clearly shows that much of the spatial variation in crime can be explained by selection processes, such as the operation of the employment and housing markets, that lead to concentrations of people with similar characteristics living in particular locations (Bottoms and Wiles 1986; Murie 1997). However, crime rates continue to show variations between areas that have been matched for their socio-economic and demographic characteristics (Hope and Foster 1992). So, once again, the area in which people live and the way that they interact with one another there also have significant influences. A community's level of social organization and its ability to exercise informal social controls over local residents play an important role in determining levels of crime (Bottoms and Wiles 1997). The community model of crime prevention is, therefore, based on the assumption that crime will go down if residents get to know and trust each other better through increased opportunities for interaction, facilitating greater informal controls on behaviour within their neighbourhoods (Donnelly and Kimble 1997).

Analysis of the British Crime Survey has revealed that areas with higher rates of crime and delinquency than would be predicted by their population profiles were characterized by sparse friendship networks, unsupervised teenage peer groups and low organizational participation (Sampson and Groves 1989). Subsequent work suggested that the key component of spatial variations in juvenile crime was a form of social capital that the researchers called 'collective efficacy'. They used this term to refer to the level of mutual trust among neighbours, combined with a willingness to intervene to supervise children and to maintain public order (Sampson *et al.* 1997). So, how have community intervention programmes attempted to translate this kind of theoretical knowledge into strategies to reduce youth crime?

When the new Labour Government came to power in 1997 they made the reduction of crime (and the reduction of the *causes* of crime) a central plank of their social policy programme, with a particular emphasis on young offenders. As part of their overall crime reduction strategy they introduced several new community programmes designed to develop models of youth crime prevention in a restricted number of 'high crime, high deprivation communities' (Home Office 1999).

One of these, Summer Plus, was an initiative designed to reduce street crime by children and young people aged 8–19 years in 34 areas across England, through the provision of 'purposeful activity' during the summer period in 2002, in which over 10,000 youngsters took part. Although the pilot projects were targeted at children and young people considered to be at high risk of becoming involved in crime, the independent evaluators have recommended that future projects should include a much broader range of children living in high crime *areas* in order to harness the benefits of wider peer interactions and relationships (CRG 2003). The initial national programme was judged to have had a positive impact, particularly when projects included educational components, rather than relying on purely diversionary activities. Participants reported improvements in their self-confidence, behaviour, attitudes towards others and future aspirations, and youth crime fell significantly more in the programme areas than in the rest of the country, although the evaluators acknowledge that the effects of other initiatives in these areas may also have played a role.

Early evaluation of parenting programmes for parents of young offenders or children at risk of becoming involved in crime also suggests positive outcomes have been achieved (Ghate and Ramella 2002). Nearly 3000 parents, who participated in

34 different programmes across England and Wales between 1999 and 2001, contributed to the initial evaluation. In the year prior to the parents' involvement, 89 per cent of their children had been convicted of an offence, compared with 61.5 per cent in the following year. There was also a reduction of 50 per cent in the number of recorded offences committed by the children over the same period (from an average of 4.4, down to 2.1). Nine out of ten parents surveyed said they would recommend such programmes to other parents in their situation. Once again, interventions like this, targeted on only a selection of parents, do not fit the definition of community programmes being used here. However, details are included because of government plans to make parenting programmes universally available in disadvantaged neighbourhoods in the future.

A more comprehensive community approach is at the centre of another promising crime reduction programme. This is Communities That Care (CTC), originally developed in the US but now being piloted in 23 areas across the UK. In addition to targeting the reduction of youth crime, the CTC approach is also designed to reduce school failure, drug abuse and teenage pregnancy. It is based on research evidence about the risk and protective factors associated with these problems (e.g. Rutter *et al.* 1998; Farrington 1996). The underlying assumption is that reductions in risk factors (and increases in protective factors) in particular locations will help to reduce the levels of problem behaviours found there (Catalano and Hawkins 1996).

The involvement of the local community and professional workers is an essential component of CTC, with the aim of enhancing social capital by promoting community investment in prevention activities, developing norms against antisocial behaviour and reducing social disorganization. After establishing a local partnership, a systematic assessment of the local community and its services is undertaken, facilitating debate between professionals and local people about the problems in the area and evidence about effective strategies for addressing them. As with other such partnership approaches, evaluators have identified the role of the partnership coordinator to be crucial in establishing programmes (France 2001). However, the most recent evidence about the impact of the CTC programme in the UK, evaluated over a three-year period, concluded that only one of the three projects studied had operated successfully and demonstrated any significant reduction in the risk factors associated with offending in that area (Crow *et al.* 2004).

Conclusion

The evidence presented in this chapter makes it clear that the most significant influences on children and families are the result of the structural inequalities, affecting particular groups of people, which run throughout British society.

However, there is also repeated evidence which shows that where people live and how they interact with one another in their local communities also have an impact on the well-being of children and parents. This means that efforts to improve the lives of children need to combine strategies to combat the inequalities experienced by individuals and groups *wherever they live*, with community programmes that can effectively address the disadvantages that affect people living in particular *areas.*

Unfortunately, evidence about the effectiveness of community programmes of this nature in the UK is quite limited at the present time. What is known indicates just how difficult it has proved, so far, to develop and maintain effective community programmes in the UK, particularly in relation to achieving the successful partnerships, between professionals and local people, upon which they are based.

In the meantime, other policy developments in the child welfare field, driven by concerns to develop more effective approaches to safeguarding children and the promotion of their welfare, are likely to lead to requirements for even more collaborative and partnership working. For example, the Green Paper on children's services, *Every Child Matters* (Cm.5860 2003) sets out the UK government's strategy for the integrated delivery of children's education, health and social services, with appropriate links to other agencies. Multidisciplinary teams, based in and around neighbourhood Children's Centres and Extended Schools will provide services for disadvantaged children, and those with additional needs, within the context of universal services for all children. These arrangements provide the potential to bridge some of the gaps that currently exist between statutory services and their local communities but that potential is only likely to be realized if there are substantial changes in organizational priorities and professional practice.

In particular, the processes for gathering and analysing information (at both individual and community levels) need to be improved, and more encouragement needs to be given to community development practice within mainstream services. Many of the measures required to assess the strengths and pressures that exist at community levels, which involve the collection of data from community surveys and the design and delivery of community programmes that address area disadvantages, demand good relationships with a wide range of community organizations and residents (Green 2000; Hawtin, Hughes and Percy-Smith 1994; Murtagh 1999 Skinner and Wilson 2002). These requirements present formidable challenges to existing arrangements within mainstream services, in which there is still an overwhelming emphasis on only the most vulnerable (or dangerous) children and adults. New initiatives, including some of the community programmes that have been reviewed here, and other community-based programmes (such as Sure Start and the Children's Fund), are helping to lead the way in developing the broader networks of relationships that are required for successful approaches to work with disadvantaged communities. However, as we have noted, these developments are still in their early stages and there is still a lot to learn about the best ways of constructing a range of different community programmes, and how to integrate this learning into the policy and practice of mainstream children's services.

CHAPTER 25

Community Programs in the US

Jacquelyn McCroskey

Introduction

Most family-centered community-based programs are designed with prevention in mind, whether they focus on primary, secondary or tertiary strategies. Primary prevention strategies, which make supports available universally to all families, are notoriously difficult to evaluate since there may be many reasons for the absence of problems. It can also be difficult to demonstrate the impact of secondary prevention strategies for at-risk children, families or neighborhoods because risk factors are not reliable, or uncomplicated, predictors of poor outcomes.

The most compelling evidence to date about the effectiveness of family-centered community-based programs is from comprehensive early intervention or maternal and child health programs where reductions in child maltreatment are only one of many benefits associated with program participation. There is also some evidence of effectiveness for tertiary prevention or treatment programs aimed at preventing more bad things from happening to already-troubled children and families. As researchers learn about the extraordinary resilience of children and families (Werner and Smith 2001), and the ripple effects of community engagement and enhancement strategies (Hess, McGowan and Botsko 2003; Medoff and Sklar 1994), evaluators are increasingly turning away from traditional research methods to "logic models" and other non-experimental research methods to describe the lessons learned from these complex interactions (Fulbright-Anderson, Kubisch and Connell 1998).

It may be especially important in an international volume to highlight differences between three strands of thought emerging in the US in regard to family-centered, community-based approaches:

1.   *Community-based supports for families.* "Supports" include things such as early childhood development, maternal and child health, and education

programs that all parents may need in order to raise healthy children. While families already known to or at risk of being known to child protection or social service agencies may participate, they are usually not there because of these connections.

2. *Building community capacity:* Efforts include mobilizing residents and key stakeholders in specific neighborhoods to address important local issues (such strategies are generally called comprehensive community initiatives), addressing the fragmentation of large-scale service systems (service integration strategies), engaging people to work together to solve their own problems (community engagement strategies), and/or developing local decision-making capacities (community development strategies).

3. *Community-based family-centered services:* Services may be designed by multi disciplinary teams of professionals, often with advice and input from clients and community members; these services provide voluntary or mandatory remediation services for high-risk families or those already involved with public social service systems.

The Interventions and their Theoretical Bases

The child welfare system in the US has developed piecemeal over time without the benefit of a systematic retooling process such as that envisioned in the UK's Children Act 1989. The three strands of 19th-century thought that helped set the stage for today's fragmented system were the settlement houses, Charity Organization Societies (COS) and Societies for the Prevention of Cruelty to Children. The premises and values of each of these approaches are still relevant but each suggests different directions for development of family-centered community-based strategies (McCroskey 2003a).

The COS casework approach suggests that family problems require professional casework "services" which may be provided directly by public agencies or through referral to community-based service providers. The settlement house approach, the inspiration for many community-based efforts, suggests that family stresses are created or exacerbated by social and economic forces, that families will take advantage of voluntary "supports," and that comprehensive approaches are needed to effectively address the underlying causes of family problems (i.e., racism, poverty, substance abuse, violence). The law enforcement approach attributed to "the Cruelty" (Folks 1902) emphasized "rescuing" children from unsafe homes with visible conse-quences for perpetrators so that other "bad" parents would be scared into judicious behavior; but inability to find safe and nurturing alternatives for these children peri-odically cycles attention back to family-centered, community-based services.

Today's family-centered, community-building approaches are rooted in concepts about ecological systems, resilience, and developmental transactions between children and the people in their environments (Sameroff and Fiese 1990). Rather than treatment or remediation, resilience-oriented transactional models provide supports for families based on a value-driven set of principles about relationships between families and professionals. In traditional programs, professionals hold the lion's share of knowledge, power and responsibility for developing therapeutic relationships. In family support and community-building programs, relationships are based on mutual respect between people in different roles seeking practical solutions to mutually identified problems.

Family Support

While the idea of supporting families is definitely not new, establishment of Family Support America (originally the Family Resource Coalition) in the early 1980s focused attention on giving families access to the support they need in welcoming surroundings in their own communities, where knowledgeable and respectful staff speak family languages and respect their cultural traditions. Such supports build on family strengths, increase stability, improve parenting skills, and thus enhance child development. The family support "movement" encourages egalitarian, flexible, and respectful interactions between families and professional helpers. Its core principles include staff and families working together with equality and respect; families serving as resources; affirmation of cultural, racial, and linguistic identities; and flexibility and responsiveness to emerging issues.

Building Community Capacity

Ecological and transactional theories posit that child development occurs over time through transactions between children and their caregivers, as well as between families and their communities. Since healthy child development requires more than even the best-functioning service delivery systems can ever provide, it is important that families, communities, and service systems acknowledge their mutual interests and purposes. Enhancing the capacity of local communities to engage people in shared problem solving is even more urgent for maltreated children and for their families who are very likely to rely on public programs. As the Executive Session on Child Protection noted, the "heart" of an improved child protective services system is "a community partnership for child protection" (Farrow 1997, p.vii).

At the same time that they build community partnerships, public agencies need to integrate services better across key domains such as health, mental health, juvenile justice, housing and employment services. The potential benefits include helping families before a crisis develops; preventing or addressing substance abuse; ensuring stable health, mental health and education services for children already in foster care, assuring employment and/or income support benefits for adult family members; and preventing children from "graduating" from dependency to juvenile delinquency.

Family-centered Community-based Child Welfare Services

Family-centered services designed to prevent child maltreatment, improve family functioning, and keep or return children home to their families have been at the core of child welfare reform efforts for decades (McCroskey 2003a; McCroskey and Meezan 1998; Schorr 1997; Walton *et al.* 2001). Popular service models include intensive family preservation services, family group conferences and wraparound, among others. Waldfogel (1998) describes community partnership and differential response efforts as providing "a customized response, depending on each family's needs and strengths" where public child welfare departments share responsibilities with a broad range of community partners.

Evidence on Program Effectiveness

There is some research to support continuing efforts in each of these three arenas, but available evidence is seldom conclusive and there are significant gaps in knowledge. There are also unanswered questions about how well prevailing standards for research fit the requirements of family support and community capacity building. Randomized clinical trials may set a reasonable standard for evaluating family-centered intervention programs, because professionals running these programs can allow or restrict access to services under relatively controlled conditions. In the other two arenas, however, professionals do not exert "control" over whether families accept or incorporate support, or whether communities have or increase capacities. Indeed, in some situations, efforts to do so would betray the basic principles of equality, respect, flexibility and responsiveness that guide this work. But while research "standards" are still controversial, even the limited evidence now available in all three arenas makes their potential hard to ignore.

Family Support

Perhaps the most compelling evidence related to family support comes from basic research on resilience rather than from applied research evaluating specific family support programs. For example, in summarizing longitudinal findings from Kauai, Werner and Smith describe a common core of individual characteristics and supports that contribute to childhood resiliency and adult "recovery" from adverse circumstances:

This core includes temperamental characteristics that elicit positive social responses from parents, peers, and teachers; efficacy, planfulness and self-esteem; competent caregivers and supportive adults (other than parents) who foster trust and a sense of coherence or faith; and "second chance" opportunities in society at large (at school, at work, in church, in the military) which enable high-risk youth to acquire competence and confidence. (Werner and Smith 1992, p.187)

Highlighting the critical roles played by caring adults who nurture and inspire children, Werner and Smith (2001) call attention to the support provided by extended family members, teachers, youth leaders, ministers, mentors, friends, and ultimately coworkers and bosses.

The considerable evaluation literature now available on family support is perhaps best summarized by Abt Associates' National Evaluation of Family Support Programs (Layzer *et al.* 2001; Layzer and Goodson 2001). Abt's meta-analysis of 665 studies representing 260 programs showed, not surprisingly, a range of effects with those for child cognitive and social development, parenting attitudes and behavior, and child safety being among the largest.

In response, authors in the spring 2002 Evaluation Exchange newsletter suggested some next steps for the field. For example, McCartney and Dearing (2002) observe that the field will need to address effect sizes more systematically—since statistical significance alone, without demonstration of practical differences for families, should not justify program implementation. Particularly in a field devoted to the well-being of families and children, research protocols need to be judged by their relevance to families and communities. This also raises a question about which conclusions from which reporters should carry most weight in understanding program impact and importance (McCroskey and Meezan 1997). Luckily, most studies of family support have employed multiple measures, both standardized and newly developed, to capture the perceptions of different reporters.

Comer and Frazer's review of three studies using random assignment and three using matched comparison groups concluded that "support services produced gains in both immediate and long-term outcomes" (Comer and Fraser 1998, p.141), as well as some "sleeper" effects that manifested two to three years after the intervention. All six programs were designed to provide a comprehensive long-term array of services, and each relied on multidisciplinary service teams that customized home visits, developmental screening, parent training and other family supports to meet the particular needs of poor (often uneducated) families in specific communities.

Eckenrode, Izzo and Campa-Muller's (2003) review described findings from family support and early intervention programs designed to improve parenting, and increase children's education and life chances. Based primarily on studies using random assignment to controlled experiments, they summarize the most persuasive research available on the short and long term benefits of early childhood education programs, including the High/Scope Perry Preschool Program, the Chicago Child–Parent Centers, and the Carolina Abecedarian Project. Taken together, the findings of these studies continue to fuel development of early education and universal pre-school programs in communities across the United States. The authors report mixed findings from programs aimed at improving maternal life course development, but at least one – David Olds' nurse home-visiting program – includes compelling findings on reduced child maltreatment as a result of early intervention (Olds *et al.* 1997). Findings from the Chicago Child–Parent Centers also show reductions in maltreatment as a result of early education and parent involvement (Horton 2003; Reynolds 1998; Reynolds and Robertson 2003).

Building Community Capacity

How important are neighborhoods in setting the context for child development and family behaviors? While both personal experiences and the stories of others suggest that neighborhoods set a crucial context for development, research on how and for whom neighborhood factors have most impact is relatively limited. Shonkoff and Phillips (2000) summarize their review of literature by suggesting that conditions in the family are generally more important than neighborhood context for children in non-inner-city neighborhoods, while neighborhood conditions make a great deal of difference for many families in poor inner-city neighborhoods. The most compelling research evidence concerns programs that move families out of high-poverty neighborhoods into low-poverty neighborhoods, thus enhancing physical and psychological health and reducing adolescent crime.

Epstein's 2003 *New York Times* article suggests that the grinding poverty of many of America's rundown urban neighborhoods may indeed be "enough to make you sick:"

> Whatever the miasma is that afflicts America's minority poor, it is at least partly a legacy of the segregation of America's cities. These neighborhoods, by concentrating the poor, also concentrate the mysterious, as yet poorly understood, factors that make them sick. (Epstein 2003, p.108)

Evidence on the impact of specific capacity building initiatives in poor neighborhoods is limited, but promising practices are emerging from a broad range of efforts (Schorr 1997). Efforts to build community capacities are generally based on at least one of the following key strategies: leadership development, organizational development, community organizing and/or inter-organizational collaboration (Chaskin *et al.* 2001). Roth and Brooks-Gunn (2003) cite evidence from 48 effective community-based youth development programs. Mentoring, apprenticeship, civic activism and leadership programs also demonstrate promising results when children and adolescents gain access to caring non-parent adults (Rhodes and Roffman 2003).

ReadBoston, a citywide Mayoral initiative focused on increasing reading proficiency, and San Antonio's efforts to improve kindergarten readiness, provide examples of how cities are mobilizing residents to work together toward improving outcomes for children and families (Weissbourd 2003; www.sanantonio.gov). Evidence of promising practices from such strengths-based activities is available from projects at different geographic levels (e.g., neighborhoods, cities, counties) (Ashcraft 2003; Mannes *et al.* 2003; McCroskey 2003b). Case histories of service integration projects in specific localities in California also suggest promising results from deliberate action strategies that span departmental silos to integrate services for children and families (Austin 1997).

Family-centered, Community-based Child Welfare Services

While there has been considerable debate about the research methods and outcome measures used to evaluate the effectiveness of specific family preservation service models (Fraser *et al.* 1996; Jacobs, Williams and Kapuscik 1997; Pecora *et al.* 1995), there is little doubt in the field as a whole that an array of family-centered service programs are needed to serve families and children in communities across the country.

Family-centered services are used throughout the child welfare system for prevention, alternative response or diversion of at-risk families from protective services, treatment services for children already in the system, reunification of families, and support for kinship or adoptive families when children cannot be protected at home. These services may be provided through referral to community-based agencies (some of which operate under contract with the public child welfare agency and some of which receive funding from other public agencies, charitable or philanthropic fundraising) or by specialized units in public child welfare agencies.

There is persuasive evidence of effectiveness for a few program models including Multisystemic Therapy (MST) which provides family-centered services for adolescents involved in the juvenile justice system. Documented effects of MST include fewer arrests and decreased aggression (Halliday-Boykins and Henggeler 2001; Henggeler *et al.* 1998).

In her review of the literature on community-based mental health services for foster children, Marsenich (2002) used the National Institute of Mental Health standards for evidence-based research including at least two controlled clinical trials, a minimum of two investigators, tests of clinical significance and long-term outcomes lasting beyond program termination. Using these rigorous standards, she found strong evidence of effectiveness for only two programs – wraparound (as designed by Hewitt Clark and colleagues at the University of South Florida) and treatment foster care (Patricia Chamberlain and colleagues at the Oregon Social Learning Center). She also found promising initial evidence for two other programs – early intervention foster care (Phil Fisher and colleagues at the Oregon Social Learning Center) and foster parent attachment training (Mary Dozier and colleagues at the University of Delaware). All of these services are provided in community settings rather than in clinics or offices, treat parents as partners, are sensitive to the families' cultures, and are less expensive than institutional care.

Decisions about where and when to place children have generally been made by individual public agency workers and court officials. Glisson (1994) used a quasi-experimental design to compare child outcomes in two pilot areas (made up of six Tennessee counties each) using multi-agency services coordination teams versus comparable areas using traditional decision-making methods. Counties were matched on per capita income, custody rates and population demographics. He showed that implementation of multi-agency service teams in the pilot areas not only improved decision making, but also improved psychosocial functioning for children. There is also limited evidence from other community-based partnership initiatives suggesting that such reforms, while extremely complex and challenging, can be beneficial both for clients and for service systems over the long run (Waldfogel 1998).

Conclusion

There is now some promising evidence that family-centered community-based approaches can be effective in supporting families, enhancing communities, and providing family-centered services, placing prevention and child protection firmly in the ecological context of local communities. There is also persuasive evidence that some of the most intensely studied early intervention programs in the US (i.e., nurse home visiting, Chicago Child–Parent Centers, High/Scope) can also be extremely effective in decreasing maltreatment over the long term. Research has shown at least short-term impact for some specialized intervention programs such as MST and wraparound that address the comprehensive treatment needs of families already involved in the child welfare system. And when children need to be removed from their birth families, it appears that similar kinds of services can enable foster, kinship and adoptive families to care effectively for these troubled and traumatized children. None of these families stands alone; they rely on the continuing support of professionals, friends, neighbors and kin to help them raise their children to healthy, happy and productive adulthood – as do we all.

PART SIX

Summary and Conclusion

CHAPTER 26

Effective Child Welfare Interventions: Evidence for Practice

Colette McAuley, Peter J. Pecora and Wendy Rose

Introduction

In this final chapter, we look at the development of evidence-based policy and practice and some of the debates around what constitutes evidence. Lessons from the evidence in this volume are then considered before some broad recommendations relating to research, policy and service delivery are made.

Evidence-based Policy and Practice

The National Service Framework for Children, Young People and Maternity Services was introduced as part of the UK government's modernization agenda for health and welfare services. Its aim is 'to improve the lives of children and young people through the development of effective, evidence-based and needs-led services' (Department of Health 2003a, p.2). In setting out national standards for health, social and educational services for children, a strong emphasis has been placed on the standards being based upon research evidence (Sloper and Statham 2004).

Evidence-based policy and practice has been the subject of considerable debate in the UK, US and Europe. Increasingly in the UK and US, there is a move towards evidence-based policy, leading to a recognition within most helping professions of the need to develop an evidence base to justify policy and practice developments. Increased scrutiny of public expenditure, coupled with concern that limited resources should be targeted where there is most likelihood of tangible benefits, has fuelled a preoccupation with determining outcomes of interventions.

Evidence-based practice as a concept originated with health academics in Canada. Their original definition described evidence-based practice as a process which considers 'the conscientious, explicit and judicious use of current best evidence in making decisions about the care of individuals' (Sackett *et al.* 1997). Writers in the field emphasize that it is a process involving a number of stages starting with the motivation to adopt this approach. Having convinced themselves of the value of this approach, agencies then need to consider their information needs and formulate these into questions. A consideration of the types of available evidence to provide answers should follow before a critical appraisal of the evidence for validity and applicability to practice. The results from the review of selected evidence should then be applied to policy and practice with the resultant performance criteria set for future practice (Greenhalgh 2001; Sackett *et al.* 1997).

On the face of it, it would be hard to argue with the intention of developing well-informed decision making based upon the best available published research to provide the most effective services for children and families (Barratt 2003; Humphries 2003). However, the collection of evidence is a complex social activity influenced by competing interests. Policy and practice are often not based on evidence but on ideology or politics which may lead to available evidence being ignored.

What Constitutes Evidence?

In both UK and US health literature, there are clear hierarchies of research evidence used to grade health care recommendations (see, for example, Guyatt *et al.* 1995; Khan *et al.* 2001). These generally place systematic reviews and randomized controlled trials (RCTs) at the top of the hierarchy, with cross-sectional surveys, case reports and expert opinion at the lower end. In the social care field, there are still very few studies involving RCTs or involving experimental or quasi-experimental designs and indeed their feasibility has been questioned for research in the community (Ghate 2001). While most people would agree that we need to try to achieve the best possible evidence to answer questions about effectiveness, there has been considerable disquiet about adopting a 'narrow' view of the evidence to be included. In the UK, some writers argue that evidence on effectiveness should be restricted to RCTs or studies with random assignment or control/comparison groups (Macdonald 1999). Others take the view that much relevant information to identify and understand problems (which remains highly relevant in many areas of social care research) can be found in wider types of studies/sources (Qureshi 2004). Yet others fundamentally question the appropriateness of examining social care interventions via methods developed to investigate health-care options and based on a positivist view of the world (Humphries 2003).

One primary concern with adopting a narrower view of relevant evidence is the likely exclusion of the views of service users and carers as well as professionals. More recent definitions of evidence-based approaches, however, have specifically addressed this. For example, *research in practice* (one of the largest children and families research implementation project in England and Wales) defines an evidence-based approach as '[one] informed by the best available evidence of what is effective, the practice expertise of professionals and the experience and views of service users' (Barratt and Cook 2001, p.2).

The Children's National Service Framework (NSF) has adopted a similar approach (Department of Health and Department for Education and Skills 2004; Sloper and Statham 2004). The NSF Research Group used a typology of evidence which identified the different types of evidence used to support the development of the NSF and thereby made explicit the need for various kinds of evidence to answer different types of research question (see Box 26.1).

Box 26.1: Classification of Types of Evidence

Evidence from Expert Opinion

A1 Systematic reviews which include at least one RCT

A2 Other systematic and high quality reviews which synthesize references

B1 Individual RCTs

B2 Individualized, non-randomized, experimental/intervention studies

B3 Individual well-designed non-experimental studies, controlled statistically if appropriate

C1 Descriptive and other research or evaluation not in B

C2 Case studies and examples of good practice

D Summary review articles and discussions of relevant literature and conference proceedings not otherwise classified

Evidence from expert opinion

P Professional opinion, including reports of committees, inquiries, Social Services Inspectorate inspections

U1 User views – children

U2 User views – parents/carers

Source: Department of Health 2005, p.9

An important point was that the classification was not intended to be a hierarchical system as the NSF Research Group took the position that the most appropriate type of evidence would be determined by the research questions posed. While they recognized that experimental and quasi-experimental designs may be particularly suitable for research on effectiveness, other studies were seen to make an important contribution. Taking account of the views of users was also clearly valued. Both qualitative and quantitative evidence were included, with the former being seen as particularly suited to gaining in-depth knowledge about the views of children and their families on their needs and services they have received. Fuller information on the National Service Framework is available on their website (www.publica-tions.doh.gov.uk/nsf/children).

In her 2004 article, Qureshi emphasizes that the relative quality of a research design should be judged according to the 'suitability of the design and methods for answering the particular question' (p.10). She goes on to stress that even when the ultimate aim is more information about effectiveness, the current state of knowledge or practice may demand prior questions and designs more appropriate. Littell's recent experience in conducting a review of Multisystemic Therapy for the Cochrane and Campbell Collaborations illustrated how statistical analysis issues such as subject attrition and examination of the effects of treatment on the treated are important to understanding the evidence base for a particular intervention approach (Littell 2005). A major challenge facing the field is that of how to evaluate increasingly more complex community-based services such as Sure Start (National Evaluation of Sure Start Team 2005; Pawson 2004; Tunstill *et al.* 2005).

Lessons from the Evidence in this Volume

In reviewing the UK and US evidence on effectiveness of the selected child welfare interventions collated in this volume, a number of predominant messages emerged concerning the availability and nature of the evidence as well as the strengths and limitations of the studies available.

1. *There is a lack of research on the effectiveness of core child welfare interventions.*
    An important message coming out of the reviews was the lack of a significant body of research into the effectiveness of many of the core interventions commonly offered to children and families (Bentovim; Biehal; Jack; McCroskey; Quinton; Sinclair; Smith; Tanner and Turney; Whittaker; Wilson). This appears to be the case particularly in the UK. Again, some of the evidence available may be outdated. For example, the lack of recent research in both residential care and adoption in the UK was of particular concern as earlier studies related to forms of residential care which no longer exist and forms of adoption which have less

relevance now. In contrast, a considerable body of research on effectiveness seemed to be available in the US on home visiting, adoption, therapeutic interventions for child sexual abuse, support for at-risk youth and their families in the community as well as for youth exiting out-of-home care. But even with the US research, few independently conducted replication studies have been completed.

2.   *Few interventions were systematically evaluated in a rigorous way so the evidence base is inconclusive.* Bearing in mind that we were looking particularly for evidence of effectiveness, the absence of rigorous evaluation was noted by many of the contributors (Barlow; Hanson, Morrow and Bandstra; Nollan; Smith; Tanner and Turney; Whittaker). Generally there were few RCTs and a limited number of studies with other kinds of comparison/control groups. This was particularly true of the UK (Barlow; DePanfilis; Hanson, Morrow and Bandstra; Nollan; Pugh and Statham; Quinton and Selwyn; Wade; Wilson). A further concern was that the comparison groups were not always thought to be equivalent (Corcoran). Few studies involved random assignment. There was an over-reliance on pre-test/post-test designs, post-test only and single subject designs in the fields of physical and sexual abuse and neglect (Corcoran; DePanfilis). The available studies in out-of-home care were mostly cross-sectional and the more rigorous studies often were based on small sample sizes; this hinders the undertaking of more comprehensive analyses (Maluccio and Pecora). In the field of adoption in the UK, retrospective studies of volunteers were viewed as being of limited value. Sinclair described the available evidence on residential care in the UK (qualitative, statistical description and cross-institutional) as a 'motley array'. There did seem to be some growth in experimental and quasi-experimental studies in the field of abuse (Corcoran). Low sample size and research studies only conducted within a single setting were highlighted as problems for generalization of findings (Corcoran; Nollan; Pugh and Statham). Interestingly, both the UK and US contributors on the community-based programmes highlighted the challenges posed in finding ways to rigorously evaluate their initiatives.

3.   *Studies involve user views but lack objective/standardized outcome measures.* In the UK in particular, there was considerable evidence available of the views of parents and children as users of services. However, few of these studies also incorporated more objective measures. while it is obviously important that users perceive the intervention positively, evidence of other aims of the intervention being achieved remain relevant (Pugh and Statham; Smith; Nollan). while user views were evident in areas relating

to out-of-home care in the US, they seemed to be less prevalent in other areas or more recently incorporated in studies (McRoy). In both countries, consultation with users provided understanding of the processes as well as the outcome from the individual's point of view.

4.   *There is a lack of longitudinal evaluations.* Several authors (Corcoran; Smith) expressed concern about the fact that most studies on effectiveness were confined to short-term follow-ups, restricting our knowledge about impact on children and families over time. Evaluations at multiple time points and longer-term follow-ups were advocated (Maluccio and Pecora; Pugh and Statham).

5.   *Confounding variables made evidence on effectiveness difficult to achieve.* In certain areas such as physical abuse and neglect, many studies included both in their samples and failed to distinguish results for each group (Corcoran; DePanfilis). Again, studies which involved treatment for children and parents failed to report separately the impact on each (Corcoran). Further, when treatment involved a cognitive behavioural package, the effectiveness of elements of the package remained unknown.

6.   *There is a need for more research into effectiveness of interventions with children of different ages and families of differing ethnic origins or communities.* Few of the contributors could find evidence of transferability of effectiveness across these groups. Small sample sizes have hindered these kinds of analyses. In addition, this seemed to be at least partly attributable to the lack of interventions actually being taken up by different groups. High drop-out rates from parenting programmes by disadvantaged groups were noted and the fact that many ethnic minority families experiencing disadvantage were likely to be included in these rates (Smith).

7.   *Some interventions lack a theoretical basis.* Several contributors emphasized that the lack of a developed theoretical or conceptual basis in their respective areas had contributed to imprecision in the research questions and hypotheses being posed as well as the absence of fundamental studies of effectiveness. Authors addressing these issues include Tanner and Turney (neglect), Whittaker (residential care) and Corcoran (child sexual abuse).

8.   *Broader evidence contains valuable information on process and user views.* Several of the UK authors, while acknowledging the lack of experimental/quasi-experimental studies of effectiveness research in their areas, strongly stressed the valuable contributions made by descriptive studies of process. For example, they emphasized the value of

studies of new services, as well as research involving the views of
children and young people in extraordinary circumstances which are
essentially exploratory in nature (Biehal; Wade; Wilson).

Recommendations

The Need for Substantial Investment in Research into Effectiveness of Social Care Interventions.

Relative to health care, funding for social work research in the UK university sector is
small scale. In 2001 the sum of £3.5 million was allocated to English universities. The
Department of Health invests about £30 million per annum into a policy research
programme, part of which is allocated to outcomes in social care. Until very recently,
the Economic and Social Research Council did not recognize social work as a disciplinary subject and its commissioned programmes were not specifically targeted at
social work or social care. The UK Charities, such as the Joseph Rowntree and
Nuffield Foundation, devote around £20 million per annum to social care research.
Fisher (2002) has highlighted the lack of a nationally coordinated programme with
agreed priorities and the absence of any agreed system of reviewing and synthesizing
knowledge. The main issue, however, is funding. The Research and Development
spending on social care is estimated to be between one eighth and one tenth that of
health care. The 2001 Research Assessment Exercises indicate that in social work
there are fewer research groups with fewer staff and fewer centres of national
excellence than in other related disciplines. In comparing the results of the 1996 and
2001 Research Assessment Exercises, the position of social work research had clearly
advanced but generating a critical mass comparable to that in other disciplines
remained the challenge. Essentially, social care in the UK lacks cumulative and programmatic research designed to throw concentrated light on specific areas (Fisher
2002).

While the funding is higher in the United States, the federal government has
lessened its investment in child welfare research, and many programmes are not being
evaluated in rigorous ways that would truly advance practice knowledge. Funding
'silos' (isolated ways of working that ignore the need to coordinate efforts) are
mirroring programme 'silos' at a time when experts increasingly recognize what
parents have endured while trying to navigate multiple service delivery systems – the
need for stronger and closer interrelationships among the education, mental health,
juvenile justice, employment, child welfare and other sectors is apparent (Hanson *et
al.* 2001).

The Need to Build Better Links Between Research, Policy and Practice

Few people would dispute the wisdom of research findings influencing policy and practice and that policies should be based on sound evidence. Nevertheless, the level of impact of research on policy can be disappointing. Davies (2003) suggests that there are a number of areas of incompatibility between researchers and policymakers which may contribute to this. While it is the role of the policymaker to implement political decisions, the academic tradition, on the other hand, is to remain distant from the business of politics. Research may complicate issues in order to explain them, while the best policymaking simplifies to the point where action is possible (Pahl 1992). Perhaps one of the greatest tensions between policymaking and research lies in the different time scales in which they operate. Policymaking increasingly operates to short-term, demanding time scales while good research often takes years to complete. Policymakers also prefer short punchy reports with firm recommendations and cost-effectiveness data while academics tend to produce lengthy reports with qualified conclusions and often are unable to provide cost-benefit data. Clearly where research can be commissioned to assist policy decisions or evaluate new initiatives, the relationship can be seen to be mutually advantageous.

The Department of Health, in its desire to build knowledge around pressing policy questions, has commissioned child welfare research on an annual basis to a budget of £2.5 to £3.5 million per year and this has continued with the transfer of policy responsibility for children's services to the Department for Education and Skills. As described in Chapter 1, overviews have been produced of the findings from groups of research studies, starting with *Social Work Decisions in Child Care* (Department of Health 1985). These overviews have brought key messages to service managers and practitioners in a highly accessible form as well as influencing the framing of new legislation, such as the Children Act 1989. More recent research initiatives have focused on themes such as Supporting Parents, Quality Protects (improving management and delivery of children's services) and Costs and Effectiveness. It is to the credit of those charged with leading research and policy in the department that so much has been achieved on such a limited budget and that mutually beneficial and respectful relationships have been developed between the department and the research community.

The Social Care Institute of Excellence (SCIE), established in October 2001, was also part of the UK government's modernization agenda and intended specifically to raise standards of practice across the social care sector through the better use of knowledge and research. It has already begun to fulfil an important role in commissioning and disseminating readily available and accessible reviews of available evidence in social care. Fisher (2005) has adopted an inclusive view of evidence to be included in reviews. He sees the importance for SCIE of reviewing evidence not only about outcomes but also process and implementation issues. How people experience interventions and indeed any unintended outcomes are also seen to be of relevance. Recent attempts to integrate qualitative and quantitative studies in reviews of effectiveness (Dixon Woods et al. 2001, 2004; Popay and Roen 2003) and the recent expansion of the Campbell Collaboration (www.campbellcollaboration.org) represent examples of strategies to expand the available, but still scant, knowledge base.

The Need to Develop an Organizational Climate Conducive to Producing Positive Service Outcomes

Glisson and Hemmelgarn's three-year study (1998) of children's services in Tennessee found that organizational climate (including low conflict, cooperation, role clarity and personalization) was the primary predictor of positive service outcomes (the children's improved psychosocial functioning) and a significant predictor of service quality. A more recent study of 13 networks of organizations in Los Angeles also suggested that organizational characteristics are potentially strong determinants of service effectiveness (Yoo and Brooks 2005). Organizations characterized as having greater routineness of work, strong leadership qualities and supervisor and co-worker support were related to better outcomes for children in a family preservation programme.

A final related point is that the recent SCIE review on improving the use of research in social care practice (Walter et al. 2004) found support amongst the social care workforce for an 'Organizational Excellence Model'. In this approach, leadership, management and organization would be key to successful research use. A research-minded culture would be developed and partnerships between universities and agencies would facilitate the creation and use of research. The need to pay attention to organizational culture and human resource development factors was also recently highlighted in the US (Johnson and Austin 2005).

Conclusion

Increasingly in the UK and US, there is a move towards evidence-based policy and practice. This volume draws together evidence from both countries on core child welfare interventions. The final chapter has highlighted the overarching themes which have emerged concerning the availability and nature of the evidence. In both countries, it was recognised that we have insufficient evidence on effectiveness for most of these interventions. However, this was particularly the case for the UK. Research from both countries indicated that the lack of recent studies, long-term follow up research and evaluations with sufficient rigour all contributed to an evidence base which was at times inconclusive. The need for more research on the effectiveness of services for children and families with special needs, or from different ethnic origins or communities, was advocated. It was recognised that information on process and user views was relatively strong in the UK.

Clearly, evidence-based policy and practice needs to be underpinned by a body of knowledge generated from rigorous research. To obtain this, substantial investment in programmes of research into effectiveness is required. Building stronger links between research, policy and practice should also ensure that the evidence base leads to the commissioning of services for children and families which really do make a difference to enhancing the well-being of vulnerable children and young people and improving their outcomes.

References

Acton, R.G. and During, S.M. (1992) 'Preliminary results of aggression management training for aggressive parents.' *Journal of Interpersonal Violence 7*, 410–17.

Administration on Children, Youth and Families, (1996) *Fact Sheet: The Personal Responsibility and Work Opportunity Reconciliation Act of 1996.* Retrieved September 1996 from: www.acf.dhhs.gov/programs/opa/facts/prwora96.htm

Adoption Register (2003) *Adoption Register for England and Wales – Annual Report.* London: Department of Health.

Adoption-UK. (2000) *It's a Piece of Cake? A New Parent Support Programme Developed by Adopters for Adopters.* Daventry: Adoption UK.

Aggleton, P., Blenkinshop, S., Chase, E., Ewggers, M., Schagen, I., Shagen, S. *et al.* (2004) *Evaluation of the Impact of the National Healthy School Standard.* London: National Foundation for Educational Research and Thomas Coram Research Unit. www.wiredforhealth.gov.uk/evidenceofimpact

Ainsworth, M.D.S. (1989) 'Attachments beyond infancy.' *American Psychologist 44*, 709–16.

Alderson, P., Brill, S., Chalmers, I., Fuller, R., Hinkley-Smith, P., MacDonald, G. *et al.* (eds) (1996) *What Works? Effective Social Interventions in Child Welfare.* Barkingside: Barnado's, SSRU.

Aldgate, J., Bradley, M. and Hawley, D. (1996) 'Respite accommodation: A case study of partnership under the Children Act 1989.' in M. Hill and J. Aldgate (eds) *Child Welfare Services.* London: Jessica Kingsley Publishers.

Aldgate, J. and Bradley, M. (1999) *Supporting Families Through Short-term Fostering.* London: The Stationery Office

Aldgate, J., Colton, M., Ghate, D. and Health, A. (1992) 'Educational attainment and long-term stability in foster care.' *Children and Society 2*, 6, 91–103.

Aldgate, J., Heath, A., Colton, M. and Simm, M. (1993) 'Social work and the education of children in foster care.' *Adoption and Fostering 17*, 3, 25–34.

Aldgate, J. and Seden, J. (2006) 'Direct work with children.' In J. Aldgate, D.P.H. Jones, W. Rose and C. Jeffery (eds) *The Developing World of the Child.* London: Jessica Kingsley Publishers.

Aldgate, J. and Tunstill, J. (1995) *Making Sense of Section 17. Implementing Services for Children in Need within the Children Act 1989.* London: HMSO.

Alexander, G. and Huberty, T.J. (1993) 'Caring for troubled children: The villages follow-up study.' In *The Villages of Indiana 22.* Bloomington, IN.

Allen, J.P., Philliber, S., Herrling, S. and Kuperminc, G.P. (1997) 'Preventing teen pregnancy and academic failure. Experimental evaluation of a developmentally based approach.' *Child Development 64*, 729–42.

Allen, J.P., Philliber, S. and Hoggson, N. (1990) 'School-based prevention of teenage pregnancy and school dropout: Process evaluation of the national replication of the Teen Outreach Program.' *American Journal of Community Psychology 18*, 4, 505–24.

Allerhand, M.E., Weber, G. and Haug, M. (1966) 'Adaptation and adaptability: The Bellefaire follow-up study. New York: Child Welfare League of America.

Altstein, H., Coster, M., First-Hartling, M., Ford, C., Glascoe, B., Hairson, S. *et al.* (1994) 'Clinical observations of adult intercountry adoptees and their adoptive parents.' *Child Welfare 73*, 3, 261–69.

Andrews, D.W. (2003) 'Selecting Evidence-Based Practices: What Constitutes Evidence?' Workshop presented at the Alternative Education Summit, Columbus, OH.

Andrews, D.W., Soberman, L.H. and Dishion, T.J. (1995) 'The Adolescent Transitions Program for high-risk teens and their parents: Toward a school-based intervention.' *Education and Treatment of Children 18*, 4, 478–98.

Arnold, L.S., Brecht, M.C., Hockett, A.B., Amspacher, K.A. and Grad, R.K. (1989) 'Lessons from the past.' *American Journal of Maternal Child Nursing 14*, 75–82.

Arnold R. and Boyd E. (2001) 'The effectiveness of nurture groups: Preliminary research findings.' *British Journal of Special Education 28*, 4, 160–166.

Asen, K., George E., Piper R. and Stevens A. (1989) 'A systems approach to child abuse: management and treatment issues.' *Child Abuse and Neglect 13*, 45–58.

Ashcraft, R.F. (2003) 'Collaborations and coalitions for positive youth development.' In D. Wertlieb, F. Jacobs and R.M. Lerner (eds) *Handbook of Applied Developmental Science, Promoting Positive Youth and Family Development*, vol. 3. Thousand Oaks, CA: Sage.

Ashton, Baroness (2003) 'Schools to provide a full range of community services by 2006.' *Lifelong Learning News* (March). www.lifelonglearning.co.uk/iln/late54.htm

Austin, M.J. (ed.) (1997) *Human Services Integration.* New York: The Haworth Press.

Austin, T. and Johnston, J. (1995) *The Effectiveness of Pennsylvania's Independent Living Initiative*. Shippensburg University, PA: Center for Juvenile Justice Training and Research, Child Welfare Division.

Avery, R. (1998) *Public Agency Adoption in New York State: Phase I Report. Foster Care Histories of Children Freed for Adoption in New York State: 1980–1993*. Ithaca, NY: Cornell University.

Azar, S.T. (1986) 'A framework for understanding child maltreatment: An integration of cognitive behavioral and developmental perspectives.' *Canadian Journal of Behavioral Science 18*, 340–55.

Azar, S.T., Barnes, K.T. and Twentyman, C.T. (1988) 'Developmental outcomes in physically abused children: Consequences of parental abuse or the effects of a more general breakdown in caregiving behaviors?' *The Behavior Therapist 11*, 27–32.

Bachrach, C.A., Stolley, K.S. and London, K.A. (1992) 'Relinquishment of premarital births: Evidence from national survey data.' *Family Planning Perspectives, 24*, 1, 27–32.

Baker, A.J., Olson, D. and Mincer, C. (2000) *The Way to Work: An Independent Living/Aftercare Program for High-Risk Youth*. Washington, DC: CWLA Press.

Baker, A.J.L., Piotrkowski, C.S. and Jeanne, B.G. (1999) 'The home instruction program for preschool youngsters (HIPPY).' *Future of Children: Home Visiting: Recent Program Evaluations 9*, 1, 116–33.

Baldry, S. and Kemmis, J. (1998) 'The quality of child care in one local authority – a user study.' *Adoption and Fostering 27*, 3, 34–41.

Baldwin, N. and Carruthers, L. (1998) *Developing Neighbourhood Support and Child Protection Strategies*. Aldershot: Ashgate.

Ball, M. (1998) *School Inclusion: The School, the Family and the Community*. York: York Publishing Services.

Barker, P. (1998) 'The future of residential treatment for children.' In C. Schaefer and A. Swanson (eds) *Children in Residential Care: Critical Issues in Treatment*. New York: Van Nostrand Reinhold.

Barlow, J., Brocklehurst, N., Stewart-Brown, S., Davis, H., Burns, C. and Mockford, C. (2002) *Working in Partnership: The Development of a Home Visiting Service for Vulnerable Families*. Oxford: HSRU.

Barlow, J., Shaw, R. and Stewart-Brown, S. (2004) *Parenting Programmes and Minority Ethnic Parents: Experiences and Outcomes*. London: National Children's Bureau for Joseph Rowntree Foundation.

Barlow, J. and Stewart-Brown, S.L. (2001) 'Understanding parenting programmes: Parents' views.' *Primary Health Care Research and Development 2*, 117–30.

Barlow, J., Stewart-Brown, S., Callaghan, H., Tucker, J., Brocklehurst, N., Davis, H. and Burns, C. (2003) 'Working in partnership: the development of a home visiting service for vulnerable families.' *Child Abuse Review 12*, 3, 172–89.

Barnard, K.E. (1997) 'Influencing parent–child interactions for children at risk.' In M.J. Guralnick (ed.) *The Effectiveness of Early Intervention*. Baltimore, MD: Paul H. Brookes Publishing Co.

Barnardo's Evidence Network (2002) *One-to-one, Non-directive Mentoring is Unlikely to Improve Behaviour in Troubled Children*. www.barnardos.org.uk

Barnett, W.S. (1995) 'Long-term effects of early childhood programs on cognitive and school outcomes.' *The Future of Children 5*, 25–50.

Barratt, M. (2003) 'Organizational support for evidence-based practice within child and family social work: a collaborative study.' *Child and Family Social Work 8*, 143–50.

Barratt, P.M. and Cook, J.C. (2001) *REAL Evidence Based Practice in Teams: Action Pack*. Sheffield: Research in Practice, Sheffield University.

Barth, R.P. (1990) 'On their own: The experience of youth after foster care.' *Child and Adolescent Social Work 7*, 5, 419–40.

Barth, R.P. (2002) 'Institutions vs. Foster Homes: The Empirical Base for the Second Century of Debate.' Paper prepared for the Annie E. Casey Foundation.

Barth, R.P. and Berry, M. (1988) *Adoption and Disruption*. New York: Aldine de Gruyter.

Barth, R.P., Blythe, B.J. and Schinke, S.P. (1983) 'Self-control training with maltreating parents.' *Child Welfare 62*, 313–25.

Barth, R.P. and Miller, J.M. (2000) 'Building effective post-adoption services: what is the empirical foundation?' *Family Relations 46*, 4, 447–55.

Bath, H.I. and Haapala, D.A. (1994) 'Family preservation services: What does the outcome research really tell us?' *Social Service Review*, 386–99.

Bath, H.I., Richey, C.A. and Haapala, D.A. (1992) 'Child age and outcome correlates in intensive family preservation services.' *Children and Youth Services Review 14*, 389–406.

Battistich, V., Schaps, E., Watson, M. and Solomon, D. (1996) 'Prevention effects of the Child Development Project: Early findings from an ongoing multisite demonstration trial.' *Journal of Adolescent Research 11*,1, 12–35.

Becker, J.V., Alpert, J.L., BigFoot, D.S., Bonner, B.L., Geddie, L.F., Henggeler, S.W. *et al.* (1995) 'Empirical research on child abuse treatment: Report by the child abuse and neglect treatment working group, American Psychological Association.' *Journal of Clinical Child Psychology 24*, 23–46.

Baxter, J. (2000) 'Needs and resources assessment: Establishing a baseline of expectation in delivering emotional support to schools.' *International Journal of Mental Health Promotion 2*, 3, 27–34.

Beckett, R. (2002) *Adolescent Sexual Abusers Protocol*. Oxford: Oxford Forensic Services.

Beek, M. (1999) 'Parenting children with attachment difficulties: Views of adoptive parents and the implications for post-adoption support.' *Adoption and Fostering 23,* 1, 16–23.

Belsky, J. (1993) 'Etiology of child maltreatment: A developmental ecological analysis.' *Psychological Bulletin 114,* 3, 413–34.

Belsky, J. and Stratton, P. (2002) 'An ecological analysis of the etiology of child maltreatment.' In K. Browne, H. Hanks, P. Stratton and C. Hamilton (eds) *Early Prediction and Prevention of Child Abuse.* Chichester: Wiley.

Ben-Arieh, A. (2002) 'Evaluating the outcomes of programs versus monitoring wellbeing: A child centred perspective.' In T. Vecchiato, A.N. Maluccio and C. Canali (eds) *Evaluation in Children and Family Services.* New York: Aldine de Gruyter.

Benson, P.L. (1993) *The Troubled Journey: A Portrait of 6th–12th Grade Youth.* Minneapolis, MN: Search Institute.

Benson, P.L. (1997) *All Kids Are Our Kids: What Communities Must do to Raise Caring and Responsible Children and Adolescents.* Minneapolis, MN: Search Institute.

Bentovim, A. (1995) *Trauma Organised Systems – Sexual, Physical Abuse in Families.* London: Karnac.

Bentovim A. (1998) 'Significant harm in context.' In M. Adcock and R. White (eds) *Significant Harm: Its Management and Outcome.* Croydon: Significant Publications.

Bentovim, A. (2002a) 'Preventing sexually abused young people from becoming abusers, and treating the victimisation experiences of young people who offend sexually.' *Child Abuse and Neglect 26,* 661–78

Bentovim, A. (2002b) 'Working with abusing families.' In K. Wilson and A. James (eds) *The Child Protection Handbook.* London: Baillière Tindall.

Bentovim, A. (2003) 'Is it possible to work with parental denial?' In P. Reder, S. Duncan and C. Luceig (eds) *Studies in the Assessment of Parenting.* Hove and New York: Brunner Routledge.

Bentovim, A., Elton, A., Hildebrand, J., Tranter, M. and Vizard, E. (1988) *Child Sexual Abuse Within the Family (Assessment and Treatment).* London: Wright.

Bentovim, A., Elton, A. and Tranter, M. (1987) 'Prognosis for rehabilitation after abuse.' *Adoption and Fostering 11,* 26–31.

Bergner, R.M., Delgado, L.K. and Graybill, D. (1994) 'Finkelhor's risk factor checklist: A cross validation study.' *Child Abuse and Neglect 18,* 4, 331–40.

Berrick, J.B., Barth, R.P., Needell, B. and Jonson-Reid, M. (1997) 'Group care and young children.' *Social Service Review 71,* 257–74.

Berrick, J.D., Needell, B., Barth, R.B. and Johnson-Reid, M. (1998) *The Tender Years: Toward Developmentally Sensitive Child Welfare Services for Very Young Children.* New York: Oxford University Press.

Berridge, D. (1985) *Children's Homes.* Oxford: Blackwell.

Berridge, D. (1997) *Foster Care: A Research Review.* London: The Stationery Office.

Berridge, D. and Brodie, I. (1998) *Children's Homes Revisited.* London: Jessica Kingsley Publishers.

Berrueta-Clement, J., Schweinhart, L., Barnett, W., Epstein, A. and Weikart, D. (1984) *Changed Lives: The Effects of the Perry Preschool Program on Youth Through Age 19.* Michigan: High/Scope Press.

Berry, M. (1991) 'The assessment of imminence of risk of placement: Lessons from a family preservation program.' *Children and Youth Services Review 13,* 239–56.

Berry, M. (1992) 'An evaluation of family preservation services: Fitting agency services to family needs.' *Social Work 37,* 314–21.

Berry, M. (1995) 'An examination of treatment fidelity in an intensive family preservation program.' *Family Preservation Journal,* 25–50.

Besharov, D.J. (1994) *When Drug Addicts Have Children: Reorienting Child Welfare's Response.* Washington, DC: Child Welfare League of America.

Biehal, N. (2005) *Working with Adolescents. Supporting Families, Preventing Breakdown.* London: BAAF.

Biehal, N., Clayden, J. and Byford, S. (2000) *Home or Away? Supporting Young People and Families.* London: National Children's Bureau.

Biehal, N., Clayden, J., Stein, M. and Wade, J. (1992) *Prepared for Living? A Survey of Young People Leaving the Care of Three Local Authorities.* London: National Children's Bureau.

Biehal, N., Clayden, J., Stein, M. and Wade, J. (1995) *Moving On: Young People and Leaving Care Schemes.* London: HMSO.

Biehal, N. and Wade, J. (1996) 'Looking back, looking forward: Care leavers, families and change.' *Children and Youth Services Review 18,* 4/5, 425–46.

Biehal, N. and Wade, J. (1999) '"I thought it would be easier": The early housing careers of young people leaving care.' In J. Rugg (ed.) *Young People, Housing and Social Policy.* London: Routledge.

Biehal, N. and Wade, J. (2000) 'Going missing from residential and foster care: Linking biographies and contexts.' *British Journal of Social Work 30,* 211–25.

Bifulco, A. and Moran, P. (1998) *Wednesday's Child: Research into Women's Experience of Neglect and Abuse in Childhood, and Adult Depression.* London and New York: Routledge.

Biglan, A., Mrazek, P.J., Carnine, D. and Flay, B.R. (2003) 'The integration of research and practice in the prevention of youth problem behaviors.' *American Psychologist 58,* 433–40.

Blank, M., Melaville, A. and Shah, B. (2003) *Making the Difference: Research and Practice in Community Schools.* Washington DC: Coalition for Community Schools.

Blaxter, M. (1990) *Health and Lifestyles.* London: Routledge.

Blome, W. (1997) 'What happens to foster kids? Educational experiences of a random sample of foster care youth and a matched group of non-foster care youth.' *Child and Adolescent Social Work Journal 14/1,* 1, 41–53.

Blumenthal, K. (1983) 'Making foster family care responsive.' In B. McGowan and W. Meezan (eds) *Child Welfare: Current Dilemmas – Future Directions.* Itasca, IL: F.E. Peacock.

Bohman, M., and Sigvardsson, S. (1980) 'A prospective longitudinal study of children registered for adoption: A 15 year follow-up.' *Acta Psychiatrica Scandanavica 61,* 339–55.

Bolen, R. and Scannapieco, M. (1999) 'Prevalence of child sexual abuse: A corrective meta-analysis.' *Social Service Review,* 281–301.

Bonnerjea, L. (1990) *Leaving Care in London.* London: London Borough's Children's Regional Planning Committee.

Bottoms, A.E. and Wiles, P. (1986) 'Housing tenure and residential community crime careers in Britain'. In A.J. Reiss and M. Tonry (eds) *Communites and Crime.* Chicago, IL: University of Chicago Press.

Bottoms. A.E. and Wiles, P. (1997) 'Environmental criminology.' In M. Maguire, R. Morgan and R. Reiner (eds) *The Oxford Handbook of Criminology.* Oxford: Clarendon Press..

Botvin, G. J., Baker, E., Filazzola, A.D. and Botvin, E.M. (1990) 'A cognitive-behavioral approach to substance abuse prevention: One-year follow-up.' *Addictive Behaviors 15,* 47–63.

Bowlby, J. (1951) *Child Care and the Growth of Love.* London: HMSO.

Boxall, M. (2002) *Nurture Groups in School: Principles and Practice.* London: Paul Chapman Educational Publishing.

Bradley, R.H., Caldwell, B.M., Fitzgerald, J.A., Morgan, A.G. and Rock, S.L. (1986) 'Behavioral competence of maltreated children in child care.' *Child Psychiatry and Human Development 6,* 171–93.

Brandford, C. (2004) *Foster Youth Transition to Independence Study.* Seattle, WA: Office of Children's Administration Research.

Brassard, J. (1982) *Beyond Family Structure: Mother-child Interaction and Personal Social Networks.* Unpublished doctoral dissertation. Cornell University, Ithaca, NY.

Bribitzer, M.P. and Verdieck, M.J. (1988) 'Home-based, family-centered intervention: Evaluation of a foster care prevention program.' *Child Welfare LXVII,* 255–66.

Brickman, E. (1996) *A Formative Evaluation of PS 5: A Children's Aid Society/Board of Education Community School .*New York: Fordham University.

Bridge Childcare Consultancy (1995) *Paul: Death through Neglect.* London: Bridge Consultancy Services.

Briere, J. (1992) *Child Abuse Trauma Theory and Treatment of the Lasting Effects.* Newbury Park, CA: Sage Publications.

Briere, J. and Elliott, D.M. (2003) 'Prevalence and psychological sequelae of self-reported children physical and sexual abuse in a general population sample of men and women.' *Child Abuse and Neglect 27,* 1205–22.

British Association for Adoption and Fostering (2005) *Statistics.* London: BAAF. www.baaf.org.uk/info/stats

Broad, B. (1994) *Leaving Care in the 1990s.* Westerham: Royal Philanthropic Society.

Broad, B. (1998) *Young People Leaving Care: Life After the Children Act.* London: Jessica Kingsley Publishers.

Broad, B. (1999) 'Improving the health of children and young people leaving care'. *Adoption and Fostering 23,* 1, 40–8.

Broad, B. (2003) *After the Act: Implementing the Children (Leaving Care) Act 2000.* Children and Families Research Unit Monograph, No. 3, Leicester: De Montfort University.

Brodie, I., Berridge, D., Ayre, P., Barrett, D., Burroughs, L., Porteous, D. and Wenman, H. (1998) *Family Support for Adolescents: An Evaluation of the Work of the Adolescent Community Support Team.* Luton: University of Luton.

Brodzinsky, D. (1993) 'Long-term outcomes in adoption.' *The Future of Children 31,* 153–66.

Brodzinsky, D.A. (1990) 'Stress and Coping Model of Adoption Adjustment.' In D. Brodzinsky, and M. Schechter (eds) *The Psychology of Adoption.* New York: Oxford University Press.

Brodzinsky, D.M. and Pinderhughes, E.E. (2002) 'Parenting and child development in adoptive families.' In M. Bornstein (ed.) *Handbook of Parenting, Second Edition,* Vol. 1. Mahwa, NJ: Lawrence Erlbaum Associates.

Bronfenbrenner, U. (1976) 'Is early intervention effective? Facts and principles of early intervention: A summary.' In A.M. Clarke and A.D.B. Clarke (eds) *Early Experiences: Myth and Evidence.* London: Open Books.

Bronfenbrenner, U. (1979) *The Ecology of Human Development. Experiments in Nature and Design.* Cambridge, MA: Harvard University Press.

Bronfenbrenner, U. (1989) 'Ecological systems theory.' In R.Vasta (ed.) *Annals of Child Development 6,* 187–249. Greenwich, CT: Jason Aronson Press.

Bronfenbrenner, U. and Morris, P.A. (1998) 'The ecology of developmental processes.' In W. Damon (ed.) *Handbook of Child Psychology, Fifth Edition.* New York: John Wiley and Sons, Inc.

Brooks, D. and Barth, R. (1998) 'Characteristics and outcomes of drug-exposed children in kinship care and non-relative foster care.' *Children and Youth Services Review 20,* 475–501.

Brooks-Gunn, J., Berlin, L.J. and Fuligni, A.S. (2000) 'Early childhood intervention programs: What about the family?' In J.P. Shonkoff and S.J. Meisels (eds) *Handbook of Early Childhood Intervention, Second Edition.* New York: Cambridge University Press.

Brown, E., Bullock, R., Hobson, C. and Little, M. (1998) *Making Residential Care Work: Structure and Culture in Children's Homes.* Aldershot: Ashgate.

Brown, J. (1998) *Family and Adolescent Support Service.* Discussion paper. London: National Institute for Social Work.

Browne, K., Hanks, H., Stratton, P. and Hamilton, C. (2002) *Early Prediction and Prevention of Child Abuse.* Chichester: Wiley.

Bruininks, R.H., Woodcock, R.W., Weatherman, R.F. and Hill, B.K. (1984) *The Scales of Independent Behavior.* Allen, TX: DLM Teaching Resources.

Brunk, M., Henggeler, S.W. and Whelan, J.P. (1987) 'Comparison of multisystemic therapy and parent training in the brief treatment of child abuse and neglect.' *Journal of Consulting and Clinical Psychology 55,* 171–8.

Buchanan, A. (1995) 'Young people's views on being looked after in out-of-home care under the Children Act 1989.' *Children and Youth Services Review 17,* 5/6, 681–96.

Bull, J., McCormick G., Swann C. and Mulvihill, C. (2004) *Ante- and Post-natal Home-visiting Programmes: A Review of Reviews.* London: Health Development Agency.

Bullock, M., Little, M. and Millham, S. (1993a) *Going Home: The Return of Children Separated From Their Foster Families.* Aldershot: Dartmouth.

Bullock, R., Little, M. and Millham, S. (1991) 'The research background to the law on parental access to children in care.' *Journal of Social Welfare and Family Law 2,* 85–93.

Bullock, R., Little, M. and Millham, S. (1993b) *Residential Care of Children: A Review of the Research.* London: HMSO.

Burns, B.J. and Hoagwood, K. (2002) *Community Treatment for Youth: Evidence-based Interventions for Severe Emotional and Behavioral Disorders.* New York: Oxford University Press.

Burns, B.J., Hoagwood, K. and Mrazek, P.J. (1998) 'Effective Treatment for Adolescents.' Paper prepared for the Surgeon General's Report on Mental Health.

Cadoret, R. (1990) 'Biologic perspectives in adoptee adjustment.' In D. Brodzinsky and E. Schecter (eds) *The Psychology of Adoption.* New York: Oxford University Press.

Cairns, L. (2001) 'Investing in children: Learning how to promote the rights of children.' *Children and Society 15,* 5, 347–60.

Cancelli, A., Brickman, E., Sanchez, A. and Rivera, G. (1999) *The Children's Aid Society/Board of Education Community Schools: Third-Year Evaluation Report.* New York City: Fordham University.

Canning, U., Millward, L., Raj, T. and Warm, D. (2004) *Drug Use Prevention Among Young People: A Review of Reviews. Evidence Briefing.* London: Health Development Agency.

Carlson, C. and Peckham, S. (2001) *Bodyzone Programme Evaluation Report (Phase 1).* Unpublished paper, Oxford Brookes University.

Carlson, V., Cicchetti D., Barnett, D. and Braunwald, K. (1989) 'Disorganised/disorientated attachment relationships in maltreated infants.' *Developmental Psychology 25,* 525–31.

Carnegie Corporation (1996) *Starting Points: State and Community Partnerships for Young Children.* New York: Carnegie Coorporation.

Carr-Hill, R., Dixon, P., Mannion, R., Rice, N., Rudat, K., Sinclair R. and Smith, P. (1997) *A Model of the Determinants of Expenditure on Children's Personal Social Services.* York: Centre for Health Economics, University of York.

Cartoof, V. and Klerman, L. (1982) *Adoption: Is it an Option for Pregnant Adolescents?* Walthan, MA: Florence Heller School for Advanced Studies in Social Welfare.

Casey Family Programs (2000) *The Casey Model of Practice.* Seattle, WA: Casey Family Programs. www.casey.org.

Casey Family Programs (2003a) *Family, Community, Culture: Roots of Permanency – A Conceptual Framework on Permanency from Casey Family Programs.* Seattle, WA: Casey Family Programs. www.casey.org.

Casey Family Programs (2003b) *Higher Education Reform: Incorporating the Needs of Foster Youth.* Seattle, WA: Casey Family Programs. www.casey.org.

Casey Family Programs (2004) *2005 Public Policy Agenda.* Seattle, WA: Casey Family Programs. www.casey.org.

Casey Family Services (1999) *The Road to Independence: Transitioning Youth in Foster Care to Independence.* Shelton, CT: Casey Family Services. www.caseyfamilyservices.org.

Casey National Resource Center for Family Support (2003) *Siblings in Out-Of-Home Care: An Overview.* Washington, DC: Casey National Resource Center for Family Support. www.casey.org.

Catalano, R.F., Berglund, M.L., Ryan, J.A.M., Lonczak, H.S. and Hawkins, J.D. (1998) *Positive Youth Development in the United States: Research Findings on Evaluations of Positive Youth Development Programs.* Seattle, WA: Social Development Research Group, University of Washington.

Catalano, R.F. and Hawkins, J.D. (1996) 'The social developmental model: A theory of antisocial behavior.' In J.D. Hawkins (ed.) *Delinquency and Crime: Current Theories.* New York: Cambridge.

Catalano, R.F., Hawkins, J.D., Berglund, L., Pollard, J.A. and Arthur, M.W. (2002) 'Prevention science and positive youth development: Competitive or cooperative frameworks?' *Journal of Adolescent Health 31,* 230–9.

Cawson, P. (2002) *Child Maltreatment in the Family: The Experience of a National Sample of Young People.* London: NSPCC.

Cawson, P., Wattam, C., Brooker, S. and Kelly, G. (2000) *Child Maltreatment in the United Kingdom. A Study of the Prevalence of Child Abuse and Neglect.* London: NSPCC.

Celano, M. Hazzard, A. Webb, C. and McCall, C. (1996) 'Treatment of traumagenic beliefs among sexually abused girls and their mothers: An evaluation study.' *Journal of Abnormal Child Psychology 24,* 1–17.

Center for Substance Abuse Prevention (CSAP) (2000) *CSAP Substance Abuse Resource Guide: Middle School and High School Youth.* Washington, DC: SAMHSA's National Clearinghouse.

Chaffin, M., Bonner, B.L. and Hill, R.F. (2001) 'Family preservation and family support programs: Child maltreatment outcomes across client risk levels and program types.' *Child Abuse and Neglect 25*, 10, 1269–89.

Chaffin, M. and Friedrich, B. (2004) 'Evidence-based treatments in child abuse and neglect.' *Children and Youth Services Review 26*, 11, 1097–113.

Chamberlain, P. (1998) *Family Connections: A Treatment Foster Care Model for Adolescents with Delinquency.* Oregon: Northwest Media Inc.

Chamberlain, P. (2003) *Treating Chronic Juvenile Offenders – Advances Made through the Oregon Multidimensional Treatment Foster Care Model.* Washington, DC: American Psychological Association.

Chamberlain, P. and Reid, J. (1991) 'Using a specialized foster care community treatment model for children and adolescents leaving a state mental hospital.' *Journal of Community Psychology 19*, 266–76.

Chandra, A., Abma, J., Maza, P. and Bachrach, C. (1999) *Adoption Seeking and Relinquishment for Adoption in the United States*, Advance data, 306. Washington, DC: National Center for Health Statistics, US DHHS.

Chaskin, R.J., Brown, P., Venkatesh, S. and Vidal, A. (2001) *Building Community Capacity.* Hawthorne, New York: Aldine de Gruyter.

Cheung, Y. and Heath, A. (1994) 'After care: the education and occupation of adults who have been in care.' *Oxford Review of Education 20*, 3, 361–74.

Chibnall, S., Dutch, N., Jones-Harden, B., Brown, A., Gourgine, R., Smith, J., Boone, A. and Snyder, S. (2003) *Children of Color in the Child Welfare System: Perspectives from the Child Welfare Community.* Washington, DC: US DHHS Administration for Children and Families Children's Bureau, ACF.

Child Trends (2002) *Helping Teens Develop Healthy Social Skills and Relationships: What the Research Shows about Navigating Adolescence.* Washington, DC: Child Trends.

Child Welfare League of America (1995) *Standards of Excellence for Family Foster Care.* Washington, DC: CWLA.

Child Welfare League of America (2003) *Making Children a National Priority: A Framework for Community Action.* Washington, DC: CWLA.

Child Welfare League of America (2004a) *Children 2004: Vision, Action, Results.* National Fact Sheet. Washington, DC: CWLA. Available online at www.cwla.org/advocacy/nationalfactsheet04.pdf

Child Welfare League of America (2004b) *Making Children a National Priority.* Washington, DC: CWLA.

Child Welfare Watch (2002) *No. 8*, Fall (From Mayor's Management Reports). New York State Office of Children and Family Services Monitoring and Analysis Profiles. New York City: City Limits Community Information Service, and New York University, Milano Graduate School.

Children's Defense Fund (2004) *How Can I Get Involved? State Fact Sheets for Grandparents and Other Relatives Raising Children.* Last retrieved August 20, 2004 from: www.childrensdefense.org/childwelfare/kinshipcare/fact_sheets/default.asp

Cicchetti, D. and Lynch, M. (1993) 'Toward an ecological/transactional model of community violence and child maltreatment: Consequences for children's development.' *Psychiatry 56*, 96–118.

Cicchetti, D. and Toth, S.I. (1995) 'A developmental psychopathology perspective on child abuse and neglect.' *Journal of the American Academy of Child and Adolescent Psychiatrist 34*, 541–65.

Clarke, R.V.G. and Martin, D. (1971) *Absconding from Approved Schools.* London: HMSO.

Clayden, J. and Stein, M. (1996) 'Self care skills and becoming adult.' In S. Jackson and S. Kilroe (eds) *Looking After Children: Good Parenting, Good Outcomes.* London: HMSO.

Cleaver, H. and Freeman, P. (1995) *Parental Perspectives in Cases of Suspected Child Abuse.* London: The Stationery Office.

Cleaver, H., Unell, I. and Aldgate, J. (1999) *Children's Needs – Parenting Capacity. The Impact of Parental Mental Illness, Problem Alcohol and Drug Use, and Domestic Violence on Children's Development.* London: The Stationery Office.

Cleaver, H. and Walker, S. (2004) 'A framework for social work assessments of children and families.' *Child and Family Social Work 9*, 1, 81–90.

Cleaver, H. and Walker, S., with Meadows, P. (2004) *The Assessment Framework – A Structured Approach to Assessing Children's Needs and Family Capacities.* London: Jessica Kingsley Publishers.

Cliffe, D. with Berridge, D. (1991) *Closing Children's Homes. An End to Residential Child Care?* London: National Children's Bureau.

Cm.5750 (2003) *The Victoria Climbié Inquiry: Report of an Inquiry by Lord Laming.* London: The Stationery Office.

Cm.5860 (2003) *Every Child Matters.* London: The Stationery Office.

Coalition for Evidence-Based Policy (2002) *Bringing Evidence-Driven Progress to Education: A Recommended Strategy for the US Department of Education.* Washington, DC: US Department of Education.

Cohen, J. (1988) *Statistical Power Analysis for the Behavioral Sciences, Second Edition.* Hillsdale, NJ: Erlbaum.

Cohen, J.A., Deblinger, E., Mannarino, A. and DeArellano, M. (2001) 'The importance of culture in treating abused and neglected children: An empirical review.' *Child Maltreatment 6*, 148–57.

Cohen, J.A. and Mannarino, A.P. (1993) 'A treatment model for sexually abused preschoolers.' *Journal of Interpersonal Violence 8*, 115–31.

Cohen, J.A. and Mannarino, A.P. (1996) 'A treatment outcome study for sexually abused preschool children: initial findings.' *Journal of the American Academy of Child and Adolescent Psychiatry 35*, 42–50.

Cohen, J.A. and Mannarino, A.P. (1997) 'A treatment study for sexually abused preschool children: outcome during a one year follow-up.' *Journal of the American Academy of Child and Adolescent Psychiatry 36*, 1228–35.

Cohen, J.A. and Mannarino, A.P. (1998) 'Interventions for sexually abused children: initial treatment outcome findings.' *Child Maltreatment 3*, 17–26.

Cohen. J.A. and Mannarino, A.P. (2000) 'Predictors of treatment outcome in sexually abused children.' *Child Abuse and Neglect 24*, 983–994.

Cohen, J.A., Mannarino, A.P. and Zhitova, A.C. (2003) 'Treating child abuse-related posttraumatic stress and comorbid substance abuse in adolescents.' *Child Abuse and Neglect 27*, 12, 1345–65.

Cohen, N. J., Muir, E., Muir, R., Parker, C. J., Barwick, M. and Brown, M. (1999) 'Watch, wait and wonder: Testing the effectiveness of a new approach to mother–infant psychotherapy.' *Infant Mental Health Journal 20*, 4, 419–51.

Cohn, A. and Daro, D. (1987) 'Is treatment too late? What ten years of evaluative research tell us.' *Child Abuse and Neglect 11*, 433–42.

Coie, J.D., Watt, N.F., West, S.G., Hawkins, J.D., Asarnow, J.R., Markman, H.J. *et al.* (1993) 'The science of prevention: A conceptual framework and some directions for a national research program.' *American Psychologist 48*, 1013–22.

Coleman, J.C. and Hendry, L.B. (1999) *The Nature of Adolescence*. London: Routledge.

Collier, F., Hutchinson, B. and Pearmain, J. (2000) *Linking Children with Adoption Parents*. London: BAAF.

Collins, M.E. (2001) 'Transition to adulthood for vulnerable youths: A review of research and implications for policy.' *Social Service Review,* June, 271–91.

Collinshaw, S., Maughan, B. and Pickles, A. (1998) 'Infant adoption: psychosocial outcomes in adulthood.' *Social Psychiatry and Psychiatric Epidemiology 33*, 57–65.

Coltoff, P. (2005) 'Why the Children's Aid Society is Involved in this Work.' in J. Dryfoos and J. Quinn (eds) *Community Schools in Action: Lessons from a Decade of Practice*. New York: Oxford University Press.

Colton, M. (1988) *Dimensions of Substitute Care: A Comparative Study of Foster and Residential Care Practice*. Aldershot: Avebury.

Colton, M., Drury, C. and Williams, M. (1995) *Children in Need: Family Support Under the Children Act 1989*. Aldershot: Avebury.

Combe, V. (2002) *Up For It: Getting Young People Involved in Local Government*. Leicester: National Youth Agency.

Comer, E.W. and Fraser, M.W. (1998) 'Evaluation of six family support programs: Are they effective?' *Families in Society: The Journal of Contemporary Human Services 79*, 2, 134–48.

Conaway, L.P. and Hansen, D.J. (1989) 'Social behavior of physically abused and neglected children: A critical review.' *Clinical Psychology Review 9*, 627–52.

Connolly, M. and McKenzie, M. (1999) *Effective Participatory Practice: Family Group Conferencing in Child Protection*. New York: Aldine de Gruyter.

Conte, J. and Schuerman, J. (1987) 'Factors associated with an increased impact of child sexual abuse.' *Child Abuse and Neglect 11*, 201–11.

Coohey, C. (1996) 'Child mistreatment: testing the social isolation hypothesis.' *Child Abuse and Neglect, 30*, 3, 241–54.

Cook, R. (1994) 'Are we helping foster care youth prepare for their future?' *Children and Youth Services Review 16*, 3–4, 213–29.

Cook, R., Fleishman, E. and Grimes, V. (1991) *A National Evaluation of the Title IV-E Foster Care Independent Living Programs for Youth: Phase 2*. Rockville, MD: Westat, Inc.

Cook, R., McLean, J.L. and Ansell, D.I. (1989) *A National Evaluation of the Title IV-E Foster Care Independent Living Programs for Youth*. Contract No. 105-87-1608. Rockville, MD: Westat, Inc.

Cook-Fong, S. (2000) 'The adult well-being of individuals reared in family foster care placements.' *Child and Youth Care Forum 29*, 1, 7–25.

Coote, A., Allen, J. and Woodhead, D. (2004) *Finding Out What Works: Building Knowledge About Complex Community-Based Initiatives (Summary)*. The King's Fund, London.

Cooper, P. (2001) *We Can Work it Out: What Works in Educating Pupils with Social Emotional and Behavioural Difficulties Outside Mainstream Classrooms?* Barkingside: Barnardo's.

Cooper, P., Arnold, R. and Byford, E. (2001) 'The effectiveness of nurture groups: preliminary research findings.' *British Journal of Special Education 28*, 4, 160–6.

Corby, B. (2000b) *Child Abuse: Towards a Knowledge Base, Second Edition*. Buckingham: Open University Press.

Corcoran, J. (1998) 'In defense of mothers of sexual abuse victims.' *Families in Society 79*, 358–69.

Corcoran, J. (2000a) *Evidence-based Social Work Practice with Families: A Lifespan Approach*. New York: Springer Publishing.

Corcoran, J. (2000b) 'Family interventions with child physical abuse and neglect: A critical review.' *Children and Youth Services Review 22*, 563–91.

Corcoran, J. (2004) 'Treatment outcome research with the non-offending parents of sexually abused children: A critical review.' *Journal of Child Sexual Abuse 13*, 59–84.

Corcoran, J. (2003) *Clinical Applications of Evidence-Based Family Treatment*. New York: Oxford University Press.

Corlyon, J. and McGuire, C. (1997) *Young Parents in Public Care*. London: National Children's Bureau.

Cornish, D. and Clarke, R. (1975) *Residential Care and its Effects on Juvenile Delinquency*. London: HMSO.

Costin, L. (1972) *Child Welfare: Policies and Practices*. New York: McGraw-Hill.

Costin, L.B., Bell, C.J. and Downs, S.W. (1991) *Child Welfare: Policies and Practices*. New York, NY: Longman Publishing Group.

Cote, S. and Healy, T. (2001) *The Well-Being of Nations. The Role of Human and Social Capital.* Paris: Organisation for Economic Co-operation and Development.

Cotterill, A.M. (1988) 'Geographical distribution of child abuse in an inner-city borough.' *Child Abuse and Neglect, 12,* 461–67.

Courtney, M. and Dworsky, A. (2005) *Midwest Evaluation of the Adult Functioning of Former Foster Youth: Outcomes at Age 19.* Chicago, IL: University of Chicago, Chapin Hall.

Coulton, C., Korbin, J.E., Su, M. and Chow, J. (1995) 'Community level factors and child maltreatment rates.' *Child Development 66,* 1262–76.

Courtney, M.E., Piliavin, I., Grogan-Kaylor, A. and Nesmith, A. (2001) 'Foster youth transitions to adulthood: A longitudinal view of youth leaving care.' *Child Welfare 80,* 6, 686–717.

Courtney, M.E., Terao, S. and Bost, N. (2004) *Midwest Evaluation of the Adult Functioning of Former Foster Youth: Conditions of Youth Preparing to Leave State Care in Illinois.* Chicago, IL: Chapin Hall Center for Children at the University of Chicago.

Cowie, H., Naylor, P., Talamelli, L., Chauhan, P. and Smith, P. (2002) 'Knowledge, use of and attitudes towards peer support: a two-year follow-up to the Prince's Trust survey.' *Journal of Adolescence 25,* 5, 453–67.

Cox, A., Pound, A., Mills, M., Puckering, C. and Owen, A. (1991) 'Evaluation of a home visiting and befriending scheme for young mothers: NEWPIN.' *Journal of the Royal Society of Medicine 84,* 217–20.

Craig, G. (2002) 'Community development with children.' In D. McNeish, T. Newman and H. Roberts (eds): *What Works for Children?* Buckingham Open University Press .

Creighton, S.J. (2002) 'Patterns and outcomes'. In K. Wilson and A. James (eds) *The Child Protection Handbook.* London: Baillière Tindall.

CRG (2003) *An Evaluation of Summer Plus: A Cross-departmental Approach to Preventing Youth Crime.* Nottingham: Department for Education and Skills Publications.

Crittenden, P. (1988) 'Distorted patterns of relationship in maltreating families: The role of internal representation models.' *Journal of Reproductive and Infant Psychology 6,* 183–99.

Crittenden, P. (1993) 'An information-processing perspective on the behavior of neglectful parents.' *Criminal Justice and Behavior 20,* 1, 27–48.

Crittenden, P. (1996) 'Research on maltreating families: implications for intervention.' In J. Briere *et al.* (eds) *The APSAC Handbook on Child Maltreatment.* Thousand Oaks, CA: Sage.

Cross, W. (1990) 'Race and ethnicity: effects on social networks.' In M. Cochran, M. Larner, D. Riley, L. Gunnarson and C. Hernderson Jr. (eds) *Extending Families: The Social Networks of Parents and their Children.* Cambridge: Cambridge University Press.

Crow, I., France, A. Hacking, S. and Hart, M. (2004) *Does Communities that Care Work? An Evaluation of a Community-based Risk Prevention Programme in Three Neighbourhoods.* York: Joseph Rowntree Foundation.

Culp, R.E., Heide, J. and Richardson, M.T. (1987) 'Maltreated children's developmental scores: Treatment versus nontreatment.' *Child Abuse and Neglect 11,* 29–34.

Culp, R.E., Little, V., Letts, D. and Lawrence, H. (1991) 'Maltreated children's self-concept: Effects of a comprehensive treatment program.' *American Journal of Orthopsychiatry 61,* 114–21.

Curry, J. (1991) 'Outcome research on residential treatment: Implications and suggested directions.' *American Journal of Orthopsychiatry 61,* 348–58.

Curry, J. (1993) 'The Current Status of Research in Residential Treatment.' Unpublished paper presented at the American Association of Children's Residential Centers, Boston, MA.

Curtis, P.A., Dale, G. Jr. and Kendall, J.C. (eds) (1999) *The Foster Care Crisis – Translating Research into Policy and Practice.* Lincoln, NE: The University of Nebraska Press, in association with the Child Welfare League of America.

Dale, P., Davies, M., Morrison, T. and Waters, J. (1986) *Dangerous Families: Assessment and Treatment of Child Abuse.* London: Tavistock.

Dale, P., Green, R. and Fellows, R. (2002) *What Really Happened? Child Protection Case Management of Infants with Serious Injuries and Discrepant Parental Explanations.* London: NSPCC.

Daniel, B. (1998) 'A picture of powerlessness: An exploration of child neglect and ways in which social workers and parents can be empowered towards efficacy.' *International Journal of Child and Family Welfare 3,* 269–85.

Daro, D.A., and Harding, K.A. (1999) 'Healthy families America: Using research to enhance practice.' *Future of Children 9,* 1, 152–76.

Davies, C. (2003) 'Policy development: making research count.' In K. Kufeldt and B.McKenzie (eds) *Child Welfare: Connecting Research Policy and Practice.* Waterloo, Ontario: Wilfred Laurier Press.

Davies, L. (2004) '"The difference between child abuse and child protection could be you": Creating a community network of protective adults.' *Child Abuse Review 13,* 426–32.

Davis, H. and Hester, P. (1996) *An Independent Evaluation of Parent-Link: A Parenting Education Programme.* London: Parent Network.

Davis, H. and Rushton, R. (1991) 'Counselling and supporting parents of children with developmental delay: A research evaluation.' *Journal of Mental Deficiency Research 35,* 89–112.

Davis, H. and Spurr, P. (1998) 'Parent counselling: An evaluation of a community child mental health service.' *Journal of Child Psychology and Psychiatry and Allied Disciplines 39,* 3, 365–76.

Davis, H., Spurr, P., Cox, A., Lynch, M.A., Roenne, A. and Hahn, K. (1997) 'A description and evaluation of a community child mental health service.' *Clinical Child Psychology and Psychiatry 2*, 2, 221–38.

Davis, S. and Fantuzzo, J.W. (1989) 'The effects of adult and peer social initiations on social behavior of withdrawn and aggressive maltreated preschool children.' *Journal of Family Violence 4*, 227–48.

Dawson, B., de Armas, A., McGrath, M.L. and Kelly, J.A. (1986) 'Cognitive problem-solving training to improve the child-care judgment of child neglectful parents.' *Journal of Family Violence 1*, 209–21.

Day, P. (2002) 'Classroom drama: acting for emotional literacy.' *Young Minds Magazine 61*, 22–33.

DeBerry, K.M., Scarr, S. and Weinberg, R. (1996) 'Family racial socialization and ecological competence: Longitudinal assessments of African American transracial adoptees.' *Child Development 67*, 2375–99.

Deblinger, E. and Heflin, A.H. (1996) 'Treating Sexually Abused Children and Their Nonoffending Parents: A Cognitive-Behavioral Approach.' Thousand Oaks, CA: Sage.

Deblinger, E., Lippmann, J. and Steer, R. (1996) 'Sexually abused children suffering posttraumatic stress symptoms: initial treatment outcome findings.' *Child Maltreatment 1*, 310–21.

Deblinger, E., Stauffer, L. and Steer, R. (2001) 'Comparative efficacies of supportive and cognitive behavioral group therapies for young children who have been sexually abused and their nonoffending mothers.' *Child Maltreatment 6*, 332–43.

Deblinger, E., Steer, R. and Lippmann, J. (1999) 'Two year follow-up study of cognitive behavioral therapy for sexually abused children suffering post-traumatic stress symptoms.' *Child Abuse and Neglect 23*, 1371–8.

DePanfilis, D. (1982) 'Clients who refer themselves to Child Protective Services.' *Children Today 11*, 2, 21–5.

DePanfilis, D. (1996a) 'Implementing child mistreatment risk assessment systems: Lessons from theory.' *Administration in Social Work 20*, 2, 41–59.

DePanfilis, D. (1996b) 'Social isolation of neglectful families: A review of social support assessment and intervention models.' *Child Maltreatment 1*, 37–52.

DePanfilis, D. (1999) 'Intervening with families when children are neglected.' In H. Dubowitz (ed.) *Neglected Children.* Newbury Park, CA: Sage.

DePanfilis, D. (2000) 'How do I assess a caregiver's motivation and readiness to change?' In H. Dubowitz and D. DePanfilis (eds) *Handbook for Child Protection Practice.* Newberry Park, CA: Sage.

DePanfilis, D. and Dubowitz, H. (2005) 'Family Connections: A program for preventing child neglect.' *Child Maltreatment 10*, 2.

DePanfilis, D. and Salus, M.K. (2003) *Child Protective Services: A Guide For Caseworkers.* Washington, DC: US DHHS, Administration for Children and Families, Administration on Children, Youth and Families, Children's Bureau, Office on Child Abuse and Neglect.

DePanfilis, D. and Zuravin, S.J. (1998) 'Rates, patterns, and frequency of child maltreatment recurrences among public CPS families.' *Child Maltreatment 3*, 27–42.

DePanfilis, D. and Zuravin, S. (2002) 'The effect of services on the recurrence of child maltreatment.' *Child Abuse and Neglect 26*, 187–205.

Department for Education and Employment (1997) *Making a Difference for Children and Families: Sure Start.* London: The Stationery Office.

Department for Education and Employment (1999a) *National Healthy School Standard: Guidance.* London: DfEE.

Department for Education and Employment (1999b) *Schools Plus: Building Learning Communities. Improving the Educational Chances of Children and Young People from Disadvantaged Areas.* A report from the Schools Policy Action Team 11. London: DfEE.

Department for Education and Employment (2001) *Promoting Children's Mental Health within Early Years and School Settings.* London: DfEE.

Department for Education and Employment/Department of Health (2000) *Guidance on the Education of Children and Young People in Public Care, LAC (2000) 13.* London: DH.

Department for Education and Skills (2001) *Statistics of Education: Public Examinations GCSE/GNVQ in England 2000.* London: The Stationery Office.

Department for Education and Skills (2004a) *Statistics of Education: Looked After Children Year Ending 31 March 2003.* London: The Stationery Office.

Department for Education and Skills (2004b) *Statistics of Education: Referrals, Assessments and Children and Young People on Child Protection Registers: Year Ending 31 March 2003.* London: The Stationery Office.

Department for Education and Skills (2005a) *Children Looked After in England (including Adoptions and Care Leavers) 2003–4.* London: DfES, National Statistics.

Department for Education and Skills (2005b) *Children Looked After in England 2004-5.* National Statistics SFR 51/2005. London: DfES.

Department for Education and Skills (2005c) *Common Assessment Framework for Children and Young People. Implementation Guidance for Directors of Children's Services in Local Areas Implementing during April 2005 – March 2006.* London: DfES (www.dfes.gov.uk/isa).

Department for Education and Skills/Coram Family (2002) *Intervening Early.* London: DfES.

Department for Work and Pensions (2004) *Households Below Average Income.* London: The Stationery Office.

Department of Health (1985) *Social Work Decisions in Child Care.* London: HMSO.

Department of Health (1991) *The Children Act 1989 Guidance and Regulations, Volume 4, Residential Care.* London: HMSO.

Department of Health (1993) *Children in Care of Local Authorities: Year Ending 31 March 1993.* London: Government Statistical Service.

Department of Health (1995a) *Child Protection: Messages from the Research.* London: HMSO.

Department of Health (1995b) *Looking After Children: Good Parenting – Good Outcomes.* London.

Department of Health (1996a) *Focus on Teenagers.* London: HMSO.

Department of Health (1996b) *Messages from Research.* London: The Stationery Office.

Department of Health (1997) *'When Leaving Home is Also Leaving Care', An Inspection of Services for Young People Leaving Care.* London: DH.

Department of Health (1998a) *Adoption: Achieving the Right Balance (LAC98).* London: DH.

Department of Health (1998b) *Caring for Children Away From Home: Messages From Research.* Chichester: John Wiley and Sons.

Department of Health (1998c) *Quality Protects: Framework for Action.* London: DH.

Department of Health (1998d) *Supporting Families: A Consultation Document.* London: The Stationery Office.

Department of Health (2000a) *Assessing Children in Need and their Families: Practice Guidance.* London: The Stationery Office.

Department of Health (2000b) *A Quality Strategy for Social Care.* London: DH.

Department of Health (2000c) *Quality Protects Management Action Plans: A Thematic Review of Leaving Care Services.* London: DH.

Department of Health (2000d) *The Children Act Report 1995–1999.* London: DH.

Department of Health (2001a) *Children (Leaving Care) Act 2000: Regulations and Guidance.* London: DH.

Department of Health (2001b) *Children Looked After by Local Authorities, Year Ending 31 March, 2001 (A/F 01/12).* London: Department of Health. Available at: www.doh.gov.uk/public/cla2001.htm

Department of Health (2001c) *Outcome Indicators for Looked After Children: Year Ending 30 September 2000.* London: DH.

Department of Health (2001d) *The Children Act Now: Messages From Research.* London: The Stationery Office.

Department of Health (2002a) *Care Leavers, Year Ending 31 March 2002, (Statistical Bulletin 2002/27).* London: DH.

Department of Health (2002b) *Children Act Report 2001.* London: Department of Health

Department of Health (2002c) *Children Adopted from Care in England: 2001/2002 (Statistical Bulletin 2002/24).* London: DH.

Department of Health (2002d) *Children Looked After by Local Authorities, Year Ending 31 March 2002. England. Volume 1: Summary and National Tables.* A/F 02/12. London: DH. Available at: www.doh.gov.uk/ public/cla2002.htm

Department of Health (2002e) *Health Minister Announces Major Review of Fostering and Placement Services.* 19 April. London: Department of Health Media Centre.

Department of Health (2002f) *Integrated Children's System – Working with Children in Need and their Families.* Consultation document. London: DH.

Department of Health (2003a) *Children Looked After by Local Authorities, March 31st 2002.* London: DH.

Department of Health (2003b) *The Adoption Support Services Regulations.* London: DH.

Department of Health (2005) *Evidence to Inform the National Service Framework for Children, Young People and Maternity Services.* London: DH.

Department of Health, Department for Education and Employment and Home Office (2000b) *Framework for the Assessment of Children in Need and their Families.* London: The Stationery Office.

Department of Health and Department for Education and Skills (2004) *The National Service Framework for Children, Young People and Maternity Services.* London: DH.

Department of Health, Home Office and Department for Education and Employment (1999) *Working Together to Safeguard Children. A Guide To Inter-Agency Working to Safeguard and Promote the Welfare of Children.* London: The Stationery Office.

DeWolff, M.S. and van Ijzendoorn, M.H. (1997) 'Sensitivity and attachment: A meta-analysis on parental antecedents of infant attachment.' *Child Development 68,* 571–91.

Dillon, S. (2003) 'State cutbacks put schools and federal law to test.' *New York Times,* August 31, p.1.

DiNitto, D. and Dye, T. (1989) *Social Welfare: Politics and Public Policy.* Englewood Cliffs, NJ: Prentice Hall, Inc.

Dishion, T.J., McCord, J. and Poulin, F. (1999) 'When interventions harm. Peer groups and problem behavior.' *American Psychologist 54,* 755–65.

Dixon, J. and Stein, M. (2002) *Just a Bairn: Throughcare and Aftercare Services in Scotland.* Final report to the Scottish Executive. Edinburgh: Scottish Executive.

Dixon-Woods, M., Agarwal, S., Young, B., Jones, D. and Sutton, A. (2004) *Integrative Approaches to Qualitative and Quantitative Evidence.* London: Health Development Agency.

Dixon-Woods, M., Fitzpatrick, R. and Roberts, K. (2001) 'Including qualitative research in Systemic reviews: Opportunities and problems.' *Journal of Evaluation in Clinical Practice 7,* 2, 125–133.

Donnelly, B.W. and Voydanoff, P. (1991) 'Factors associated with releasing for adoption among adolescent mothers.' *Family Relations 40,* 4, 404–10.

Donnelly, P.G. and Kimble, C.E. (1997) 'Community organizing, environmental change and neighbourhood crime.' *Crime and Delinquency 43,* 4, 493–511.

Donohue, B. (2004) 'Coexisting child neglect and drug abuse in young mothers.' *Behavior Modification 28*, 206–33.

Donovan, J., Jessor, R. and Costa, F. (1988) 'Syndrome of problem behavior in adolescence: A replication.' *Journal of Consulting and Clinical Psychology 56*, 762–5.

Doueck, H.J., English, D.J., DePanfilis, D. and Moote, G.T. (1993) 'Decision-making in child protective services: A comparison of selected risk-assessment systems.' *Child Welfare 72*, 441–52.

Downs, A.C. and Pecora, P.J. (2004) *Application of Erikson's Psychosocial Theory to the Effects of Child Abuse and Ameliorative Foster Care. Working Paper No. 2.* Seattle, WA: Casey Family Programs. www.casey.org/research

Doy, E., Gilbert, D. and Aitland, L. (2001) *Empowering Young People in Rural Suffolk: An Evaluation Report for the Home Office.* London: Home Office.

Dryfoos, J. (1990) *Adolescents at Risk: Prevalence And Prevention.* New York: Oxford University Press.

Dryfoos, J. (2003) *Quitman Street Community School: Rallying Around the Whole Village Serving the Whole Child.* Newark, NJ: Prudential Foundation.

Dryfoos, J. and Maguire, S. (2003) *Inside Full-service Community Schools.* Thousand Oaks, CA: Corwin Press.

Dubowitz, H. (1999) *Neglected Children: Research, Practice and Policy.* Thousand Oaks, CA: Sage.

Dubowitz, H., Feigelman, S. and Zuravin, S. (1993) A profile of kinship care. *Child Welfare 72*, 153–69.

Duchnowski, A.J., Kutash, K. and Friedman, R.M. (2002) 'Community-based interventions in a system of care and outcomes framework.' In B.J. Burns and K. Hoagwood *Community Treatment for Youth: Evidence-Based Interventions for Severe Emotional and Behavioral Disorders.* New York: Oxford University Press.

Duggan, A.K., McFarlane, E.C., Windham, A.M., Rohde, C.A., Salkever, D.S., Fuddy, L., Rosenberg, L.A., Buchbinder, S.B., and Sia, C.C.J. (1999) 'Evaluation of Hawaii's Healthy Start Program.' *The Future of Children 9*, 1, 66–90.

Duerr-Berrick, J. and Barth, R.P. (1994) 'Research on kinship foster care: What do we know? Where do we go from here?' *Children and Youth Services Review 15*, 1–5.

Dumaret, A.C., Coppel-Batsch, M. and Couraud, S. (1997) 'Adult outcome of children cared for long-term periods in foster families.' *Child Abuse and Neglect 21*, 911–27.

Dunlop, A.B. (1975) *The Approved School Experience.* London: HMSO.

Dunst, C.J., Trivette, C.M. and Jodry, W. 1997 'Influences of social support on children with disabilities and their families.' In M.J. Garulnick (ed.) *The Effectiveness of Early Intervention.* Baltimore, MA: Paul H. Brookes.

Durlak, J.A. and Wells, A.M. (1997) 'Primary prevention mental health programs for children and adolescents: A meta-analytic review.' *American Journal of Community Psychology 25*, 115–52.

Dworsky, A. and Courtney, M.E. (2000) *Self-Sufficiency of Former Foster Youth in Wisconsin: Analysis of Unemployment Insurance Wage Data and Public Assistance Data.* Washington, DC: Office of the Assistant Secretary for Planning and Evaluation, US Department of Health and Human Services. Available at aspe.hhs.gov/hsp/fosteryouthWI00/

Dyson, A., Millward, A. and Cummings, C. (2003) *The Role of Schools in Area Regeneration: A Working Paper.* www.ncl.ac.uk/ecls/research/education/snrc/research/current role_area-regen.htm

Dyson A., Millward A. and Todd, L. (2002) *A Study of Extended Schools Demonstration Projects.* Research Report 381. London: DfES

Dyson, A. and Robson, E. (1999) *School, Family and Community: Mapping School Inclusion in the UK.* York: Joseph Rowntree Foundation.

Eastham, D. (1990) 'Plan it or suck it and see.' In G. Darvill and G. Smale (eds) *Partners in Empowerment: Networks of Innovations in Social Work.* London: National Institute of Social Work.

Eckenrode, J., Izzo, C. and Campa-Muller, M. (2003) 'Early intervention and family support programs.' In F. Jacobs, D. Wertlieb and R.M. Lerner (eds) *Handbook of Applied Developmental Science, Enhancing the Life Chances of Youth and Families*, vol. 2. Thousand Oaks: Sage.

Edwards, J.J. and Alexander, P.C. (1992) 'The contribution of family background to the long-term adjustment of women sexually abused as children.' *Journal of Interpersonal Violence 7*, 306–20.

Edwards, R. (in press) *Recidivisms Following Residential Treatment of Young Sex Offenders.*

Eeklaar, J. (2003) 'Contact and adoption reform.' In A. Bainham, B. Lindley, M. Richards and L. Trinder (eds) *Children and their Families: Contact, Rights and Welfare.* Oxford and Portland, OR: Hart Publishing.

Eisenberg, N. (1998) 'Parental socialisation of emotion.' *Psychological Enquiry 9*, 241–73.

Ellen, I. and Turner, M. (1997) 'Does neighbourhood matter? Assessing recent evidence.' *Housing Policy Debate 8*, 833–66.

Elmer, E. (1986) 'Outcome of residential treatment for abused and high-risk infants.' *Child Abuse and Neglect 10*, 351–60.

Emde, R.N. and Robinson, J. (2000) 'Guiding principles for a theory of early intervention: A developmental-psychoanalytic perspective.' In J.P. Shonkoff and S.J. Meisels (eds) *Handbook of Early Childhood Intervention, Second Edition.* New York: Cambridge University Press.

Emond, A., Pollock, J., Deave, T., Bonnell, S., Peter, T.J. and Harvey, I. (2002) 'An evaluation of the first parent health visitor scheme.' *Archives of Disease in Childhood 86*, 150–7.

English, D.J., Kouidou-Giles, S. and Plocke, M. (1994) 'Readiness for independence: A study of youth in foster care.' *Children and Youth Services Review 16*(3/4), 1–5.

English, M.J. (2002) 'Policy implications relevant to implementing evidence-based treatment.' In J. Burns and K. Hoagwood *Community Treatment for Youth: Evidence-Based Interventions for Severe Emotional and Behavioral Disorders,* 301–27. New York: Oxford University Press.

Epstein, H. (2003) 'Enough to make you sick?' The *New York Times Magazine,* October 12, section 6: 74 through 108.

Epstein, N., Baldwin, L. and Bishop, D. (1983) 'The McMaster Family Assessment Device.' *Journal of Marital and Family Therapy 9,* 2, 171–80.

Erickson, M.F. and Kurz-Riemer, K. (1999) *Infants, Toddlers, and Families: A Framework for Support and Intervention.* New York: The Guilford Press.

Erikson, E.H. (1968) *Identity: Youth and Crisis.* New York: W. W. Norton and Company.

Erikson, E.H. (1985) *The Life Cycle Completed.* New York: Norton.

Eslea, M. and Smith, P. (1998) 'The long-term effectiveness of anti-bullying work in primary schools.' *Educational Research 40,* 2, 203–18.

Essen, J., Lambert, L. and Head, J. (1976) 'School attainment of children who have been in care.' *Child Care, Health and Development 2,* 339–51.

European Early Promotion Project (2005). *International Journal of Mental Health Promotion. Special Issue 7,* 1.

Everson, M.D., Hunter, W.H., Runyon, D.K., Edelsohn, G.A. and Coulter, M.A. (1989) 'Maternal support following disclosure of incest.' *American Journal of Orthopsychiatry 59,* 197–207.

Fahlberg, V. (1988) *Fitting the Pieces Together.* London: BAAF.

Family Support America (2003) *Evidence Along the Way Project Report.* Chicago, IL: Robert Wood Johnson Foundation.

Fanshel, D., Finch, S.J. and Grundy, J.F. (1990) *Foster Children in a Life Course Perspective.* New York: Columbia University Press.

Fanshel, D. and Shinn, E.B. (1978) *Children in Foster Care: A Longitudinal Investigation.* New York: Columbia University Press.

Fantuzzo, J., Jurecic, L., Stovall, A., Hightower, A., Goins, C. and Schactel, D. (1988) 'Effects of adult and peer social intitiations on the social behavior of withdrawn, maltreated preschool children.' *Journal of Consulting and Clinical Psychology 56,* 34–9.

Fantuzzo, J., Sutton-Smith, B., Atkins, M. and Meyers, R., Stevenson, H., Coolahan, K. *et al.* (1996) 'Community-based resilient peer treatment of withdrawn maltreated preschool children.' *Journal of Clinical and Consulting Psychology 64,* 6, 1377–86.

Fantuzzo, J., Weiss, A. and Coolahan, K. (1998) 'Community-based partnership-directed research. Actualizing community strengths to treat victims of physical abuse and neglect.' In R.J. Lutzker (ed.), *Child Abuse: A Handbook of Theory, Research, and Treatment.* New York: Pergamon Press.

Fantuzzo, J.W., Wray, L., Hall, R., Goins, C. and Azar, S. (1986) 'Parent and social-skills training for mentally retarded mothers identified as child maltreaters.' *American Journal of Mental Deficiency 91,* 135–40.

Farmer, E., Moyers, S. and Lipscombe, J. (2001) *The Fostering Task with Adolescents.* Bristol: SPS.

Farmer, E., Moyers, S. and Lipscombe, J. (2004) *Fostering Adolescents.* London: Jessica Kingsley Publishers.

Farmer, E. and Parker, R. (1991) *Trials and Tribulations.* London: HMSO.

Farmer, E. and Pollock, S. (1998) *Substitute Care for Sexually Abused and Abusing Children.* London: Wiley.

Farran, D. (1990) 'Effects of intervention with disadvantaged and disabled children: a decade review.' In S. Meisels and J. Shonkoff (eds) *Handbook of Early Childhood Intervention.* Cambridge: Cambridge University Press.

Farrington, D.P. (1996) *Understanding and Preventing Youth Crime. Social Policy Research 93.* York: Joseph Rowntree Foundation.

Farrow, with the Executive Session on Child Protection (1997) *Child Protection: Building Community Partnerships, Getting from Here to There.* Cambridge, MA: John F. Kennedy School of Government, Harvard University.

Featherstone, B. (1999) 'Taking mothers seriously: The implications for child protection.' *Child and Family Social Work 4,* 1, 43–55.

Fein, E., Maluccio, A.H. and Kluger, M.P. (1990) *No More Partings: An Examination of Long-Term Foster Family Care.* Washington, DC: Child Welfare League of America.

Feldman, L.H. (1991) *Evaluating the Impact of Intensive Family Preservation Services in New Jersey, xxiii.* Newbury Park, CA: Sage Publications, Inc.

Fergusson, D., Lynskey, M., and Horwood, L. (1995) 'The adolescent outcomes of adoption: A 16 year longitudinal study.' *Journal of Child Psychology and Psychiatry and Allied Disciplines 36,* 597–615.

Ferleger, N., Glenwick, D.S., Gaines, R.R.W. and Green, A.H. (1988) 'Identifying correlates of reabuse in maltreating parents.' *Child Abuse and Neglect 12,* 41–9.

Festinger, T. (1983) *No One Ever Asked Us: A Postcript to Foster Care.* New York: Columbia University Press.

Fields, J. (2001) *Living Arrangements of Children. Current Population Reports.* Washington, DC: US Census Bureau.

Finkelhor, D. (1980) 'Risk factors in the sexual victimisation of children.' *Child Abuse and Neglect 4,* 265–73.

Finkelhor, D. and Berliner, L. (1995) 'Research on treatment of sexually abused children.' *Journal of the American Academy of Child and Adolescent Psychiatry 34,* 1408–23.

Finkelhor, D. and Browne, A. (1985) 'The traumatic impact of child sexual abuse: A conceptualization.' *American Journal of Orthopsychiatry 55,* 530–41.

First Key (1987) *A Study of Young Black People Leaving Care.* Leeds: First Key.

Fisher, M. (2002) 'The Social Care Institute for Excellence: The role of a national institute in developing knowledge and practice in social care.' *Social Work and Social Sciences Review 10*, 1, 36–64.

Fisher, M. (2005) 'Knowledge production for social welfare: Enhancing the evidence base.' In P. Sommerfield (ed.) *Evidence-based Social Work: Towards a New Professionalism?* Bern: Peter Lang.

Fisher, M., Marsh, P. and Phillips, D. (1986) *In and Out of Care.* London: Batsford/BAAF.

Fisher, P., Gunnar, M., Chamberlain, P. and Reid, J. (2000) 'Preventive intervention for maltreated preschool children: Impact on children's behavior, neuroendocrine activity and foster parent functioning.' *Journal of the American Academy of Child and Adolescent Psychiatry 39*, 1356.

Fitzpatrick, S., Hastings, A. and Kintrea, K. (1998) *Including Young People in Regeneration: A Lot to Learn?* Bristol: The Policy Press.

Flango, V.E. and Flango, C.R. (1995) 'How many children were adopted in 1992?' *Child Welfare 75*, 5, 1018–32.

Folks, H. (1902) *The Care of Destitute Neglected and Delinquent Children.* Washington DC: NASW Classics Series.

Fonagy, P. and Kurtz, Z. (2002) 'Disturbance of conduct.' In P. Fonagy, M. Target, D. Cottrell, J. Phillips and Z. Kurtz (eds) *What Works for Whom? A Critical Review of Treatments for Children and Adolescents.* New York: The Guilford Press.

France, A. (2001) 'Involving communities in the evaluation of programmes with "at risk" children and young people.' *Children and Society 15*, 39–45.

Fraser, C. (1993) *Corporate Parents: Inspection of Residential Child Care Services in 11 Authorities November 1992 to March 1993.* London: DH.

Fraser, M., Walton, E., Lewis, R.E., Pecora, P. and Walton, W.K. (1996) 'An experiment in family reunification correlates of outcomes at one-year follow-up.' *Children and Youth Services Review 18*, 4/5, 335–62.

Fraser, M.W. (1990) 'Program outcome measures.' In Y.T. Yuan and M. Rivest (eds) *Preserving Families: Evaluation Resources for Practitioners and Policy Makers 117*, 77–101. Newbury Park, CA: Sage Publications.

Fraser, M.W., Pecora, P.J. and Haapala, D.A. (1991) *Families in Crisis: The Impact of Intensive Family Preservation Services.* Hawthorne, NY: Adline de Gruyter.

Fraser, M.W. (ed.) (2004) *Risk and Resilience in Childhood: An Ecological Perspective. Second Edition.* Washington, DC: NASW Press.

Freundlich, M. and Wright, L. (2003) *Post-permanency Services.* Washington, DC: Casey Family Programs National Resource Center for Resource Family Support.

Frost, N. (1997) 'Delivering family support: issues and themes in service development.' In N. Parton (ed.) *Child Protection and Family Support.* London: Routledge.

Fry, E. (1992) *After Care: Making the Most of Foster Care.* London: National Foster Care Association.

Fulbright-Anderson, K., Kubisch, A.C. and Connell, J.P. (1998) *New Approaches to Evaluating Community Initiatives, volume 2, Thory, Measurement and Analysis.* Washington DC: Aspen Institute.

Fuller, R. (1989) 'Problems and possibilities in studying preventive work.' *Adoption and Fostering 13*, 9–13.

Furlong, A. and Cartmel, F. (1997) *Young People and Social Change.* Buckingham: Open University Press.

Furniss, T., Bingley Miller, L. and Van Elburg, A. (1988) 'Goal-orientated group treatment for sexually abused adolescent girls.' *British Journal of Psychiatry 152*, 97–106.

Gallagher, B. (1998) *Grappling With Smoke: Investigating and Managing Organised Child Sexual Abuse: A Good Practice Guide.* London: NSPCC.

Garbarino, J. (1992) *Children and Families in the Social Environment. Second Edition.* New York: Aldine de Gruyter.

Garbarino, J. and Kostelny, K. (1992) 'Neighbourhood and community influences on parenting.' In T. Luster and L. Okagaki (eds) *Parenting: An Ecological Perspective.* Hillsdale, NJ: Lawrence Erlbaum Associates.

Garmezy, N. and Masten, A. (1991) 'The protective role of competence indicators in children at risk.' In E.M. Cummings, A.L. Greene and K.H. Karraker (eds) *Life-Span Developmental Psychology: Perspectives on Stress and Coping,* Hillsdale, NJ: Lawrence Erlbaum Associates.

Garnett, L. (1992) *Leaving Care and After.* London: National Children's Bureau.

Gaudin, J.M. Jr. (1993a) *Child Neglect: A Guide for Intervention.* Washington, DC: US DHHS.

Gaudin, J.M. Jr. (1993b) 'Effective intervention with neglectful families.' *Criminal Justice and Behavior 20*, 66–89.

Gaudin, J.M. Jr. (1999) 'Child neglect: Short-term and long-term outcomes.' In H. Dubowitz (ed.) *Neglected Children: Research, Practice and Policy.* Thousand Oaks, CA: Sage.

Gaudin, J., Wodarski, J., Arkinson, M. and Avery, L. (1990–1) 'Remedying child neglect: Effectiveness of social network interventions.' *Journal of Applied Social Sciences 15*, 97–123.

Geen, R. (2004) 'The evolution of kinship care policy and practice.' *Future of Children 14*, 1, 131–49. www.futureofchildren.org

Gelardo, M.S. and Sanford, E.E. (1987) 'Child abuse and neglect: A review of the literature.' *School Psychology Review 16*, 137–55.

Gelles, R. (1973) 'Child abuse as psychopathology: A sociological critique and reformulation.' *American Journal of Orthopsychiatry 43*, 611–21.

Gelles, R.J. (1987) *Family Violence.* London: Sage.

Gelles, R.J. and Cornell, C.P. (1997) *Intimate Violence in Families, Third Edition.* Beverly Hills, California: Sage.

Gershater-Molko, R.M., Lutzker, J.R. and Sherman, J.A. (2003) 'Assessing child neglect.' *Aggression and Violent Behavior* 8, 563–85.

Gershater-Molko, R.M., Lutzker, J.R. and Wesch, J.R. (2002) 'Using recidivism data to evaluate Project Safecare: Teaching bonding, safety, and health care skills to parents.' *Child Maltreatment 7*, 277–85.

Ghate, D. (2001) 'Community-based evaluations in the UK: Scientific concerns and practical constraints.' *Children and Society 15*, 23–32.

Ghate, D. and Hazel, N. (2002) *Parenting in Poor Environments: Stress, Support and Coping.* London: Jessica Kingsley Publishers.

Ghate, D. and Ramella, M. (2002) *Positive Parenting: The National Evaluation of the Youth Justice Board's Parenting Programme.* London: Youth Justice Board.

Gibbons, J., Gallagher, B., Bell, C. and Gordon, D. (1995) *Development after Physical Abuse in Early Childhood.* London: HMSO.

Gibbons, J. (1990) *Family Support and Prevention. Studies in Local Areas.* London: HMSO.

Gibbons, J. and Thorpe, S. (1989) 'Can voluntary support projects help vulnerable families? The work of Home-Start.' *British Journal of Social Work 19*, 189–202.

Gibbs, I. and Sinclair, I. (1998a) 'Private and local authority children's homes: A comparison.' *Journal of Adolescence 21*, 5, 517–27.

Gibbs, I. and Sinclair, I. (1998b) 'Treatment and treatment outcomes in children's homes.' *Child and Family Social Work 4*, 1, 1–8.

Gill, O., Tanner, C. and Bland, L. (2000) *Family Support: Strengths and Pressures in a 'High-Risk' Neighbourhood.* Barkingside: Barnardo's,

Gilligan, R. (2000) 'Adversity, resilience and young people: The protective value of positive school and spare time experiences.' *Children and Society 14*, 1, 37–47.

Glantz, M.D. and Johnson, J.L. (1999) *Resilience and Development: Positive Life Adaptations.* New York, NY: Kluwer Academic/Plenum.

Glaser, D. (2002) 'Emotional abuse and neglect – a conceptual framework.' *Child Abuse and Neglect 67*, 697–714.

Glass, N. (2001) 'What works for children – the political issues.' *Children and Society 15*, 14–20.

Glisson, C. (1994) 'The effects of services coordination teams on outcomes for children in state custody.' *Administration in Social Work 18*, 4, 1–23.

Glisson, C. and Hemmelgarn, A. (1998) 'The effects of organizational climate and interorganizational coordination on the quality and outcomes of children's service systems.' *Child Abuse and Neglect 22*, 5, 401–21.

Godek, S. (1976) *Leaving Care.* Barkingside: Barnardo's.

Goerge, R., Bilaver, L., Lee, B.L., Needell, B., Brookhart, A. and Jackman, W. (2002) *Employment Outcomes for Youth Aging Out of Foster Care – Final Report.* Chicago, IL and Berkeley, CA: Chapin Hall Center for Children at the University of Chicago, and Center for Social Services Research, University of California Berkeley. Last retrieved 15 April 2004 from: aspe.hhs.gov/hsp/fostercare-agingout02/

Goffman, E. (1961) *Asylums.* New York. Doubleday.

Gold, E.R. (1986) 'Long-term effects of sexual victimization in childhood: An attributional approach.' *Journal of Consulting and Clinical Psychology 54*, 471–5.

Goldberg, D. and Williams, P. (1988) *A User's Guide to the General Health Questionnaire.* Windsor: NFER-Nelson.

Goldstein, J., Freud, A. and Solnit, A. (1980) *Beyond the Best Interests of the Child.* New York: Burnett Books.

Goldstein, J.A., Solnit, J., Goldstein, S. and Freud, A. (1996) *The Best Interests of the Child: The Least Detrimental Alternative.* New York: Free Press.

Golub, J.S., Espinosa, M.A., Damon, L. and Card, J. (1987) 'A videotape parent education program for abusive parents.' *Child Abuse and Neglect 11*, 255–65.

Gomby, D. (1999) 'Understanding evaluations of home visitation programs.' *The Future of Children 9*, 1, 27–43.

Gomby, D. (2000) 'Promise and limitations of home visitation.' *Journal of the American Medical Association 284*, 11, 1430–1.

Gomby, D.S., Culross, P.L. and Behrman, R.E. (1999) 'Home visiting: Recent program evaluations – Analysis and recommendations.' *The Future of Children 9*, 1, 4–43.

Gomby, D.S., Larner, M.B., Stevenson, C.S., Lewit, E.M. and Behrman, R.E. (1995) 'Long-term outcomes of early childhood programs: Analysis and recommendations.' *The Future of Children 5*, 6–24.

Goodman, R. (1997) 'The strengths and difficulties questionnaire: A research note.' *Journal of Child Psychology and Psychiatry 38*, 5, 581–86.

Goodson, B.D., Layzer, J.I., St. Pierre, R.G., Bernstein, R.S. and Lopez, M. (2000) 'Effectiveness of a comprehensive, five-year family support program for low-income children and their families: Findings from the Comprehensive Child Development Program.' *Early Childhood Research Quarterly 15*, 1, 5–39.

Gordon, D. (2000) 'Inequalities in income, wealth and standard of living in Britain.' In D. Gordon and C. Pantazis (eds) *Tackling Inequalities: Where are We Now and What Should be Done?* pp. 13–28. Bristol: The Policy Press.

Gottfredson, G.D. and Gottfredson, D.C. (2001) 'What schools do to prevent problem behavior and promote safe environments.' *Journal of Educational and Psychological Consultation 12*, 313–44.

Gough, D. (1993) *Child Abuse Interventions: A Review of the Research Literature.* London: HMSO.

Graham, B., Tanner, G., Cheyne, B., Freeman, I., Rooney, M. and Lambrie, A. (1998) 'Unemployment rates, single parent density and indices of child poverty: their relationship to different categories of child abuse and neglect.' *Child Abuse and Neglect 22*, 2, 79–90.

Graham, J. and Bowling, B. (1995) *Young People and Crime. Research Study 145.* London: HMSO.

Graziano, A.M. and Mills, J.R. (1992) 'Treatment for abused children: When is a partial solution acceptable?' *Child Abuse and Neglect 16*, 217–28.

Green, R. (2000) 'Applying a community needs profiling approach to tackling service user poverty.' *British Journal of Social Work 30*, 3, 287–303.

Greenberg, M.T., Domitrovich, C. and Bumbarger, B. (2001) 'The prevention of mental disorders in school-aged children: Current state of the field.' *Prevention and Treatment 4*.

Greenberg, M.T., Weissberg, R.P., O'Brien, M.U., Zins, J.E., Fredericks, L., Resnik, H., and Elias, M.J. (2003) 'Enhancing school-based prevention and youth development through coordinated social, emotional, and academic learning.' *American Psychologist 58*, 466–74.

Greenhalgh, T. (2001) *How to Read a Paper: The Basics of Evidence Based Medicine, Second Edition.* London: BMJ Books.

Grimshaw, R. and McGuire, C. (1998) *Evaluating Parenting Programmes: A Study of Stakeholders' Views.* London: NCB.

Grotevant, H. (2000) 'Openness in adoption: Research with the adoption kinship network.' *Adoption Quarterly 4*, 45–66.

Grotevant, H. and McRoy, R. (1998) *Openness in Adoption: Exploring Family Connections.* Thousand Oaks, CA: Sage.

Grotevant, H., Ross, N., Marchel, M., and McRoy, R. (1999) 'Adaptive behavior in adopted children: predictors from early risk, collaboration in relationships within the adoptive kinship network, and openness arrangements.' *Journal of Adolescent Research 14*, 2, 231–47.

Groze, V. (1996) 'A one- and two-year follow-up study of adoptive families and special needs children.' *Children and Youth Services Review 18*, 57–82.

Groze, V. and Illeana, D. (1996) 'A follow-up study of adopted children from Romania.' *Child and Adolescent Social Work Journal 13*, 6 541–65.

Gunnar, M. (1998) 'Quality of early care and buffering of neuroendocrine stress reactions: potential effects on the developing human brain.' *Preventive Medicine 27*, 208–11.

Guralnick, M. (ed.) (1997) *The Effectiveness of Early Intervention.* Baltimore, MD: Brookes.

Guyatt, G.H., Sackett, D.L., Sinclair, J.C., Hayward, R., Cook, D.J. and Cook, R.J. (1995) 'Users' guides to the medical literature XI A method for grading health care recommendations.' *Journal of the American Medical Association 174*, 1800–4.

Hahn, A. (1994) 'The use of assessment procedures in foster care to evaluate readiness for independent living.' *Children and Youth Services Review 16*, 3/4, 171–79.

Hai, N. and Williams, A. (2004) *Implementing the Children Leaving Care Act 2000: The Experience of Eight London Boroughs.* London: National Children's Bureau.

Hallfors, D. and Godette, D. (2002) 'Will the "principles of effectiveness" improve prevention practice? Early findings from a diffusion study.' *Health Education Review 17*, 461–70.

Halliday-Boykins, C.A. and Henggeler, S.W. (2001) 'Multisystemic therapy, Theory, research and practice.' In E. Walton, P. Sandau-Beckler and M. Mannes (eds) *Balancing Family-centered Services and Child Well-being.* New York: Columbia University Press.

Halpern, R. (1993) 'The societal context of home visiting and related services for families in poverty.' *Future of Children 3*, 3, 158–71.

Halpern, R. (2000) 'Early intervention for low-income children and families.' In J.P. Shonkoff and S.J. Meisels (eds) *Handbook of Early Childhood Intervention, Second Edition.* New York: Cambridge University Press.

Halsey, A.H. (ed.) (1972) *Educational Priority: EPA Problems and Practices.* London: HMSO.

Hanson, K.L., Vogel, A.L., Morrow, C.E., Windham, A.M. and Bandstra, E.S. (2003) 'Caregiver–Infant Interaction in At-Risk Dyads.' Abstract presented at the meeting of the College on Problems of Drug Dependence, Miami Beach, FL.

Hanson, L., Deere, D., Lee, C., Lewin, A. and Seval, C. (2001) *Key Principles in Providing Integrated Behavioral Health Services for Young Children and Their Families: The Starting Early Starting Smart Experience.* Washington, DC: Casey Family Programs and the US Department of Health and Human Services, Substance Abuse and Mental Health Services Administration.

Harper, R. (2001) *Social Capital: A Review of the Literature.* London: Office for National Statistics.

Harrington, R., Peters, S., Green, J., Byford, S., Woods, J. and McGowan, R. (2000) 'Randomised comparison of the effectiveness and costs of community and hospital based mental health services for children with behavioural disorders.' *British Medical Journal 321*, 1047–50.

Hart, B. and Risley, T. (1995) *Meaningful Differences in the Everyday Experience of Young American Children.* Baltimore, MD: Brookes.

Hart, A. and Thomas, H. (2000) 'Controversial attachments: The indirect treatment of fostered and adopted children via parent co-therapy.' *Attachment and Human Development 2*, 3, 306–27.

Haugaard, J. (1998) 'Is adoption a risk factor for the development of adjustment problems?' *Clinical Psychology Review 18*, 1, 47–69.

Hawkins, J.D., Catalano, R.F., Kosterman, R., Abbott, R. and Hill, K.G. (1999) 'Preventing adolescent health-risk behaviors by strengthening protection during childhood.' *Archives of Pediatrics and Adolescent Medicine 153*, 3, 226–32

Hawkins, J.D., Catalano, R.F. and Miller, J.Y. (1992) 'Risk and protective factors for alcohol and other drug problems in adolescence and early adulthood: implications for substance abuse prevention.' *Psychological Bulletin 112*, 64–105.

Hawtin, M., Hughes, G. and Percy-Smith, J. (1994) *Community Profiling: Auditing Social Needs.* Buckingham: Open University Press.

Headlam Wells, C. (2001) Unpublished report, Institute of Education, University of London.

Heal, K., Sinclair, I. and Troop, J. (1973) 'The development of a social climate questionnaire for use in community homes and approved schools.' *British Journal of Sociology 24*, 222–31.

Healy, K., Kennedy, R., and Sinclair, J. (1991) 'Child physical abuse observed, with and without history of child abuse. Treatment in an in-patient family unit.' *British Journal of Psychiatry 158*, 234–237.

Heath, A., Colton, M. and Aldgate, J. (1994) 'Failure to escape: A longitudinal study of foster children's educational attainment.' *British Journal of Social Work 24*, 241–60

Hebbeler, K.M. and Gerlach-Downie, S.G. (2002) 'Inside the black box of home visiting: A qualitative analysis of why intended outcomes were not achieved.' *Early Childhood Research Quarterly 17*, 1, 28–51.

Hellinckx, W., Broekaert, E., Vanden Berge, A. and Colton, M. (eds) (1991) *Innovations in Residential Care.* Acco Leuven, Netherlands: Amersfoort.

Henderson, A. and Mapp K.L. (2002) *A New Wave of Evidence: The Impact of School, Family, and Community Connections on Student Achievement.* Austin, TX: National Center for Family and Community Connections with Schools, Southwest Educational Development Laboratory.

Henderson, P. (ed.) (1995) *Children and Communities.* Pluto Press/Community Development Foundation, London.

Henggeler, S., Cunningham, P., Pickrel, S., Schoenwald, S. and Brondino, M.J. (1996) 'Multisystemic therapy: An effective violence prevention appraoch for serious juvenile offenders.' *Journal of Adolescence 19*, 47–61.

Henggeler, S.W., Schoenwald, S.K., Borduin, C., Rowland, M. and Cunningham, P.B. (1998) *Multisystemic Treatment of Antisocial Behavior in Children and Adolescents.* New York: The Guilford Press.

Henggeler, S., Schoenwald, S., Rowland, M. and Cunningham, P. (2002) *Serious Emotional Disturbance in Children and Adolescence: Multisystemic Therapy.* New York: Guilford.

Henricson, C. (2003) *Government and Parenting: Is There a Case for a Policy Review and A Parent's Code.* York: Joseph Rowntree Foundation.

Henricson, C., Katz, I., Mesie, J., Sandison, M. and Tunstill, J. (2001) *National Mapping of Family Services in England and Wales – A Consultation Document.* London: National Family and Parenting Institute.

Hersov, L. (1990) 'Aspects of adoption: The 7th Jack Tizard Memorial Lecture.' *Journal of Child Psychology and Psychiatry 31*, 493–510.

Hess, P.M., McGowan, B.G. and Botsko, M. (2003) *Nurturing the One, Supporting the Many, The Center for Family Life in Sunset Park Brooklyn.* New York: Columbia University Press.

Hill, M. (1997) 'Participatory research with children.' *Child and Family Social Work 2*, 171–83.

Hill, R.B. (2001) 'The Role of Race in Foster Care Placements.' Paper presented at The Race Matters Forum sponsored by the University of Illinois at Urbana-Champaign, January 9–10.

Hines, A.M., Lemon, K., Wyatt, P. and Merdinger, J. (2004) 'Factors related to the disproportionate involvement of children of color in the child welfare system: A review and emerging themes.' *Children and Youth Services Review 26*, 507–27.

HM Government (2004a) *Department for Education and Skills: Five Year Strategy for Children and Learners.* London: The Stationery Office.

HM Government (2004b) *Every Child Matters: Change for Children.* London: DfES.

Hodges, J., Steele, M., Hillman, S., Henderson, K. and Neil, M. (2000) 'Effects of abuse on attachment representations: narrative assessments of abused children.' *Journal of Child Psychotherapy 26*, 422–55.

Hodges, J. and Tizard, B. (1989a) 'IQ and behavioural adjustment of ex-institutional adolescents.' *Journal of Child Psychology and Psychiatry 30*, 53–75.

Hodges, J. and Tizard, B. (1989b) 'Social and family relationships of ex-institutional adolescents.' *Journal of Child Psychology and Psychiatry 30*, 77–97.

Hoge, J. and Idalski, A. (1999) 'How Boysville of Michigan specifies and evaluates its supervised independent living program.' In *Preparing Youths for Long-term Success: Proceedings from the Casey Family Program National Independent Living Forum.* Washington DC: Child Welfare League of America.

Hollingsworth, L.D. (1997) 'Effect of transracial/transethnic adoption on children's racial and ethnic identity and self-esteem: A meta-analytic review.' *Marriage and Family Review 25*, 99–130.

Holloway, J. (1997) 'Outcomes in placements for adoption and long-term fostering.' *Archives of Disease in Childhood 76*, 227–30.

Home Office (1998) *Supporting Families.* London: Stationery Office.

Home Office (1999) *On Track Programme: Invitations to Bid.* London: Home Office Family Policy Unit.

Hope, T. and Foster, J. (1992) 'Conflicting forces: Changing the dynamics of crime and community on a "problem estate".' *British Journal of Criminology 32*, 4, 488–504.

Horton, C. (2003) *Protective Factors Literature Review: Early Care and Education Programs and the Prevention of Child Abuse and Neglect*. Washington DC: Center for the Study of Social Policy. (www.cssp.org/uploadFiles/horton.pdf)

Horwath, J. (2002) 'Maintaining a focus on the child: first impressions of the "Framework for the Assessment of Children In Need and their Families" in cases of child neglect.' *Child Abuse Review 11*, 195–213.

Horwath, J. (2005) 'Identifying and assessing cases of child neglect: Learning from the Irish experience.' *Child and Family Social Work 10*, 99–110.

House of Commons (1984) *Children in Care. Second Report from the Social Services Committee Session 1983–84*. London: HMSO.

Howe, D. (1990) 'The Post Adoption Centre: the first three years.' *Adoption and Fostering 14*, 32–6.

Howe, D. (1997) 'Parent Reported Problems in 211 Adopted children: some risk and protective factors.' *Journal of Child Psychology and Psychiatry 38*, 401–412.

Howe, D. (1998) *Patterns of Adoption: Nature Nurture and Psychosocial Development*. Oxford: Blackwell Science.

Howe, D., Brandon, M., Hinings, D. and Schofield, G. (1999) *Attachment Theory, Child Maltreatment and Family Support*. Basingstoke: Macmillan.

Howe, D. and Hinings, D. (1987) 'Adopted Children Referred to a Child and Family Centre.' *Adoption and Fostering 20*, 35–43.

Hudson, J. and Galaway, B. (eds) (1995) *Child Welfare in Canada – Research and Policy Implications*. Toronto: Thompson Educational Publishing.

Hughes, M. and Traynor, T. (2000) 'Reconciling process and outcome in evaluating community initiatives.' *Evaluation 6*, 1, 37–49.

Hughes, W.H. (1985) *Report of the Committee of Enquiry into Children's Homes*. Belfast: HMSO.

Humphries, B. (2003) 'What else counts as evidence in evidence based social work.' *Social Work Education 22*, 81–91.

Hurry, J., Lloyd C. and McGurk, H. (2000) 'Long-term effects of drugs education in primary schools.' *Addiction Research 8*, 2, 183–202.

Hurry, J. and McGurk, H. (1997) 'An evaluation of a primary prevention programme for schools.' *Addiction Research 5*, 1, 23–38.

Hurry, J. and Sylva, K. (1998) *The Long-term Effects of Two Interventions for Children with Reading Difficulties*. London: Qualifications and Curriculum Authority (QCA).

Hutson, S. (1995) *Care Leavers and Young Homeless People in Wales: The Exchange of Good Practice*. Swansea: University of Wales.

Hutson, S. (1997) *Supported Housing: The Experience of Young Care Leavers*. Barkingside: Barnardo's.

Huxley, P.J., Evans, S., Burns, T., Fahy, T. and Green, J. (2001) 'Quality of life outcome in a randomized controlled trail of case management.' *Social Psychiatry and Psychiatric Epidemiology 36*, 249–55.

Hyland, J. (1993) *Yesterday's Answers*. London: Whiting and Birch Ltd.

Iglehart, A.P. (1994) 'Adolescents in foster care: Predicting readiness for independent living. Special Issue: Preparing Foster youth for adulthood.' *Children and Youth Services Review 16*, 3/4, 159–69.

Immigration and Naturalization Service, US Dept. of Justice (2000) *Statistical Yearbook of the Immigration and Naturalization Services*. Available at www.ins.usdoj.gov/graphics/aboutins/ statistics/1998yb.pdf.

Ince, L. (1999) 'Preparing black young people for leaving care.' In R. Barn (ed.) *Working with Black Children and Adolescents in Need*. London: British Agencies for Adoption and Fostering.

Ingersoll, B. (1997). Psychiatric disorders among adopted children: A review and commentary. *Adoption Quarterly 1*, 1, 57–73.

Institute of Medicine (1994) *Reducing Risks for Mental Disorders: Frontiers for Prevention Intervention Research*. Washington, DC: National Academy Press.

Irueste-Montes, A.M. and Montes, F. (1988) 'Court-ordered vs. voluntary treatment of abusive and neglectful parents.' *Child Abuse and Neglect 12*, 33–9.

Iszatt, J. and Wasileska, T. (1997) 'Nurture Groups: an early intervention model enabling children with emotional and behavioural difficulties to integrate successfully in schools.' *Educational and Child Psychology 14*, 3, 121.

Ives, R. and Clements, I. (1996) 'Drugs education in schools: A review.' *Children and Society 10*, 1, 14–27.

Iwaniec, D. (1995) *The Emotionally Abused and Neglected Child: Identification, Assessment and Intervention*. Chichester: John Wiley and Sons.

Iwaniec, D. (2004) *Children Who Fail to Thrive: A Practice Guide*. Chichester: John Wiley and Sons.

Iwaniec, D., Herbert, M. and Sluckin, A. (2002) 'Helping emotionally abused and neglected children and abusive carers.' In K. Browne, H. Hanks, P. Stratton and C. Hamilton (eds) *Early Prediction and Prevention of Child Abuse: A Handbook*. Chichester: John Wiley and Sons Ltd.

Iwaniec, D. and Sneddon, H. (2001) 'Attachment style in adults who failed to thrive as children: outcomes of a 20-year follow-up study of factors influencing maintenance or change in attachment style.' *British Journal of Social Work 31*, 179–95.

Jack, G. (1997a) 'Ecological approach to social work.' In M. Davies (ed.) *The Blackwell Encyclopaedia of Social Work 105*. Oxford: Blackwell.

Jack G. (1997b) 'An ecological approach to social work with children and families.' *Child and Family Social Work 2*, 109–20.

Jack, G. (2000) 'Ecological influences on parenting and child development.' *British Journal of Social Work 30*, 703–20.

Jack, G. (2004) 'Child protection at the community level.' *Child Abuse Review 13*, 363–83.

Jack, G. and Jordan, B. (1999) 'Social capital and child welfare.' *Children and Society 13*, 242–56.

Jack, G. and Gill, O. (2003) *The Missing Side of the Triangle: Assessing the Importance of Family and Environmental Factors in the Lives of Children*. London: Barnardo's.

Jackson, S. (1994) 'Educating children in residential and foster care.' *Oxford Review of Education 20*, 3, 267–79.

Jackson, S. (2002) 'Promoting stability and continuity in care away from home.' In T. Newman, H. Roberts and D. McNeish (eds) *What Works for Children?* Buckingham: Open University Press.

Jackson, S. (2003) 'Late foster placements – a second chance for stability and educational success.' In *Stability in Foster Care*, papers prepared for seminar. Norwich: University of East Anglia.

Jackson, S. and Martin, P.Y. (1998) 'Surviving the care system: education and resilience.' *Journal of Adolescence 21*, 5, 569–83.

Jacobs, F.H., Williams, P.H. and Kapuscik, J.L. (1997) 'Evaluating family preservation services: Asking the right questions.' In W. Hellinckx, M. J. Colton and M. Williams (eds) *International Perspectives on Family Support*. Aldershot, England: Arena.

James, S., Landsverk, J. and Slymen, D.J. (in press) 'Placement movement in out-of-home care: patterns and predictors.' *Children and Youth Services Review*.

James, S. and Mennen, F. (2001) 'Treatment outcome research: How effective are treatments for abused children?' *Child and Adolescent Social Work Journal 18*, 73–95.

Jensen, P.S, Weersing, R., Hoagwood, K.E. and Goodman, E. (2005) 'What is the evidence for evidence-based treatment? A hard look at our soft underbelly.' *Mental Health Services Research 7*, 1, 53–74.

Jenson, J. and Whittaker, J.K. (1987) 'Parental involvement in children's residential treatment: From pre-placement to aftercare.' *Children and Youth Services Review 9*, 2, 81–100.

Jessor, R. and Jessor, S.L. (1977) *Problem Behavior and Psychosocial Development: A Longitudinal Study of Youth*. New York: Academic Press.

Jessor, R., Van Den Bos, J., Vanderryn, J., Costa, F.M. and Turbin, M.S. (1997) 'Protective factors in adolescent problem behavior: Moderator effects and developmental change.' *Developmental Psychology 31*, 6, 923–33.

Jinich, S. and Litrownik, A. (1999) 'Coping with sexual abuse: Development and evalutation of a videotape intervention for nonoffending parents.' *Child Abuse and Neglect 23*, 175–90.

Johnson, K., Knitzer, J. and Kaufmann, R. (2003) *Making Dollars Follow Sense: Financing Early Childhood Mental Health Services to Promote Healthy Social and Emotional Development in Young Children*. New York: Columbia University, National Center on Children in Poverty.

Johnson, K., Strader, T., Berbaum, M., Bryant, D., Bucholtz, G., Collins, D. and Noe, T. (1996) 'Reducing alcohol and other drug use by strengthening community, family, and youth resiliency: An evaluation of the Creating Lasting Connections Program.' *Journal of Adolescent Research 11*, 1, 36–67.

Johnson, Z., Howell, F. and Molloy, B. (1993) 'Community mothers' programme: randomised controlled trial of non-professional intervention in parenting.' *British Medical Journal 306*, 1449–52.

Johnson, Z., Molloy, B., Scallan, E., Fitzpatrick, P., Rooney, B., Keegan, T. and Byrne, P. (2000) 'Community Mothers Programme – seven year follow-up of a randomised controlled trial of non professional intervention in parenting.' *Journal of Public Health Medicine 22*, 3, 337–42.

Johnson, M. and Austin, M.J. (2005) *Evidence-based Practice in the Social Sciences: Implications for Organizational Change*. Berkeley, CA: School of Social Welfare, University of California, Berkeley.

Jones, D.P.H. (1997) 'Treatment of the child and the family where child abuse or neglect has occurred.' In R. Helfer, R. Kempe and R. Krugman (eds) *The Battered Child, Fifth Edition*. Chicago: University of Chicago.

Jones, D.P.H. (1998) 'The effectiveness of intervention.' In M. Adcock and R. White (eds) *Significant Harm: Its Management and Outcome*. Croydon: Significant Publications.

Jones, D.P.H. (2003) *Communicating with Vulnerable Children: A Guide for Practitioners*. London: Gaskell.

Jones, D.P.H. and Newbold, C. (2001) 'Assessment of abusing families' In G. Adshead, and D. Broake (eds) *Assessment of Abusing Families in Munchausen Syndrome by Proxy*. London: Imperial College.

Jones, D.P.H. and Ramchandani, P. (1999) *Child Sexual Abuse: Informing Practice from Research*. Abingdon: Radcliffe.

Jones, G. (1995) *Leaving Home*. Buckingham: Open University Press.

Jones, J. and Gupta, A. (1998) 'The context of decision-making in cases of child neglect.' *Child Abuse Review 7*, 2, 97–110.

Jones, L. (2001) *An Evaluation of the Youth Empowerment Services Program (YES)*. Seattle, WA: Casey Family Programs.

Jones, M.A. and Moses, B. (1984) 'West Virginia's former foster children: Their experiences in care and their lives as young adults.' Washington, D.C: CWLA.

Jordan, B. (1997) 'Partnership with service users in child protection and family support.' In N. Parton (ed) *Child Protection and Family Support: Tensions, Contradictions and Possibilities*. London: Routledge.

Jowitt, S. (2003) *Child Neglect: Contemporary Themes and Issues. Policy and Practice in Child Welfare Literature Review Series 2*. Glasbury-on-Wye: The Bridge Publishing House Ltd.

Jumper, S.A. (1995) 'A meta-analysis of the relationship of child sexual abuse to adult psychological adjustment.' *Child Abuse and Neglect 19*, 715–28.

Kadushin, A. (1980) *Child Welfare Services, Third Edition,* New York: Macmillan.

Kahan, B. (1979) *Growing Up in Care.* Oxford: Blackwell.

Kahan, B. (1994) *Growing Up in Groups.* London: HMSO.

Kaniuk, J. (1992). 'The use of relationship in the preparation and support of adopters.' *Adoption and Fostering 16,* 2, 47–52.

Kaniuk J., Steele M., and Hodges J. (2004) 'Report on a longitudinal research project, exploring the development of attachments between older, hard-to-place children and their adopters over the first two years of placement.' *Adoption and Fostering 28,* 61–67.

Karoly, L.A., Greenwood, P.W., Everingham, S.S., Hoube, J., Kilburn, M.R., Rydell, C.P. *et al.* (1998) *Investing in Our Children: What We Know and Don't Know About the Costs and Benefits of Early Childhood Interventions.* Santa Monica, CA: RAND.

Karoly, L.M., Kilburn, R.M., Caulkins, J.P. and Cannon, J.S. (2000) *Assessing Costs and Benefits of Early Childhood Intervention Programs: Overview and Application.* Santa Monica, CA: RAND.

Kaufman, K.L. and Rudy, L. (1991) 'Future directions in the treatment of physical child abuse.' *Criminal Justice and Behavior 18,* 82–97.

Kazdin, A. (1997) 'Practitioner review: Psychosocial treatments for conduct disorder in children.' *Journal of Child Psychology and Psychiatry 38,* 161–78.

Kelly, B. (1999) 'Circle Time.' *Educational Psychology in Practice 15,* 1, 40–4.

Kelly, J.F. and Barnard, K.E. (1999) 'Parent education within a relationship-focused model-response.' *Topics in Early Childhood Special Edition 19,* 3, 151–57.

Kempe, C.H., Silverman, F.N., Steele, B., Droegmuller, W. and Silver, H.H. (1962) 'The battered child syndrome.' *Journal of the American Medical Association 181,* 17–24.

Kendall-Tackett, K.A., Williams, L.M. and Finkelhor, D. (1993) 'Impact of sexual abuse on children: A review and synthesis of recent empirical studies.' *Psychological Bulletin 113,* 164–80.

Kessler, R.C. and Magee, W.J. (1993) 'Childhood adversities and adult depression.' *Psychological Medicine 23,* 679–90.

Khan, K.S., ter Riet, G., Popay, J., Nixon, J. and Kleijnen, J. (2001) 'Study quality assessment.' In NHS Centre for Reviews and Dissemination *Undertaking Systematic Reviews of Research on Effectiveness: CRD's Guidance for Those Carrying Out or Commissioning Reviews.* Sections 2.5. York: University of York.

Kim, W.J., Davenport, C., Joseph, J., Zrull, J. and Woolford, E. (1988) 'Psychiatric disorder and juvenile delinquency in adopted children and adolescents.' *Journal of the American Academy of Child and Adolescent Psychiatry 27,* 111–15.

King, J. and Taitz, L. (1985) 'Catch-up growth following abuse.' *Archives of Disease in Childhood 60,* 1152–4.

King, N., Tonge, B., Mullen, P., Myerson, N., Heyne, D., Rollings, S. *et al.* (2000) 'Treating sexually abused children with posttraumatic stress symptoms: A randomized clinical trial.' *Journal of the American Academy of Child and Adolescent Psychiatry 39,* 1347–55.

Kirby, D., Barth, R.P., Leland, N. and Fetro, J.V. (1991) 'Reducing the risk: Impact of a new curriculum on sexual risk-taking.' *Family Planning Perspectives 23,* 6, 253–63.

Kirk, S., Gallagher, J. and Aastasiow, N. (1993) *Educating Exceptional Children, Seventh Edition.* Boston: Houghton-Mifflin.

Kirk, R.S., Reed-Ashcraft, K.B. and Pecora, P.J. (2003) 'Implementing family preservation services: A case of infidelity.' *Family Preservation Journal 6,* 2, 59–81.

Kirkwood, A. (1993) *The Leicestershire Enquiry 1992.* Leicester: Leicestershire County Council.

Kitchin, H. (ed.) (2000) *Taking Part: Promoting Children and Young People's Participation for Safer Communities.* Local Government Information Unit, London.

Knitzer, J. (2001) *Building Services and Systems to Support the Healthy Emotional Development of Young Children: An Action Guide for Policymakers.* New York: National Center for Children in Poverty.

Knutson, J.F. (1995) 'Psychological characteristics of maltreated children: Putative risk factors and consequences.' *Annual Review of Psychology 46,* 401–31.

Kolko, D. (1993) 'Further evaluation of inpatient child behavior ratings: Consistency across settings, time, and sources.' *Journal of Emotional and Behavioral Disorders 1,* 4, 251–9.

Kolko, D.J. (1996) 'Clinical monitoring of treatment course in child physical abuse: psychometric characteristics and treatment comparisons.' *Child Abuse and Neglect 20,* 23–43.

Kolko, D. and Swenson, C. (2002) *Assessing and Treating Physically Abused Children and their Families: A Cognitive Behavioral Approach.* Newbury Park, CA: Sage Publications.

Korfmacher, J., O'Brien, R., Hiatt, S., Olds, D. (1999) 'Differences in program implementation between nurses and paraprofessionals providing home visits during pregnancy and infancy: A randomized trial.' *American Journal of Public Health 89,* 12, 1847.

Kumpfer, K.L. and Alvarado, R. (2003) 'Family-strengthening approaches for the prevention of youth problem behaviors.' *American Psychologist 58,* 457–65.

Kutash, K. and Robbins Rivera, V. (1996) *What Works in Children's Mental Health Services?* Baltimore, MD: Paul H. Brookes Publishing Company.

Lambert. R., Millham, S. and Bullock, R. (1970) *A Manual to the Sociology of the School.* London: Weidenfeld and Nicholson.

Larner, M.B., Stevenson, C.S. and Behrman, R.E. (1998) 'Protecting children from abuse and neglect: Analysis and recommendations.' *The Future of Children 8*, Spring, 4–22.

Laughlin, J. and Weiss, M. (1981) 'An outpatient milieu therapy approach to treatment of child abuse and neglect problems.' *Social Casework 62*, 106–109.

Layton M. (1996) *An Evaluation of the Effectiveness of the 'School and Family Links Programme'*. Unpublished MA dissertation: Oxford Brookes University, School of Education.

Layzer, J.I. and Goodson, B.D. (2001) *National Evaluation of Family Support Programs*. Cambridge, MA: Abt Associates. www.abt assoc.com

Layzer, J.I., Goodson, B.D., Bernstein, L. and Price, C. (2001) *National Evaluation of Family Support Programs, Final report volume A: The meta-analysis*. Cambridge, MA: Abt Associates.

Lehman, C. and O'Dell, K. (2002) *Powerhouse Evaluation Final Report*. Seattle, WA: Casey Family Programs.

Leibold, J. and Downs, A.C. (2002a) *San Antonio PAL Program Evaluation Report*. Seattle, WA: Casey Family Programs.

Leibold, J. and Downs, A.C. (2002b) *Rapid City Stepping Stones Life Skills Program Evaluation Report*. Seattle, WA: Casey Family Programs.

Lerner, R.M. (1995) *America's Youth in Crisis: Challenges and Options for Programs and Policies*. Thousand Oaks, CA: Sage.

Leslie, L., Landsverk, J., Horton, M., Ganger, W. and Newton, R. (2000) 'The heterogeneity of children and their experiences in kinship care.' *Child Welfare LXXIX*, 315–34.

Leventhal, J., Garber, R.B. and Brady, C.A. (1989) 'Identification during the postpartum period of infants who are at high risk of child maltreatment.' *Journal of Pediatrics 114*, 481–7.

Levine, C.I., Brandt, A. and Whittaker, J.K. (1998) *Staying Together, Living Apart: New Perspectives on Youth Group Living from the AIDS Epidemic (from Planning and Placement Project)*. Available from Carol Levine, The United Hospital Fund, 23rd Floor, 350 Fifth Avenue, New York, NY 10118, USA.

Levy, A. and Kahan, B. (1991) *The Pindown Experience and the Protection of Children. The Report of the Staffordshire Child Care Inquiry 1990*. Stafford: Staffordshire County Council.

Lewis, A. and Lindsay, G. (eds) (2000) *Researching Children's Perspectives*. Buckingham: Open University Press.

Lewis, J. (1998) 'Building an evidence-based approach to social interventions.' *Children and Society 12*, 136–40.

Lewis, J. and Utting, D. (2001) 'Made to measure? Evaluating community initiatives for children: Introduction.' *Children and Society 15*, 1–4.

Lieberman, A.F. (1993) *The Emotional Life of the Toddler*. New York: The Free Press.

Light, R. (1973) 'Abused and neglected children in America: A study of alternative policies.' *Harvard Educational Review 43*, 556–98.

Lindon, J. and Nourse, C.A. (1994) 'Multidimensional group work for children who have been sexually abused.' *Child Abuse and Neglect 18*, 180–5.

Lindsey, E.W. and Ahmend, F.U. (1999) 'The North Carolina Independent Living Program: A comparison of outcomes for participants and non-participants.' *Children and Youth Services Review 21*, 5, 389–412.

Littell, J. (2005) 'Lessons from a systematic review of effects of multisystemic therapy.' *Children and Youth Services Review 27*, 445–63.

Littell, J., Forsythe, B. and Popa, M. (2004) *A Systematic Review of the Effects of Multisystemic Treatment*. Eighth Annual Conference of the Society for Social Work and Research, New Orleans, 16–19 January. Retrieved 3 May 2004 from www.sswr.org/papers2004/papers.htm

Littell, J.H., Popa, M. and Forsythe, B. (2005) 'Multisystemic therapy for social, emotional and behavioral problems in youth aged 10–17 (Cochrane Review).' In *The Cochrane Library*, Issue 3. Chichester: John Wiley and Sons.

Little, M. and Mount, K. (1999) *Prevention and Early Intervention with Children in Need*. Aldershot: Ashgate.

Lloyd, S. 1993 'Facing the facts: Self-help as a response to childhood sexual abuse'. In L. Waterhouse (ed.) *Child Abuse and Child Abusers*. London: Jessica Kingsley Publishers.

Loeber, R. (1990) 'Development and risk factors of juvenile antisocial behavior and delinquency.' *Clinical Psychology Review 10*, 1–41.

LoSciuto, L., Freeman, M.A., Harrington, E., Altman, B. and Lanphear, A. (1997) 'An outcome evaluation of the Woodrock Youth Development Project.' *Journal of Early Adolescence 17*, 1, 51–66.

LoSciuto, L., Rajala, A.K., Townsend, T.N. and Taylor, A.S. (1996) 'An outcome evaluation of across ages: An intergenerational mentoring approach to drug prevention.' *Journal of Adolescent Research 11*, 1, 116–29.

Lowe, N., Murch, M. and Borkowski, M. (1993) *Pathways to Adoption*. London: HMSO.

Lowe, N., Murch, M. and Thomas, C. (1999) *Supporting Adoption: Reframing the Approach*. London: BAAF.

Lupton, C. (1985) *Moving Out*. Portsmouth: Portsmouth Polytechnic.

Luttrell, J., Hull, S. and Wagner, D. (1995) 'The Michigan Department of Social Services Structured Decision Making System. An Evaluation of its Impact on Child Protection Services.' Paper presented at the Ninth National Roundtable on CPS Risk Assessment 14–16 June. San Francisco, CA.

Lutzker, J.R. (1994) 'Project 12-Ways: Treating child abuse and neglect from an ecobehavioral perspective.' In R.F. Dangel and R.F. Polster (eds) *Parent Training: Foundations of Research and Practice*, 260–97. New York: Guilford.

Lutzker, J.R. and Bigelow, K.M. (2002) *Reducing Child Maltreatment, A Guidebook for Parent Services*. New York: Guilford.

Lutzker, J., Bigelow, K.M., Doctor, R.M. and Kessler, M.L. (1998) 'Safety, health care, and bonding within an ecobehavioral approach to treating and preventing child abuse and neglect.' *Journal of Family Violence 13*, 163–85.

Lutzker, J. and Rice, J. (1984) 'Project 12-ways: Measuring outcome of a large in-home service for treatment and prevention of child abuse and neglect.' *Child Abuse and Neglect 18*, 519–24.

Lutzker, J.R. and Rice, J.M. (1987) 'Using recidivism data to evaluate Project 12-ways: An ecobehavioral approach to the treatment and prevention of child abuse and neglect.' *Journal of Family Violence 2*, 283–90.

Lutzker, J.R., Wesch, D. and Rice, J.M. (1984) 'A review of Project 12-Ways: An ecobehavioral approach to the treatment and prevention of child abuse and neglect.' *Advanced Behavior Residential Therapy 6*, 63–72.

Lynch, M. and Roberts, J. (1982) *Consequences of Child Abuse*. London: Academic Press.

Lynes D. and Goddard J. (1997) *The View From the Front*. Norwich: Norfolk County Council Social Services Department.

Lyon, J., Dennison, C. and Wilson, A. (2000) *Tell Them So They Listen: Messages From Young People in Custody*. Home Office Research Study 201. London: Home Office.

Maas, H.S. and Engler, R.E. (1959) *Children in Need of Parents*. New York, NY: Columbia University Press.

Maattanen, K. (2001) *Dialogical Baby Dance – A Parent's Guide*. South-Eastern Health Centre at Herttoneime.

Macdonald, G. (1999) 'Evidence-based care: wheels off the runway?' *Public Money and Management 19*, 25–32.

Macdonald, G. (2000) *Effective Interventions for Child Abuse and Neglect: An Evidence-Based Approach*. Chichester: Wiley.

Macdonald, G. (2003) 'Helping foster carers to manage challenging behaviour: An evaluation of a cognitive-behavioural training programme for carers.' In *Stability in Foster Care*. Papers from a seminar funded by the Nuffield Foundation and organized by members of the Centre for Research on the Child and Family, University of East Anglia.

Macdonald, G. (2004) 'Intervening in neglect.' In J. Taylor and B. Daniel (eds) *Child Neglect: Practice Issues for Health and Social Care*. London: Jessica Kingsley Publishers.

Macdonald, G. and Kakavelakis, I. (2004) *Helping Foster Carers Manage Challenging Behaviour: An Evaluation of a Cognitive-Behavioural Training Programme for Foster Carers*. Exeter: Centre for Evidence-Based Research, University of Exeter.

Macdonald, G. and Roberts, H. (1995) *What Works in the Early Years?* Barkingside: Barnardo's.

Macdonald, G., Sheldon, B. and Gillespie, J. (1992) 'Contemporary studies of social work effectiveness.' *British Journal of Social Work 22*, 6, 615–43.

Macdonald, G. and Winkley, A. (1999) *What Works in Child Protection?* Barkingside: Barnardo's.

MacLeod, J. and Nelson, G. (2000) 'Programs for the promotion of family wellness and the prevention of child maltreatment: A meta-analysis.' *Child Abuse and Neglect 24*, 9, 1127–49.

MacMillan, H.L., MacMillan, J.H., Offord, D.R., Griffith, L. and MacMillan, A. (1994) 'Primary prevention of child sexual abuse: A critical review. Part 2.' *Journal of Child Psychology and Psychiatry 35*, 5, 857–76.

Magee, S., and Thoday, R. (1995). 'How one local authority developed post-adoption services.' *Adoption and Fostering, 19*, 37–40.

Makins V. (1997) *The Invisible Children: Nipping Failure in the Bud*. London: David Fulton Publishers.

Malek, M. (1996) *Making Home–School Work: Home–School Work and the East London Schools Fund*. London: National Children's Bureau.

Malinosky-Rummell, R. and Hansen, D.J. (1993) 'Long-term consequences of childhood physical abuse.' *Psychological Bulletin 114*, 68–79.

Mallon, G.P. (1998) 'After care, then where? Outcomes of an independent living program.' *Child Welfare 77*, 1, 61–78.

Mallon, G.P. (1999) *Let's Get This Straight: A Gay- and Lesbian-Affirming Approach to Child Welfare*. New York: Columbia University Press.

Maluccio, A.N., Ainsworth, F. and Thoburn, J. (2000) *Child Welfare Outcome Research in the United States, the United Kingdom, and Australia*. Washington, DC: CWLA Press.

Maluccio, A.N., Fein, E. and Olmstead, K.A. (1986) *Permanency Planning for Children: Concepts and Methods*. London and New York: Routledge, Chapman and Hall.

Maluccio, A.N., Pine, B.A. and Tracy, E.M. (2002) *Social Work Practice with Families and Children*. New York: Columbia University Press.

Mannes, M., Benson, P.L., Kretzman, J.P. and Norris, T. (2003) 'The American tradition of community development.' In R. M. Lerner, F. Jacobs and D. Wertlieb (eds) *Handbook of Applied Developmental Science, Applying Developmental Science for Youth and Families*, Vol. 1. Thousand Oaks, CA: Sage.

Marsenich, L. (2002) *Evidence-based Practices in Mental Health Services for Foster Youth*. Sacramento, CA: California Institute for Mental Health. www.cimh.org/downloads/fostercaremanual.pdf

Marsh, P. and Peel, M. (1999) *Leaving Care in Partnership: Family Involvement with Care Leavers*. London: The Stationery Office.

Mash, E.J. and Wolfe, D.A. (1991) 'Methodological issues in research on physical child abuse.' *Criminal Justice and Behavior 18*, 8–29.

Mason, M., Castrianno, L.M., Kessler, C., Holmstrand, L., Huefner, J., Payne, V. *et al.* (2003) 'A comparison of foster care outcomes across four child welfare agencies.' *Journal of Family Social Work 7*, 2, 55–72.

Massinga, R. and Pecora, P.J. (2003) 'Providing better opportunities for older children in the child welfare system.' *The Future of Children 30*, 14, 151–73. Available at www.futureofchildren.org

Mather, M., Humphrey, J. and Robson, J. (1997) 'The statutory medical and health needs of looked after children.' *Adoption and Fostering 21*, 2, 36–40.

Matthews, H., Limb, M., Harrison, L. and Taylor, M. (1998) 'Local places and the political engagement of young people: Youth councils as participatory structures.' *Youth and Policy 62*, 16–29.

Maughan, B., Collishaw, S., and Pickles, A. (1998) 'School achievement and adult qualifications among adoptees: a longitudinal study.' *Journal of Child Psychology and Psychiatry 39*, 669–86.

Maughan, B., and Pickles, A. (1990) 'Adopted and illegitimate children growing up.' In L. Robins and M. Rutter (eds), *Straight and Devious Pathways from Childhood to Adulthood*. Cambridge: Cambridge University Press.

Maughan, B. and Rutter, M. (2001) 'Antisocial children grown up.' In J. Hill and B. Maughan (eds) *Conduct Disorders in Childhood and Adolescence*. Cambridge: Cambridge University Press.

McArdle, P., Moseley, D., Quibell, T., Johnson, R., Allen, A., Hammal, D. and LeCouteur, A. (2002) 'School-based indicated prevention: a randomised trial of group therapy'. *Journal of Child Psychology and Psychiatry 43*, 6, 705–12.

McAuley, C. (1996) *Children in Long-Term Foster Care: Emotional and Social Development*. Aldershot: Avebury.

McAuley, C. (1998) 'Child participatory research: Ethical and methodological issues.' In D. Iwaniec and J. Pinkerton (eds) *Making Research Work: Promoting Child Care Policy and Practice*. Chichester: John Wiley and Sons.

McAuley, C. (1999) *The Family Support Outcomes Study*. Ballymena: Northern Health and Social Services Board.

McAuley, C. (2005) *Pathways and Outcomes: A Ten Year Follow Up of Children Who Have Experienced Care*. Belfast: DHSSPSNI.

McAuley, C. (in press) 'Outcomes of long-term foster care: Young people's views.' In D. Iwaniec (ed.) *Children's Care Pathways: Stability or Drift?* Chichester: John Wiley and Sons.

McAuley, C., Knapp, M., Beecham, J., McCurry, N. and Sleed, M. (2002) *Evaluating the Outcomes and Costs of Home-Start Support to Young Families Experiencing Stress: A Comparative Cross Nation Study*. York: Joseph Rowntree Foundation.

McAuley, C., Knapp, M., Beecham, J., McCurry, N. and Sleed, M. (2004) *Young Families Under Stress: Outcomes and Costs of Home-Start Support*. York: Joseph Rowntree Foundation.

McAuley, C., McCurry, N., Knapp, M., Beecham, J. and Sleed, M. (in press) 'Young families under stress: assessing maternal and child well-being using a mixed methods approach.' *Child and Family Social Work*.

McCann, J., James, A., Wilson, S. and Dunn, G. (1996) 'Prevalence of psychiatric disorders in young people in the care system.' *British Medical Journal 313*, 14 December, 1529–30.

McCartney, K. and Dearing, E. (2002) 'Evaluation effect sizes in the policy arena.' *The Evaluation Exchange Newsletter VIII*, 1. www.gse.Harvard.edu/hfrp/eval/issue18/index.html

McCroskey, J. (2003a) 'Child welfare: Controversies and possibilities.' In F. Jacobs, D. Wertlieb and R.M. Lerner (eds). *Handbook of Applied Developmental Science, Enhancing the Life Chances of Youth and Families*, Vol. 2. Thousand Oaks: Sage.

McCroskey, J. (2003b) *Walking the Collaboration Talk: Ten Lessons Learned from the Los Angles County Children's Planning Council*. Los Angles, CA: Children's Planning Council. (www.childrensplanningcouncil.org)

McCroskey, J. and Meezan, W. (1997) *Family Preservation and Family Functioning*. Washington, DC: Child Welfare League of America.

McCroskey, J. and Meezan, W. (1998) 'Building a continuum of family services: Approaches and effectiveness.' *The Future of Children 8*, 1, 54–71.

McDonald, J., Salyers, N. and Shaver, M. (2004) *The Foster Care Straitjacket: Innovation, Federal Financing and Accountability in State Foster Care Reform – A Report by Fostering Results* Urbana-Champaign, IL. Children and Family Research Center at the School of Social Work, University of Illinois at Urbana-Champaign. Available at www.fosteringresults.org/results/reports/pewreports_03-11 04_straightjacket.pdf

McDonald, T., Allen, R., Westerfelt, A. and Piliavin, I. (1996) *Assessing the Long-Term Effects of Foster Care: A Research Synthesis*. Washington, DC: CWLA.

McGee, F. (2001) *Involving Young People in Community Safety*. London: London Borough of Camden, Housing Department.

McIvor, G. and Moodie, K. (2002) *Interchange 77: Evaluation of the Matrix Project*. Stirling: Social Work Research Centre, University of Stirling.

McLaren, L. (1988) 'Fostering mother-child relationships.' *Child Welfare League of America LXVII*, 4, 353–65.

McMillen, C. (1992) 'Attachment theory and clinical social work.' *Clinical Social Work Journal 20*, 2, 205–18.

McMillen, J.C., Rideout, G.B., Fisher, R.H. and Tucker, J. (1997) 'Independent-living services: The views of former foster youth.' *Families in Society: The Journal of Contemporary Human Services 78*, 5, 471–9.

McMillen, J.C. and Tucker, J. (1999) 'The status of older adolescents at exit from out-of-home care.' *Child Welfare 78*, 3, 339–59.

McRoy, R.G. (1999) *Special Needs Adoptions: Practice Issues*. New York: Garland Publishing.

McRoy, R. (2005) 'African American adoptions' In J. Everett, S. Chipungu and B. Leashore (eds) *Child Welfare: An Africentric Perspective*. New Brunswick, NJ: Rutgers University.

McRoy, R.G., Oglesby, Z., and Grape H. (1997) 'Achieving same-race adoptive placements for African American children: Culturally sensitive practice.' *Child Welfare 76*, 85–106.

McRoy, R.G. and Zurcher, L. (1983) *Transracial and Inracial Adoptees*. Springfield IL: Charles C. Thomas.

Meadowcroft, P., Thomlison, B. and Chamberlain, P. (1994) 'Treatment foster care services: A research agenda for child welfare.' *Child Welfare 73*, 565–81.

Meadowcroft, P. and Trout, B.A. (eds) (1990) *Troubled Youth in Treatment Homes: A Handbook of Therapeutic Foster Care.* Washington, DC: Child Welfare League of America.

Mech E.V. (ed.) (1988) 'Independent-living services for at-risk adolescents.' *Child Welfare 67,* 483–634.

Mech, E.V. (1994) 'Foster youths in transition: Research perspectives on preparation for independent living.' *Child Welfare 73,* 5, 606–23.

Mech, E.V. and Fung, C.C. (1999) 'Placement restrictiveness and educational achievement among emancipated foster youth.' *Research on Social Work Practice 9,* 2, 213–28.

Mech, E.V., Ludy-Dobson, C. and Hulseman, F.S. (1994) 'Life skills knowledge: A survey of foster adolescents in three placement settings.' *Children and Youth Services Review 16,* 181-200.

Medoff, P. and Sklar, H. (1994) *Streets of Hope, The Fall and Rise of an Urban Neighborhood.* Boston, MA: South End Press.

Meezan, W. and O'Keefe, M. (1998) 'Multifamily group therapy: Impact on family functioning and child behavior.' *Families in Society: The Journal of Contemporary Human Services 79,* 32–44.

Meisels, S. and Shonkoff, K. (1990) *Handbook of Early Childhood Intervention.* Cambridge: Cambridge University Press.

Meisels, S.J. and Shonkoff, J.P. (2000) 'Early childhood intervention: A continuing evolution.' In J.P. Shonkoff and S.J. Meisels (eds) *Handbook of Early Childhood Intervention, Second Edition.* New York: Cambridge University Press.

Melosh, B. (2002) *Strangers and Kin: The American Way of Adoption.* Cambridge, MA: Harvard University Press.

Meltzer, H., Corbin, T., Gatward, R., Goodman, R. and Ford, T. (2003) *The Mental Health of Young People Looked After by Local Authorities in England: Summary Report.* London: HMSO.

Meltzer, H., Harrington, R., Goodman, R. and Jenkins, R. (1999) *Children and Adolescents Who Try to Harm, Hurt or Kill Themselves.* Newport: National Statistics.

Mental Health Foundation (MHF) (2002) *Peer Support: Someone to Turn To: An Evaluation Report of the Mental Health Foundation Peer Support Programme.* London: MHF.

M. H. Treasury (2003) *Every Child Matters.* London: The Stationery Office.

Millen, L. and Roll, S. (1985) 'Solomon's mothers: A special case of pathological bereavement.' *American Journal of Orthopsychiatry 55,* 3, 411–18.

Miller, D.L., Hoffman, F. and Turner, D. (1980) 'A perspective on the Indian Child Welfare Act.' *Social Casework 61,* 468–71.

Miller, W.R. and Rollnick, S. (1991) *Motivational Interviewing.* New York: Guilford.

Millham, S., Bullock, R. and Cherrett, P. (1975) *After Grace Teeth: A Comparative Study of Residential Experience of Boys in Approved Schools.* London: Human Context Books.

Mills, M. and Puckering, C. (2001) *Evaluation of Mellow Parenting. Report to the UK.* London: DH.

Minnis, H. and Devine, C. (2001) 'The effect of foster carer training on the emotional and behavioural functioning of looked after children.' *Adoption and Fostering 25,* 1 44–54.

Minow, M. (1994) 'Home visiting.' *The Future of Children 4,* 2, 243–6.

Moffit, T.E., Caspi, A., Dickson, N., Silva, P. and Stanton, W. (1996) 'Childhood-onset versus adolescent-onset antisocial conduct problems in males: Natural history from ages 3 to 18 years.' *Developmental Psychology 8,* 399–24.

Monck, E. and New, M. (1996) *Sexually Abused and Abusing Children Treated in Voluntary Community Facilities.* London: HMSO.

Monck, E., Sharland, E., Bentovim, A., Goodall, G., Hyde, C. and Lewin, B (1994) *Child Sexual Abuse : A Descriptive and Treatment Outcome Study.* London: HMSO

Moore, E., Armsden, G., and Gogerty, P. (1998) 'A twelve-year follow-up study of maltreated and at-risk children who received early therapeutic child care.' *Child Maltreatment 3,* 3–16.

Mordock, J.B. (2002) *Managing for Outcomes: A Basic Guide to the Evaluation of Best Practices in the Human Services.* Washington, DC: CWLA.

Morgan, L.J., Spears, L.S. and Kaplan, C. (2003) *A Framework for Community Action: Making Children a National Priority.* Washington, DC: CWLA.

Morgan-Klein, B. (1985) *Where Am I Going to Stay?* Edinburgh: Scottish Council for Single Homeless.

Morrell, C.J., Siby. H., Sewart, P., Walters, S. and Morgan, A. (2000) 'Costs and effectiveness of community postnatal support workers: Randomised controlled trial.' *British Medical Journal 321,* 593–8.

Morris, J. (1998) *Still Missing? The Experiences of Disabled Children and Young People Living Away From Their Families. Volume 1.* London: Who Cares? Trust.

Morris, S. and Wheatley, H. (1994) *Time to Listen: The Experiences of Young People in Foster and Residential Care.* London: ChildLine.

Mosley, J. (1993) *Turn Your School Around.* Wisbech: LDA.

Moss, P. and Petrie, P. (2002) *From Children's Services to Children's Spaces.* London: Routledge Falmer.

Mott, P.E. (1976) *Meeting Human Needs: The Social and Political History of Title XX.* Columbus, OH: National Conference on Social Welfare.

Mueller, E. and Silverman, N. (1989) 'Peer relations in maltreated children.' In D. Cicchetti and V. Carlson (eds) *Child Maltreatment: Theory and Research on the Causes and Consequences of Child Abuse and Neglect,* 529–78. Cambridge: Cambridge University Press.

Munro, E. (1999) 'Common errors of reasoning in child protection work.' *Child Abuse and Neglect 23,* 8, 745–58.

Murie, A. (1997) Linking housing change to crime. *Social Policy and Administration 31*, 5, 22–36.

Murtagh, B. (1999) Listening to communities: Locality research and planning. *Urban Studies 36*, 7, 1181–93.

Musick, J. and Stott, F. (2000) 'Paraprofessionals revisited and reconsidered.' In J.P. Shonkoff and S.J. Meisels (eds), *Handbook of Early Childhood Intervention, Second Edition.* New York: Cambridge University Press.

Muskie School of Public Service (1998) *Improving Economic Opportunities for Young People Served by the Foster Care System: Three Views of the Path to Independent Living (Phase One and Phase Two).* Portland, ME: University of Southern Maine.

Myeroff, R.L., Mertlich, G. and Gross, G. (1999) Comparative effectiveness of holding therapy with aggressive children. *Child Psychiatry and Human Development 29*, 303–13.

Nash, M., Zivney, O. and Hulsey, T. (1993) 'Characteristics of sexual abuse associated with greater psychological impairment among children.' *Child Abuse and Neglect 17*, 401–8.

Nastasi, B.K. (2002) 'The realities of large-scale change efforts.' *Journal of Educational and Psychological Consultation 13*, 219–26.

Nation, M., Crusto, C., Wandersman, A., Kumpfer, K.L., Seybolt, D., Morrissey-Kane, E. and Davino, K. (2003) 'What works in prevention: Principles of effective prevention programs.' *American Psychologist 58*, 449–56.

National Adoption Information Clearinghouse (2000) *Cost of Adopting.* Washington, DC: National Adoption Information Clearinghouse.

National Center for Children in Poverty, Columbia University (2003) *Low-income Children in the United States (2003).* New York: National Center for Children in Poverty.

National Clearinghouse on Child Abuse and Neglect Information (2004) *About CAPTA: A Legislative History.* US Department of Health and Human Services, Administration for Children and Families. Downloaded 28 March 2005 from nccanch.acf.hhs.gov/pubs/factsheets/about.cfm

National Commission of Inquiry into the Prevention of Child Abuse (NCIPCA) (1996) *Childhood Matters.* London: HMSO.

National Evaluation of Sure Start Team (2005) *Early Imapcts of Sure Start Local Programmes on Children and Families. Report of the Cross-sectional Study of 9- and 36-month-old Children and their Families.* London: DFES.

National Foster Care Awareness Project (2000) *Frequently Asked Questions About the Foster Care Independence Act of 1999 and the John H. Chafee Foster Care Independence Program.* February, April. Seattle, WA: The Casey Family Program.

National Research Council (1993) *Understanding Child Abuse and Neglect.* Washington, DC: National Academy Press.

National Research Council and Institute of Medicine (NRCIM) (2000) *From Neurons to Neighborhoods: The Science of Early Childhood Development.* Committee on Integrating the Science of Early Childhood Development. J.P. Shonkoff and D.A. Phillips (eds) Board on Children, Youth, and Families, Commission on Behavioral and Social Sciences and Education. Washington, DC: National Academy Press.

National Statistics (2003) *Social Trends UK.* London: The Stationery Office.

National Statistics (2005) *Children Looked After by Local Authorities.* Year Ending 31st March 2004. London: DfES.

Naylor, P. and Cowie, H. (1999) 'The effectiveness of peer support systems in challenging school bullying: the perspectives and experiences of teachers and pupils.' *Journal of Adolescence 22*, 4, 467–79.

Neighbors, H.W. and Jackson, J.S. (1984) 'The use of informal and formal help: Four patterns of illness behavior in the black community.' *American Journal of Community Psychology 12*, 629–44.

Neil, E. (2003) 'Adoption and contact: a research review.' In A. Bainham, B. Lindley, M. Richards and L. Trinder (eds) *Children and Their Families: Contact, Rights and Welfare.* Oxford: Hart Publishing.

Nelki, J and Waters, J. (1988) 'A group for sexually abused children.' *Child Abuse and Neglect 13*, 369–77.

Nelson, E., Heath, A., Madden, P., Cooper, M., Dinwiddie, S., Bucholz, K. *et al.* (2002) 'Association between self-reported childhood sexual abuse and adverse psychosocial outcomes.' *Archives of General Psychiatry 59*, 139–45.

Nelson, K.E. (1991) 'Populations and outcomes in five family preservation programs.' In K. Wells and D.E. Biegel (eds) *Family Preservation Services: Research and Evaluation.* Newbury Park, CA: Sage Publications.

Nelson, K.E., Emlen, A., Landsman, M., Hutchinson, J., Zalenski, A., Black, R., *et al.* (1988) *Family-based Services: A National Perspective on Success and Failure.* Iowa City, IA: The National Resource Center on Family-Based Services.

Nelson, K.E. and Landsman, M.J. (1992) *Alternative Models of Family Preservation: Family-Based Services in Context.* Springfield, IL: Charles C. Thomas.

Nelson, K.E., Landsman, M.J. and Deutelbaum, W. (1990) 'Three models of family-centered placement prevention service.' *Child Welfare LXIX*, 3–19.

Nelson, S. and Baldwin, N. (2002) 'Comprehensive neighbourhood mapping: Developing a powerful tool for child protection.' *Child Abuse Review 11*, 214–29.

Nelson, S. and Baldwin, N. (2004) 'The Craigmillar project: Neighbourhood mapping to improve children's safety from sexual crime.' *Child Abuse Review 13*, 415–25.

NESS (National Evaluation of Sure Start) (2004) *The Impact of Sure Start Local Programmes on Child Development and Family Functioning: A Report on Preliminary Findings.* Available at www.ness.bbk.ac.uk/documents/activities/impact/397.pdf

Neumann, D.A., Houskamp, B.M., Pollock, V.E. and Briere, J. (1996) 'The long-term sequlae of childhood sexual abuse in women: A meta-analytic review.' *Child Maltreatment 1*, 6–16.

Newburn, T. (2001) 'What do we mean by evaluation?' *Children and Society 15*, 5–13.

Newman, T. and Roberts, H. (1997) 'Assessing social work effectiveness in child care practice: the contribution of randomised controlled trials.' *Child Care, Health and Development 23*, 4, 287–96.

NHS Centre for Reviews and Dissemination (1997) *Preventing and Reducing the Adverse Effects of Unintended Teenage Pregnancies.* York: CRD.

Nicol, A.R., Smith, J., Kay, B., Hall, D., Barlow, J. and Williams, B. (1988) 'A focused casework approach to the treatment of child abuse: A controlled comparison. *Journal of Child Psychology and Psychiatry 29*, 703–11.

Nollan, K.A. (1996) 'Self-Sufficiency Skills among Youth in Long-Term Foster Care.' Doctoral dissertation University of Washington, Seattle, WA: The University of Washington.

Nollan, M., Horn, M., Downs, A.C. and Pecora, P.J. (2002a) *Ansell-Casey Life Skills Assessment Manual, Version 3.0.* Seattle, WA: Casey Family Programs.

Nollan, K.A., Nurius, P., Pecora, P.J. and Whittaker, J. (2002b) 'Risk and protective factors influencing life skills among youth in long-term foster care.' *The International Journal of Child and Family Welfare 5*, 1–2, 5–19.

Nollan, K.A., Wolf, M., Ansell, D., Burns, J., Barr, L., Copeland, W. and Paddock, G. (2000) 'Ready or not: Assessing youth's preparedness for independent living.' *Child Welfare 79*, 2, 159–78.

Northern Ireland Department of Health, Social Services and Public Safety (NIDHSSPS) (2005) *Community Statistics, 1 April 2003 – 31 March 2004.* Belfast: NIDHSSPS.

Oakley, A. (1996) 'Who's afraid of the randomised controlled trial? The challenge of evaluating the potential of social interventions.' In P. Alderson *et al. What Works: Effective Social Interventions in Child Welfare.* London: SSRU, Institute of Education and Barnardo's.

Oakley, A., Mauthner, M., Rajan, L. and Turner, H. (1995) 'Supporting vulnerable families: an evaluation of NEWPIN.' *Health Visitor 68*, 188–91.

Oakley, A., Rajan, L., Turner, H. (1998) 'Evaluating parent support initiatives: Lessons from two case studies.' *Health and Social Care in the Community 6*, 5, 318–30.

O'Connor, T. and Zeahah, C. (2003) Attachment disorders: assessment strategies and treatment approaches. *Attachment and Human Development 5*, 223–44.

Ofsted and Audit Commission (2003) *The Children's Fund: First Wave Partnerships.* www.ofsted.gov.uk

O'Hagan, K. and Dillenburger, K. (1995) *The Abuse of Women Within Childcare Work.* Buckingham: Open University Press.

Olds, D.L., Henderson, C.R., Kitzman, H.J., Exkenrode, J.J., Cole, R.E. and Tatelbaum, R.C. (1999) *Prenatal and Infancy Home Visitation by Nurses: Recent Findings. Future of Children 9*, 1, 44–65.

Olds, D.L., Henderson, C.R., Tatelbaum, R. and Chamberlin, R. (1986a) 'Improving the delivery of prenatal care and outcomes of pregnancy: A randomized trial of nurse home visitation.' *Pediatrics 77*,1, 16–28.

Olds, D.L., Henderson, C., Tatelbaum, R. and Chamberlin, R. (1986b) 'Preventing child abuse and neglect: A randomized trial of nurse home visitation.' *Pediatrics 78*, 65–78.

Olds, D., Hill, P., Robinson, J., Song, N. and Little, C. (2000) 'Update on home visiting for pregnant women and parents of young children.' *Current Problems in Pediatrics 30*, 107–41.

Olds, D.L. and Kitzman, H. (1993) 'Review of research on home-visiting for pregnant women and parents of young children.' *The Future of Children, 3*, 3, 53–91.

Olds, D., Kitzman, H., Cole, R. and Robinson, J. (1997) 'Theoretical foundations of a program of home visitation for pregnant women and parents of young children.' *Journal of Community Psychology 25*, 1, 9–25.

Oliver, C. and Smith, M. (2000) *The Effectiveness of Early Interventions.* (No. 10: Perspectives on Education Policy.) London: Institute of Education.

Onzawa, K., Glover, V., Adams, D., Modi, N. and Kumar, R.C. (2001) 'Infant massage improves mother–infant interaction for mothers with postnatal depression.' *Journal of Affective Disorders 63*, 1–3, 201–7.

Osofsky, J.D. and Thompson, M.D. (2000) 'Adaptive and maladaptive parenting: Perspectives on risk and protective factors.' In J.P. Shonkoff and S.J. Meisels (eds), *Handbook of Early Childhood Intervention, Second Edition.* New York: Cambridge University Press.

Owen, G. and Fercello, C. (1999) *The Family Support Project Evaluation: Final Report.* Report produced for the McKnight Foundation and the Minnesota Department of Human Services. Retrieved 26 April, 2004 from the Wilder Research Center's web page at www.wilder.org/research/reports.html?summary=78

Owen, M. (1999) *Novices, Old Hands and Professionals: Adoption by Single People.* London: BAAF.

Packman, J. and Hall, C. (1998) *From Care to Accommodation – Support, Protection and Control in Child Care Services.* London: The Stationery Office.

Pahl, J. (1992) 'Force for change or optional extra? The impact of research on policy in social work and social welfare.' In P. Carter, T. Jeffs and M.K. Smith (eds) *Changing Social Work and Welfare.* Buckingham: Open University Press.

Pain, R., Francis, P., Fuller., I., O'Brien, K. and Williams, S. (2002) '*Hard to Reach' Young People and Community Safety: A Model for Participatory Research and Consultation.* London: Home Office.

Painter, C. and Clarence, E. (2001) 'UK local action zones and changing urban governance.' *Urban Studies 38*, 8, 1215–32.

Panayiotopoulos, C. and Kerfoot, M. (2004) 'A home and school support project for children excluded from primary and first year secondary school.' *Child and Adolescent Mental Health 9*, 3, 109–14.

Paolucci, E.O., Genuis, M.L. and Violato, C. (2001) 'A meta-analysis of the published research on the effects of child sexual abuse.' *The Journal of Psychology 135*, 1, 17–36.

Paredes, M., Leifer, M. and Kilbane, T. (2001) 'Maternal variables related to sexually abused children's functioning.' *Child Abuse and Neglect 25*, 1159–76.

Parish, S.L., Pomeranz, A.E. and Braddock, D. (2003) 'Family support in the United States: Financing trends and emerging initiatives.' *Mental Retardation 41*, 174–87.

Parish, S.L. and Whisnant, A.L. (2005) 'Policies and programs for children and youth with disabilities.' In J. Jenson and M. Fraser (eds) *Policies and Programs for Children, Youth and Families: An Ecological Perspective on Integrated Service Delivery.* Newbury Park, CA: Sage Press.

Park, A. and Roberts, C. (2002) *British Social Attitudes* (19th Report). London: Sage.

Parker, R. (1991) 'Trends in residential care.' In B. Kahan (ed.) *Residential Care for Children: Report of a Department of Health Seminar,* held on 30 October–1 November at Dartington Hall, Devon. London: DH.

Parker, R., Ward, H., Jackson, S., Aldgate, J. and Wedge, P. (eds) (1991) *Looking After Children: Assessing Outcomes in Child Care.* London: HMSO.

Parton, N. (1991) *Governing the Family: Child Care, Child Protection and the State.* London: Macmillan.

Parton, N. (1997) 'Child protection and family support. Current debates and future prospects.' In N. Parton (ed.) *Child Protection and Family Support: Tensions, Contradictions and Possibilities.* London: Routledge.

Patterson, G.R. (1982) *Coercive Family Process.* Oregon: Castalia Publications.

Pawson, R. (2004) 'Simple principles for the evaluation of complex programmes.' In *Research Education: What Works?* DfES Research Conference. London: DfES.

Pawson, R. and Tilley, N. (1994) 'What works in evaluation research?' *British Journal of Criminology 34*, 3, 291–306.

Pawson, R. and Tilley, N. (1997) *Realistic Evaluation.* London: Sage.

Pecora, P.J., Fraser, M.W. and Haapala, D.A. (1991) 'Client outcomes and issues for program design.' In K. Wells and D.F. Biegel (eds) *Family Preservation Services.* Newbury Park, CA: Sage.

Pecora, P.J., Fraser, M.W. and Haapala, D.A. (1992) 'Intensive home-based family preservation services: An update from the FIT project.' *Child Welfare LXXI*, 177–88.

Pecora, P.J., Fraser, M.W., Nelson, K., McCroskey, J. and Meezan, W. (1995) *Evaluating Family-based Services.* New York: Aldine de Gruyter.

Pecora, P.J., Kessler, R.C., Williams, J., Downs, A.C., English, D., White, J., *et al.* (2005) *Improving Family Foster Care: Findings from the Northwest Foster Care Alumni Study.* Seattle, WA: Casey Family Programs. Available from www.casey.org

Pecora, P.J., Kessler, R.C., Williams, J., Downs, A.C., English, D. and White, J., and O'Brien, K. (forthcoming) *What Works in Foster Care?* Oxford: Oxford University Press.

Pecora, P.J., Kingery, K., Downs, A.C., Nollan, A.C., Huff, S., Touregenau, J. and Sim, K. (2003b) *Examining the Effectiveness of Family Foster Care: A Select Literature Review.* Working Paper No.1. Seattle, WA: University of Washington, School of Social Work, and the Casey Family Programs.

Pecora, P.J. and Maluccio, A.N. (2000) 'What works in family foster care?' In M.P. Kluger, G. Alexander and P.A. Curtis (eds) *What Works in Child Welfare?* Washington, DC: CWLA.

Pecora, P.J., Selig, W., Zirps, F. and Davis, S. (eds) (1996) *Quality Improvement and Program Evaluation in Child Welfare Agencies: Managing into the Next Century.* Washington, DC: CWLA.

Pecora, P.J., Whittaker, J.K., Maluccio, A.N. and Barth, R.P. (2000) *The Child Welfare Challenge – Policy, Practice and Research, Second Edition.* New York: Aldine de Gruyter.

Pecora, P.J., Williams, J., Downs, A.C., Kessler, R.J., Kirk O'Brien, K. Hiripi, E. and Morello, S. (2003c) *What Casey Family Programs Intervention Components Provide the Most Leverage towards Achieving Key Program Outcomes?* Working Paper No. 8. Seattle, WA: Casey Family Programs. Available from www.casey.org/research

Pecora, P.J., Williams, J., Kessler, R.J., Downs, A.C., O'Brien, K., Hiripi, E. and Morello, S. (2003a) *Assessing the Effects of Foster Care: Early Results from the Casey National Alumni Study.* Seattle, WA: Casey Family Programs. Available from www.casey.org

PEEP (2000) *Learning Together With Babies.* Oxford: PEEP.

Pentz, M.A., Trebow, E.A., Hansen, W.B., MacKinnon, D.P., Dwyer, J.H., Johnson, C.A. *et al.* (1990) 'Effects of program implementation on adolescent drug use behavior: The Midwestern Prevention Project (MPP).' *Evaluation Review 14*, 3, 264–89.

Percy, P. and Barker, W. (1986) 'The child development programme.' *Midwife, Health Visitor and Community Nurse 22*, 235–40.

Perry, B. (1995) *Maltreated Children: Experience, Brain Development and the Next Generation.* New York: W.W. Norton.

Perry, B. (2000) 'The neuroarchaeology of childhood maltreatment: the neurodevelopmental costs of adverse childhood events.' In B. Geffner (ed.) *The Cost of Child Maltreatment: Who Pays? We All Do.* New York: Haworth Press.

Perry, B. and Pollard, R. (1997) 'Altered Brain Development Following Global Neglect in Early Childhood.' Proceedings from the Society of Neuroscience Annual Meeting, New Orleans.

Perry, C.L., Williams, C.L., Veblen-Mortenson, S., Toomey, T.L., Komro, K.A., Anstine, P.A. *et al.* (1996) 'Project Northland: Outcomes of a communitywide alcohol use prevention program during early adolescence.' *American Journal of Public Health 86*, 7, 956–65.

Peters, S.D. (1988) 'Child sexual abuse and later psychological problems.' In G.E. Wyatt and G.J. Powell (eds) *Lasting Effects of Child Sexual Abuse,* 101–17. Newbury Park, CA: Sage Publications.

Petit, M.R. and Curtis, P.A. (1997) *Child Abuse and Neglect: A Look at the States: 1997 CWLA Stat Book.* Washington, DC: CWLA Press.

Pinderhughes, E. (1998) 'Short term placement outcomes for children adopted after age five.' *Children and Youth Services Review 20,* 3, 223–49.

Pine, B.A. (1986) 'Child welfare reform and the political process.' *Social Service Review 60,* 339–59.

Pine, B.A., Healy, L.M. and Maluccio, A.N. (2002) 'Developing measurable program objectives: A key to evaluation of family reunification programs.' In T. Vecchiato, A.N. Maluccio and C. Canali (eds) *Evaluation in Child and Family Services – Comparative Client and Program Perspectives.* New York: Aldine de Gruyter.

Pinkerton, J. and McCrea, R. (1999) *Meeting the Challenge? Young People Leaving Care in Northern Ireland.* Aldershot: Ashgate.

PIPPIN (2000) *Your Baby as a Person.* Training notes. London: PIPPIN.

Pithouse, A., Lowe, K. and Hill Tout, J. (2002) 'Training foster carers in challenging behaviour: a case study in disappointment?' *Journal of Child and Family Social Work 7,* 3, 203–14.

Pittman, K. (1991) *Promoting Youth Development: Strengthening the Role of Youth Serving and Community Organizations.* Washington, DC: Academy for Educational development, Center for Youth Development and Policy Research.

PIU (2000) *The Prime Minister's Review of Adoption.* London: The Cabinet Office.

Plantz, M.C., Hubbell, R., Barrett, B.J. and Dobrec, A. (1989) 'Indian Child Welfare Act: A status report.' *Children Today 18,* 24–9.

Pleace, N. and Quilgars, D. (1999) 'Youth homelessness.' In J. Rugg (ed.) *Young People, Housing and Social Policy.* London: Routledge.

Popay, J. and Roen, K. (2003) *Using Evidence from Diverse Research Designs.* London: SCIE Report 3. [q26]

Popple, K. (1995) *Analysing Community Work: Its Theory and Practice.* Buckingham: Open University Press.

Portes, A. (1998) 'Social capital: Its origins and applications in modern sociology.' *Annual Review of Sociology 24,* 1–24.

Poulin, F., Dishion, T.J. and Burraston, B. (2001) 'Three year iatrogenic effects associated with aggregating high-risk adolescents in cognitive-behavioral preventive interventions.' *Applied Developmental Science 5,* 4, 214–24.

Powell, D.R. (1993) 'Inside home visiting programs.' *The Future of Children 3,* 3, 23–38.

Powers, S. and Fenichel, E. (1999) *Home Visiting: Reaching Babies and Families Where They Live.* Washington, DC: Zero to Three.

Prilleltensky, I. and Nelson, G. (2000) 'Promoting child and family wellness: Priorities for psychological and social interventions.' *Journal of Community and Applied Social Psychology 10,* 85–105.

Prilleltensky, I., Nelson, G. and Peirson, C. (2001) *Promoting Family Wellness and Preventing Child Maltreatment. Fundamentals for Thinking and Action.* Toronto: University of Toronto Press.

Prison Reform Trust (1991) *The Identikit Prisoner.* London: Prison Reform Trust.

Pritchard, C. and Williams, R. (2001) 'A three year longitudinal study of a school-based social work family service to reduce truancy, delinquency and school exclusions.' *Journal of Social Welfare and Family Law 23,* 1, 23–43.

Prout, A. (2002) 'Researching children as social actors: An introduction to the children 5–16 programme.' *Children and Society 16,* 67–76.

Puckering, C., Rodgers, J., Mills, M. and Cox, A. (1994) 'Process and evaluation of a group intervention for mothers with parenting difficulties.' *Child Abuse Review 3,* 299–310.

Pugh, G., De'Ath, E. and Smith, C. (1994) *Confident Parents, Confident Children. Policy and Practice in Parent Education and Support.* London: National Children's Bureau.

Putnam, R. (2000) *Bowling Alone – The Collapse and Revival of American Community.* New York: Simon and Schuster.

Puura, K., Davis, H., Papadopoulou, K., Tsiantis, J., Ispanovic-Radojkovic, V., Tamminen, T. *et al.* (2002) 'The European Early Promotion Project: A new primary health care service to promote children's mental health.' *Infant Mental Health Journal 23,* 6, 606–24.

Quinton, D. (2004) *Supporting Parents: Messages from Research.* London: Jessica Kingsley Publishers.

Quinton, D., Rushton, A., Dance, C. and Mayes, D. (1997) 'Contact between children placed away from home and their birth parents: Research issues and evidence.' *Clinical Child Psychology and Psychiatry 2,* 3, 393–413.

Quinton, D., Rushton, A., Dance, C. and Mayes, D. (1998) *Joining New Families: Adoption and Fostering in Middle Childhood.* Chichester: Wiley.

Quinton, D. and Rutter, M. (1988) *Parenting Breakdown: The Making and Breaking of Inter-generational Links.* Aldershot: Avebury.

Qureshi, H. (2004) 'Evidence in policy and practice: What kinds of research designs?' *Journal of Social Work 4,* 1, 7–23.

Rabiee, P., Priestley, M. and Knowles, J. (2001) *Whatever Next? Young Disabled People Leaving Care.* York: York Publishing Services.

Ramchandani, P. and Jones, D.P.H. (2003) 'Treating psychological symptoms in sexually abused children. From research findings to service provision.' *British Journal of Psychiatry 183,* 484–90.

Ramey, C.T. and Ramey, S.L. (1993) 'Home visiting programs and the health and development of young children.' *Future of Children 3,* 3, 129–39.

Ramey, C.T. and Ramey, S.L. (1998) 'Early intervention and early experience.' *American Psychologist 53,* 109–20.

Randall, G. (1989) *Homeless and Hungry*. London: Centrepoint.

Raychuba, B. (1987) *Report on the Special Needs of Youth in the Care of the Child Welfare System*. Toronto: National Youth in Care Network.

Reams, R. and Friedrich, W. (1994) 'The efficacy of time-limited play therapy with maltreated preschoolers.' *Journal of Clinical Psychology 50*, 889–99.

Rector-Staerkel, F. (2002) 'Early Head Start: Home visiting and parenting group program uptake – an implementation study.' *UMI Dissertation Services, 240*. Seattle, WA.

Reder, P., Duncan, S. and Gray, M. (1993) *Beyond Blame: Child Abuse Tragedies Revisited*. London and New York: Routledge.

Reeker, J., Ensing, D. and Elliott, R. (1997) 'A meta-analytic investigation of group treatment outcomes for sexually abused children.' *Child Abuse and Neglect*, 669–80.

Reilly, T. (2003) 'Transition from care: Status and outcomes of youth who age out of foster care.' *Child Welfare 82*, 6, 727–46.

Reitz, M. and Watson, K. (1992) *Adoption and the Family System*. New York: Guilford.

Renwick, F. and Spalding, B. (2002) '"A Quiet Place" project: An evaluation of early therapeutic intervention within mainstream schools.' *British Journal of Special Education 29*, 3, 144–9.

Report to the NHS Central Research and Development Committee (1995) *Improving the Health of Mothers and Children: NHS Priorities for Research and Development*. London: HMSO.

Reynolds, A.J. (1998) 'Resilience among black urban youth. Prevalence, intervention effects, and mechanisms of influence.' *American Journal of Orthopsychiatry 68*, 1, 84–100.

Reynolds, A.J. (2004) 'Research on early childhood interventions in the confirmatory mode.' *Children and Youth Services Review 26*, 1, 15–38.

Reynolds, A.J. and Robertson, D.L. (2003) 'School-based early intervention and later child maltreatment in the Chicago Longitudinal Study.' *Child Development 74*, 1, 3–26.

Reynolds, A.J., Temple, J.A., Robertson, D.L. and Mann, E.A. (2001) 'Long-term effects of an early childhood intervention on educational achievement and juvenile arrest – A 15-year follow-up of low-income children in public schools.' *Journal of American Medical Association 285*, 18, 2339–46.

Rhodes, J.E. and Roffman, J.G. (2003) 'Relationship-based interventions: The impact of mentoring and apprenticeship on youth development.' In F. Jacobs, D. Wertlieb and R. M. Lerner (eds) *Handbook of Applied Developmental Science, Enhancing the Life Chances of Youth and Families*, Vol. 2. Thousand Oaks, CA: Sage.

Rhodes, J., Tyler, P., Brennan, A., Stevens, S., Warnock, C. and Otero-Garcia, M. (2002) *Lessons and Valuation Evidence from Ten Single Regeneration Budget Case Studies*. London: Department for Transport, Local Government and the Regions.

Rispens, J., Aleman, A. and Gourdena, P.P. (1997) 'Prevention of child sexual abuse victimisation: A meta-analysis of school programs.' *Child Abuse and Neglect 21*, 10, 975–87.

Rivara, F.P. (1985) 'Physical abuse in children under two: A study of therapeutic outcomes.' *Child Abuse and Neglect 9*, 81–7.

Rivers K., Aggleton, P., Chase, E., Downie, A., Mulvihill, C., Sinkler, P. *et al.* (2000) *Setting the Standard: Research Linked to the Development of the National Healthy School Standard (NHSS)*. London: DH/DfEE.

RMC Research Corporation (2003) *Washington State Readiness to Learn: School-linked Models for Integrated Family Services 2001–2002 Evaluation Report*. Olympia, WA: Office of the Superintendent of Public Instruction.

Robbins, D. (2001) *Transforming Children's Services: An Evaluation of Local Responses to the Quality Protects Programme, Year 3*. London: DH.

Roberts, I., Kramer, M.S. and Suissa, S. (1996) 'Does home-visiting prevent childhood injury? A systematic review of randomised controlled trials.' *British Medical Journal 312*, 29–33.

Roberts, J. (1996) 'Behavioural and cognitive-behavioural approaches.' In R. Phillips and E. McWilliam (eds), *After Adoption: Working with Adoptive Families*. London: BAAF.

Rohrbach, L.A., D'Onofrio, C.N., Backer, T.E. and Montgomery, S.B. (1996) 'Diffusion of school-based substance abuse prevention programs.' *American Behavioral Scientist 39*, 919–34.

Rooney, R.H. (1992) *Strategies for Work with Involuntary Clients*. New York: Columbia University Press.

Rooney, R.H. (2000) 'How can I use authority effectively and engage family members?' In H. Dubowitz and D. DePanfilis (eds) *Handbook for Child Protection Practice*. Newberry Park, CA: Sage.

Rose, G. (1992) *The Strategy of Preventive Medicine*. Oxford: Oxford Medical Publications.

Rose, W. (2001) 'Assessing children in need and their families. An overview of the framework.' In J. Horwath (ed.) *The Child's World*. London: Jessica Kingsley Publishers.

Rosenthal, J.A. (1993) Outcomes of adoption of children with special needs. *The Future of Children 3*, 77–88.

Rosenthal, J. and Groze, V. (1992) *Special Needs Adoption: A Study of Intact Families*. New York: Praeger.

Rossi, P.H. (1992) 'Assessing family preservation programs.' *Children and Youth Services Review 14*, 77–98.

Roth, J.L. and Brooks-Gunn, J. (2003) 'What is a youth development program? Identification of defining principles.' In F. Jacobs, D. Wertlieb and R.M. Lerner (eds) *Handbook of Applied Developmental Science, Enhancing the Life Chances of Youth and Families*, Vol. 2. Thousand Oaks, CA: Sage.

Roth, J., Brooks-Gunnn, J., Murray, L. and Foster, W. (1998) 'Promoting healthy adolescents: Synthesis of youth development program evaluations.' *Journal of Research on Adolescence 8*, 4, 423–59.

Rowe, J., Cain, H., Hundleby, M. and Garnett, L. (1989) *Child Care Now: A Survey of Placement Patterns*. London: BAAF.

Rowe, J., Caine, M., Hundleby, M. and Keane, A. (1984) *Long-Term Foster Care*. London: Batsford.

Rubin, D.M., Alessandrini, E.A., Feudtner, C., Mandell, D.S., Russell Localio A.R. and Hadley, T. (2004) 'Placement stability and mental health costs for children in foster care.' *Pediatrics 113*, 1336–41.

Rushton, A. (2000) *Adoption as a Placement Choice: Arguments and Evidence*. Maudsley Discussion Paper.

Rushton, A. (2003) 'Support for adoptive families: A review of current evidence on problems, needs and effectiveness.' *Adoption and Fostering 27*, 41–50.

Rushton, A. and Dance, C. (2002) *Adoption Support Services for Families in Difficulty: A Literature Review and UK survey*. London: BAAF.

Rushton, A. and Dance, C. (2004) 'The outcomes of later permanent placements: the adolescent years.' *Adoption and Fostering 28*, 1, 49–58

Rushton, A., Dance, C., Quinton, D. and Mayes, D. (2001) *Siblings in Late Permanent Placements*. London: BAAF.

Rushton, A., Mayes, D., Dance, C., and Quinton, D. (2003) 'Parenting late-placed children: the development of new relationships and the challenge of behavioural problems.' *Clinical Child Psychology and Psychiatry 8*, 389–400.

Rutter, M. (1987a) 'Psychosocial resilience and protective mechanisms.' *American Journal of Orthopsychiatry 57*, 3, 316–31.

Rutter, M. (1987b) 'Temperament, personality, and personality disorder.' *British Journal of Psychiatry 150*, 443–58.

Rutter, M. (1989) 'Intergenerational continuities and discontinuities in serious parenting difficulties.' In D. Cicchetti and V. Carlson (eds) *Child Maltreatment: Theory and Research on the Causes and Consequences of Child Abuse and Neglect*. Cambridge: Cambridge University Press.

Rutter, M. (2005) 'How the environment affects mental health.' *British Journal of Psychiatry 186*, 4–6.

Rutter, M. and ERA Study Team. (1998) 'Developmental catch-up and deficit following adoption after severe global early deprivation.' *Journal of Child Psychology and Psychiatry 39*, 465–76.

Rutter, M., Giller, H. and Hagell, A. (1998) *Anti-social Behaviour by Young People*. Cambridge: Cambridge University Press.

Rutter, M., Maugham, B., Mortimore, P. and Ouston, J. (1979) *Fifteen Thousand Hours: Secondary Schools and Their Effects on Children*. London: Open Books.

Rutter, M. and O'Connor, T. (1999) 'Implications of attachment theory for child care policies.' In J. Cassidy and P. Shaver (eds), *Handbook of Attachment: Theory, Research and Clinical Applications*. New York: Guildford Press.

Rutter, M. and Smith, D. (eds) (1995) *Psychosocial Disorders in Young People and Their Causes*. Chichester: Wiley.

Ryan, J. and Schuerman, J. (2004) 'Matching family problems with specific family preservation services: A study of services effectiveness.' *Children and Youth Services Review 26*, 4, 347–72.

Ryan, J. and Testa, M. (2004) *Child Maltreatment and Juvenile Delinquency: Investigating the Role of Placement and Placement Instability*. Champaign-Urbana, IL: University of Illinois at Urbana-Champaign School of Social Work, Children and Family Research Center.

Ryan, P., McFadden, E.J., Rice, D. and Warren, B.L. (1988) 'The role of foster parents in helping young people develop emancipation skills.' *Child Welfare 67*, 6, 563–72.

St. Pierre, R.G. and Layzer, J.I. (1999) 'Using home visits for multiple purposes: The Comprehensive Child Development Program.' *The Future of Children 9*, 1, 134–51.

St. Pierre, T.L., Kaltreider, D.L., Mark, M.M. and Aitkin, K.J. (1992) 'Drug prevention in a community setting: A longitudinal study of the relative effectiveness of a three-year primary prevention program in Boys and Girls Clubs across the nation.' *American Journal of Community Psychology 20*, 673–706.

St. James-Roberts I. and Singh C.S. (2001) *Can Mentors Help Primary School Children with Behaviour Problems?* Home Office Research Study 233. London: Home Office.

Sackett, D.L., Straus, S.E., Richardson, W.S., Rosenberg, W. and Haynes, R.B. (1997) *Evidence-Based Medicine: How to Practice and Teach EBM, Second Edition*. Edinburgh: Churchill Livingstone.

Salter, D., McMillan, D., Richards, M., Talbot, T., Hodges, J., Bentovim, A. *et al.* (2003) 'Development of sexually abusive behaviour in sexually victimised males: A longitudinal study.' *The Lancet 361*, 471–6.

Sameroff, A.J. and Fiese, B.H. (1990) 'Transactional regulation and early intervention.' In S.J. Meisels and J.P. Shonkoff (eds) *Handbook of Early Childhood Intervention*. Cambridge: Cambridge University Press.

Sameroff, A.J. and Fiese, B.H. (2000) 'Models of development and developmental risk.' In C.H. Zeanah, Jr. (ed.) *Handbook of Infant Mental Health, Second Edition*. New York: The Guilford Press.

Sameroff, A.J. and Seifer, R. (1990) 'Early contributors to developmental risk.' In J. Rolf, A.S. Masten, D. Cichetti, K.H. Nuechterlein and S. Weintraub (eds) *Risk and Protective Factors in the Development of Psychopathology*. New York: Cambridge University Press.

Sammons, P., Power, S., Robertson, P., Elliot, K., Campbell, C. and Whitty, G. (2002) *National Evaluation of the New Community Schools Pilot Programme in Scotland: Phase 1 Interim Findings (Interchange 76)*. Edinburgh: Scottish Executive Education Department.

Sampson, R.J. and Groves, W.B. (1989) 'Community structure and crime: Testing social disorganization theory.' *American Journal of Sociology 94*, 4, 774–802.

Sampson, R.J. and Laub, J.H. (1993) *Crime in the Making: Pathways and Turning Points Through Life.* Cambridge, MA: Harvard University Press.

Sampson, R.J., Raudenbush, S.W. and Earls, F. (1997) 'Neighbourhoods and violent crime: A multi-level study of collective efficacy.' *Science 277*, 1–7.

Saunders, B.E., Berliner, L. and Hanson, R.F. (eds) (2001) *Child Physical and Sexual Abuse: Guidelines for Treatment* (final report: January 15, 2003). Charleston, SC: National Crime Victims Research and Treatment Center. Retrieved 17 June 2003 from www.musc.edu/cvc/TreatmentGuidelines01-15-03.pdf

Saunders, B., Berliner, L. and Hanson, R. (eds) (2003) *Child Physical and Sexual Abuse: Guidelines for Treatment* (final Report: January 15, 2003). Charleston, SC: National Crime Victims Research and Treatment Center. Retrieved 4 January 2004 from www.musc.edu/cvc/

Saunders, L. and Broad, B. (1997) *The Health Needs of Young People Leaving Care.* Leicester: De Montfort University.

Scannapieco, M., Schagrin, J. and Scannapieco, T. (1995) 'Independent living programs: Do they make a difference?' *Child and Adolescent Social Work Journal 12*, 5, 381–9.

Schinke, S.P., Schilling, R.F., Kirkham, M.A., Gilchrist, L.D., Barth, R.P. and Blythe, B.J. (1986) 'Stress management skills for parents.' *Journal of Child and Adolescent Psychotherapy 3*, 293–8.

Schofield, G. (2003) *Part of the Family: Pathways Through Foster Care.* London: BAAF.

Schofield, G., Beek, M., Sargent, K. with Thoburn, J. (2000) *Growing Up in Foster Care.* London: BAAF.

Schore, A.N. (1996) 'The experience-dependent maturation of a regulatory system in the orbital prefrontal cortex and the origin of developmental psychopathology.' *Development and Psychopathology 8*, 59–87.

Schorr, L.B. (1997) *Common Purpose, Strengthening Families and Neighborhoods to Rebuild America.* New York: Anchor Books.

Schuerman, J., Rzepnicki, T. and Littell, J. (1991) *From Chicago to Little Egypt: Lessons from an Evaluation of a Family Preservation Program.* Newbury Park, CA: Sage.

Schuerman, J.R., Rzepnicki, T. and Littell, J. (1994) *Putting Families First. An Experiment in Family Preservation.* New York: Aldine de Gruyler.

Schwartz, I.M., AuClaire, P. and Harris, L.J. (1991) *Family Preservation Services as an Alternative to the Out-of-home Placement of Adolescents: The Hennepin Count Experiences.* Newbury Park, CA: Sage.

Schweinhart, L., Barnes, H. and Weikart, D. (1993) *A Summary of Significant Benefits: The High/Scope Perry Pre-school Study through Age 27.* Michigan: High/Scope Press.

Schweinhart, L. and Weikart, D. (1980) *Young Children Grow Up: The Effects of the Perry Pre-School Program on Youths Through Age 15.* Monographs of the High/Scope Educational Research Foundation, No. 7. Ypsilanti: High/Scope Educational Foundation.

Schweinhart, L., Weikart, D. and Larner, M.B. (1986) 'Consequences of three pre-school curriculum models through age 15.' *Early Childhood Research Quarterly 1*, 15–45.

Scott, S. (1998) 'Aggressive behaviour in childhood.' *British Medical Journal 16*, 202–6.

Scott, S. and Sylva, K. (forthcoming) *The 'Spokes' Project: Supporting Parents on Kids' Education.* Final report to the Department of Health.

Scott, S., Spender, Q., Doolan, M., Jacobs, B. and Aspland, H. (2001) 'Multicentre controlled trial of parenting groups for childhood antisocial behaviour in clinical practice.' *British Medical Journal 323*, 194–7.

Scottish Executive (2002) *Children Looked After in the Year to 31 March 2002.* Edinburgh: Scottish Executive.

Scottish Executive (2004) *Children's Social Work Statistics 2003–4.* Edinburgh: Scottish Executive.

Sedlak, A. and Broadhurst, D. (1992) *Study of Adoption Assistance Impact and Outcomes: Final Report.* Contract No. 105-89-1607, Westat, Inc. Washington, DC: US DHHS.

Seglow, J., Pringle, M. and Wedge, P. (1972) *Growing Up Adopted.* London: National Foundation for Educational Research.

Sellick, C. and Thoburn, J. (1996) *What Works in Family Placement?* Ilford: Barnado's.

Selwyn, J., Sturgess, W., Quinton, D. and Baxter, K. (2006) *Costs and Outcomes of Non-Infant Adoption.* London: BAAF.

Sharland E., Seal H., Croucher, M., Aldgate, J. and Jones, D. (1998) *Professional Intervention in Child Sexual Abuse.* London: HMSO.

Shaw, C. (1998) *Remember my Messages... The Experiences and Views of 2000 Children in Public Care in the UK.* London: Who Cares? Trust.

Sheehy, A.M., Oldham, E., Zanghi, M., Ansell, D., Correia, P. and Copeland, R. (2002) *Promising Practices: Supporting Transition of Youth Served by the Foster Care System.* Baltimore, MD: National Foster Care Awareness Project.

Shireman, J. and Johnson, P. (1988) *Growing Up Adopted.* Chicago: Child Care Society.

Shonkoff, J.P., Lippitt, J.A. and Cavanaugh, D.A. (2000) 'Early childhood policy: Implications for infant mental health.' In C.H. Zeanah, Jr. (ed.) *Handbook of Infant Mental Health, Second Edition.* New York: The Guilford Press.

Shonkoff, J.P. and Meisels, S.J. (eds) (2000) *Handbook of Early Childhood Intervention, Second Edition.* New York: Cambridge University Press.

Shonkoff, J.P. and Phillips, D.A. (eds) (2000) *From Neurons to Neighborhoods: The Science of Early Childhood Development.* Washington, DC: National Academy Press.

Shouls, A., Congdon, P. and Curtis, S. (1996) 'Modelling inequality in reported long term illness: combining individual and area characteristics.' *Journal of Epidemiology and Community Health 50*, 3, 366–76.

Simon, R.J. and Altstein, H. (1994) *The Case for Transracial Adoption.* Washington, DC: The American University Press.

Sinclair, I. (1971) *Hostels for Probationers.* London: HMSO.

Sinclair, I. (1975) 'The influence of wardens and matrons on probation hostels.' In J. Tizard, I. Sinclair and R.V.G. Clarke (eds) *Varieties of Residential Experience.* London: Routledge and Kegan Paul.

Sinclair, I. (2005) *Fostering Now: Messages from Research.* London: Jessica Kingsley Publishers.

Sinclair, I., Baker, C., Wilson, K. and Gibbs, I. (2005a) *Foster Children: Where They Go and How They Get On.* London: Jessica Kingsley Publishers.

Sinclair, I. and Clarke, R. (1973) 'Acting out and its significance for the residential treatment of delinquents.' *Journal of Child Psychiatry and Psychology 14,* 283–91.

Sinclair, I.A.C. and Gibbs, I. (1998) *Children's Homes: A Study in Diversity.* Chichester: Wiley.

Sinclair, I., Wilson, K. and Gibbs, I. (2000) *Supporting Foster Placements: Report Two.* York: Social Work Research and Development Unit, University of York.

Sinclair, I., Wilson, K. and Gibbs, I. (2001) 'A life more ordinary: What children want from foster placements.' *Adoption and Fostering 25,* 4, 17–26.

Sinclair, I., Wilson, K. and Gibbs, I. (2003) 'Matches and mismatches: The contribution of foster carers and children to the success of foster placements.' *British Journal of Social Work 33,* 7, 871–84.

Sinclair, I., Wilson, K. and Gibbs, I. (2005b) *Foster Placements: Why Some Succeed and Some Fail.* London: Jessica Kingsley Publishers.

Sinclair, R. (1998) 'Involving children in planning their care.' *Child and Family Social Work 3,* 137–42.

Sinclair, R. (2003) 'Who takes care of education? Looked after children's perceptions of support for educational progress.' In *Stability in Foster Care.* Papers from a seminar funded by the Nuffield Foundation and organized by members of the Centre for Research on the Child and Family, University of East Anglia.

Sinclair, R., Garnett, L. and Berridge, D. (1995) *Social Work and Assessment with Adolescents.* London: National Children's Bureau.

Singer, J.D. and Butler, J.A. (1987) 'The education for all handicapped children act: Schools as agents of social reform.' *Harvard Educational Review 57,* 125–52.

Skinner, S. and Wilson, M. (2002) *Assessing Community Strengths: A Practical Handbook for Planning Capacity Building.* London: Community Development Foundation.

Skinner T. *et al.* (1996) 'Beneficial effects of therapeutic activity groups for children at risk of maladjustment: retrospective evaluation of the National Pyramid Trust model.' Paper presented at British Psychological Society conference, Oxford.

Skuse, D., Bentovim, A., Hodges, J., Stevenson, J., Andreou, C., Lanyardo, M. *et al.* (1998) 'Risk factors for development of sexually abusive behaviour in sexually victimised adolescent boys: Cross sectional study.' *British Medical Journal 317,* 175–9.

Sloper, P. and Statham, J. (2004) 'The national service framework for children, young people and maternity services: Developing the evidence base.' *Child: Care, Health and Development 30,* 6, 567–70.

Smith, C. (1994) *Partnership in Action: Developing Effective Aftercare Projects.* Westerham: Royal Philanthropic Society.

Smith, C. and Pugh, G. (1996) *Learning to be a Parent: A Survey of Group-Based Parenting Programmes.* London: Family Policy Studies Centre.

Smith, C. (ed.) (1998) *Leaving Care: Messages from Young People.* London: Royal Philanthropic Society.

Smith, G. (1994) 'Parent, partner, protector: Conflicting role demands for mothers of sexually abused children.' In T. Morrison, M. Erooga and R. C. Becket (eds) *Sexual Offending Against Children: Assessment and Treatment of Male Abusers.* London: Routledge.

Smith, J., Gilford, S., Kirby, P., O'Reilly, A. and Ing, P. (1996) *Bright Lights and Homelessness.* London: YMCA.

Smith, P. and Sharp, S. (eds) (1994) *School Bullying: Insights and Perspectives.* London: Routledge.

Smith, T. (1996) *Family Centres and Bringing Up Young Children.* London: HMSO.

Social Security Administration (2000) 'Supplemental security income. Determining disability for a child under 18. Final rules.' *Federal Register, September 11, 65,* 54747–90.

Social Services Inspectorate (SSI) (1996) *For Children's Sake.* London: Department of Health.

Social Services Inspectorate (SSI) (1998) *Someone Else's Children. Inspections of Planning and Decision Making for Children Looked After and the Safety of Children Looked After.* London: Department of Health.

Social Services Inspectorate (SSI) (1999) *Getting Family Support Right. Inspection of the Delivery of Family Support Services.* London: Department of Health.

Social Services Inspectorate (SSI) (2000) *Adopting Changes: Survey and Inspection of Local Councils' Adoption Services.* London: Stationary Office.

Sorosky, A.D., Baran, A. and Pannor, R. (1978) 'Adopted children.' In D. Cantwell and P. Tanguay (eds) *Clinical Child Psychology.* Jamaica, NY: Spectrum Publications.

Southern Regional Educational Board (no date) *Helping Families to Help Students: Kentucky's Family Resource and Youth Services Centers,* prepared for the state of Kentucky by David Denton for SREB. Atlanta, GE.

Spalding B. (2000) 'The contribution of a "Quiet Place" to early intervention strategies for children with emotional and behavioural difficulties in mainstream school.' *British Journal of Special Education 27,* 3, 129–34.

Speak, S. (2000) 'Children in urban regeneration: Foundations for sustainable participation.' *Community Development Journal 35*, 1, 31–40.

Spencer, N. (2003) 'Parenting programmes.' *Archives of Disease in Childhood 88*, 99–100.

Statham, J. (2000) *Outcomes and Effectiveness of Family Support Services: A Research Review.* London: Thomas Coram Research Unit, Institute of Education, University of London.

Stauffer, L.B. and Deblinger, E. (1996) 'Cognitive behavioural groups for nonoffending mothers and their sexually abused children: A preliminary treatment outcome study.' *Child Maltreatment 1*, 65–76.

Stein, M. (1990) *Living Out of Care.* Barkingside: Barnardo's.

Stein, M. (1997) *What Works in Leaving Care?* Barkingside: Barnardo's.

Stein, M. (2002) 'Leaving care.' In D. McNeish, T. Newman, and R. Roberts (eds) *What Works for Children?* Buckingham: Open University Press.

Stein, M. and Carey, K. (1986) *Leaving Care.* Oxford: Blackwell.

Stein, M. and Wade, J. (2000) *Helping Care Leavers: Problems and Strategic Responses.* London: Department of Health.

Stein, T. (1984) 'The Child Abuse Prevention and Treatment Act.' *Social Service Review 58*, 2, 302–14.

Stein, T. (1991) *Child Welfare and the Law.* New York and London: Longman.

Stein, T. (1998) *Child Welfare and the Law (Revised Edition).* Washington, DC: Child Welfare League of America.

Stephenson, J., Strange, V., Forrest, S., Oakley, A., Copas, A., Allen, E. *et al.* (2004) 'Pupil-led sex education in England (RIPPLE study): Cluster-randomised intervention trial.' *Lancet 364*, 338–46.

Stevenson J. (1999) 'The treatment of the long-term sequelae of child abuse.' *Journal of Child Psychology and Psychiatry 40*, 89–111.

Stevenson, O. (1998) *Neglected Children: Issues and Dilemmas.* Oxford: Blackwell.

Stier, D.M., Leventhal, J.M., Berg, A.T., Johnson, L. and Mezger, J. (1993) 'Are children born to young mothers at increased risk of maltreatment.' *Pediatrics 91*, 642–8.

Stone, B. (1998) *Child Neglect: Practitioners' Perspectives.* London: NSPCC.

Stone, B. (2003) 'A framework for assessing neglect.' In M. Calder and S. Hackett (eds) *Assessment in Childcare: Using and Developing Frameworks for Practice.* Lyme Regis: Russell House Publishing.

Stone, M. (1990) *Young People Leaving Care.* Redhill: Royal Philanthropic Society.

Strathdee, R. and Johnson, M. (1994) *Out of Care and on the Streets: Young People, Care Leavers and Homelessness.* London, Centrepoint.

Stroul, B.A. and Goldman, S.K. (1990) 'Study of community-based services for children and adolescents who are severely emotionally disturbed.' *The Journal of Mental Health Administration 17*, 61–77.

Susser, E., Lin, S., Conover, S. and Strueing, E. (1991) 'Childhood antecedents of homelessness in psychiatric patients.' *American Journal of Psychiatry 148*, 8, 1026–30.

Sykes, J., Sinclair, I., Wilson, K. and Gibbs, I. (2002) 'Kinship and stranger foster carers: how do they compare?' *Adoption and Fostering 26*, 2, 39–48.

Sylva, K., Melhuish, E., Sammons, P., Siraj-Blatchford, I. and Taggart, B. (2004) *The Effective Provision of Pre-School Education (EPPE) Project: Final Report.* Available at www.dfes.gov.uk/research/data/uploadfiles/SSU_FR_2004_01.pdf

Sylvester, J., Bentovim, A., Stratton, P. and Hanks, H.G (1995) 'Using spoken attributions to classify abusive families.' *Child Abuse and Neglect 19*, 10, 1221–32.

Szykula, S.A. and Fleischman, M.J. (1985) 'Reducing out-of-home placements of abused children: Two controlled field studies.' *Child Abuse and Neglect 9*, 277–83.

Taber, M.A. and Proch, K. (1988) 'Parenting: An essential child welfare service.' *Social Work 33*, 1, 63–4.

Tanner, K. and Turney, D. (2000) 'The role of observation in the assessment of child neglect.' *Child Abuse Review 9*, 5, 337–48.

Tanner, K. and Turney, D. (2003) 'What do we know about child neglect? A critical review of the literature and its application to social work practice.' *Child and Family Social Work 8*, 25–34.

Tarling, R., Davison, T. and Clarke, A. (2004) *Mentoring Projects: The National Evaluation of the Youth Justice Board's Mentoring Projects.* London: Youth Justice Board.

Testa, M.F. (2002) 'Subsidized guardianship: Testing an idea whose time has finally come.' *Social Work Research 26*, 3, 145–58.

Taylor M.J. (2003) *Going Round in Circles: Implementing and Learning from Circle Time.* Slough: NFER.

Thoburn, J. (1990) *Success and Failure in Permanent Family Placement.* Brookfield, VT: Gower Publishing Company.

Thoburn, J., Louis, A. and Shemmings, D. (1995) *Paternalism or Partnership? Family Involvement in the Child Protection Process.* London: HMSO.

Thoburn, J., Norford, L. and Rashid, S. (2000b) *Permanent Family Placement for Children of Minority Ethnic Origin.* London: Jessica Kingsley Publishers.

Thoburn, J. and Rowe, J. (1991) 'Survey findings and conclusions.' In J. Fratter, J. Rowe, D. Sapsford and J. Thoburn *Permanent Family Placement: A Decade of Experience.* London: BAAF.

Thoburn, J., Wilding, J. and Watson, J. (2000a) *Family Support in Cases of Emotional Maltreatment and Neglect.* London: The Stationery Office.

Thomas, G. (1994) 'Travels in the trench between child welfare theory and practice: A case study of failed promises and prospects for renewal.' *Child and Youth Services Review 17*, 1–260.

Thomlison, B. (1997) 'Risk and protective factors in child maltreatment.' In M.W. Fraser (ed.) *Risk and Resilience in Childhood.* Washington, DC: National Association of Social Workers.

Thomlison, B. (2003) 'Characteristics of evidence-based child maltreatment interventions.' *Child Welfare 82*, 541–69.

Thompson, R.A. (1995) *Preventing Child Maltreatment Through Social Support.* London: Sage.

Thompson, R.W., Huefner, J.C., Ringle, J.L. and Daly, D.L. (in press). 'Adult outcomes of girls and boys town youth: A follow-up report.' In C. Newman, C. Liberton, K. Kutash, and R. Friedman (eds) *Proceedings of the 17th Annual Florida Mental Health Institute Research Conference. A System of Care for Children's Mental Health: Expanding the Research Base.* Tampa, FL: University of South Florida.

Tilbury, C. (2004) 'The influence of performance measurement on child welfare policy and practice.' *British Journal of Social Work 34*, 2, 225–41.

Tizard, B. (1977) *Adoption: A Second Chance.* London: Routledge.

Tobler, N.S., Roona, M.R., Ochshorn, P., Marshall, D.G., Streke, A.V. and Stackpole, K.M. (2000) 'School-based adolescent drug prevention programs: 1998 meta-analysis.' *Journal of Primary Prevention 20*, 275–337.

Tobler, N.S. and Stratton, H.H. (1997) 'Effectiveness of school-based drug prevention programs: A meta-analysis of the research.' *Journal of Primary Prevention 18*, 71–128.

Toroyan, T., Roberts, I., Oakley, A., Laing, G., Mugford, M. and Frost, C. (2003) 'Effectiveness of out-of-home day care for disadvantaged families: Randomised controlled trial.' *British Medical Journal 327*, 906–11.

Toth, S.L., Manly, J.T. and Cicchetti, D. (1992) 'Child maltreatment and vulnerability to depression.' *Development and Psychopathology 4*, 97–112.

Tracy, E.M. (1991) 'Defining the target population for family preservation services.' In K. Wells and D.E. Biegel (eds) *Family Preservation Services: Research and Evaluation.* Newbury Park, CA: Sage Publications.

Trieschman, A.E., Whittaker, J.K. and Brendtro, L.K. (1969) *The Other 23 Hours: Child Care Work with Emotional Disturbed Children in a Therapeutic Milieu.* New York: Aldine de Gruyter.

Triseliotis, J. (1980) 'Growing up in foster care.' In J. Triseliotis (ed.) *New Developments in Foster Care and Adoption.* London: Routledge and Kegan Paul.

Triseliotis, J. (2002) 'Long-term foster care or adoption? The evidence examined.' *Child and Family Social Work 7*, 1, 23–33.

Triseliotis, J., Borland, M., Hill, M. and Lambert, L. (1995b) *Teenagers and Social Work Services.* London: HMSO.

Triseliotis, J. and Hill, M. (1990) 'Contrasting adoption, foster care, and residential rearing.' In D. Brodzinsky and M. Shechter (eds), *The Psychology of Adoption*, 107–20. New York: Oxford University Press.

Triseliotis, J. and Russell, J. (1984) *Hard to Place: The Outcome of Adoption and Residential Care.* London: Heinemann Educational Books.

Triseliotis, J., Sellick, C. and Short, R. (1995a) *Foster Care: Theory and Practice.* London: Batsford.

Trolley, B., Wallin, J. and Hansen, J. (1995) 'International adoptions: Issues of acknowledgement of adoption and birth culture.' *Child and Adolescent Social Work Journal 12*, 6, 465–79.

Trowell, J., Kolvin, I., Weeramanthri, T. Sadowski, H., Berelowitz, M., Glasser, D. and Leitch, I. (2002) 'Psychotherapy for sexually abused girls: psychopathological outcome findings and patterns of change.' *British Journal of Psychiatry 180*, 3, 234–47.

Tufts New England Medical Center, Division of Child Psychiatry (1984) *Sexually Exploited Children.* Final report for the Office of Juvenile Justice and Delinquency Prevention. Washington, DC: US Department of Justice. Service and Research Project.

Tunstill, J. and Aldgate, J. (2000) *Services for Children in Need. From Policy to Practice.* London: The Stationery Office.

Tunstill, J., Allnock, D., Akhurst, S. and Garbers, C. (2005) 'Sure Start local programmes: Implications of case study data from the national evaluation of Sure Start.' *Children and Society 19*, 158–71.

Turney, D. (2004) 'Who cares? The role of mothers in cases of child neglect.' In J. Taylor and B. Daniel (eds) *Child Neglect: Practice Issues for Health and Social Care.* London: Jessica Kingsley Publishers.

Turney, D. and Tanner, K. (2001) 'Working with neglected children and their families.' *Journal of Social Work Practice 15*, 2, 193–204.

US Census Bureau (2000) 'QT-P2: Single years of age under 30 years and sex: 2000.' Washington, DC: US Bureau of the Census.

US Census Bureau, Population Division (2003) *Table NA-EST2002-ASRO-03: National Population Estimates. Characteristics.* 18 June. Washington, DC: US Census Bureau. Available at eire.census.gov/popest/data/national/tables/asro/NA-EST2002-ASRO-03.php

US Census Bureau (2003a) *Household Relationship and Living Arrangements of Children Under 18 Years, by Age, Sex, Race, Hispanic Origin, and Metropolitian Residence: March 2002 (Table 2).* June. Washington, DC: US Census Bureau.

US Census Bureau (2003b) *People in Families with Related Children Under 18 by Family Structure, Age and Sex, Iterated by Income-to-poverty Ratio and Race: 2002 below 100% of Poverty – All Races (Table POV03).* September. Washington, DC: US Census Bureau.

US Census Bureau (2005) *Selected Social Characteristics: 2004 Data Set: 2004 American Community Survey.* Retrieved September 28, 2005 from http://factfinder.census.gov/servlet/ADPTable?_bm= y&-geo_id=01000US&-qr_name=ACS_2004_EST_G00_DP2&-ds_name=ACS_2004_EST_G00_&-_lang=en&-_sse=on

US Census Bureau, American Community Profile (2003) *Table 1. General demographic characteristics.* 2002 Community Population Survey. Retrieved August 19, 2004 from www.census.gov/acs/www/Products/ Profiles/Single/2002/ACS/Tabular/010/01000US1.htm

US Census Bureau, Population Division (2005) *Table 1-RES: Estimates of the Resident Population by Selected Age Groups for the United States and States and for Puerto Rico: July 1, 2004 (SC-EST2004-01-RES).* 25 February. Washington, DC: US Census Bureau. www.census.gov/popest/states/asrh/sc-est2004-01.html

US Department of Health and Human Services (1999a) *Blending Perspectives and Building Common Ground. A Report to Congress on Substance Abuse and Child Protection.* Washington, DC: US Government Printing Office.

US Department of Health and Human Services (1999b) *Mental Health: A Report of the Surgeon General.* Rockville, MD: DHHS, Substance Abuse and Mental Health Services Administration, National Institutes of Health, National Institute of Mental Health.

US Department of Health and Human Services (2000) *A Commitment to Supporting the Mental Health of our Youngest Children: Report of the Infant Mental Health Forum.* Washington, DC: DHHS.

US Department of Health and Human Services (2003) *Child Maltreatment 2001.* Retrieved December 23, 2003 from www.acf.hhs.gov/programs/cb/publications/CM01/chapterone.htm

US Department of Health and Human Services (2004a) *AFCARS Report 9.* Available from: www.acf.dhhs.gov/programs/cb/cwrp/results.htm

US Department of Health and Human Services (2004b) *Children's Bureau Child and Family Services Reviews: Summary of Key Findings Fiscal Years 2003 and 2004.* Washington, DC: Administration for Children and Families, Children's Bureau.

US Department of Health and Human Services (2005) *Child Maltreatment 2003: Reports from the States to the National Child Abuse and Neglect Data Systems – National Statistics on Child Abuse and Neglect.* Washington, DC: US Census Bureau.

US Department of Health and Human Services, Administration for Children and Families, Administration on Children, Youth and Families, Children's Bureau (2000) *The AFCARS Report: Current Estimates As of March 31, 1999.* Available at www.acf.dhhs.gov/programs/cbdata.

US Department of Health and Human Services, Administration for Children and Families, Administration on Children, Youth and Families, Children's Bureau (2004) *Adoption and Foster Care Analysis and Reporting System (AFCARS).* Data as of May 2004. Washington, DC: US Government Printing Office.

US Department of Health and Human Services, Administration for Children and Families, Administration on Children, Youth and Families, Children's Bureau (2005a) Adoption and Foster Care Analysis and Reporting System (AFCARS). *2003 Data.* Washington, DC: US Government Printing Office. Available at www.acf.hhs.gov/programs/cb/dis/afcars/publications

US Department of Health and Human Services, Administration for Children and Families, Administration on Children, Youth and Families, Children's Bureau (2005b) *Adoption and Foster Care Analysis and Reporting System (AFCARS).* Data as of May 2004. Washington, DC: US Government Printing Office.

US Department of Health and Human Services, Administration for Children and Families, Children's Bureau, National Clearinghouse on Child Abuse and Neglect Information (2005c) *Child Maltreatment 2003.* Washington, DC: US DHHS.

US Department of Health and Human Services, Administration for Children and Families, Children's Bureau (2005d) *The AFCARS Report: Preliminary FY 2003 Estimates as of August 2005.* Washington, DC: US Department of Health and Human Services. Retrieved August 15, 2005 from www.acf.hhs.gov/programs/cb/publications/afcars/report10.htm

US Department of Health and Human Services, Administration on Children and Families, Children's Bureau (2000) *Rethinking Child Welfare Practice under the Adoption and Safe Families Act of 1997.* Washington, DC: US Government Printing Office.

US Department of Health and Human Services, Administration for Children and Families, National Clearinghouse on Child Abuse and Neglect Information (2004) *Child Maltreatment 2002.* Washington, DC: US Government Printing Office.

US Department of Health and Human Services, Administration on Children, Youth and Families (2004) *Child Maltreatment 2002.* Washington, DC: US Government Printing Office.

US Department of Health and Human Services, Administration on Children, Youth and Families, Children's Bureau (2003a) *Safety, Permanency and Well-Being: Child Welfare Outcomes 1998, 1999 and 2000.* Washington, DC: US Government Printing Office.

US Department of Health and Human Services, Administration on Children, Youth and Families, Children's Bureau, Adoption and Foster Care Analysis and Reporting System (AFCARS) (2003b) *The AFCARS Report – Preliminary FY2001 estimates as of March 2003* 8, 1–7. Washington, DC: US Government Printing Office.

US Department of Health and Human Services, Administration on Children, Youth and Families, National Clearinghouse on Child Abuse and Neglect Information (2001) *Child Maltreatment 1999 – Ten Years of Reporting.* Washington, DC: US Government Printing Office. Available at: www.calib.com/nccanch/whatsnew.cfm, p.vii.

US Department of Health and Human Services, Children's Bureau (1997) *National Study of Protective, Preventive, and Reunification Services Delivered to Children and Their Families.* Washington, DC: US Government Printing Office.

US Department of Health and Human Services, Children's Bureau, Administration on Children, Youth and Families, National Clearinghouse on Child Abuse and Neglect Information (2003a) *Child Maltreatment 2001.* Washington, DC: US Government Printing Office.

US Department of Health and Human Services, Children's Bureau, Administration on Children, Youth and Families, National Clearinghouse on Child Abuse and Neglect Information (2003b) Child Maltreatment 2002. Washington, DC: US DHHS.

US General Accounting Office (1994) *Residential Care: Some High-risk Youth Benefit, but More Study Needed.* Gaithersburg, MD: GAO.

US Government Accounting Office (2004) *Child and Family Services Reviews: Better Use of Data and Improved Guidance Could Enhance HHS's Oversight of State Performance.* Report No. GAO-04-333. Washington, DC: US Government Printing Office.

US Public Health Service (2000) *Report of the Surgeon General's Conference on Children's Mental Health: A National Action Agenda.* Washington, DC: DHHS.

US State Department. Immediate relative visas issued, FY 1990, FY 2001. Available at: www.adoptioninstitute.org/FactOverview/International_print.html

Utting, W. (1991) *Children in the Public Care.* London: HMSO.

Utting, W. (1997) *People Like Us: Report of the Review of Safeguards for Children Living Away from Home.* London: DH and the Welsh Office.

Utting, W., Rose, W. and Pugh, G. (2001) *Better Results for Children and Families.* London: NCVCCO.

van der Eyken, W. (1990) *Home-start: A Four-year Evaluation.* Leicester, UK: Home-start Consultancy.

Verhulst, F., Althaus, M. and Versluis-den-Bieman, H. (1992) 'Damaging backgrounds: Later adjustment of international adoptees.' *Journal of the American Academy of Child and Adolescent Psychiatry 31,* 518–24.

Vinson, T., Baldry, E. and Hargreaves, J. (1996) 'Neighbourhoods, networks and child abuse.' *British Journal of Social Work 26,* 523–43.

Vizard, E., Monck, E. and Misch, P. (1995) 'Child and adolescent sex abuse perpetrators: A review of the research literature.' *Journal of Child Psychology and Psychiatry 36,* 731–56.

Vogel, A.L., Morrow, C.E., Windham, A.M., Hanson, K.L. and Bandstra, E.S. (2003) 'The Starting Early Starting Smart Program: Impacting caregiver responsiveness in at-risk families with infants and toddlers.' Poster presented at the 11th Annual Meeting of the Society for Prevention Research, Washington, DC.

Wade, J. (1997) 'Developing leaving care services: Tapping the potential of foster carers.' *Adoption and Fostering 21,* 3, 40–9.

Wade, J. and Biehal, N. with Clayden, J. and Stein, M. (1998) *Going Missing: Young People Absent from Care.* Chichester: Wiley.

Wagner, M.M. and Clayton, S.L. (1999) 'The Parents as Teachers program: Results from two demonstrations.' *Future of Children 9,* 91–115.

Wald, M.S. and Wolverton, M. (1990) 'Risk assessment: The emperor's new clothes.' *Child Welfare 69,* 483–511.

Waldfogel, J. (1998) *The Future of Child Protection, How to Break the Cycle of Abuse and Neglect.* Cambridge, MA: Harvard University Press.

Waldinger, G. and Furman, W.M. (1994) 'Two models of preparing foster youth for emancipation.' *Children and Youth Services Review 16,* 3, 201–21.

Walker, M., Hill, M. and Triseliotis, J. (2002) *Testing the Limits of Foster Care: Fostering as an Alternative to Secure Accommodation.* London: BAAF.

Waller, S., Naidoo, B. and Thorn, B. (2002) *Prevention and Reduction of Alcohol Misuse: Evidence Briefing.* London: Health Development Agency.

Walsh, M., Brabeck, M., Howard, K., Sherman, E. Montes, C. and Garvin, T. (2000) 'The Alston College-Allston/Brighton Partnership: Description and challenges.' *Peabody Journal of Education 75,* 3, 6–32.

Walter, I., Nutley, S., Percy-Smith, J, Mcneish, D. and Frost, S. (2004) *Improving the Use of Research in Social Care Practice. Knowledge Review 4.* London: SCIE.

Walton, E. (1996) 'Family functioning as a measure of success in intensive family preservation services.' *Journal of Family Social Work 1,* 67–82.

Walton, E., Fraser, M.W., Lewis, R.E., Pecora, P.J. and Walton, W.K. (1993) 'In-home family-focused reunification: An experimental study.' *Child Welfare 72,* 5, 473–87.

Walton, E., Sandau-Beckler, P. and Mannes, M. (eds) (2001) *Balancing Family-centered Services and Child Well-being: Exploring Issues in Policy, Practice, and Research.* New York: Columbia University Press.

Wandersman, A. and Florin, P. (2003) 'Community interventions and effective prevention.' *American Psychologist 58,* 441–8.

Ward, H. (ed.) (1995) *Looked After Children: Research into Practice.* London: HMSO.

Ward, J., Henderson, Z. and Pearson, G. (2003) *One Problem Among Many: Drug Use Among Care Leavers in Transition to Independent Living.* Home Office Research Study 260. London: Home Office.

Warner, N. (1992) *Choosing with Care: Report of the Committee of Inquiry into the Selection and Management of Staff in Children's Homes.* London: HMSO.

Warren, S. (1992) 'Lower Thresholds for referral for psychiatric treatment for adopted adolescents.' *Journal of the American Academy of Child and Adolescent Psychiatry 31*, 512–7.

Waterhouse, S. (1997) *The Organisation of Foster Services.* London: NFCA.

Wattam, C. (1999) 'The prevention of child abuse.' *Children and Society 13*, 317–29.

Weare, K. and Gray, G. (2003) *What Works in Developing Children's Emotional and Social Competence and Wellbeing? DfES Research Report 456.* London: DfES.

Webb, R. and Vulliamy, G (2001) *A Multi-agency Approach to Reducing Disaffection and Exclusions from School.* Research Report 568. London: DfES

Webster-Stratton, C. (1985) Predictors of treatment outcome in parent training for conduct disordered children. *Behaviour Therapy 16*, 223–43.

Webster-Stratton, C. (1998) 'Parent training with low-income families: Promoting parental engagement through a collaborative approach.' In J.R. Lutzker (ed.) *Handbook of Child Abuse Research and Treatment, 183–211.* New York: Plenum.

Webster-Stratton, C. (2000) *The Incredible Years Training Series.* Washington, DC: Office of Juvenile Justice and Delinquency Prevention.

Webster-Stratton, C. and Hancock, L. (1998) 'Training for parents of young children with conduct problems: content, methods, and therapeutic processes.' In J.M. Breismeister and C.E. Shaefer (eds) *Handbook of Parent Training, Second Edition.* New York: Wiley.

Webster-Stratton, C., Hollinsworth, T. and Kolpacoff, M. (1989) 'The long-term effectiveness and clinical significance of three cost-effective training programmes for families with conduct-problem children.' *Journal of Consulting and Clinical Psychology 57*, 550–3.

Webster-Stratton, C. and Taylor, T. (2001) 'Nipping early risk factors in the bud: Preventing substance abuse, delinquency, and violence in adolescence through interventions targeted at young children (0–8).' *Prevention Science 2*, 165–92.

Weekes, D. and Wright, C. (1998) *Improving Practice: A Whole School Approach to Raising the Achievement of African Caribbean Youth.* London: Runnymede Trust.

Weinfield, N.S., Ogawa, J.R. and Sroufe, L.A. (1997) 'Early attachment as a pathway to adolescent peer competence.' *Journal of Research on Adolescence 7*, 3, 241–65.

Weiss, A. and Manz, P. (1998) 'Community-based resilient peer treatment of withdrawn maltreated preschool children.' *Journal of Counseling and Clinical Psychology 64*, 1377–86.

Weiss, H. (1993) 'Home visits: Necessary but not sufficient.' *The Future of Children – Home Visiting 3*, 3, 113–28.

Weissberg, R.P., Caplan, M. and Harwood, R.L. (1991) 'Promoting competent young people in competence-enhancing environments: A systems-based perspective on primary prevention.' *Journal of Consulting and Clinical Psychology 59*, 830–41.

Weissberg, R.P. and Greenberg, M.T. (1997) 'School and community competence-enhancement and prevention programs.' In W. Damon, I.E. Sigel and K.A. Renninger (eds) *Handbook of Child Psychology: Child Psychology in Practice, Fifth Edition.* New York: John Wiley and Sons.

Weissberg, R.P., Kumpfer, K.L., and Seligman, M.E.P. (2003) 'Prevention that works for children and youth: An introduction.' *American Psychologist 58*, 6/7, 425–32.

Weissbourd, R. (2003) 'How cities can improve children's outcomes: The case of ReadBoston.' In F. Jacobs, D. Wertlieb and R.M. Lerner (eds) *Handbook of Applied Developmental Science, Enhancing the Life Chances of Youth and Families,* Vol. 2. Thousand Oaks, CA: Sage.

Wellard, S., Tearse, M. and West, A. (1997) *All Together Now: Community Participation for Children and Young People.* London: Save the Children.

Wells J., Barlow J. and Stewart-Brown S. (2003) 'A systematic review of universal approaches to mental health promotion in schools'. *Health Education 103*, 4, 197–220.

Wells, K. (1995) 'Family preservation services in context: Origins, practices, and current issues.' In I.M. Schwartz and P. AuClaire (eds) 'Home-based services for troubled children.' *Child, Youth, and Family Services Series.* University of Nebraska Press.

Wells, K. and Biegel, D.E. (1991) *Family Preservation Services.* Newbury Park, CA: Sage.

Wells, K. and Biegel, D.E. (1992) 'Intensive family preservation services research: Current status and future agenda.' *Special Issue: Children Social Work Research and Abstracts 28*, 21–7.

Wells, K., Wyatt, E. and Hobfoll, S. (1991) 'Factors associated with adaptation of youths discharged from residential treatment.' *Children and Youth Services Review 13*, 199–216.

Welsh Assembly (2003) *Social Services Statistics, 2003.* Cardiff: National Assembly for Wales.

Welsh Assembly (2005) *Adoptions, Outcomes and Placements for Children Looked After by Local Authorities: Year Ending 31 March 2004.* Cardiff: National Assembly for Wales.

Welsh Office (1996) *The Report of the Examination Team on Child Care Procedures and Practice in North Wales.* Cardiff: Welsh Office.

Werner, E.E. (1989) 'High risk children in young adulthood: A longitudinal study from birth to 32 years.' *American Journal of Orthopsychiatry 59*, 1, 72–81.

Werner, E.E. (2000) 'Protective factors and individual resilience.' In J.P. Shonkoff and S.J. Meisels (eds) *Handbook of Early Childhood Intervention, Second Edition.* New York: Cambridge University Press.

Werner, E.E. and Smith, R.S. (1982) *Vulnerable but Invincible: A Longitudinal Study of Resilient Children and Youth.* New York: McGraw-Hill.

Werner, E.E. and Smith, R.S. (1992) *Overcoming the Odds, High Risk Children from Birth to Adulthood.* Ithaca, NY: Cornell University Press

Werner, E.E. and Smith, R.S. (2001) *Journeys from Childhood to Midlife, Risk, Resilience and Recovery.* Ithaca, NY: Cornell University Press.

Whitaker, D., Archer, L. and Hicks, L. (1998) *Working in Children's Homes: Challenges and Complexities.* Chichester: Wiley.

Whiteman, M., Fanshel, D. and Grundy, J.F. (1987) 'Cognitive-behavioral interventions aimed at anger of parents at risk of child abuse.' *Social Work 32,* 469–74.

Whittaker, J.K. (2000) 'What works in residential child care and treatment: Partnerships with families.' In M. Kluger, G. Alexander and P. Curtis (eds) *What Works in Child Welfare?* Washington, DC: CWLA.

Whittaker, J.K. and Maluccio, A.N. (2002) 'Rethinking "child welfare": A reflective essay.' *Social Service Review 76,* 107–34.

Whittaker, J.K. and Pfeiffer, S.I. (1994) 'Research priorities for residential group child care.' *Child Welfare 73,* 583–601.

Whittaker, J.K. and Savas, S.A. (1999) 'Community links for troubled youth: A neglected dimension in service planning.' In E. Knorth and M. Smit (eds) *Handbook on Structured Residential Care* (English version). Leuven-Apeldoorn, Netherlands: Garant.

Widom, C.S. and Ames, M.A. (1994) 'Criminal consequences of childhood sexual victimization.' *Child Abuse and Neglect 18,* 4, 303–18, 307, 310.

Wierzbicki, M. (1993) 'Psychological adjustment of adoptees: A meta-analysis.' *Journal of Clinical Child Psychology 22,* 4, 447–54.

Wiggins, M., Oakley, A., Roberts, I., Turner, H., Rajan, L., Austerberry, H. *et al.* (2004) *Postnatal Support for Mothers Living in Disadvantaged Areas: A Randomised Controlled Trial and Economic Evaluation.* Southampton: Health Technology Assessment.

Wiggins, R. D., Bartley, M. and Gleave, S. *et al.* (1998) 'Limiting long-term illness: A question of where you live or who you are? A multilevel analysis of the 1971-1991 ONS Longitudinal Study.' *Risk, Decision and Policy 3,* 3, 181–98.

Wilkin, A., Kinder, K., White, R., Atkinson, M. and Doherty, P. (2003) *Towards the Development of Extended Schools. DfES Research Report 408.* London: DfES.

Williams, G. and Macreadie, J. (1992) *Ty Mawr Community Home Inquiry.* Gwent: Gwent County Council.

Williams, J., Jackson, S. and Maddocks, S. (2001) 'Case-control study of the health of those looked after by local authorities.' *Archives of Disease in Childhood 85,* 4, 280–5.

Wilkinson, R.G. (1996) *Unhealthy Societies.* London: Routledge.

Wilson, K., Petrie, S. and Sinclair, I. (2003) 'A kind of loving: A model of effective foster care.' *British Journal of Social Work 33,* 8, 991–1004.

Wilson, K. and Sinclair, I. (2004) 'Contact in foster care.' In E. Neil and D. Howe *Contact in Adoption and Permanent Foster Care.* London: Jessica Kingsley Publishers.

Wind, T.W. and Silvern, L. (1994) 'Parenting and family stress as mediators of the long-term effects of child abuse.' *Child Abuse and Neglect 18,* 439–53.

Winkler, R. and Van Keppel, M. (1984) *Relinquishing Mothers in Adoption: Their Long-term Adjustment.* Melbourne: Institute of Family Studies.

Wolf, M., Copeland, W. and Nollan, K.A. (1998) 'All in a day's work: Resources for teaching life skills.' *Journal of Child and Youth Care 12,* 4, 1–10.

Wolfe, D.A. (1994) 'The role of intervention and treatment services in the prevention of child abuse and neglect.' In G.B. Melton and F.D. Barry (eds) *Protecting Children From Abuse and Neglect Foundations for a New National Strategy.* New York: Guilford.

Wolfe, D.A., Edwards, B., Manion, I. and Koverola, C. (1988) 'Early intervention for parents at-risk for child abuse and neglect: A preliminary investigation.' *Journal of Consulting and Clinical Psychology 56,* 40–57.

Wolfe, D.A., Jaffe, P., Wilson, S. and Zak, L. (1985) 'Children of battered women: The relation of child behavior to family violence and maternal stress.' *Journal of Consulting and Clinical Psychology 53,* 657–64.

Wolfe, D.A. and Wekerle, C. (1993) 'Treatment strategies for child physical abuse and neglect: A critical progress report.' *Clinical Psychology Review 13,* 473–500.

Wolfe, V.V. (1998) 'Child sexual abuse.' in E.J. Mash and R.A. Barkley (eds) *Treatment of Childhood Disorders, Second Edition.* New York: The Guilford Press.

Wolins, M. (1974) *Successful Group Care: Explorations in the Powerful Environment.* Chicago, IL: Aldine.

Wood, S., Barton, K. and Schroeder, C. (1988) 'In-home treatment of abusive families: Cost and placement at one year.' *Psychotherapy 25,* 409–14.

Wooden, K. (1976) *Weeping in the Playtime of Others.* New York, NY: McGraw-Hill.

Woolf, G.D. (1990) 'An outlook for foster care in the US' *Child Welfare 69,* 75–81.

Wulczyn, F., Barth, R.P., Yuan, Y.Y., Jones-Harden, B. and Landsverk, J. (in press) *Evidence for Child Welfare Policy Reform.* New York: Transaction De Gruyter.

Wulczyn, F. and Brunner Hislop, K. (2001) *Teens In Out-of-home Care: Background Data and Implications.* Chicago, IL: University of Chicago, Chapin Hall Center for Children.

Wulczyn, F.H., Harden, A. and Goerge, R.M. (1997) *Foster Care Dynamics: 1983–1994: An Update from the Multistate Foster Care Archive.* Chicago, IL: The Chapin Hall Center for Children.

Yoo, J. and Brooks, D. (2005) 'The role of organizational variables in predicting service effectiveness: An analysis of a multilevel model.' *Research on Social Work Practice 15*, 4, 267–77.

Yoshikawa, H. (1995) 'Long-term effects of early childhood programs on social outcomes and delinquency.' *The Future of Children 5*, 51–75.

Yuan, Y.Y. and Struckman-Johnson, D.L. (1991) 'Placement outcomes for neglected children with prior placements in family preservation programs.' In K. Wells and D.E. Biegel (eds) *Family Preservation Services: Research and Evaluation.* Beverly Hills, CA: Sage.

Zeanah, C.H. (ed.) (2000) *Handbook of Infant Mental Health, Second Edition.* New York: The Guilford Press.

Zero To Three National Center for Infants, Toddlers, and Families (1994) *Diagnostic Classification of Mental Health and Developmental Disorders of Infancy and Early Childhood (DC: 0–3).* Washington, DC: Zero To Three.

Zima, B., Bussing., R., Freeman, S., Yang., X., Belin, T. and Forness, S. (2000) 'Behavior problems, academic skill delays and school failure among school-aged children in foster care: Their relationship to placement characteristics.' *Journal of Child and Family Studies 9*, 1, 87–103.

Zimmerman, R.B. (1982) 'Foster care in retrospect.' *Tulane Studies in Social Welfare 14*, 1–119.

Zoritch, B., Roberts, I. and Oakley, A. (2002) 'Day care for preschool children (Cochrane Review).' In *The Cochrane Library 4.* Oxford: Update Software.

The Contributors

Dawn Anderson-Butcher is an Associate Professor in the College of Social Work at Ohio State University (OSU). Her primary research interests include school–family–community partnerships; youth development; after-school programming; and interprofessional collaboration. Dawn is the lead principal investigator for the Ohio Department of Education's Community Collaboration Model for School Improvement project, an expanded school improvement model focused on addressing non-academic barriers to learning through school–family–community partnerships. Dawn's work is published in key journals such as Social Work, Children and Schools, Social Work in Education, and Journal of Community Psychology. She also is a member of the Society for Social Work Research; National Association of Social Workers; and the American Alliance for Health, Physical Education, Recreation and Dance.

Emmalee S. Bandstra, is Professor of Pediatrics and Obstetrics and Gynecology, Attending Neonatologist, and Director of the Perinatal Chemical Addiction Research and Education (CARE) Program at the University of Miami's Miller School of Medicine. Emmalee is medically licensed and board-certified in pediatrics and neonatal medicine. She received her undergraduate degree at the University of Alabama in Tuscaloosa and medical degree and postgraduate training at the University of Alabama School of Medicine in Birmingham. She is a past president of the Southern Society for Pediatric Research and a member of the Society for Pediatric Research and the American Pediatric Society. Emmalee is Principal Investigator of a National Institutes of Health/National Institute on Drug Abuse grant entitled 'Neurodevelopmental Outcome of In Utero Cocaine Exposure' and has been principal investigator or co-investigator on numerous research and service projects dealing with perinatal substance abuse and mental health issues.

Jane Barlow recently joined Warwick Medical School, Division of Health in the Community as a Reader in Public Health. Her main research interest is in the field of mental health in particular the effectiveness of early interventions aimed at improving parenting practices and their role in the primary prevention of mental health problems, and the reduction of inequalities in health. Her programme of research focuses on interventions that are provided around infancy, and she is currently undertaking long-term follow-up (at age 3 years) of an intensive home-visiting programme that was provided by health visitors across two southern counties in the UK.

Arnon Bentovim is a Child Psychiatrist also trained as a Psycho-analyst and Family Therapist. For many years he was a Consultant at the Great Ormond Street Children's Hospital and the Tavistock Clinic. Being responsible for management of Child Protection in the hospital he helped establish services for the unfolding pattern of presentation of child abuse including physical abuse, neglect patterns, the induction of illness states and sexual abuse. He and his colleagues conducted descriptive and outcome studies and established approaches to training professionals in this complex field.

Nina Biehal is a Senior Research Fellow at the Social Work Research and Development Unit (SWRDU), University of York and editor of the journal *Child and Family Social Work*. Her research interests focus in particular on social work with older children and adolescents. She has completed studies on family support, running away from care, leaving care and missing persons. Her current research interests include treatment foster care, adoption, long-term fostering and the reunification of looked after children with their families. Publications include: *Working with Adolescents. Supporting Families, Preventing Breakdown* (2005), London: BAAF; *Reuniting Looked After Children with their Families: A Research Review* (2006) London: National Children's Bureau; Wade, J. and Biehal, N. with Clayden, J., Stein, M. (1998) *Going Missing.* Chichester: Wiley and Biehal, N., Clayden, J., Stein, M. and Wade, J. (1995) *Moving On. Young People and Leaving Care Schemes.*

Scottye J. Cash is an Associate Professor of Social Work in the College of Social Work at the Ohio State University (OSU). Scottye has been involved in evaluations of child welfare populations, assessment instruments, and services throughout her career. She has focused specifically on evaluating family preservation services, adoption practice, and managed care in child welfare. While at OSU she has worked with Dawn Anderson-Butcher to design and evaluate positive youth development opportunities and parental participation initiatives in OSU's University District Neighborhood.

Jacqueline Corcoran is an Associate Professor at the School of Social Work at Virginia Commonwealth University where she teaches human behaviour, direct practice, and research. From 1996 to 2000, she was on faculty at the University of Texas at Arlington School of Social Work and prior to that she completed her doctoral work at the University of Texas at Austin. Jacqueline writes in the areas of evidence-based practice, strengths-based practice, and child and family services. Her publications include *Building Strengths and Skills* (Oxford, 2005), *Clinical Applications of Evidence-Based Family Interventions* (Oxford, 2004), and *Evidence-Based Social Work Practice with Families* (Springer, 2000).

Diane DePanfilis is an Associate Professor at the University of Maryland School of Social Work and Co-Director of the Center for Families, an interdisciplinary center that combines service, education, and research to promote the safety, health, and well-being of children, families, and communities. She also has appointments as Associate Dean for Research and Director of the Institute for Human Services Policy. Diane is particularly interested in ways to bridge the gap between research, policy, and practice. She has published extensively about methods for assessing, preventing, and responding to child abuse and neglect. She is Past President of the American Professional Society on the Abuse of Children, an interdisciplinary association that works to assure that everyone affected by child maltreatment receives the best possible professional response.

Joy G. Dryfoos is an unaffiliated researcher and writer from Brookline, Massachusetts. She received support from Carnegie Corporation and Grant Foundation for a long-term 'youth-at-risk' project with a focus on prevention of substance abuse, delinquency, school failure, and teen pregnancy. In addition to more than 100 published articles and book chapters, Joy has written: *Adolescents-at-Risk: Prevalence and Prevention; Full Service Schools: A Revolution in Health and Social Services for Children, Youth, and Families; Safe Passage: Making it Through Adolescence in a Risky Society; Inside Full-Service Community Schools; Community Schools in Action; and Adolescence:Growing up in America Today*. She serves on the steering committees of the Coalition for Community Schools and the Boston Roundtable for Full Service Schools.

Jenny Gray has a professional child care background and joined the Government in 1990. Her current responsibility is to provide professional advice on child protection policy within the Department for Education and Skills. She had lead responsibility for *The Framework for the Assessment of Children in Need and their Families*. She has co-lead responsibility for the Integrated Children's System.

K. Lori Hanson is Director of Research, Evaluation and Training at The Children's Trust, and Voluntary Assistant Professor of Pediatrics at the University of Miami. She is a licensed psychologist, having completed her PhD at Saint Louis University, and clinical psychology internship at the University of Miami's Mailman Center for Child Development specializing in pediatric and child populations. She has been a Principal Investigator and Program Coordinator of multiple early intervention studies and service programs, including Miami's Starting Early Starting Smart/Healthy Start Initiative. Dr. Hanson currently oversees all research and evaluation priorities and provider capacity-building and quality improvement activities of The Children's Trust, a dedicated source of funding created by voter referendum to improve the lives of children and families in Miami-Dade county, Florida.

Gordon Jack is Principal Lecturer in Social Work at the University of Plymouth and Leader of the post-qualifying Peninsula Child Care Award Programme. He was previously Head of Social Work at the University of Exeter, where he had been working since 1991. Gordon also has extensive experience in child-care practice and management, having worked in three local authority social services departments in the North of England between 1975 and 1991. He has researched and published widely on the ecological approach to social work with children and families, focusing in particular on the influence of disadvantage and inequality on the welfare of children and the functioning of families and communities. He is co-author, with Owen Gill, of *The Missing Side of the Triangle: Assessing the Importance of Wider Family and Environmental Factors in the Lives of Children*, published by Barnardo's in 2003.

Anthony N. Maluccio is Professor Emeritus of Social Work at the University of Connecticut and Boston College. His teaching and research interests focus on service delivery and outcome evaluation in the area of child and family services, particularly family preservation, family foster care, residential treatment of children and youths, and family reunification of children in out-of-home care. He has coauthored a number of books on the above topics, including, most recently, *Teaching Family Reunification; Reconnecting Families: A Guide to Strengthening Family Reunification Services; The Child Welfare Challenge: Policy, Practice, and Research;* and *Child Welfare Outcome Research in the United States, the United Kingdom, and Australia*.

Maureen Marcenko is an associate professor at the University of Washington School of Social Work located in Seattle, Washington. Maureen has conducted research on a number of community-based programs addressing the needs of young children and their families. The current focus of her work is on the mental health needs of children in the child welfare system. She also teaches advanced practice with children and families in the graduate social work program. Maureen can be reached at: mmarcenk@u.washington.edu.

Colette McAuley lectures in the School of Sociology, Social Policy and Social Work at Queen's University Belfast and was Head of Research at the former School of Social Work for three years. Prior to that she worked as a practitioner and manager in child welfare services. Her predominant research interests include outcomes for looked after children and young families under stress and the evaluation of effectiveness and cost-effectiveness of child welfare services. Colette has recently completed studies in these areas and related publications include *Pathways and Outcomes: A Ten Year Follow-Up of Children who Have Experienced Care* (2005) Belfast: DHSSPHNI, and McAuley, C., Knapp, M., Beecham, J., McCurry, N. and Sleed, M. (2004), *Young Families Under Stress: Outcomes and Costs of Home-Start Support* York: Joseph Rowntree Foundation. She is a member of the International Association for Outcome Based Evaluation and Research in Family and Children's Services and sits on the Editorial Board of the *International Journal of Child and Family Welfare*.

Jacquelyn McCroskey, the John Milner Professor of Child Welfare at the University of Southern California School of Social Work, is active in developing community-based supports and services for children and families in Los Angeles County. Her research includes numerous studies of service organization and financing, as well as development and application of performance measurement systems for public agencies serving children and families. She was one of the co-developers of the Family Assessment Form, has studied the effectiveness of family-centered services, and the impact of inter-professional training on professional development. Recent publications include *Walking the Collaboration Talk: Ten Lessons Learned from the Los Angeles County Children's Planning Council* (www.childrensplanningcouncil.org).

Ruth G. McRoy is currently a Research Professor and the Ruby Lee Piester Centennial Professor Emeritus at the University of Texas School of Social Work at the University of Texas at Austin. She served on the UT faculty for 26 years and held a joint appointment with the Center for African and African American Studies and was a member of the University of Texas Academy of Distinguished Professors. For 13 years she served as the Associate Dean for Research, and Director of the Center for Social Work Research and Director of the Diversity Institute at the UT School of Social Work. She has authored or co-authored seven books and numerous articles and book chapters on adoptions, has presented many invited papers at national and international conferences. Her books include: *Transracial and Inracial Adoptees: The Adolescent Years* (with L. Zurcher, 1983); *Emotional Disturbance in Adopted Adolescents: Origins and Development* (with H. Grotevant and L. Zurcher, 1988); *Openness in Adoption: New Practices, New Issues* (with H. Grotevant and K. White, 1988), *Social Work Practice with Black Families* (with Sadye Logan and Edith Freeman, 1990); *Openness in Adoption: Exploring Family Connections* (with H. Grotevant, 1998); *Special Needs Adoptions: Practice Issues* (1999); and *Does Family Preservation Serve a Child's Best Interests?* (with H. Altstein, 2000). Her latest co-edited book (with Rowena Fong and Carmen Ortiz-Hendricks), *Intersecting Child Welfare, Substance Abuse and Family Violence: Culturally Competent Approaches,* will be published in early 2006. She is currently writing a new book on transracial adoptions.

Connie E. Morrow is Research Associate Professor of Pediatrics at the University of Miami and a licensed psychologist specializing in pediatric and child clinical psychology. She completed her PhD at the University of Miami, and her Clinical Psychology Internship at the University of North Carolina-Chapel Hill. Connie has more than a decade of experience implementing research and service programs for at-risk infants and young children. She is Principal Investigator of the Starting Early Starting Smart/Healthy Start Initiative, initially funded by SAMHSA and the Casey Family Program to enhance early childhood development for infants and young children at-risk due to caregiver mental health or substance abuse issues by providing comprehensive, family-centered parenting and behavioral health services. Connie has published extensively in the area of prenatal cocaine exposure and child development, and has been the Psychology Research Director on the NIDA-funded Miami Prenatal Cocaine Study since 1992.

Helen Nissani is a senior advisor to Caliber Associates' Education Studies Division, and a national family support advocate and researcher. She is currently the project manager for the national evaluation study of Communities in Schools. As a senior education advisor to Family Support America, and program director of the Child/Family and Community program of the Northwest Regional Educational Laboratory, Helen published several articles describing family-friendly schools and the integration of education and human services leading to positive student outcomes.

Kimberly A. Nollan, Momentum Partners Consulting, Seattle, WA, consults in the areas of child welfare, program evaluation, and research and development. Prior to consultation, she worked for Casey Family Programs, leading efforts to develop the internationally used *Ansell-Casey Life Skills Assessment,* an assessment for youth and caregivers that has helped over 70,000 people in preparing youth for living independently. She also co-authored the *Life Skills Guidebook, Supplemental Guidebook Learning Plans, and Ready, Set, Fly! A Parent's Guide to Teaching Life Skills.* She led numerous research studies to better understand the outcomes and life skills of youth in out-of-home care.

Peter J. Pecora has a joint appointment as the Senior Director of Research Services for Casey Family Programs, and as Professor in the School of Social Work, University of Washington, Seattle, Washington. He was a line worker and later a program coordinator in a number of child welfare service agencies. He has worked with the state departments of social services to implement intensive home-based services, child welfare training, and risk assessment systems for child protective services. He has served as an expert witness for the states of Florida, New Mexico, Washington and Wisconsin. His co-authored books and articles focus on child welfare program design, administration, and research. Currently, he is completing a study of foster care alumni with the states of Oregon and Washington in conjunction with Harvard Medical School and the University of Michigan, benchmarking data on the progress of children in foster care, testing a caregiver empowerment approach to helping youth in foster care access evidence-based mental health services, and participating in a national effort to reduce racial disproportionality in the child welfare system.

Gillian Pugh has recently retired as Chief Executive of Coram Family, a leading children's charity which aims to develop and promote best practice in the care and support of very vulnerable children and their families. She worked previously at the National Children's Bureau where she was responsible for a broad range of work in the children's field, especially services for young children and support for parents. Over the past 30 years, Gillian has advised governments in the UK and overseas on the development of policy for children and families and has published widely. She was a founder member and is chair of the Parenting Education and Support Forum and a trustee of the National Family and Parenting Institute. She has been an advisor to the Children, Young People and Families Directorate at the Department of Education and Skills, is a member of the new Children's Workforce Development Council, and is visiting Professorial Fellow at the Institute of Education. She was awarded the DBE in 2005 for services to children and families.

David Quinton is Emeritus Professor of Psychosocial Development in the School for Policy Studies at the University of Bristol. His interest is in continuities and discontinuities in social adaptation, especially following poor parenting experiences, and in interventions and supports for those who experience them. He is the founder of the Hadley Centre for Adoption and Foster Care studies at Bristol.

Wendy Rose is a Senior Research Fellow in the Faculty of Health and Social Care at The Open University. She was previously a senior civil servant advising on children's policy. She has a background in social work practice, and social services management and policy development. She currently works on national and international child welfare research and development projects. Most recently, she has worked with UK government departments on the development of a national framework for assessing children in need and their families, and is completing a national study of reviews of deaths and serious injuries to children. She has published widely on policy and practice issues concerned with improving outcomes for children and families.

Julie Selwyn is Director of the Hadley Centre for Adoption and Foster Care Studies, at the University of Bristol. The centre aims to link research, policy, practice and training in all aspects of permanence and planning for looked after children (www.bristol.ac.uk/hadley). She is currently working on a number of research studies including a study funded by the Department for Education and Skills on 'Pathways to Permanence for Children of Black, Asian and Mixed Parentage: Dilemmas, Decision-making and Outcomes.' Julie qualified as a social worker in 1981 after lengthy residential childcare experience and then worked in local authority children's services until joining the University in 1993.

Ian Sinclair worked initially in teaching, probation social work and counseling. His recent posts have been as Director of Research at the National Institute of Social Work, Professor of Social Work at the University of York and Co-director of the Social Work Research and Development Unit at the same university. He is currently a research professor at the same unit. His most recent work has focused on residential work and fostering for children and the movements and outcomes of children 'in care'.

Marjorie Smith is Deputy Director of the Thomas Coram Research Unit, and Professor of the Psychology of the Family, at the Institute of Education, University of London. Marjorie is a psychologist who has been carrying out research relating to children and families for nearly 30 years. Her particular interests are family and other influences on child development, including outcomes such as educational attainment, health, behaviour and well-being. She is not an active interventionist, but did contribute to the development of Sure Start in the UK, by writing with a colleague a review for the UK Treasury of the research evidence of effective interventions. Marjorie has conducted a number of normative studies involving randomly selected community samples. These have included an investigation of punishment and control within the home; a study of stepchildren and step-parenting, and a normative study of minor injuries in children.

Fredi Staerkel has been an Assistant Professor at University of Wisconsin-Oshkosh since August 2002. She came to UW-Oshkosh after receiving her PhD in Social Welfare from the School of Social Work at the University of Washington, in Seattle. She has 25 years of social work practice experience in the areas of child and family welfare, early childhood development, and prevention science. She has been involved in research related to implementation of the Early Head Start program, prevention of acquaintance rape/sexual assault, and foster care relationships. Fredi teaches in both the undergraduate Social Work and Master of Social Work Programs at UW-Oshkosh. Specifically, her teaching has focused on family life cycles, research methods, generalist practice with groups, and macro level social work practice.

June Statham is a Reader in Education and Family Support and a Senior Research Officer at the Thomas Coram Research Unit, Institute of Education, University of London. She has over 25 years' experience of research into early childhood services and support for vulnerable children and their families, including children in need in the community and children who are cared for away from home, as well as informal care within families for grandchildren or older relatives. June manages the research unit's programme of responsive research studies for government policy makers on issues of immediate or strategic policy relevance for the development of children's services.

Karen Tanner is a Senior Clinical Lecturer in Social Work at the Tavistock Clinic and a tutor on the post qualifying social work programmes at Royal Holloway College, London University. Her clinical and academic interests are in child neglect and the use of observation in working with complex child-care cases.

Danielle Turney is a Senior Lecturer (Children and Families) in the Faculty of Health and Social Care at The Open University. She worked initially as a local authority social worker and then, after PhD research exploring anti-racist practice, she moved into social work education and training. She has taught on social work programmes at both qualifying and post-qualifying levels and is currently involved in writing teaching materials that focus on work with children and young people. Her current research interests are in child neglect and broader issues of child welfare and protection.

Jim Wade is a Senior Research Fellow in the Social Work Research and Development Unit, University of York. For the past 15 years he has researched and published widely in the area of social work and related services for vulnerable groups of children and young people, including looked after children, care leavers, young runaways and unaccompanied asylum-seeking children. He has also conducted research into adults who go missing from their families. He has been involved in the preparation of best practice guides and official guidance on services for care leavers and young runaways and acted as consultant to other national and international research initiatives in these areas.

James K. Whittaker is The Charles O. Cressey Endowed Professor at the University of Washington School of Social Work, Seattle, where he has served as a member of senior faculty since 1970. His research and teaching interests encompass child and family policy and services, and the integration of evidence-based practices into contemporary child and family services. A frequent contributor to the professional literature, James is author/co-author/editor of eight books and nearly 100 peer-reviewed papers and book chapters. In all, Dr. Whittaker's works have been translated into eight languages and he presently serves on the editorial review boards of a number of social service journals including: *Social Service Review* (U.S.); *The British Journal of Social Work* (U.K.); *Child and Family Social Work* (U.K.) and *International Journal of Child and Family Welfare* (Belgium).

Kate Wilson is Professor of Social Work at the Centre for Social Work, University of Nottingham and Non-executive Director of the Nottinghamshire Healthcare NHS Trust, one of the largest Trusts with responsibility for mental health services in the UK. Her practice and research interests are in child welfare and therapeutic work, particularly with children and adolescents. Her recent, jointly authored books include three on foster care and the second edition of a practice guide to non-directive play therapy with children and adolescents.

Subject Index

Author Index

Page references followed by n indicate note numbers